QUEEN ELIZABETH
THE QUEEN MOTHER

Queen Elizabeth
The Queen Mother

And Her Support To The Throne
During Four Reigns

Dorothy Laird

The author is grateful for the gracious permission and assistance
given to her by Her Majesty Queen Elizabeth The Queen Mother
in preparing this first authorised biographical study of Her Majesty.

CORONET BOOKS
Hodder and Stoughton

First published in Great Britain
by Hodder and Stoughton Limited 1966

Revised Coronet edition 1975
Third impression 1985

Printed and bound in Great Britain for
Hodder and Stoughton Paperbacks,
a division of Hodder and Stoughton Ltd,
Mill Road, Dunton Green, Sevenoaks, Kent
(Editorial Office: 47 Bedford Square,
London, WC1 3DP) by
Richard Clay (The Chaucer Press) Ltd,
Bungay, Suffolk

ISBN 0 340 19919 9

CONTENTS

CONTENTS

ILLUSTRATIONS

Glamis Castle (*Author*)
St Paul's Walden Bury (*Ziemsen*)
Lady Elizabeth and the Hon David Bowes-Lyon (*Lafayette*)
As bridesmaid to Princess Mary (*Lafayette*)
The Duke and Duchess of York (*PA-Reuter*)
The wedding day, April 26, 1923 (*Camera Press*)
The newly married Duchess in Belgrade (*Central Press Photos*)
A family group at Liverpool Street Station (*Radio Times Hulton Picture Library*)
The opening of the Federal Parliament of Australia in 1927 (*Central Press Photos*)
On the moors at Glamis with the Prince of Wales (*The Times*)
The Duke and Duchess of York with Princess Elizabeth (*Marcus Adams*)
A family group at Windsor in June 1936 (*Radio Times Hulton Picture Library*)
Queen Elizabeth seated in state (*Central Press Photos*)
The Royal Family on the balcony of Buckingham Palace, May 12, 1937 (*Central Press Photos*)
Windsor Castle (*The Times*)
Balmoral (*James Reid, Ballater*)
Sandringham (*J. Salmon, Sevenoaks*)

FOREWORD

ACCORDING to the calendar, the eighty-fifth anniversary of the birth of Queen Elizabeth the Queen Mother falls on August 4, 1985. When Lady Elizabeth Bowes-Lyon married the Duke of York in 1923 she possessed a serenity unusual in a young woman. Today she retains a vitality which many people never possessed nor ever will possess. For vitality and serenity are not merely a matter of years, and both—like much else in her personality—are family traits.

Queen Elizabeth the Queen Mother is exactly a woman of the twentieth century, her experiences and her memories matching this era of unparalleled change. She is old enough to remember the carefree days before the First World War. She knew the anguish of that time through the death of a much-loved brother, and through personal contact with the wounded in body and spirit when her home at Glamis became a hospital.

In the hectic depressed twenties she became the first commoner for generations to marry into the Royal family, making the transition from her informal, happy home into the rigid structure of the royal circle of that day.

She lived through the traumas which followed the death of her father-in-law King George V and the abdication of her brother-in-law King Edward VIII, which thrust kingship upon her shy husband, and forced upon him an irrevocable loss of privacy. Hardest of all, she saw her daughters lose their quiet childhood. Yet she maintained even within the unlikely confines of a palace, the simple happiness of her family circle.

With King George VI she unflinchingly supported and uplifted the country during the Second World War. Afterwards, when peaceful years might be hoped for, she suffered the decline in health and early death of the husband she loved so deeply, and for whom she was always life's centre and joy.

As mother of the young Queen she surmounted the anguish of loss, and the re-establishment of her new and narrower life as a widowed Queen. Always she has lived life to the full. Her reward is the affection in which she is held by millions who have never met her, and the deep and personal love she has kindled among the many, many people who have personal knowledge of her joyous spirit.

Hampstead
January 1985

AUTHOR'S ACKNOWLEDGEMENTS

THIS book could not have been written without the gracious permission of Her Majesty Queen Elizabeth the Queen Mother, whose wonderful record of service to the Commonwealth I have been privileged to recount.

Members of Her Majesty's family and past and present Members of her Household have given invaluable help. Indeed very many people have unstintingly given their memories, time and trouble to make this book possible and I am most grateful to them all. Some of them have asked to remain anonymous, and as it would seem invidious to thank some by name and not others I have reluctantly decided not to name my sources.

Among those who helped me with the actual writing and correction of the book I owed much to Mrs. Martin Secker, who has made corrections to the original typescript with such sympathetic skill; to Miss Elsie Herron and Miss Jane Osborne of Messrs Hodder and Stoughton for their unfailing quiet help; and to Miss Alexandra Mitchell, who was my principal assistant and support during the years of writing.

Dorothy Laird
Hampstead, 1959–1966
Originally published 1966

The author and publishers are grateful to the following for permission to quote copyright material: the *Auckland Star*, the *Glasgow Herald*, *The Times*, Canadian Pacific Steamships Limited for an extract from the Log Book of the *Empress of Australia*, and Methuen and Company Limited for an extract from *The Royal Embassy* by Ian F. M. Lucas. The description of *Special Cargo*'s win of the Whitbread Gold Cup in 1984 is by kind permission of Brough Scott and *The Sunday Times*. Lady Clarke has kindly made available her account of Queen Elizabeth's visit to Venice in October 1984, published in *Rivista*, the Journal of the British-Italian Society.

CHAPTER ONE

QUEEN ELIZABETH TODAY

Queen Elizabeth has inward grace and it appears in outward graces

The Very Rev. Dr. F. R. V. Scott, Formerly Minister of St. Columba's Church of Scotland, Pont Street, London

WHEN Queen Elizabeth the Queen Mother is in London, her personal standard—the Royal Standard impaled with the blue lions and the black archers' bows of the Bowes-Lyon family—flies, languid with its own length and weight, in the prevailingly western wind, from the flagstaff over Clarence House.

Here, in the cream-painted, stucco-covered Clarence House with its flower-filled window-boxes, Queen Elizabeth is in the centre of a circle of memories. From her windows she looks across a stretch of lawn and a drop-wall to the Mall and the trees of St. James's Park. Only a mile to the north-west is the site of her father's house in Bruton Street, which she left on the morning of April 26, 1923, to become the bride of King George V's second son, the Duke of York. Just over half a mile to the south-east stands Westminster Abbey, in which she was married, where she was crowned Queen, and where she saw her children married and her elder daughter crowned Queen. Half a mile due west of Clarence House, at Hyde Park Corner, the traffic speeds over the site of the tall Piccadilly house in which she learned that she was Queen. Six furlongs away, along the Mall, lies Buckingham Palace, which was her home for over sixteen years, in which she was bombed, where she lived in great anxiety during the illnesses of her husband, and which also holds many happy and splendid memories. There she held the last of the Evening Courts: there on V.E. night she stood on the balcony with King George VI and Winston Churchill, looking down on the upturned faces of a vast, jubilant and thankful crowd.

She has lived in Clarence House since it was made ready for

her after the death of her husband. Princess Margaret was married from here, and returned here for the birth of her first child.

Queen Elizabeth lives in a circle of unique memories, yet hers is not a life of retirement, given over to recollection and reflection. She is an active and hard-working member of an active and hard-working Royal family.

No other woman in our history has been successively daughter-in-law, sister-in-law and consort of three Sovereigns, and finally Queen Mother of a Sovereign Queen. Her public duty has been splendidly given under many different circumstances, in times of physical danger and mental anguish; of constitutional uncertainty; of peace and war; of austerity and great happiness. Her unflinching courage and her warm heart, her sparkling dresses and her reputed unpunctuality, her gay smile, are part of the British legend of our times. She is greatly loved and widely popular, a world personality who commands respect as well as affection, and yet possibly we owe even more to her than we realise.

Wherever Queen Elizabeth lives, she implants her own atmosphere. It has something to do with the scent of the massed flowers with which she is always surrounded, with the fresh air coming through the open windows, with the subtle, delicate colours she likes, and the ornaments, often birds and animals, chosen for their individuality and character as much as their beauty as works of art.

When I was given permission to write this book, Her Majesty decided to see me.

On the morning of my audience, I came to the black Household door in Ambassador's Court, at the back of Clarence House. The footman who answered the bell led me past the portraits of Cavendish-Bentinck relatives of Queen Elizabeth into the Equerries' sitting room, where I waited with the Equerry (being far, far too early) until the time for my audience approached and Lord Adam Gordon came to take me to the Queen.

Because Clarence House consists of three back-to-back houses joined into one, the way into Queen Elizabeth's part of Clarence House is actually through the Equerries' sitting room, where a short flight of steps adjusts the different levels of the houses.

I emerged through a swing door, stepping over a leopard rug, into a corridor, which stretches like a broad shaft, cool and dim, leading from the light of the garden into the heart of the house.

I did not see much of this corridor, its pictures and furniture on that first occasion. Indeed I saw nothing at all except a very well-known lady in a blue lace dress, who was crossing the hall with a tall, pretty girl in yellow, and making to mount the stairs. She hesitated for a second, then crossed the hall and shook hands with me, and presented me to her companion, whom I only then recognised to be Princess Alexandra. Then, with a smiling word of excuse, Queen Elizabeth continued on her way.

That morning, from my vantage point in the Equerries' room, I had seen a procession of people assembling and going through and returning from audiences with Her Majesty. It was at a time when her daughter, the Queen, was overseas, and Queen Elizabeth, as a Counsellor of State, was undertaking an even more crowded programme than usual, including a Privy Council meeting at Clarence House.

My audience with Queen Elizabeth took place in the morning room. It is across the wide lower corridor, the corner room on the ground floor, facing the garden and Stable Yard, a long, sunlit room with pale grey walls and off-white woodwork. Dominating the room are the display cabinets, flanking the fireplace, built for Queen Elizabeth's extensive and beautiful collection of Red Anchor period Chelsea china. Here are a large number of the plates and dishes depicting fruit and flowers in Sir Hans Sloane's Chelsea Physic Garden, some of which were taken from the engravings in *Figures of Plants* by Philip Miller, gardener to the Apothecaries. This is some of the most beautiful china ever made in England, and is now almost prohibitively expensive, even for a Queen's purse. It was collected piece by piece by the Queen herself and by her husband and family as presents for her, when it was less widely recognised. There are also two fine Chelsea clocks decorated with shepherds and shepherdesses from the more ornate Gold Anchor period.

The furniture, some of which came from Marlborough House, is gilt-wood, made in England in the eighteenth century.

The outstanding modern paintings are possibly unexpected. Over the mantelpiece is an unusual and fine Sickert, showing a young man and a girl in fancy dress. This is one of two paintings by Sickert in the room; the other is a conversation piece of King George V and his racing manager, Major Fetherstonhaugh, a former occupier of The Royal Lodge.

There is an unusual and haunting Monet of a high hillside, reminiscent of Scotland and called *Le Rocher*, and a fine Paul Nash, *The Vernal Equinox*, bought by Queen Elizabeth during the war. A study of George Bernard Shaw painted between the wars by Augustus John, who has long been one of Her Majesty's favourite modern painters, hangs on the wall beside the door.

It must be confessed that on the morning Her Majesty received me, I saw hardly any of these things, with the exception of two of the paintings, which Her Majesty pointed out, and an astonishing glimpse of the reds and greens and creamy-white of the Sloane Chelsea china.

I had eyes only for Queen Elizabeth. Like everyone else, I had heard of her gift for putting people at ease, now I was experiencing it. Nervous and tense, but determined to make use of every second of this invaluable time, what was I doing? Telling Her Majesty about a personal anxiety of which one would normally speak only to friends, an approaching operation on my daughter, and gaining courage from her very genuine sympathy. It was an experience both unexpected and strengthening.

Queen Elizabeth is not so tall as I had expected, and is very erect, both standing and sitting. She is extremely young-looking, nor is her young appearance due to excessive make-up, but to her smooth skin and even more to her vitality. She bends her whole, complete attention upon you, and I was held most of all by her eyes, grey-blue and very direct. Her voice is light, clear, warm and expressive, with bell-like emphasis on certain words. I was to find later that it is the Bowes-Lyon family voice, which says decided things gently, and which quickly bubbles into humour. Queen Elizabeth has an enjoyment of words, which she chooses quickly, but with care.

She is extremely perceptive and receptive in conversation. Still inexplicably blundering through a potted life history, I mentioned that I had made a long voyage in a square-rigged sailing ship. She immediately responded, 'One of the grain ships? . . . from what country? . . . how fortunate you were! It must have been beautiful with the silence and the creaking.' It is those little noises in the working of a sailing ship in a sea which, without an engine to overwhelm them, become audible and important, but one does not expect a Queen instantly and exactly to pin-point the memory. Queen Elizabeth went on, 'You would have long periods to think . . . Everything is so broken up today, that it is so difficult to find time, and it is so important.'

Queen Elizabeth spoke of her rôle as Queen in a way which brought home to me just how much intelligence and thought she pours into her life-work. Most of all, I was impressed with her deep love of country, of Commonwealth and of all of us.

She spoke of the many continual changes to meet new conditions in the position of Monarchy. She spoke of the importance of the Commonwealth and of the Monarchy to the Commonwealth and of London as the heart of the Commonwealth. She said how glad she was when people here could learn more about Commonwealth countries.

She spoke of the technique of Queenship, of ways 'in which one learns with practice how to do things better, such as seeing people who are at different levels in the crowd', of the little skills by which she could appear fresh, however long the day, perhaps by having a crisp coat to slip on top of the coat in which she had been travelling.

'I love meeting people,' she said. 'I have met people of every possible kind and it is so easy to get on with them after the first moment, isn't it?' Queen Elizabeth went on, 'Nearly everyone is pleasant. When one is eighteen, one has very definite dislikes, but as one grows older, one becomes more and more tolerant, and finds that nearly everyone is, in some degree, nice.' She paused and then said, 'The only regret one has as one grows older is that things do not matter so strongly.'

She has an intimate and skilled way of drawing you to share her comments. When she described, in a way that made it seem extremely amusing, emerging from a dark aircraft into the unfamiliar blaze of a tropical sun, so that 'one's eyes filled with tears, and one inspected a guard of honour half-blinded', I found I was laughing with her.

She deftly turned compliments, so that several times when I began speaking about her, her remarks were made to refer instead to others. When I spoke of the bombing, and was thinking of her own narrow escapes at Buckingham Palace, she spoke instead of her deep admiration of the courage of the bombed-out, adding, 'The people of London were perfectly marvellous in the way they *endured*, don't you think?

'Yet times were almost worse,' she added, 'at the end of the war, when the people were all tired; they had been through so much.'

She spoke with remembered enjoyment about her tours to Australia and New Zealand and to Africa and said, 'We had a wonderful trip to Canada before the war. Canada is so . . . so up-lifting,' and she lifted her hands high.

Air travel now makes tours much more exacting. She was in-clined to think that future Royal tours might well have to be shorter and more rapid, confining themselves to one district of a Commonwealth country, rather than attempting to go round the whole country. 'On these tours,' she said, 'you know you will go on getting more tired; you get no chance to win any rest back.'

Television, she thought, had been a great help for people in understanding the duties as well as the privileges of the Royal family. 'People forget that the Queen has to do with so many sides of life, and that really everything that goes on in the country is the concern of the Queen. She comes into contact with all facets of life here and in the Commonwealth.

'But the Queen especially,' she added, 'should not be seen on television too often, as it does impose an extra strain.'

It must, I suggested, be difficult and hard work continually to be in the public eye, carrying through a heavy and often repetitive programme.

'It is very tiring—and very exciting,' Her Majesty replied. Then she paused, and said, slowly and memorably, 'If one loves one's country—as one does—such service is something one is proud to do and to give.'

Much of Queen Elizabeth's personality—her continual and sympathetic interest in people, her love of warm rather than austere beauty, her love of flowers and animals—is very evident in her own home. Yet it is surprisingly difficult to describe the character of the homemaker. So much is known about her—and yet so little. Although she gives of herself so freely, she has spent her life in avoiding the comparisons which, like the poet, she believes are odious. Queen Elizabeth always tells her entourage when she has enjoyed something, but she will never be drawn into saying what she has liked best.

Best known, most indescribable of Queen Elizabeth's characteristics is her charm, which a dictionary defines as 'that which fascinates or attracts, exciting love and admiration'. One can only illustrate it by its effect on those around her. Look at photographs of Queen Elizabeth—how often she has smiling faces round her. She adds lustre and joy to everything she does: she has what, in another way of life, is known as 'star quality'.

Queen Elizabeth has a quite extraordinary effect upon all sorts of people, old and young, sophisticated and simple. A Commonwealth Prime Minister remarked, 'She's a real corker!', a Major-General said, 'To me, she's the most wonderful woman in the world'; a patient in the Royal Hospital and Home for Incurables said the same, and added, 'She was really interested in us—not like some of the ladies who come and speak to you as a duty: we can tell.'

This charm is not an acquired quality; it was born in her. People who knew her when she was growing up, her contemporaries as well as officers who convalesced at Glamis when it was a hospital during the First World War, vividly recall that Lady Elizabeth Bowes-Lyon had a perfectly fascinating power of charming everyone. Nor is this effect upon people confined to her own circle—such different people as South African Cabinet Ministers, French Canadians in Quebec, businessmen and cab-drivers in New York, Senators in Washington, gold-miners in Australia, sheep-farmers in Australia and shipyard workers on the Clyde all have, in their different ways, recognised and paid tribute to it.

At the worst time of the Depression the Duke and Duchess of York visited an unemployed men's club in industrial Scotland. The Duke, with his interest in the human problems of men in industry, was specially interested in the project, but when the Chief Constable of the town heard what was being planned, he went to see the Staffs of both King George V and of the Duke and Duchess of York, and told them that as a result of crippling unemployment and poor housing conditions, the district was particularly restless, and that policemen went there in couples. He said that in his opinion the visit would be untimely. The matter was raised with the Duke and Duchess of York: he listened and she said, 'But Bertie, all the more reason why we should go.'

On the day, the atmosphere in the club appeared tense and awkward, and it seemed desirable that the visit should not be prolonged. The Duke of York said, however, that he would like to see the tennis court and other sports facilities. As they passed the bowling green, where the unemployed men's wives were playing bowls, one woman called out, 'Wud ye care to try a wood?'

'Do you think I should?' the Duchess asked her husband.

'Yes, do,' said the Duke and then, as the Duchess of York in her high-heeled shoes moved towards the bowling green, he called quickly after her, 'No, Elizabeth—not in those shoes.'

The Duchess of York slipped off her shoes and went on to the green in her stockinged soles.

Someone asked, 'Who will throw the jack?'

'I will,' said the Duke of York, and to the dismay of his Staff, he threw it about thirty yards, a considerable distance.

'Now try yer luck!'

The Duchess of York said, 'Now do show me, have I got the bias right?' The wood was examined and approved. The Duchess of York laid off the wood, which went off at an angle of twenty degrees, but at last took the bias, turned and finally nestled not a breadth from the jack. The atmosphere was transformed, there was merry music and a good tea, and everyone enjoyed a thoroughly happy afternoon.

When Queen Elizabeth was a comparatively new but enthusiastic Chancellor, she attended the President's Ball at the University of London. She was suffering from a very heavy cold and had intimated that she would leave early, when it was learnt that a university delegation from an Iron Curtain country was coming on to the ball at a late hour. Queen Elizabeth immediately agreed to stay on, and received each delegate individually. 'They looked a bit resistant as they went up to her,' said an official of London University, 'but what a transformation afterwards in those rather tough-looking faces!' In an account of their visit given afterwards on their home radio, the presentation to Queen Elizabeth came over as the highlight of their time in London.

Queen Elizabeth has the same effect upon a crowd as upon one or two individuals. She often gets letters from people who have been in the crowd saying, 'How wonderful it was that you had a special smile for me', and she never leaves a room without everyone feeling they have met her.

Queen Elizabeth is interested in all sorts of people, enjoys them whole-heartedly and does not think there is a bore in the world. This again is a trait continuing from her childhood. Lady Strathmore, her remarkable mother, taught her family, 'If you find a person a bore, the fault lies in you.'

A connoisseur in people, Queen Elizabeth likes them to be full of character, 'different', even a bit off-key; she likes them simple and homely; she likes the expert in some esoteric field; or wise in commonsense or in deep learning. She likes people shy, cheerful, grumpy, tolerant, old, young, of whatever creed or colour, she even likes them voluble, though she prefers them not to be dogmatic and self-important. Genuinely liking people—which is quite different from making oneself like them—is a more uncommon quality than one might think, and it is an integral part of Queen Elizabeth's special charm.

Opposition lends her zest. Members of her Household speak of her belief that she could go right into the heart of any opposition, meet it face to face, and find it not nearly so formidable as its reputation. 'Though her human knowledge is tremendous, her political acumen is possibly sometimes not so great,' said a senior Member of the Sovereign's Household. 'It is never hard to get her to go to some trouble-spot: it is much harder to persuade her that in the circumstances it may be better for her to stay away.'

During her visit to the United States in 1939, one old Senator of strongly Republican viewpoint swore he would *not* be presented, but eventually came up: he not only shook her hand, but held it in both of his. In South Africa an anti-British Boer came up to her brusquely at a reception and said, 'I am sorry, but I really hate the English.' She at once replied, 'I do sympathise—you see I'm Scots.'

Queen Elizabeth appreciates people for what they are, and does not expect them to be something different. She talks with the same ease and animation to all types of people. She will not say the same thing to a Durham miner's wife as to a New Zealand farm worker, to a Prime Minister or to an actor, but she talks to each in the same natural manner, about something in which both she and they are interested. Her subject of conversation may alter, but never her manner. Her simple and natural good manners have a complete lack of that petty snobbery found in those insecure in themselves. Queen Elizabeth meets people on their own ground and has a remarkable ability to make enjoyment flow out around her.

Queen Elizabeth is an immediately warm and friendly person. She creates an aura of well-being about her, and she has almost a genius for relaxing the tense and nervous, and creating an air of gaiety and enjoyment in stiff official circumstances. But it would be wrong to assume from this that she gives her friendship—her deep and personal friendship—lightly. She does not. But when she has given her friendship, nothing will make her withdraw it. Her loyalty is absolute, however much the circumstances may change, or perhaps the person become involved in difficulties.

One thing she simply will not allow and that is one member of the family criticising another in his or her absence.

Queen Elizabeth has a gay wit, delighting in the absurd, readily sharing a joke, or indeed creating a special joke apt to the occasion. Unfortunately lightheartedness and spontaneous gaiety flower and die in the moment: it is almost impossible to transplant them to the printed page.

A retired Member of the Household, entertaining her to tea, showed her with pride the labour of his hands, a newly-laid terrace of paving-stones. 'Oh, how clever of you,' she exclaimed warmly, and then, with a wicked glance, 'and they *fit*!'

When President Daladier of France was entertained at Windsor, he was taken round the Castle and shown some historic documents of Anglo-French interest in the library. Monsieur Daladier's English was not of the conventional variety, but he was doing his best, and he explained 'Ah yes—abiocobus!' Everyone looked bewildered, but Queen Elizabeth grasped what he meant. '*Ah oui, Monsieur,*' and she continued the conversation in French. The others looked at her hopefully for a lead, but she talked and twinkled, deliberately refusing to enlighten them. Afterwards, she explained that what he had meant was the Habeas Corpus Act.

When she was arranging details of her arrival in a certain public building, in which the reception rooms are at a great distance from the entrance, she wrote in a note to her Lady-in-Waiting, 'I shall arrive at 3.30 and proceed (by roller skate!) . . .'

Queen Elizabeth is imperturbable and serene in conditions which, with less adept handling, might deteriorate into chaos. She rises gladly to an emergency, and with her tremendous dignity, grace and charm she averts what might be an incident. She can cope with anything.

When a Lord Mayor lost his place in the proceedings, and called for a vote of thanks before Queen Elizabeth had spoken, she was enchanted—she beamed. When a lady's hat blew off just as she was presented, Queen Elizabeth said quietly, 'Don't worry about it—it's quite all right,' and continued speaking to her longer than to anyone else. When a confused man, coming at the end of a long line of women who were being presented, also dropped a curtsey, she smiled delightedly at him as if it were a private joke between them. When, at an inspection of the London Scottish, of which she is Honorary Colonel, the Provost's 'lum hat' blew off and bowled across the parade ground, she turned to the officers of her Regiment beside her and said, 'That's made the afternoon.' She immensely enjoyed the moment when a newly-appointed Deaconess of the Forces during the war, when asked her biggest problem, replied promptly, 'King's Regulations, Ma'am.' 'But he does not *write* them you know,' she said with a broad smile.

On a day in Australia, when the gremlins were loose and everything went wrong that could—a guard of honour had suddenly turned about to face away from her; the gusty wind had blown away the hats of the women being presented and indeed had blown their skirts over their heads; fire engines with sirens screaming had suddenly broken through the official motorcade; a public address system had broken down during her speech—the Queen Mother, serene and smiling, said sincerely as she finished what had been a long and exhausting day of constant crisis, 'I had a wonderful day and enjoyed everything.'

A newspaper report which gave her the greatest pleasure and amusement described her launching the *Ark Royal* in these words: 'On the dais stood the Queen, chatting to the Bishop and waving to the crowd. Suddenly, silently she was in the sea, surrounded by a mass of broken wreckage and the comments of the dockyard workers.'

When dignity is required, she gives it to the full. Those present when she presented Colours to the Royal Inniskilling Fusiliers Fifth Battalion (T.A.) and to the Royal Irish Fusiliers Fifth Battalion (T.A.), the first occasion on which Territorial Army Colours had been presented in Ulster, remember the appalling conditions of mud below and rain above and how Queen Elizabeth carried on with her duties as if everything overhead and underfoot were perfect.

Queen Elizabeth has a deep love of tradition: it is with reluctance that she sees history slip away. She knows that, while it may be just possible to carry on an old tradition, once continuity has been broken it becomes almost impossible to revive it. She is reluctant to see change for the sake of change, and accepts it only when she is sure it will lead to growth or betterment.

She has a great love of history, and her own roots are deep and strong. She has bought back portraits and possessions of the Bowes and the Lyons when they have come upon the market from time to time, and it was the plight of the historic little Barrogill Castle, to which she gave back its old name of Castle of Mey, that impelled her to buy and restore it when it was threatened with demolition.

Queen Elizabeth is very lucky; she likes simple things but she also likes great grandeur. She enjoys and graces the great occasions, formal and dignified during such ceremonies as a church service or a Presentation of Colours, relaxed and delightful in the social events which follow.

Yet she will pull on 'one of her dear, dreadful old felt hats', and at the end of a long day, battle out against wind and weather with her dogs. She loves fresh air, and she loves the country, where she relaxes and is at peace. She loves the blue distances of Africa; the swirling currents of the Pentland Firth with the cliffs of Orkney rising beyond; the blazing autumn colours of Deeside. She enjoys finding beautiful views with which to surprise and please her friends. She thought out a circuitous route at Invercauld, designed to show Queen Ingrid its special beauties—but alas, on the day of the Queen of Denmark's visit, the mist was down and there was nothing to be seen. When she had a relative staying on Deeside one wet autumn, and the sun was hidden day after day she really *longed* for the sun to shine again, so that one could see the full glory of the gold and red of the trees.

Queen Elizabeth is not a simple but a complex person. She has the simple qualities to a high degree—courage; a sense of duty; a deep love and sympathy with all living things; but she has subtler and hidden facets as well. The turbulent, mystic, complex blood of her Highland ancestry and the Scottish kings beats in her arteries. For all that she loves people and delights in the company of her friends, she also needs solitude from time to time. She is a very Highland person: some things are very private and secret.

She dislikes all things being known about her at all times, and will keep little inconsequential matters to herself, even from her own Household. She dislikes being forced in advance to decide and reveal her decisions about every single matter that concerns her private life, from the number of people coming to lunch, to the time she may or may not want to leave for her week-end at The Royal Lodge. It is, perhaps, the last revolt of the private person who was Lady Elizabeth Bowes-Lyon and who has been for over sixty years a Member of the Royal family.

Queen Elizabeth herself considers that one of her weak points is that, 'I am terribly *lazy*, and always have to drive myself to do things.' Laziness is the last defect of which the outside observer would accuse her, but perhaps there is a battle between her inner desire for quietude and the need to prepare for her next under-

taking. If she arrives a few minutes late, she occasionally ration-
alises this by saying, 'They are never ready for one.'

She refuses to be hurried or to stick too rigidly to a planned
programme. 'It is much more important not to miss anyone than
to be five or ten minutes late,' she once said to a Lady-in-Waiting. Programmes broken down into such precise timings as
10.53 a.m. and 3.42 p.m. are not at all to her liking. 'Timing to
the nearest five minutes is quite the limit,' she has said.

Queen Elizabeth may occasionally be a little over-optimistic
about the time factor, but nothing—nothing—could make her
deflect from her duty. Within is steel: a sense of duty unflinching
and absolute; and which expects the same selfless execution of
duty from others that she demands from herself. The fundamental integrities are all-powerful to her. If her duty is to do this
—and she sees duty in simple terms, not blurred with conditional
clauses and excuses—then she will unflinchingly fulfil it, come
what may. She has faced great crises in her life with the courage
of one of her own Black Watch going into battle.

Her life is founded upon her faith. In her home, her father, the
Earl of Strathmore, was a very religious man, while 'her mother
lived her faith', as an old family friend expressed it. When Lady
Elizabeth Bowes-Lyon married, the Christian faith was a strength
and joy she shared with her husband, the Duke of York. They
never undertook any great commitment or faced any great
danger or decision without prayer for God's blessing and
strength. Yet Queen Elizabeth is not a narrow churchwoman and
has always found it possible to understand and appreciate the
differing ways in which humanity reaches up to God.

This great inner strength has a complementary weakness—
because of course she must have weaknesses—in a refusal to
believe the worst or acknowledge anything wrong or evil until
it has absolutely overwhelmed her. This has been interpreted as a
refusal to face facts, but is a disinclination to cross a bridge from a
well-loved landscape before it is unavoidable. When, or if, no
alternative remains she will resolutely cross over the bridge to the
new life beyond; until then she may well ignore its very presence.

Queen Elizabeth has a simple belief that no one would do anything really nasty by design. It takes her a very long time to

believe that she has been thoroughly let down. Once she realises that the trust has been misplaced, the wound goes deep: she can forgive any act but treachery, but then she is implacable as any Scot.

Queen Elizabeth can sometimes take a long time to make up her mind. She is a person whom it is difficult to force into a decision. If she is not ready for it, or if she believes that the situation will be solved by time better than by premature decision, she will slide the discussion away from the disputed subject, not refusing to discuss it but instead somehow talking about something else. Her opinion is not lightly shaken nor changed, even though she may not always express it. When her standpoint has been taken she will not argue nor dispute, it will somehow just be very much easier to do the thing in her way. Perhaps her philosophy towards opposition might be summed up in the old Scottish proverb, 'Wha tholes, wins' (he who endures will win).

She has an iron will with regard to health. Although she was not considered strong as a girl, she has great physical stamina. Even on days when she sets out from the Royal train about 9.30 in the morning and does not get back to it until the end of a full and crowded day at 8.30 p.m., she can still return as fresh, amusing and cheerful as she started out. Queen Elizabeth does not burden other people with her tiredness, believing that if she pays attention to her fatigue, she will only intensify it and realise how exhausted she really is.

Cosseting and pampering one's health are utterly foreign to her. She would neither want for herself nor expect you to want overmuch sympathy for any minor ailment. She considers it a kind of unseemly self-indulgence to give in and admit you are not well unless you are absolutely forced to do so. She also believes that much can be achieved by mind over matter, and that by refusing to recognise an ailment, it will cease to have any importance. (One disability she does understand is asthma, from which several of the Bowes-Lyon family suffered: an asthmatic Member of her Household is often told quietly, 'Don't hurry—take it easy.') A cold in the head, a headache or any minor upset would simply be disregarded in the course of duty: sometimes she suffers from heavy bronchial colds, to which she gives in with extreme reluctance. Her eldest sister, Lady Elphinstone, remembered a truly dreadful day of wind and rain at Carberry Tower when Queen Elizabeth, who had recently been ill, stood facing into the gale with her head back, saying, 'This really makes you recover from the flu.'

When she broke a small bone in her foot in the summer of 1961, although the foot caused her considerable pain, she insisted on fulfilling every possible engagement. Wearing a bandage and a special wooden-soled shoe, she made the journey to Walker-on-Tyne that June to launch the liner *Northern Star*. Queen Elizabeth was pushed in a wheel-chair up a special ramp to the launching platform, but because she noticed that the shipyard workers and their wives could not see her from the wheelchair, she insisted on walking back.

In a quiet way Queen Elizabeth can dislike things, but as she seldom says so, it is not easy to enumerate them. She certainly dislikes a show of officious bossiness or unnecessary fuss, albeit for her benefit. Her Ladies-in-Waiting know how to interpret her glance if officials or police get carried away with over-enthusiasm on a public occasion. She dislikes strongly held and expressed prejudices which are unsupported by adequate knowledge. Incidentally, she is not easily convinced in argument.

Many people who have known her for half their lives have never seen her angry. One of her sisters said, 'I have never seen Queen Elizabeth angry. She *must* have been angry at some time, but she must have bottled it up. I am sure cruelty would make her angry.' Although the other sides of her character can be illustrated again and again, I learnt only of the following two instances on which she had been perceptibly angry. Once a very young person was put on a pony, took fright and showed it. Again, she watched three of her nephews and nieces trying to climb down a dangerous cliff face at Loch Muick. 'Then, she was *very* angry.'

She has an instinctive abhorrence of disease and maiming, a characteristic which is very often found in men and is by no means uncommon in women. This dislike has never made her shrink from doing far more than her duty in visiting the sick and wounded. When she visited hospitals for the war-wounded during the Second World War she insisted on seeing all the wounded men, however disfigured, and she brought them sympathy and courage; but it was not easy for her.

This was a lesson she had had to learn while a schoolgirl, when Glamis was a military hospital during the First World War. The soldiers who spent their convalescence at Glamis remember to this day how she teased and charmed them into good spirits, how she played and sang for them, wrote letters for those unfit to write and generally helped to restore them to normality, because some of the men were badly shattered in body and spirit. She then had her early lessons in complete, selfless control, in the iron discipline and sense of duty that lie under her smile.

Queen Elizabeth learnt how to meet life and its duties from her family, and particularly from her mother. Lady Strathmore's creed was expressed in such family sayings as, 'If you give of your maximum, you then do it as well as possible' and 'If you give of your maximum, you receive more in return.' Creating gaiety and happiness are Queen Elizabeth's particular delights. She belongs to a family which enjoys life: she enjoys it, and feels it a positive charge upon her to make all others enjoy it to the full. She brought to her husband undreamed of and lasting happiness which sustained him through the crushing responsibilities of kingship and war, and through the weary frustrations of failing health. She provided a natural and happy childhood to her children, and the Queen has built her life on the absolute security of those foundations. Queen Elizabeth shares her gift with those around her on innumerable occasions, so that a formal occasion in the phrase I was to hear time and time again, 'becomes a party when she is there'.

Queen Elizabeth shows a wonderful gentle understanding; an extreme sympathy towards her own family. She is the person to whom her large family of brothers and sisters turned for advice, knowing she will do anything she can to help—and she *does* help. She is much more interested in other people than in herself. A member of the family said that the qualities she most deeply values in Queen Elizabeth are 'sympathy, first and foremost . . . then she has a great sense of humour—she can be very, very funny when she lets herself go'.

Yet Queen Elizabeth, for all her intelligence, quickness and sympathy is not 'a doing sort of person'. She seems to have no compulsion to identify herself with nature in the practical, detailed or creative ways which draw most people of such intelligence and personality. She neither paints nor photographs nor collects wild flowers, nor does she plant and sow, weed and grub in the soil, the primitive urge of most country people—and she is very much a countrywoman. Nor is she an ornithologist or any other kind of 'ologist'. She is the person who brings her fuel to your fire: she does not take your fuel for her fire. She brings her personality and adds it to yours, making your aims higher, your achievement greater, your courage brighter and your spirit happier.

It is fortunate that, through her marriage with King George V's second son, Prince Albert, Duke of York, the great gifts of Lady Elizabeth Bowes-Lyon should have become of more than family and local importance. The members of the Royal family do not just have 'a job to do', they are dedicated to the unity of the Commonwealth, to the service of all of us—not any section or class or group. They aid the Sovereign in the task of presenting unity, dignity, and the simple virtues of a good family life to the millions of diversified subjects and citizens of the Commonwealth; they create a national image to the world. Our national emblem is not a flag or an anthem, but a family; it is a human and changing ideal, and it requires many differing kinds of service from many differing members of the Royal family.

There is, and can be, no ideal British Royal personage. All qualities are needed, drawing attention to achievement and hard work, rewarding courage, condoling with disaster and bereavement, adding interest and glamour in the original sense in which Sir Walter Scott introduced it, meaning 'magic, enchantment, spell'.

The world-wide interest in the British Royal family springs from just this diversity, from the effects of personality upon high and exacting office. Every quality is of value—the dignity and sound commonsense of Queen Victoria; the charm and generosity of Queen Alexandra; the high sense of duty and courage of Queen Mary; the dedication and steadfastness of Queen Elizabeth II.

Queen Elizabeth, with her spontaneous smile and her infectious friendliness, her motherliness, her unflinching sense of duty, her courage, her gaiety is beloved by millions. Her contribution to her Sovereign and her country is as individual and as valuable as any in the long line of British Royalty, and it is the unique story of her constant support to the Sovereign, as daughter-in-law of King George V, as sister-in-law of King Edward VIII, as wife and Consort of King George VI and as mother of Queen Elizabeth II which will be told in the pages to follow.

CHAPTER TWO

BETROTHAL TO THE KING'S SON

I am quite certain that Elizabeth will be a splendid partner in your work and share with you and help you in all you have to do

King George V in a letter to the Duke of York, quoted by Sir John Wheeler-Bennett

ON Saturday, January 13, 1923, in the leafless Bury Woods of her father's home of St. Paul's Walden Bury in the county of Hertfordshire, a young man of twenty-seven proposed to a girl of twenty-two. She accepted him.

He was His Royal Highness Prince Albert Frederick Arthur George, Duke of York, second son of the reigning monarch, King George V; and she was Lady Elizabeth Angela Marguerite Bowes-Lyon, ninth child and fourth daughter of the fourteenth Earl of Strathmore and Kinghorne, who was also Viscount Lyon, and Baron Glamis, Tannadyce, Sidlaw and Strathdichtie.

On Monday, January 15, the Duke of York followed the telegram by which he had told his parents of his successful wooing, from St. Paul's Walden to Sandringham, where he confirmed and amplified the news that he was at last officially engaged.

'We are delighted, and he looks beaming,' wrote Queen Mary in her diary.

On the same day, the Court Circular formally announced:

'It is with the greatest pleasure that the King and Queen announce the betrothal of their beloved son, the Duke of York, to the Lady Elizabeth Bowes-Lyon, daughter of the Earl and Countess of Strathmore and Kinghorne, to which union the King has gladly given his consent.'

The engagement came as a complete surprise to the public, but it was not unexpected by the Bowes-Lyon family. As one of them remarked, 'Courtings are as old as the hills, and just as obvious.'

It was a very big step for Lady Elizabeth to take. She belonged to a large, warm-hearted, closely-knit family, and was a girl of exceptional charm. She had attracted many suitors. She made a brave decision when she accepted the Duke of York, and so decided to leave her unusually happy and informal family life and to enter the Royal circle. Royalty lived then, much more than now, a life apart.

Moreover, there was no precedent to help her; for over two centuries the British Royal family had always married royal, and generally foreign wives. For the first time since King James II, when Duke of York, had married Lady Anne Hyde, daughter of Edward, Earl of Clarendon, as his second wife, the son of an English King had chosen as his officially recognised wife a woman of pure British stock and a commoner.

At that time the Duke of York was extremely shy. Bedevilled by his stutter, in the public eye he was very much an 'also-ran' to his god-like elder brother, the Prince of Wales. The Duke of York's qualities of pluck and perseverance, tested in battle when he served with the Royal Navy at the Battle of Jutland during the still-recent First World War, and his sincere interest in men in industry, were mildly recognised. But the world-wide love and respect in which he was held by the end of his life were undreamt-of in 1923.

Newspapers on the following day contained a scrambled gleaning of stray grains of fact and fancy, as the Press strove desperately to comment on the engagement. Outside her family and county circles, nothing had been known of Lady Elizabeth Bowes-Lyon. She was not a member of those circles publicised in the gossip columns, which were themselves less powerful and less acid than they are today. The reference books had shown that Lady Elizabeth Bowes-Lyon was of extremely long and noble lineage, and was through her father descended from King Robert II of Scotland (as was the Duke of York); and that, through her mother, she was close kin with the Dukes of Portland. But of her personality and interests, the Press could discover virtually nothing.

To us today, accustomed to the publicity surrounding royalty, the most surprising thing about the engagement is that nothing much happened at all. The Duke of York was second in the Succession, and he was the first of the King's sons to become engaged: the marriage of a Prince of the Blood Royal, son of King, to a commoner with the willing consent of the Sovereign, was an event without precedent for several hundred years. Yet St. Paul's Walden was not besieged: it was possible for the Bowes-Lyon family to continue to lead their normal lives.

The actions of Press and public were pleasantly cordial, but there was no great excitement. Even the newly-engaged Duke of York and Lady Elizabeth Bowes-Lyon had only to contend with a heavy post of letters of goodwill, and some amiable cheering when they were seen in public.

One reason was that the Prince of Wales was then only twenty-eight years old, his early engagement was confidently expected, and so the marriage of a younger brother was not so important. A stronger reason still was the much slower tempo of life in those days, and the less fervent interest taken in the private lives of public personalities.

Prince Albert first met Lady Elizabeth when they were children, but it was only when they grew up that they came to know each other well, through the friendship of the Duke of York with the Bowes-Lyon brothers, and through Lady Elizabeth's friendship with Princess Mary, the Duke's sister. Lady Elizabeth had been bridesmaid at the marriage of Princess Mary to Viscount Lascelles. Mr. Frank Salisbury had been chosen to paint a picture of the wedding: he tells in his reminiscences, *Sarum Chase*, that he had difficulty in including the many persons connected with the ceremony in a harmonious group, and, on the suggestion of King George V, he eventually omitted some of the bridesmaids— among them Lady Elizabeth Bowes-Lyon!

The Duke of York, through his friendship with the Bowes-Lyon family, had entered a magical world—a world which never lost its savour for him as long as he lived. The Court in which the young Prince had grown up was formal, and life was conducted within a set pattern. Much though the Duke of York admired his father he had not at this time established that steadfast relationship on which King George V relied increasingly as the years went by. The Duke of York was devoted to his mother, Queen Mary, but her intense shyness, her austere sense of duty, came between her and a fully uninhibited relationship with her children.

How different it was with the Bowes-Lyon family at Glamis or at St. Paul's Walden. 'That family is a clan,' said one of their oldest friends. One who married a Bowes-Lyon stressed their fantastically happy family life. Not particularly wealthy, and certainly not interested in 'fashionable society', the Bowes-Lyon family enjoyed each other's company to the full. 'It was like an enormous family party,' said one of them. 'It was the nicest way of life in the world. And as we were stuck with each other every day from Alpha to Omega absolutely constantly, a lot of head-knocking went on which was very good for us. We learnt that most important fact, that family life is a tremendous thing—and enormous fun.'

Through his long friendship with Lady Elizabeth's brothers, the Duke of York already fitted in well with this lively family, who had seen a good deal of him over the past few years. With his sister Princess Mary, the Duke of York had first come to stay at Glamis in 1920, when the Countess of Strathmore had been ill, and so Lady Elizabeth had had to act as hostess. After that he had stayed regularly—very regularly—at St. Paul's Walden and at Glamis.

The give-and-take of the large household had been quite new to him: it warmed and expanded him. Above all, he found that the sun always shone for him—then and always—in the company of Lady Elizabeth.

Family photograph albums of the period show the Duke of York and Lady Elizabeth Bowes-Lyon playing tennis together, standing next to each other in groups taken on the steps below the circular staircase turret at Glamis. All the other girls are wearing little round hats with little round brims, but Lady Elizabeth is wearing a sun-bonnet. In every photograph, the Duke of York is noticeably looking very happy.

The Bowes-Lyon family was led, by power of personality, by the Countess of Strathmore, mother of Lady Elizabeth. There is no need to jog the memory of anyone who knew the Countess of Strathmore—mention her name and out tumble the memories and the stories, told with an irrepressible smile of remembered happiness. Her sons and daughters adored her.

'Mother was a very wonderful woman, very talented, very go-ahead and so upright,' said one of her daughters. 'She had a terrific sympathy: the young used to pour their troubles out to her and ask her for advice, often when they would not go to their own parents. She was extremely artistic. She sewed lovely embroidery, which she designed herself. She had an extremely good ear for music, she would go to a concert and listen to the music, and come back and play it perfectly.'

Lady Strathmore could not describe anything without using her hands. Her sons used to make her tell them stories. There was one about burglars, which they loved, where at one point she always picked up an imaginary pistol and went bang-bang-bang on the trigger. Queen Elizabeth also uses her hands, but does not use them as vivaciously as her mother did.

The Countess of Strathmore was quickly sparked into enthusiasm. 'She was always finding something fresh to interest her,' said another member of her family. 'Something new—not necessarily something prudent . . . buying a house . . . going to a sale . . . entering a fresh field. Mother retained this immense zest for living, this intense interest in everything going on—particularly to the people whom she loved—just as she kept her sense of gaiety, right to the end.'

She had a tremendous capacity for making friends and a complete lack of snobbery; she took strong and intuitive likes and dislikes to people.

Lady Strathmore had a delightful casualness about the things which did not seem to her to be very important. One friend, sitting with her in one of the fine rooms at St. Paul's Walden, could not take her eyes from water streaming down one wall from a burst pipe or some other mishap. At last she could not contain herself any longer, and drew Lady Strathmore's attention to it. 'Oh dear,' she said with mild interest. 'We must move that sofa.'

Her part in bringing up her large family of ten children was fundamental. Like many mothers of a large family, she was distinctly stricter with the older members than she was with the younger—or so the older members thought. She led by example, however, and not by punishment. 'I never heard her say a harsh word in my life,' said an older sister. 'But we had to obey her, we knew that. We were brought up with very definite principles.'

Lady Elizabeth and her younger brother David were so much the youngest of her children that Lady Strathmore used to call them 'my Benjamins'. It was only natural that they were treated with greater indulgence than the older children, but they never became spoilt. One of her older sisters said: 'As Elizabeth was the youngest daughter, she was very much with our mother. She was such an attractive little thing that an old friend of my mother asked, "What *can* you do to punish Elizabeth?" My mother said, "It is quite enough just to say *Elizabeth!* in a very sad way: then she will hang her head and be sorry." It is quite true, I have heard her myself. My father adored her too, but it was really my mother who brought her up.'

Queen Elizabeth greatly resembles her mother in a number of ways: the comparison is invariably made by those who also knew Lady Strathmore. A member of the Bowes-Lyon family said, 'Queen Elizabeth resembles her mother in her capacity for making friends, in the friendliness of her character, in her sense of humour. I think both of them have exactly the same sort of constructive mind . . . and of course the same gaiety.'

In comparison with the strong personality of the Countess of Strathmore, recollections of the Earl of Strathmore, Queen Elizabeth's father, are less pronounced. Lord Strathmore was a quiet, courteous, religious man, conscientious to a degree in carrying out his duties to the County of Angus, of which he was Lord Lieutenant for a large part of his life. So, too, was he vigilant in attending to his responsibilities as a landowner and took infinite care of the well-being of all whose livelihood stemmed from his property.

He was a keen sportsman, being a better than average cricketer, and an excellent shot, and these and his other country interests—particularly his devotion to forestry, of which he was an acknowledged authority—earned him a considerable reputation for his knowledge of rural affairs.

His sense of duty was developed to a high degree, a characteristic he perpetually instilled in his children, and one which Queen Elizabeth unquestionably possesses.

Lord and Lady Strathmore's family consisted of four daughters and six sons, who inherited in full measure the vitality and personality of their mother. All the Bowes-Lyon family have great charm, and it came in a special degree to the daughters.

The oldest child, Violet Hyacinth, died when she was eleven years old, before Queen Elizabeth was born. There is a memorial to her in the church of St. Paul's Walden Bury.

The second child was also a daughter—but she was followed by six sons. She was Mary Frances, who married the sixteenth baron Elphinstone in 1910, and who died in 1961. As the eldest surviving child, she was given considerable responsibility, and was regarded by the nursery end of the family as almost one of the older generation.

To the end of her life Lady Elphinstone retained her good looks, her vivacity and the easy friendliness which makes it such a particular pleasure to meet any member of the Bowes-Lyon family. She was a keen, active and knowledgeable gardener, who wrote a delightful book about British plants for children. It was at her suggestion that the tubs of giant thistles, one for each Knight of the Thistle, are placed round the walls of the Palace of Holyroodhouse, as though on guard, whenever it is occupied by a member of the Royal family.

Lord Elphinstone, who died in 1955, was Lord High Commissioner to the General Assembly of the Church of Scotland in 1923; and Captain General of the Royal Company of Archers from 1935 to 1953. Their five children all adored their very young aunt, who was only a few years older than they were. They remain close friends of Queen Elizabeth and of the Queen and Princess Margaret.

The eldest son, Patrick, was born in 1884. He married Lady Dorothy Godolphin Osborne, and died in 1949. The present sixteenth Earl of Strathmore is his second (twin) son. The second son, John Herbert, was born in 1886, married Miss Fenella Hepburn-Stuart-Forbes-Trefusis, and died in 1930. The third son, Alexander Francis, was born in 1887, and died in 1911, at the age of twenty-four. The fourth son, Fergus, was born in 1889 and married Lady Christian Norah Dawson-Damer; he was killed in action with The Black Watch at Loos in 1915.

The seventh child, Lady Rose Bowes-Lyon, married the Hon. William Spencer Leveson Gower, who succeeded his brother as fourth Earl Granville. Lord Granville had a distinguished career in the Royal Navy, and Lady Granville consequently spent much of her married life abroad 'following the flag'.

After his retirement from the Navy, Lord Granville was Lieutenant-Governor of the Isle of Man from 1937 to 1945, and then in September 1945 succeeded the Duke of Abercorn as Governor of Northern Ireland. He filled both posts with exceptional success, while Lady Granville, as Governor's wife, showed just that warm brilliance which her younger sister showed as Queen. Lord Granville was sworn in for a second term of office, but he became so ill that he was unable to take part in the Accession ceremonies of Queen Elizabeth II and he resigned in 1952. The Queen conferred the Garter on him in December of that year, and he died in June 1953.

Rose, Lady Granville, lived in a remote glen in Angus, where her garden tumbles in a riot of flowers down a hillside, and the white Bonnie Prince Charles roses (also loved by Queen Elizabeth who has planted a bush at Balmoral) grow against the thick walls of her sturdy stone house. She closely resembled her sister Queen Elizabeth, both in characteristics and in interests, and like her, had the gift of attracting and holding affection and love.

The eighth child and fifth son was Michael Claude, who was inclined to be delicate as he suffered from asthma, but had one of the keenest senses of humour in the gay family. He married Miss Elizabeth Margaret Cator, and died in 1954.

Then, seven years after the birth of her brother Michael, Lady Elizabeth Angela Marguerite was born on August 4, 1900, ninth child and fourth daughter of the Earl and Countess of Strathmore.

The member of the family closest to Lady Elizabeth in age, and also without doubt in 'togetherness', was her youngest brother, David (the late Sir David Bowes-Lyon), born in 1902. He married

Miss Rachel Pauline Spender-Clay. Sir David's death at the early age of fifty-nine in the summer of 1961 was a tragic blow.

'Although two years separated them, they were almost like twins as children,' said an older sister. 'They had rooms next to each other at Glamis, and spent all possible time together. They had a wonderful and very close relationship.' There is a family photograph which shows them as young children, her arm round his neck and shoulder, which illustrates well the protective and loving relationship between them.

Lady Elizabeth, as the elder, naturally took the lead. 'We grew up together, did all the usual country-life things together,' the late Sir David Bowes-Lyon told me. 'We looked after our gardens and our bantams, played indifferent tennis, and in London went to the theatre together. We were never separated if we could avoid it.'

They were not, however, carbon copies of each other. Lady Elizabeth loved riding, her brother David disliked horses. She loved parties: he did not. She liked to stay up late: he did not. 'But everything we did together was fun, and we did everything possible together.' It would be difficult to over-stress the love and interdependence of the two youngest Bowes-Lyon children.

Sir David Bowes-Lyon inherited Lady Strathmore's active enjoyment of the good earth. His deep love and understanding of landscape gardening was firmly founded on what he learnt from his mother and also on a practical training at Kew. Fittingly, he was President of the Royal Horticultural Society. Although Sir David had an eminent career in the City, he rose early each morning to plan the day's work in his garden at St. Paul's Walden, before travelling to London.

The Bowes-Lyon family gathered together whenever possible. They enjoyed everything as it came, all the more so when it could be shared with other members of the family, and with the close family friends who came year after year to Glamis or St. Paul's Walden. To be sure, considering their position and responsibilities, there was not very much money, but that was not important to them. Although the Bowes-Lyon family moved in differing paths through life, the happy relationship between them was never altered.

Lady Elizabeth Bowes-Lyon is of ancient family. It must be rare for two young people to marry, each brought up in houses in which Shakespeare set scenes of his plays, Windsor and Glamis. Both were directly descended from King Robert the Bruce, through his grandson, King Robert II of Scotland, an unusually wise king for the troubled times in which he lived; he reigned from 1370 or 1371 to 1390. King Robert II secured his position by marrying his large family wisely and widely among the great families of Scotland. His daughter Jean, by his first marriage, married as her second husband the King's Secretary, Sir John Lyon, called by reason of his fair colouring 'The White Lyon'. He was created Lord Lyon and received the royal hunting lodge of Glamis in dowry. From this union Lady Elizabeth Bowes-Lyon is directly descended.

By the time of their alliance with the Scottish Royal family in the fourteenth century, the Lyons were already a family of distinction in Scotland. The White Lyon's grandson was created first Lord Glamis in 1445. A century later, the widow of the sixth Lord Glamis, Lady Jean Douglas, who had subsequently married Campbell of Skipnish, and whose two Douglas brothers were hated by King James V, was accused by the King of treason and of mixing potions and witchcraft. She and her son were seized and, after four trials, condemned to death, while her second husband was killed in an attempt to escape from Edinburgh Castle. On December 3, 1540, Lady Glamis was burnt alive as a witch on the Castle Hill of Edinburgh:

'With the great commiseration of the people, being in the prime of her years, of a singular beauty, and suffering all, though a woman, with manlike courage, all men conceiving that it was not this act [witchcraft] but the hatred which the King carried to her brothers.'

During the imprisonment of her son, whose sentence of death had been turned into life imprisonment on the grounds of his youth, King James V and Queen Marie of Lorraine stayed at Glamis, which they ransacked, so that when the seventh Lord Glamis was released and his lands restored, following the death of James V, he returned to an empty Castle and impoverished lands. There is a portrait of him, with his secretary, in the drawing room at Glamis.

Patrick, the ninth Lord Glamis, was created first Earl of Kinghorne by James VI of Scotland and I of England in 1606; he was a prominent public servant and set in hand much rebuilding of Glamis. John, tenth Lord Glamis and second Earl of Kinghorne, was a follower and great personal friend of the great Marquess of Montrose, but eventually parted from him on grounds of conscience and subsequently volunteered to pay large sums for maintaining the arms of the Covenant against Montrose. Coming to his inheritance the wealthiest peer in Scotland he left it the poorest.

His son, eleventh Lord Glamis and third Earl of Kinghorne, was created Earl of Strathmore by King Charles II. He came into his estate hampered by a debt of £400,000, but paid off most of it 'by prudence and frugality'. He later altered and enlarged the Castle and improved the estate. It was John, nineteenth Lord Glamis, eleventh Earl of Kinghorne and ninth Earl of Strathmore, who married Mary Eleanor, only child and heiress of the wealthy Member of Parliament George Bowes of Streatham and Gibside in County Durham, on February 14, 1767, and who thereupon took, by Act of Parliament, the surname of Bowes. The Bowes were a very well-known North of England family, and Sir J. Bowes, an ancestor of the heiress, had been Ambassador to Russia for Queen Elizabeth I. His son, Thomas, Earl of Strathmore, resumed the surname of Lyon before Bowes, and the thirteenth Earl assumed the present Bowes-Lyon.

The Countess of Strathmore was the daughter of the Rev. C. W. F. Bentinck—he seldom used the double name of Cavendish-Bentinck, granted by Royal Licence to the third Duke of Portland in 1801. Lady Strathmore's father was heir to his unmarried kinsman, the fifth Duke of Portland, but died before him, and as he had no sons, the title passed to his younger brother's son. Through the Portland family, Lady Elizabeth Bowes-Lyon is connected with most of the great families of England. She is a descendant of the third Duke of Portland, who was Prime Minister twice, in 1783 and again in 1807-9; of William, fourth

Duke of Devonshire, and of Robert Harley, Lord High Treasurer to Queen Anne, and created Earl of Oxford.

It is impossible not to be aware of the past at Glamis. Glamis Castle is built halfway along the flat, rich Great Glen from which the family title of Strathmore is taken, close to Hunter's Hill, from which its warm pink stone was quarried. Glamis is believed to take its name from the Gaelic *glamhus* meaning 'wide gap'. Two burns, the Glamis Burn and Dean Water, amble through the grounds. The Castle is approached by a long, tree-lined avenue through Angles Park. The towers on the lawn near the house are the remains of the wall which once completely surrounded the Castle, and was pulled down—to the great indignation of Sir Walter Scott—when the grounds were laid out, it is believed by Capability Brown, around the year 1770.

The present imposing Castle is built in the original sturdy Scots Baronial style—not to be confused with its ornate Victorian counterfeit any more than 'Gilbert Scott Gothic' with medieval Gothic. It is on the site of a hunting lodge built for the Scottish Kings in the eleventh century, but the oldest parts remaining today are the L-shaped wings, which date from the fifteenth century. The circular staircase was built into the angle of the L in the early seventeenth century. Up the tower runs a staircase of one hundred and forty-three steps, each cut from a single stone, and each so wide that five men can walk up it abreast. By an early form of central heating, a fire could be lit at the base of the staircase and heat travelled up the hollow newel and came out of gratings on the landings.

So there was to be nothing strange in living in historic surroundings to Elizabeth Bowes-Lyon. Of all the Royal homes in which she was to live, only Windsor Castle and the Palace of Holyroodhouse can compare, in tradition and history, with Glamis Castle. Glamis knew the Kings of Scotland from the eleventh until the fourteenth century. Mary, Queen of Scots, was entertained here, and with her four Maries embroidered the covers of a chair. The English Ambassador privately reported to Queen Elizabeth I that, 'In spite of extreme Fowle and Colde weather, I never saw her merrier, never dismayed.'

There is a legend that Shakespeare visited Glamis Castle before writing *Macbeth*, and set the scene of the murder of King Duncan I by Macbeth, the Thane of Glamis (but not an ancestor of Lady Elizabeth's) in 1034 in Duncan's Hall. This is the original Guard Room of the Palace, through which all had to pass on entering before the new entrance and staircase were built in the seventeenth century. This is a gloomy vault with walls eight feet thick, off which lies the Castle's prison. It contains a stuffed brown bear, which was a family pet in the nineteenth century. Later, after the marriage of the Duke and Duchess of York and during one of their frequent visits to Glamis, two men of the Duke's Household sat chatting late at night, until the lights in the Castle were extinguished, as everyone was thought to be in bed. They continued their talk by candlelight, and when their candles were guttering, they went off to find their rooms. Eventually they were reduced to finding their way down the stone stairs, striking matches, and when these also ran short, they lost their way—one, to his extreme fright, ending up in the arms of the stuffed bear in Duncan's Hall!

Although Glamis was so old and full of history and ancient treasures, it was very far from being a museum. It was a lively and happy family home, whose inhabitants spent as many hours as possible out of doors, on the hills, in the policies or in the gardens created by Lady Strathmore. It was here that the Duke of York learnt what fun life can be when it is very simple.

After a day spent in the open air, the family used to take tea in the Blue Room, so called from its blue sofas, which overlooked the North-West Park and Warren Wood. On the walls were paintings of the family's famous horses, such as *West Australian*, one of John Bowes' four winners of the Derby, and the first winner of the Triple Crown.

Dinner was served in the great dining room, in the most modern part of the Castle, which had been burnt down and rebuilt in the early nineteenth century. On the walls were the family arms, their changes recalling the family history of the centuries. Food was prepared in a vast, Gothic-windowed kitchen much older than the dining room.

After dinner, the family used to gather in the barrel-vaulted drawing room, once the Great Hall of the Castle, which has an ornate plaster ceiling made by Italian craftsmen in 1621; a room dominated by the enormous fireplace, thirteen feet wide and as high as the spring of the ceiling, in which a huge log fire blazed against the chill of the Scottish evenings. At St. Paul's Walden there is an evocative picture painted in 1909 of Lord and Lady Strathmore and their family in this room. Lady Strathmore is pouring tea, and the family is grouped about the room. In the foreground Lady Elizabeth and her youngest brother are kneeling by a stool, building card houses.

The family used to gather round the piano, and Lady Strathmore or one of her daughters would play, while everyone sang. They often sang the old Scottish songs in the *Scottish Students' Song Book*, which remain favourites with Queen Elizabeth, and which she has taught her daughters. Sometimes they sang the lighthearted songs of the day, which are still kept in the mother-of-pearl canterbury beside the grand piano—'The Gaby Glide' by Irving Berlin, 'Would you like me for a father, Mary Ann?', 'The Little Nipper' by Arthur Chevalier, and 'The Vamp' from *Bran Pie*. There is also 'The Glamis Castle Waltz' by Virginia Gabriel, but it does not show signs of such constant use as the other sheets.

An unusual and fascinating feature at Glamis were the 'scrapbook walls' in what was known as 'the boys' wing', where the plain walls of the landing and staircase had been completely covered with a jigsaw of pictures cut from illustrated magazines, showing modest 'pin-up girls' in black picture hats and swathes of tulle, 'Old Bill' cartoons and *Punch* pictures in an ingenious medley, capturing the exact flavour of its age far better than any historian. There used to be similar scrapbook walls at St. Paul's Walden Bury.

The Chapel was an integral part of Glamis, where prayers were said daily. The women all wore little white caps made of thick crochet lace, fastened onto the hair with two skewers of hairpins —a cap was provided in the bedroom of each woman guest. On Sunday, Lady Strathmore, with this little cap on her head, used to sit at the harmonium and play accompaniments to the hymns.

Normally Lord Strathmore and his family only spent the late

summer and autumn at Glamis, but because of the Great War, Lady Elizabeth lived there for some years. Similarly Princess Elizabeth and Princess Margaret were to spend more of their formative years in the historic surroundings of Windsor Castle, because of the Second World War.

Most of the rest of the year the Bowes-Lyon family lived at St. Paul's Walden Bury in Hertfordshire. Although St. Paul's Walden is about thirty miles from London, and only a few miles from Letchworth, Hitchin, and the bustling satellite town of Stevenage, it is still rural. Set in undulating, pretty countryside of wood and field, it has changed remarkably little in this century. Walden was a village named in Domesday Book, and was originally held by the Abbot of St. Albans under the King. Afterwards Walden passed to the Dean and Chapter of St. Paul's, when its name was changed to St. Paul's Walden.

The Bury estate was owned in the early eighteenth century by one Edward Gilbert who left it, when he died in 1762, to his daughter Mary, who married George Bowes of County Durham. It was their daughter Mary Eleanor who married John Lyon, Earl of Strathmore.

The history of the house of St. Paul's Walden Bury is obscure. The present house is of old red brick, built between 1720 and 1740. It is a dignified and pleasant country seat, built for the arts of peace and not of war. The dark past of Glamis, vanquished only by the vitality of Lady Strathmore, 'who had exorcised the ghosts', as a family friend expressed it, has a very different atmosphere from this pleasant English country house in its delightfully laid-out grounds. There was nothing eerie or wildly romantic about St. Paul's Walden Bury. The clank and bump of opening shutters in the morning, the cough of pheasants, the songs of birds were its sounds.

In *The Times* Coronation Supplement of 1937 there was a pleasant description, for which one may hazard a family source, of Lady Elizabeth Bowes-Lyon's childhood there:

'Home was not Glamis (for holidays) or Streatlam Castle, Durham (for visits) but St. Paul's Waldenbury, a comely red-brick Queen Anne house, much grown upon by magnolia and honeysuckle, in pleasant Hertfordshire. Here were all the things that children could desire—dogs and tortoises, Persian kittens and "Bobs" the Shetland pony, hay to make, chickens to feed, a garden, a friendly stillroom, the attic of a tumble-down brew house to play truant in, bullfinches to tame, fields to roam, flowers to love, ripe apples to drop, providentially, about the head, and on wet days, the books that are best read on the floor in front of the fire, and a wonderful chest full of period costumes and the wigs that went with their gorgeous-ness.'

Sir David and Lady Bowes-Lyon lived in St. Paul's Walden Bury, and Queen Elizabeth often visited them there. Her brother was with her on public as well as private occasions in Hertford-shire, as he was Lord Lieutenant of the county in which, in her own words, she has spent 'so many happy years of my life'.

Lady Elizabeth Bowes-Lyon emerged from this exceptionally happy background, and made her first step into the public gaze, on Saturday, January 20, 1923, when she left Liverpool Street Station in London in a special saloon attached to the 11.50 train, bound for Sandringham, where she would be introduced to King George V, Queen Mary and Queen Alexandra.

Sir John Wheeler-Bennett described the meeting with the King and Queen Mary as 'an ordeal not to be underestimated but Lady Elizabeth came through it with flying colours'. 'Elizabeth is charming, so pretty and engaging and natural. Bertie is supremely happy,' Queen Mary wrote that night, and the King's comment was no less enthusiastic. 'She is a pretty and charming girl and Bertie is a very lucky fellow.'

There was nothing to hinder an early marriage: on February 8 it was announced that the wedding of the Duke of York with Lady Elizabeth Bowes-Lyon would take place at Westminster Abbey on Thursday, April 20, and The Times commented that it was understood that the wedding would be in the Abbey at the Queen's wish.

It was 1923, less than five years after the tragedy of the Great War. Mr. Bonar Law was Prime Minister, having succeeded Mr. Lloyd George, who had been Leader of a Coalition Government, in October 1922. The Lord Chancellor was Lord Cave, who had succeeded Lord Birkenhead; The Lord President was Lord Salisbury, and Lord Curzon was Secretary of State for Foreign Affairs, and busily involved in the Lausanne Conference, which was attempting a peace treaty between the Allies and Turkey, and running into trouble, although a treaty of peace was to be successfully concluded that summer.

1923 was to see a further General Election and (a major political crisis) Mr. Bonar Law contracted cancer of the throat. The King was informed that he was ill, though it was not known to be so grave, only a week after the Royal Wedding. But soon, on May 20, the Prime Minister had to resign. King George V, after weighing the qualities of Mr. Stanley Baldwin, then little known, and Lord Curzon, brilliant but by no means easy to work with, and a peer, sent for Mr. Baldwin, who became Prime Minister. Towards the end of the year Mr. Baldwin decided to go to the country, attempted a second period of office, but had to resign almost at once, a defeat which resulted in the establishment in January 1924 of the first Labour Government under Mr. Ramsay MacDonald.

The Earl of Carnarvon died that year, shortly after opening the tomb of Tutankhamen and so supposedly incurring a curse, thus furthering widespread speculation on witchcraft and superstition. Reasonably good claret was 3/- a bottle. 'An exceptionally good Dressmaker, needlewoman and hairdresser, very willing, obliging and attentive Ladies' maid', aged thirty-two, advertised her services for £45-£50 a year. Skirts were nearer the ankle than the knee, waists at the top of the hips. Hats were round, with shady brims which eliminated the top of the face. Letters to the editors dealt with smokeless cities, danger in the use of lead paints and cruelty to animals. There was a strike of Norfolk farm labourers; railway traffic was declining; fourteen million Great War Medals had been issued, involving 1,800 miles of ribbon; a six-room and kitchen flat in South Kensington—one of many—was offered at £150 per annum; Hamlet was showing at the Old Vic, Tons of Money at the Aldwych, Lilac Time at the Lyric, and Mr. Victor Sylvester had won a dancing championship. A Handley Page twin-engine air service operated to Paris daily at 12 noon and could accommodate your cabin trunk. It cost 45/- to turn a suit. An ex-Captain's wife ('new poor') advertised for a secondhand layette at moderate cost. 240,000 women were out of work.

Meanwhile Lady Elizabeth and her family found life suddenly crowded with decisions and engagements. The post brought them letters of congratulation and good wishes from the whole of their acquaintanceship and from many strangers.

Many friends and public bodies wrote to ask what they could give for wedding presents. Suitably Forfar (now Angus), the county in which Glamis was situated, was first off the mark, and after a meeting had been specially called the County Clerk wrote to Lord Strathmore, requesting suggestions for a suitable wedding present. His reply shows a thoughtful and unselfish girl.

'Lady Elizabeth wishes me to say that she is deeply touched and most grateful for the kind thoughts, which prompted the calling of a meeting, and that she would dearly love to have some token of her marriage from friends and well-wishers in the county, but that she would infinitely prefer that no money be spent on a wedding gift for her when unemployment and distress are so prevalent and when almost everyone is feeling the pinch of bad times. I entirely agree with these sentiments which Lady Elizabeth holds strongly, although she does not wish to tie the hands of those at the meeting unduly, and, above all, does not wish to appear ungrateful.'

The letter was submitted at a public meeting at Forfar, when it was decided to confine the wedding gift of the county to an illuminated address.

Many beautiful wedding presents were received. The King gave the Duchess of York a tiara and complete suite of diamonds and turquoises; and also other pieces of jewellery. Queen Mary gave her a diamond and sapphire necklace and Queen Alexandra a very long necklace of amethysts and pearls. The Duke of York gave her a necklace of diamonds and pearls, with a pendant to match; while Lady Elizabeth gave to the Duke of York a dress watch chain of platinum and pearls.

The bride's parents were determined worthily to do their part by their loved daughter. The Earl of Strathmore gave Lady Elizabeth a diamond tiara, and a rope necklace of pearls and diamonds, while the Countess of Strathmore's present to the bridegroom was particularly happily chosen: a beautiful miniature of the bride, framed in diamonds, which he always treasured.

Lady Elizabeth enjoyed all her presents with the unspoilt pleasure of one to whom such possessions were new, unexpected and delightful, not least because they represented so many friendly feelings towards them both. There were a thousand gold-eyed needles from the Livery Company of Needlemakers; an ostrich-feather mantelet, tied with ribbons, from South African ostrich farmers; and an English oak chest, stacked with twenty-four pairs of goloshes, wellingtons and other rubber shoes from the Pattenmakers, which was 'handed to her', in the unlikely verb reported, in the Bow Room at Buckingham Palace. This was the occasion on which Lady Elizabeth made her first speech, other than those she had occasionally made in familiar surroundings to her Girl Guides in Glamis or to the members of other local activities. Lady Elizabeth spoke clearly and naturally, and ended, 'I look forward to an opportunity of putting to a practical test the contents of this beautiful chest which you have so generously given me.'

She also opened a Sale of Work in aid of funds for the National Orthopaedic Hospital, at which she received a warm welcome and close scrutiny:

> 'She looked such a sweet-faced, pretty, gentle-natured girl as she appreciatively handled the lovely work and thanked the organisers. She wore a café-au-lait brown duvetyn skirt and loose Russian-shaped coat to match, a row of pearls round her lovely neck and a big black straw hat trimmed with soft black and gold ribbon.'

One is struck by the sympathy between the Duke and Duchess of York and the industrial world. The Duke of York was keenly and deeply interested in industrial conditions, and it was perhaps the factory worker, at all levels, who first realised his worth. The Duke of York's interest in men in industry and in the youth of the country were integral parts of his life. He wrote, as President of the Council of the Industrial Welfare Society, to the secretary, saying, 'I wish with all my heart for a large increase in the membership of the society. If I am able to propose for membership at the next Council, the names of many firms who at present stand aloof, I shall feel that the Industrial Welfare Society has honoured the occasion of my marriage and my personal happiness in a manner which I very deeply appreciate.'

A few days before his wedding, the Duke of York paid the first visit by a member of the Royal family to a Trade Union, the Amalgamated Engineering Union. The visit came about because the Duke of York had met the President and others of the Union at his seaside camp for boys from public schools and from industry. *The Times* reported:

> 'Mr. J. Brownlie said that it was the first time to his knowledge that a member of the Royal House had visited trade union headquarters. The union had 320,000 members and 1,800 branches. The Duke might suppose that in coming to the headquarters of a great trade union he was visiting some sort of Bolshevik organisation more concerned to promote strife than peace. But nothing could be further from the fact.'

After a detailed tour, in which the Duke of York showed great interest:

> ' "Now come into my workshop," said Mr. Brownlie, leading the way to his office. Here refreshments were "handed out for a special purpose," as the president put it. Turning to the Duke, he said, "May the step you are about to take be the happiest of your life and may it continue so. Take my assurance that you are perfectly safe in the hands of a Scots lassie." '

Meanwhile Lady Elizabeth Bowes-Lyon was already doing her part. She had quickly realised that, by herself wearing and using products of distressed industries, she could give a fillip to the trade. There was great unemployment in the Nottingham lace industry. *The Times* wrote:

'For the past three years 75 per cent of the machinery of this great and beautiful industry has been lying idle owing to the state of the Continental exchanges which worked a double injury, preventing our exports and making it worth retailers' while to import cheap Continental laces. In 1906 there were 37,500 people employed in the trade, of whom over 22,000 were women; in 1914 there were 50,000 and today only part-time work can be found for 17,000.'

Lady Elizabeth Bowes-Lyon therefore chose Nottingham lace for her wedding train.

Furthermore, she co-operated with her kinswomen, the Duchess of Portland and Lady Henry Bentinck, who had arranged an 'At Home' and exhibition of Nottingham lace all day for two days at 3 Grosvenor Square, a month before the wedding, by allowing the lace woven for her wedding to be on view there. This lace was a copy of Malines lace, made in several widths—wide for train and veil, in narrow edgings and insertions for trimming, in the finest Sea Island yarns in natural cotton by Birkin and Company of Nottingham.

The wedding dress, trousseau and bridesmaids' dresses were made by Madame Handley Seymour of New Bond Street. A woman reporter wrote:

'The note of the trousseau is simplicity. The Bride's dresses are of the lightest and flimsiest materials and are of great beauty but no splendour.'

There was a garden party dress of white organdie and broderie anglaise with cape. A tennis dress with a wide skirt of apple-green cotton crepon, edged with periwinkle blue silk, had an enormous hook-and-eye in place of a buckle. There were many tea-gowns, one of a pretty mushroom colour made of needlerun lace, with a long panel at the back forming a short train, which was fastened with a low-waisted girdle finishing in tassels of white beads. Many of the hats were 'of the same Quaker cloche bonnet shape of which Lady Elizabeth is so fond'. For furs, Lady Elizabeth chose two full-length coats at Ujhelyls in the Brompton Road.

'A full-length sable squirrel with a roll collar gathered into the revers, the coat hanging in simple lines from the shoulders and lined in striped biscuit crêpe de chine.

'The second is an evening wrap of white lapin. It has a wide band of velvet brocaded crêpe de chine upon which are worked roses of fur, let into the skirt of the wrap. The collar is made to fasten military fashion or form a roll collar. The lining is of printed satin and has pockets which, when in use, keep it wrapped over.'

The provision of a suitable trousseau for the bride of the King's son must have imposed no little financial strain upon a quiet-living and by no means wealthy peer.

Gradually the Duke's fiancée was drawn forward into partici-pation in Royal life. On Wednesday, April 4, Lady Elizabeth Bowes-Lyon was first mentioned in the Court Circular as one of those in the Royal party, when she attended Mendelssohn's *Elijah*, sung by Mme. Agnes Nicholls, Dame Clara Butt, Mr. John Coates, Mr. Robert Radford and a chorus of two hundred and eighty, in the School Hall of Eton College, in aid of St. George's Chapel Restoration Fund. The Royal Party included King George V and Queen Mary, the Prince of Wales, the Duke of York, Prince George and Princess Helena Victoria.

Soon the wedding festivities began. On April 23 the King and Queen gave an evening party for six hundred persons, and on the afternoon of April 24 there was a party at Buckingham Palace for the Staffs of both the Royal Household and the Strathmores. On April 25, a larger afternoon party was held at Buckingham Palace. Selections of the wedding presents, which had been re-ceived at the bride's London home in Bruton Street, and sorted there with the aid of Boy Scouts, were shown at each Bucking-ham Palace party.

Wedding guests were arriving from all over the world, and London was preparing to celebrate. Five Indian Princes had arrived at the Savoy Hotel, where, on the wedding night, there would be dancing in four ballrooms to the music of five bands. Selfridge's was illuminated with searchlights. Barker's was 'a

Palace of Flowers'. Whiteleys had engaged the band of the Scots Guards to play, and Harrods the band of the Irish Guards.

King George V appointed the Duke of York a Knight of the Thistle, and made the Earl of Strathmore a Knight Commander of the Royal Victorian Order.

The last hours of private citizenship had come. If Lady Elizabeth Bowes-Lyon had any inner qualms, she never showed them, and she must at all times have been reassured and sustained by the transparent and radiant joy of her fiancé.

CHAPTER THREE

THE WEDDING OF THE DUKE AND DUCHESS OF YORK

You will think not so much of enjoyment as achievement. You will have a great ambition to make this one life given to you something rich and true and beautiful

*The Archbishop of York, the Most Rev. Cosmo Gordon Lang,
in his wedding address to the Duke and Duchess of York*

THURSDAY, April 26, 1923 dawned cold and showery, but the frequent bursts of rain died into occasional snatches of raindrops as the sun gained altitude. Where the houses gave protection from the keen wind, it was reasonably warm.

From 7 in the morning, crowds began to collect in the streets; they were thickest outside Westminster Abbey and Buckingham Palace, but they waited in unexpected numbers in Bruton Street, Mayfair, in front of the bride's London home.

Inside the tall London house, the whole Bowes-Lyon family were gathered, and there was a tremendous flurry of preparation. Then, at their appointed times, the family went off in little groups to the Abbey, and gradually the bustle and excitement died away, until Lady Elizabeth Bowes-Lyon was left with her father, the Earl of Strathmore, in a silent house.

At last 11.12 a.m. arrived; the precise moment laid down for Lady Elizabeth Bowes-Lyon to leave her family home. When the door opened, the crowds outside the house were densely packed and cheered her loudly while her neighbours, probably for the first time in their lives, leant out of their open windows. Lady Elizabeth seemed surprised and touched by the warmth of her welcome.

Because she was not yet a Royal person, Lady Elizabeth rode to her wedding in a State landau, 'modestly escorted' by four mounted Metropolitan Policemen, and the troops lining the route did not present arms to the bride on her journey to the Abbey.

Spring was late that year; although it was the end of April the bare branches of the trees were just misting with green. The troops were wearing their greatcoats. But the crowds were large and cordial, and cheers rang out loudly for her—especially from groups of Scots—as the landau bowled along at a fair pace. The pealing of the Abbey bells, carried in gusts by the wind, was coming closer. The bride could be seen smilingly acknowledging the cheers, and talking animatedly to cheer the Earl of Strathmore, who was in low spirits, as a father is apt to be when his cherished daughter marries, however happy or 'good' the marriage.

Converging on Westminster Abbey were three other processions. At 11.07 a.m. Queen Alexandra, wearing violet and gold, and accompanied by her sister, Her Imperial Majesty the Empress Marie Dagmar of Russia, had left Marlborough House. One minute later, King George V and Queen Mary, with Prince George, had driven out of the gates of Buckingham Palace, with their Sovereign's Escort of the Household Cavalry. At 11.13 a.m. the bridegroom, the Duke of York, attended by the Prince of Wales and Prince Henry, had followed them from Buckingham Palace.

This was the first marriage of a King's son—and only the third Royal marriage—to take place in the Royal Peculiar of Westminster Abbey since King Richard II had married 'Good Anne of Bohemia' there on January 20, 1382. Until the end of the First World War, Royal marriages were almost invariably celebrated privately, generally in the Chapel Royal of whichever Palace the Sovereign was using at the time.

Princess Patricia of Connaught, when she married Captain Alexander Ramsay, R.N. in Westminster Abbey on February 27, 1919, was the first Royal bride of modern times to be married in Westminster Abbey.

Three years later, on February 28, 1922, Lady Elizabeth Bowes-Lyon had, as a bridesmaid, followed Princess Mary up the aisle of Westminster Abbey, at her wedding to Viscount Lascelles. The twenty-one-year-old girl could hardly have prophesied that the next Royal marriage in Westminster Abbey, fourteen months later, would be her own; that at the next Coronation she would be crowned Queen; and that there she would see her daughter crowned Queen.

When the Duke of York married, it was so rare for the King of England's son to marry a commoner that the authorities had been disputing among themselves about the future rank and status of the Duke of York's bride. If it had not been for three factors it is unlikely that the marriage would have been permitted at all. Firstly, the war had shown King George and the British people the difficulties caused by the alliances with foreign Royal Houses which had been the almost invariable pattern of the British Royal family for centuries. Then Princess Mary's marriage with an English peer had paved the way. Also, the Duke of York was not heir to the Throne, but the second of the four surviving sons of the King.

Indeed there were only five recent marriages of a commoner to any member of the Royal family, those of Princess Louise, daughter of King Edward VII, who married the Duke of Fife; Princess Patricia of Connaught with Captain Ramsay; the Marquess of Carisbrooke with Lady Irene Denison, and the Marquess of Cambridge with Lady Margaret Grosvenor. The Marquess of Carisbrooke and the Marquess of Cambridge were descendants of King George III, but they were not the sons of the Sovereign.

In the eighteenth century, a number of unsuitable marriages with subjects among the brothers of King George III had resulted in the Royal Marriage Act of 1772, by which the marriage of any person in the Succession is virtually prohibited without the formal consent of the Sovereign.

It had been reported by the Press Association, shortly before the wedding of the Duke of York and Lady Elizabeth Bowes-Lyon, that:

'The future style and title of the bride is a matter for the King's decision. Recent times supply no precedent . . . but the Press Association believes that Lady Elizabeth will share her husband's rank and precedence, but until the King's wishes are known, no official information is available.'

This supposition proved to be correct, and the Duchess of York on marriage took her husband's style and title.

Inside Westminster Abbey the three thousand guests were in their places. They included thirty factory boys, each wearing a new suit, who had been specially invited by the Duke of York, as President of the Industrial Welfare Society; twenty boys chosen from his camps; and a representative party of Boy Scouts. Prominently seated among the guests was Miss Boynard, Lady Elizabeth Bowes-Lyon's governess. Among the well-known people present were:

'Lord and Lady Carson, Mr. Lloyd George, Mr. Asquith in Trinity House uniform, Mrs. Asquith with an almond green marocain wrap drawn tightly round her . . . the Duchess of Rutland, in a ruby cloak, Lady Diana Duff Cooper, Mr. Ramsay MacDonald, Mr. Clynes, Captain Towse, V.C., in Scottish uniform.

'. . . Everywhere one noticed that feathers were worn more than flowers; paradise and trailing shaded ostrich mounts were to be seen on large and small hats, of which there were about equal numbers.' (*The Times.*)

'One of the last of the great ladies was the Marchionesss of Lansdowne, in pearl-grey embroidered in cut steel . . . she wore the badges of the Royal Order of Victoria and Albert, the Imperial Order of the Crown of India, The Companion of Honour, that of Lady of Justice of the Order of St. John of Jerusalem in England and the ribbon and star of the Order of the British Empire. Lady Lansdowne wore pearl and diamond ornaments, but the puzzle must have been to get all the badges on the left side of her bodice.' (*The Times.*)

There were three processions into the Abbey.

First came that of the dignified Archbishop of Canterbury, the Most Rev. Randall Davidson, who had just celebrated his twenty-fifth anniversary as Primate of all England; the Archbishop of York, the Most Rev. Cosmo Gordon Lang; and the Primus of the Episcopal Church of Scotland, to which the bride belonged, the Most Rev. Walter John Forbes Robberds, Bishop of Brechin, who had been Bishop of Brechin for twenty years and Primus for fifteen.

Then came the procession of King George V, wearing the uniform of an Admiral of the Fleet, and Queen Mary. The Queen was magnificently regal in an aquamarine-blue and silver dress with lace overdress embroidered with blue crystals on the corsage and skirt, and glorious diamonds, among which blazed the superb brooch made of the third and fourth parts of the Star of Africa (a cushion-shaped diamond of 62 carats, and a pear-shaped drop of 92 carats) known as the Lesser Star of Africa.

The King and Queen took their places on the south side of the Sanctuary. With them was Prince George, in the uniform of a naval cadet.

'Princess Mary . . . was looking very bright and charming in a dress of cream-coloured old lace over satin, having a sash of pale-gold tissue, and a cloak of gold cloth embroidered in gold and lined with pale blue crepe-de-Chine. A cream-coloured crepe-de-Chine hat was worn, finished with cream-coloured ostrich feathers.

'Princess Louise, Duchess of Argyll, always a charming and a graceful figure . . . was wearing sapphire-blue satin with panels of grey chiffon beautifully embroidered in grey.'

Opposite to the Royal family, on the north side of the Sanctuary, were the bride's family. The bride's mother, the Countess of Strathmore, wore:

'A handsome gown of black marocain and georgette embroidered in jet and blue paillettes, with a cloak of black lace and marocain, with collar composed of shaded blue roses.'

Around her were her family and the bride's kinsmen, including the Duke of Portland. Lady Elphinstone, the strikingly handsome eldest sister of the bride, was wearing:

'A draped frock of satin Byzantine, a material resembling georgette, with a satin back, in dove grey. The dress has wonderful embroideries on the corsage, and on the right side of the skirt draperies consisting of large Oriental roses shaded

in pale and deep jade and gold. As this shade of grey carries
brown tones, a wide brown hat with a plumage mount is worn
with it, and a sable wrap . . .

'Lady Glamis, the bride's sister-in-law, wore one of the most
successful costumes in the Abbey. It was all silver—soft, almost
liquid-looking silver. The silver cloak had a grey pleated
chiffon collar, and a white rose of York on the left shoulder.
A small hat of auburn-hued velvet was worn, with a sweeping
aquamarine feather at one side flecked all over with silver.'
(Descriptions of these dresses from *The Illustrated London News*.)

It is an interesting sidelight on (half of) human nature that a
woman guest present that day retains only vague memories of
the impressiveness of the ceremony, the sincerity of bride and
groom, the beauty of the bride and her maids—but can accurately
and minutely describe her own hat!

The bridegroom entered in procession. The Duke of York was
wearing the uniform of a Group Captain of the Royal Air Force
(which later earned him a particularly lusty cheer as he passed the
R.A.F. Club in Piccadilly) with the Garter Riband and Star, and
the Thistle Star, which had been newly bestowed on him by the
King in honour of his Scottish bride. He wore the gold aiguillettes
over his right shoulder, which showed that he was a Personal Aide-
de-Camp to the Sovereign. His single row of medals included
his Service Medals from the Great War.

The Duke of York was supported, in the official phrase, by the
Prince of Wales, who was wearing the uniform of the Grenadier
Guards, and by Prince Henry in the uniform of the Tenth
Hussars. Even on this day of the younger brother's wedding, it
was the fair-haired Prince of Wales who was the focal point for
many eyes.

Precisely at 11.30, punctual to the minute, the bride's landau
drew up at the west door of Westminster Abbey, where a large
crowd vigorously cheered her. At that moment, King George V
noted in his diary, the sun came out.

Lady Elizabeth Bowes-Lyon passed into the dark Abbey,
where her eight bridesmaids—two of whom had already been
bridesmaids at both the Royal marriages held in Westminster

Abbey—were awaiting her. They wore dresses of georgette, trimmed with machine-made Nottingham lace. One of the bridesmaids recalls that these were chosen without any of the usual acrimony when one pattern of dress is being decided upon for a number of girls of differing heights and colouring. The colour was ivory; the leaf-green tulle sashes at the waist were held in place by a white rose and a silver thistle. On their hair they wore bandeaux of silver roses, and leaves—'We had sprigs of white heather mixed with the roses,' remembered a bridesmaid: 'the Duke of York did not like the little veils which were then popular.'

The bridegroom's gift to each bridesmaid was an extremely pretty carved crystal brooch formed by the white rose of York, with a diamond centre embodying the initials E and A (for Albert) which each bridesmaid wore in the front of her dress. The senior bridesmaids wore silver shoes, but the two child train-bearers had white shoes. They all carried bouquets of white roses and white heather.

The two trainbearers were nieces of the bride—the Hon. Elizabeth Elphinstone, daughter of Lord and Lady Elphinstone, and the Hon. Cecilia Bowes-Lyon, daughter of Lord and Lady Glamis, who afterwards married Major Kenneth Harrington.

The six senior bridesmaids were led by Lady Mary Cambridge, daughter of the Marquess and Marchioness of Cambridge, whose engagement had just been announced to the Marquess of Worcester, later Duke of Beaufort; and Lady May Cambridge, daughter of Princess Alice and the Earl of Athlone, who afterwards married Colonel Sir Henry Abel Smith, later Governor of Queensland.

Behind them, in order of height with the smaller bridesmaids first, came Lady Mary Thynne, daughter of the Marquess and Marchioness of Bath, afterwards Lady Mary Alexander; and Miss Betty Cator, who afterwards married the bride's brother, the Hon. Michael Bowes-Lyon.

Tallest of the bridesmaids were Lady Katharine Hamilton, daughter of the third Duke of Abercorn, then Lady Katharine Seymour, and a Woman-of-the-Bedchamber for many years, and the Hon. Diamond Hardinge, daughter of Lord Hardinge of

Penshurst, who married Captain Robert Alexander Abercromby, M.C., that summer, but who died only four years later. She owed her unusual christian name to King Edward VII's horse *Diamond Jubilee*, which had won the Derby just about the time of her birth.

Lady Elizabeth left her white 'handkerchief bag' behind in the carriage, and this was now brought to her—her daughter, Queen Elizabeth II, also forgot her handbag in the coach on the day of her Coronation.

There was a pause, caused by the fainting of one of the clerics in the bride's procession. While Lady Elizabeth waited on her father's arm while the procession re-formed, she suddenly left him and went forward alone, spontaneously laying her bouquet of white York roses upon the Tomb of the Unknown Warrior at the west end of the Nave, in memory of the British dead who had no known grave, fallen in the Great War which had ended less than five years before. Perhaps she was thinking particularly of her brother Fergus, who had died at Loos. It had been planned that the Duchess of York should pause at the Cenotaph on her way back from the wedding, and that her bouquet should be laid there in remembrance. This unplanned tribute left her empty-handed on the long walk through the Abbey to the steps of the Sanctuary.

There were no flowers decorating Westminster Abbey, a decision made by King George V and Queen Mary at the time of Princess Mary's wedding, and adhered to for Lady Elizabeth Bowes-Lyon's wedding because it was thought they would detract from the austere beauty of the ancient Abbey. (But a generation later flowers were used with great effect at the wedding of Princess Margaret.)

Lady Elizabeth was composed and quietly happy. As a Royal bride, her veil was thrown back, showing her very beautiful eyes and fair complexion. She wore a tulle veil, with a wreath of orange blossom, with a white rose at each side.

The bride's dress was in a simple medieval style, with a square neckline. It was made of a fine chiffon moiré, the colour of old ivory, and embroidered with silver thread and pearls. It had long, medieval sleeves of very fine Nottingham lace. The train was very light: it was made of beautiful old *point de Flandres* lace (mounted on tulle), which had been lent by Queen Mary, who was a great lover and collector of old lace. Below it was a longer train of Nottingham lace. The bride's shoes were of ivory moiré, with a silver rose embroidered on them.

At last the signal came, as the choir began to sing 'Lead us, Heavenly Father, lead us'. On the arm of her father, who was wearing the scarlet uniform of a Lord Lieutenant, Lady Elizabeth Bowes-Lyon moved forward, 'with radiance and gentle confidence', as one of the wedding guests described it.

'The Duke of York faced with shining eyes and a look of happiness the girl who, hand in hand with her father, was advancing in her lovely old-fashioned dress, gleaming with silver and veiled in old lace . . . they seemed to think of no one but each other.' (*The Times.*)

The service was exactly as it would be for any other man and woman married according to the rites of the Church of England. The marriage vows were repeated word for word, but the responses were inaudible in the body of the church.

'The Prince of Wales is ready to the second with the ring. It is put upon the bride's finger. They are man and wife.'

The two small trainbearers followed as the Duke and Duchess of York went forward together to the altar, to kneel before the Precentor of the Abbey for the Lord's Prayer.

Then the Archbishop of York, Dr. Lang, a very handsome and venerable figure in his white cope, made an inspiring and prophetic address, which King George V wrote in his diary was 'beautiful' and Queen Mary noted was 'charming'. The Duke and Duchess of York followed it with marked attentiveness and resolution, and it was to be a guiding principle in their lives.

'Will you take and keep this gift of wedded life as a sacred trust? . . . with all our hearts we wish that it may be happy. You can and will resolve that it will be noble. You will not think so much of enjoyment as of achievement. You will have a great ambition to make this one life now given to you something rich and true and beautiful.'

After referring in particular to the Duke of York's work for 'the welfare of our working people' the Archbishop of York turned to the bride and said:

'And you, dear bride, in your Scottish home, have grown up from childhood among country folk and friendship with them has been your native air. So have you both been fitted for your place in the people's life. The nations and classes which make up our Commonwealth too often live their lives apart. It is . . . a great thing that there should be in our midst one family which, regarded by all as in a true sense their own, makes the whole Empire kin and helps to give it the spirit of family life.

'But above all, it is to yourselves, as simple man and maid, now husband and wife, that our heart turns as you go forth to meet the years that are to come. On behalf of a nation happy in your joy, we bid you Godspeed.'

There followed the signing of the Registers, when the bride and bridegroom, again accompanied only by the trainbearers, were followed to the Chapel of Edward the Confessor by an imposing procession of royalty and relatives. Meanwhile the cheerful anthem, 'Beloved, Let us Love one Another', which had been written for Princess Mary's wedding, was sung by the choir.

Four books were laid out for signature on an old oak table, below the tomb of Edward the Confessor. There were the Abbey Registers which were signed in duplicate, and also the Abbey's special, white-bound Visitors' Book. The special Royal Register, in which the baptisms and marriages of the Royal family are recorded, had been brought from the Chapel Royal, St. James's Palace. The marriage was 'No. 22 of 1923 . . . solemnised at Westminster Abbey in the Close of St. Peter, Westminster in the County of Middlesex.'

One of the child bridesmaids recalls a moment of acute youthful crisis when Queen Mary and Queen Alexandra were chatting to each other across the bride's train in the Chapel, when the bride moved forward, and in order to follow her with the train, the trainbearers both had to pass between and part the two Queens.

The principal guests returned to the Sanctuary and took their places. Almost at once Mendelssohn's 'Wedding March' rang out: the Duke and Duchess of York returned hand in hand. Both smiled to Lady Strathmore, who had tears in her eyes. Then, facing the King and Queen, the Duke of York bowed and the Duchess curtseyed, as her two youngest bridesmaids arranged her train.

The bride and bridegroom emerged from the Abbey to find a fine, sunny day, and enthusiastic crowds. They entered their coach and proceeded at walking pace, escorted by Household troops, by way of Marlborough Gate, St. James's Street, Piccadilly, Hyde Park Corner and Constitution Hill to Buckingham Palace.

'She drove to the Abbey in the simplest possible manner. On her return all was changed. From a commoner she became as if by magic the fourth lady in the land, and she returned to the same spot which she had passed with such little ostentation an hour before, in the gorgeous Royal scarlet and gold coach and with an imposing escort of cavalry.

'The large crowds cheered them heartily, the Scots among them vociferously.'

When the bride arrived at Buckingham Palace, her friends and bridesmaids who had driven there direct and arrived first, came forward to greet her, but each made a curtsey as she did so. The young Lady Elizabeth Bowes-Lyon was now Her Royal Highness the Duchess of York; she had stepped across the barrier into the closed circle of the Royal family for ever.

As the processions disappeared through the archway into the Palace courtyard, the crowd suddenly swept over the open space between the Victoria Memorial and the railings that guard the forecourt of Buckingham Palace. There was a pause while the Duke and Duchess of York and the Royal party made their way along the long, red-carpeted corridors to the Balcony Room. The bride and bridegroom first came out onto the balcony, and afterwards King George V, Queen Mary, Queen Alexandra, and the bride's parents, joined them, but withdrew before the Duke and Duchess of York, who could be seen, but not heard, to be repeating 'Thank you . . . thank you' to the cheering crowds.

A wedding breakfast was held for one hundred and twenty-three people. Sixty-six of the closest relatives sat at six circular tables in the State Dining Room, the remainder in the Ball Supper Room. The tables were decorated with pink tulips and white lilac. The gay and elaborate menu cards were painted with roses, thistles and shamrocks, entwined round the cipher of the King and Queen, and with the crests of the Duke and Duchess of York.

There were eight courses:

Consommé à la Windsor
Suprêmes de saumon Reine Mary
Côtelettes d'agneau, Prince Albert
Chapons à la Strathmore
    (boiled chicken in jelly, garnished with truffles and tongue)
Jambon et Langue découpées à l Aspic
Salade Royale
Asperges, Sauce Crême Mousseuse
Fraises, Duchesse Elizabeth
Pâtisserie
Fruits

There was only one simple Toast, proposed by King George V:
'I ask you to drink to the health, long life and happiness of the bride and bridegroom.'

It was drunk, in the Royal tradition, in silence, and the bridegroom did not reply.

In the Green Drawing Room, which overlooks the quadrangle, the wedding cake was cut with a silver knife. This was a splendid cake, nine feet high and weighing eight hundred pounds. It had four richly ornamented tiers, and the Duke and Lady Elizabeth had selected the designs when visiting McVitie and Price in Edinburgh. The lowest tier, representing the union of the Houses, was decorated with their combined coats of arms; the second tier with the Strathmore coat of arms; the third the Duke of York's, while the top symbolised love and peace, and the whole was topped with a vase of white flowers.

The guests in Buckingham Palace were not the only wedding guests of the Duke and Duchess of York. The Duke of York had given a cheque of £500 each to the Lord Mayors of London, York, and Belfast, and the Lord Provost of Glasgow, and had asked them to entertain, at his expense, as many young people as possible, not forgetting those who were physically handicapped or mentally sick. Each child received a piece of wedding cake, its ingredients identical with those in the principal cake, and a box of chocolates.

The Duke of York sent a message to his guests:

'It is a real pleasure to me to think that you are my guests on my wedding day. My wife and I both hope that you will have a jolly good time now and good luck in the future.'

After the wedding breakfast, the Duchess of York changed into her going-away dress, described as:

'A soft shade of dove grey crêpe romain, which has a slightly beige tinge in it, and is embroidered all in its own colour. The bodice has short sleeves, and there is a coatee made on a band at the back. A travelling coat wrap of the same shape in crêpe marocain . . . which has wheels of drawn thread work of its own material trimming it . . . Her going away hat is a small affair in tones of brown with upturned brim and a feather mount at the side. She made this choice so that those in the crowd . . . may not have their view impeded by a brim. With this dress are worn shoes of beige antelope . . . in a sandal shape.'

The bride and bridegroom left Buckingham Palace in an open landau drawn by four grey horses. As the landau moved off, the guests pelted them with quantities of rose petals, which had been made by the blind. The bridegroom's brothers and the bridesmaids ran into the arch into the forecourt, brothers at one side, bridesmaids at the other, and energetically pelted them with petals, the Prince of Wales finishing off by hitting his brother in the face with a screwed-up bag. Then the escort of cavalry clashed through the arch after the carriage, catching the bridesmaids by surprise, and for an alarming moment they were caught between the stone wall and the quarters of the great black horses.

Queen Mary, Princess Mary and Princess Victoria had made their way to the Balcony Room, immediately above the central archway, and as the carriage emerged below them they too showered it with rose petals.

At Waterloo station a special train was waiting.

'. . . The special train was drawn up at one of the platforms adjoining the carriageway . . . The train itself was an ordinary local train to which had been attached a saloon carriage upholstered in old gold brocade and decorated with white roses, white heather, white carnations and lilies of the valley.' (*The Times.*)

A footman solemnly carried into the carriage two odd shoes, which had been flung for luck into the open landau! The Duke and Duchess of York bowed and waved to the few privileged onlookers, mostly railway officials and their ladies, who had been admitted to the platform, and at 4.35 p.m. Driver Wiggs took the train out.

At 5.10 p.m. the special train drew gently into Bookham station, and the Duke and Duchess of York alighted. But they had not yet reached their destination: there were at least two more bouquets and an address of welcome to receive before a fast car carried them past hedgerows in full leaf to the seclusion of Polesden Lacey, the spacious, richly furnished early nineteenth-century house (now belonging to the National Trust; it was damaged by fire in 1960, and re-opened in 1962) lent to them by the Hon. Mrs. Ronald Greville, where they spent the first part of their honeymoon.

In London that night there was a family dinner party in the bride's home in Bruton Street. A close friend, who was present, said, 'I was deeply impressed by the attitude of the Bowes-Lyon family. They were not concerned with the great match that Lady Elizabeth had made, but with something basically far more important. As one of the family put it. "Thank God, she has married a good man".'

CHAPTER FOUR

ENTRY INTO ROYAL LIFE

In 1923 my brother Bertie had married the daughter of a Scottish
Earl, Lady Elizabeth Bowes-Lyon, who had brought into the family
a lively and refreshing spirit

A King's Story *by H.R.H. The Duke of Windsor*

AFTER the Duke and Duchess of York had spent the first part of
their honeymoon at Polesden Lacey they passed through London
on Monday, May 7, 1923, on their way north to Glamis, and that
evening the Prince of Wales, wearing a pirate-like black shade
over one eye as a result of a mishap at squash racquets, drove with
them to Euston station to see them off for the north.

The suite of rooms prepared for them (always afterwards used
by them when they stayed at Glamis) is on the first floor of
the Castle, in one of the original wings and overlooking the
Angles Park. In the sitting room latticed windows are on either
side of the fireplace, which has old blue and white Dutch tiles
and a heavily carved seventeenth-century Dutch chimneypiece.
Eighteenth-century tapestries hang on the walls, and cabinets
display Sèvres porcelain and Canton china. The fine Chippendale
chairs are all worked in different tapestry designs by Lady
Strathmore.

In the principal bedroom, the four-poster bed has hangings
embroidered with the names of Lady Strathmore's children, and
a beautiful patchwork quilt, all made by the Countess of Strathmore. The original dressing room, which opens off the bedroom,
was specially converted for the Duke and Duchess of York into a
comfortable, carpeted bathroom, and the walls hung with water-
colours of Highland scenery. A new dressing room was made
out of a lattice-windowed bedroom nearby, and hung with an
almond-blossom wallpaper.

The weather during the Duke and Duchess's honeymoon visit

to Glamis was appalling, with snow, rain and a biting cold wind, furthermore the Duchess of York developed a sharp attack of whooping cough. 'Not a very *romantic* disease,' the Duchess afterwards commented to a friend.

When the Duke and Duchess returned south on May 19, White Lodge in Richmond Park, which had been lent to them by King George V, was not yet ready, so they went first to Frogmore House in Windsor Little Park. The present Frogmore House, the third on the site, was designed by Wyattville for Queen Charlotte. The Duchess of Kent, Queen Victoria's mother, lived here, and so did King George V and Queen Mary when they were Duke and Duchess of York. It has a curving artificial lake in front of it, and is surrounded by pleasant grounds where the earth removed in making the lake has been used to introduce a variety of mounds and banks in the naturally flat landscape. Although the Duke and Duchess of York lived for only a time at Frogmore House, they were always fond of it, and took great interest in the grounds. It was a sorrow to them when the gardens had to revert to hay and tangled undergrowth during the Second World War, although the house itself did useful service in providing accommodation for Royal employees and their families evacuated from London.

The young Duchess of York's immediate entry into Royal life was delayed not only by her attack of whooping cough but by the four-week period of Court mourning which followed the death of Princess Christian on June 9. Princess Christian, fifth child and third daughter of Queen Victoria, was the Princess Helena Augusta Victoria on whom Queen Victoria had particularly relied after the death of the Prince Consort. In 1886 she married Prince Christian of Schleswig-Holstein, who made his home in this country and who died in 1917. Their children were Princess Helena Victoria and Princess Marie Louise.

Princess Christian had greatly interested herself in nursing and in the care of children. She was greatly and widely loved, and at her death Mr. Asquith said, rising without preparation to speak in the House of Commons:

'Her Royal Highness will be regretted in every quarter of this House, but nowhere more than in the homes of the poor of this country.'

To which Mr. Clynes added, speaking on behalf of the Labour Party in the House:

'She was devoted to humanitarian and to womanly duties and never wearied in well-doing and for one so elevated in station and social position she has left a memory of acts of benevolence and kindly social services.'

Princess Christian's interests are by no means irrelevant to an account of the Duchess of York's public duties. A number of the organisers of Societies with which Princess Christian had been connected turned after her death to the newest member of the Royal family, to ask her to become their new Patron or President. Some of the links which the Duchess of York formed in this un-expected way continue to this day.

On Thursday, June 7, the Duchess was well enough, and the White Lodge ready enough, for the Duke and Duchess of York to move in. It was at the instigation of Queen Mary that King George V had given the young people the White Lodge for their first home.

This was much more than an available Royal residence: it was Queen Mary's old home. In 1869 Queen Victoria had offered the White Lodge to Queen Mary's parents, the Duke and Duchess of Teck, and there Queen Mary had grown up; had mourned the death of her fiancé, the Duke of Clarence; and later had prepared for her marriage to his younger brother. Queen Mary's eldest son, the Prince of Wales, now Duke of Windsor, was born there; and at the White Lodge Queen Mary's mother, the vivacious, exuberant, popular Duchess of Teck, had died suddenly after an operation which she herself had believed would be only minor. Although all the times she had spent there had not been happy, the White Lodge was especially dear to Queen Mary, who had an almost obsessional love and regard for all family history and treasures. The loan of the White Lodge to the Duke and Duchess of York was therefore a marked expression of approval and affection.

While the Duke and Duchess of York were on their honeymoon, Queen Mary busied herself in her indefatigable and skilled way with the furnishings of the house, although she tactfully left details to be decided by the young bride. Nevertheless, entry into Royal life as a bride cannot have been made easier by setting up house in one's mother-in-law's family home, especially when she was such an outwardly formidable person as Queen Mary, nor was Queen Mary's exquisite taste for formal furnishing necessarily the choice of a young girl in whose home family treasures were treated with a more casual affection. It was fortunate that the Duke of York's bride was a person so sensitive to other people's feelings and who understood so well the deep love held for familiar family things.

Richmond Park, in which the White Lodge stands, has a long Royal history. It is believed to have been Crown property when Domesday Book was compiled, and was then known as Sheen, meaning 'splendid' or 'beautiful'. It was used as a place of hunting and recreation by the Kings. Edward III lived in Sheen Palace, and died there, abandoned and almost alone, in 1377. Richard II, who married 'the beautiful and entirely beloved Anne' in Westminster Abbey in 1382 (the last prince to be married there before the Duke of York) lived at Sheen. When Queen Anne died there in 1394—it was she who introduced the side-saddle into England —her sorrowing husband was so violently afflicted by her death that he cursed the place, and ordered the buildings to be thrown down. Sheen Palace was restored on a nearby site by Henry V, and rebuilt, after a fire in 1498, by Henry VII, after whom (he being Henry of Richmond) it was renamed. Queen Elizabeth I died there.

Charles I had the present Richmond Park enclosed, in spite of considerable opposition from the local inhabitants, although he left roads open for the people to pass through it, and allowed the poor to collect firewood as before. Enclosure was completed in 1637. Only twelve years later, the Commonwealth Parliament had most of Richmond Palace pulled down, and gave the Park to the citizens of London. At the Restoration of Charles II in 1660 the metropolitan corporation returned Richmond Park to the King, saying tactfully, 'The City had only kept it as stewards for His Majesty'.

Quite a number of Lodges, of which eight or ten remain, were built at various times, for varying purposes, within Richmond Great Park, just as they were built in Windsor Great Park. The White Lodge is the most isolated, standing right in the middle of the Park (Richmond Palace was much closer to the river) and looking towards Richmond Hill across the Deer Park. It was built by George II between 1727-29 'from a design of the Earl of Pembroke as a place of refreshment after the fatigues of the chace'. Originally it was a small house, called successively 'Stone Lodge', 'New Lodge', and then 'White Lodge'. Later George II's wife, Queen Caroline, liked Richmond and came to live at the Lodge. The Queen's Walk, the splendid elm avenue nearly a mile long that led to the Richmond Gate, was named after her. It was there that Sir Walter Scott, in *The Heart of Midlothian*, set Queen Caroline's meeting with Jeanie Deans, who intercepted the Queen to beg a pardon for her sister, condemned to death.

Afterwards Princess Amelia, King George II and Queen Caroline's daughter, was made Ranger—which is the official title of the Keeper of a Royal Park—of Richmond Park and lived at the Lodge. She built on the two brick wings on either side of the main building, and changed its name to White Lodge.

Later, the house had a succession of occupiers, including Mr. Addington the Prime Minister, afterwards Viscount Sidmouth, whose name survives in the jingle:

> Pitt is to Addington
> As London is to Paddington.

Nelson visited Lord Sidmouth at White Lodge, and drew, in wine on a polished table, his plans for a battle with the French Navy. The battle took place as he planned it, and is known as the Battle of Trafalgar.

In 1850 the Duchess of Gloucester, widow of William Frederick, Duke of Gloucester and Edinburgh, son of George III, became Ranger of Richmond Park and received the residence of White Lodge, and lived there until her death seven years later.

Queen Victoria came to White Lodge in distress after the death of her mother, the Duchess of Kent, so shortly before the great loss of her husband, the Prince Consort. Later she installed her son Albert, Prince of Wales, here, with his formidable entourage, in what was somewhat misleadingly termed his first independent residence.

But it was with the Duke and Duchess of Teck and Queen Mary that people now associated White Lodge.

White Lodge was a capacious (one of those who tried to run it goes so far as to call it a monstrous) house. The main block was two storeys high, with single-storey wings on either side of the entrance. But the ground dropped away, permitting a third storey on the garden frontage, where a flight of steps led from the principal rooms to the gardens, which included a sunk garden and a Dutch garden with yew-trees trimmed into pyramids, and a hard tennis court, which was particularly enjoyed by the Duke.

In good weather, there was a fine view over Richmond Park to the river. The drawing room was particularly light and pleasant, and contained a white marble chimneypiece incorporating the cypher of King George II and Queen Caroline.

The Duke and Duchess of York enjoyed arranging their possessions and wedding presents in their new home. With some apprehension they entertained King George V and Queen Mary, who had Prince Henry and Prince George with them, to luncheon on July 28, 1923. The Duke wrote to Queen Mary, in a letter quoted by Sir John Wheeler-Bennett:

'I had better warn you that our cook is not very good but she can do the plain dishes well, & I know you like that sort.'

In that single sentence can be felt the trepidation of the young bride and the reassurances of her husband. The visit was a great success. King George was charmed. Queen Mary thought that they had made their home 'very nice'.

The Duchess of York regarded all her new possessions with the natural and unspoilt pleasure of one who had been brought up without overabundance of wealth. She showed her jewels and presents to her friends with a young girl's delight. She enjoyed the cars in the garage, on which was painted the badge used by her husband, a white rose, encircled by golden rays, known heraldically as 'a white rose en soleil'.

The Duchess of York characteristically interested herself in the wellbeing of those working for her. A housemaid lost a relative and she was wonderfully sympathetic and helpful about it. Family conversation and letters are full of interest in everyone including the servants, who were in many cases family friends. Part of the atmosphere of Glamis was the Earl of Strathmore's butler, Barson, a delightful if not always predictable man, who never lost his dignity in any circumstances, and was the confidant and friend of the whole family. Then as always throughout her life, the Duchess of York concerned herself with the well-being of everyone she met. One of the Household, who has been with her on several tours, remarked, 'Wherever one went, in South Africa or Canada or Australia, we were always coming up against tenants or servants of the Strathmore family from Scotland or Hertfordshire. They always turned up, and she always spoke with them. It was obvious that it was not a formality, that she knew them most frightfully well.'

Among the early guests at White Lodge was a party of senior girls from Dr. Barnardo's Homes, of which the Duke of York was President, who were about to emigrate to Australia. The girls were in Girl Guide uniform, and saluted the Duchess of York in Guide fashion, as she stood smiling at them. After she had spoken to each one she took them round her new house with the same pleasure with which she showed it to her relatives and friends.

It was not long, however, before disadvantages to living in the White Lodge became apparent. It was enormous, it was also inconvenient, and proved extremely costly to run. The servants hated it. It would have needed fifty servants to run it properly. On holidays and at week-ends, Richmond Park was crowded. Even when the weather was good, it took quite a time to get into and out of London, through heavy traffic. (Once going up to town to a public duty, their car was in collision with a two-horse brewer's dray at the corner of New King's Road and Munster Road, Fulham. With a loud crash the draypole cracked the near-side door, but fortunately no one was injured. After an afternoon engagement, or a cocktail party, the Duke and Duchess of York often had to drive the whole way to Richmond to change and then back to town for a dinner party. When winter came, the White Lodge was often lost in fog. Several times the Duke and Duchess of York lost their way in Richmond Park, and drove round and round among the ghostly trees trying to find the isolated Lodge.

Soon, the Duke and Duchess began to wish for another home, at once more convenient and more private, but it was not so easy to move without hurting the feelings of the King and Queen, and when the 'official channels' of the Crown Commissioners and the Ministry of Works were involved. The Duchess of York had an early initiation into the complexity of negotiations, and the indirect approach necessary for those whose lives are governed by protocol and by the State.

It was a time of change and upheaval, violent in many parts of the world although less so in Britain. Between the older generation and the survivors of the Great War the slaughter of the trenches lay like no-man's land. Many ex-servicemen had returned restless and bitter; they were having difficulties in finding work and homes. Those who had remained in Britain during the war found it hard to understand them. The division between generations was present in the Royal family, and caused tension between the King and the Prince of Wales. It did not make it easier for the Duchess of York to take her place as a member of the Royal family.

The first occasion on which the Duchess of York appeared publicly as a member of the Royal family when King George V and Queen Mary were present was on June 30, 1923, when the King and Queen and the Duke and Duchess of York went to the Royal Air Force Pageant at Hendon. It was a popular and successful occasion at which eighty thousand people were present, and the very latest aircraft were on view. The crack Squadron 39, the first squadron formed for the aerial defence of London, demonstrated their de Havilland 9 machines, which had a speed of over 150 m.p.h., and could reach an altitude of two miles!

King George V and Queen Mary thoughtfully drew the Duke and Duchess of York into the ceremonies of their stay at the

Palace of Holyroodhouse in July. Owing in great measure to the efforts of Queen Mary, Holyroodhouse was again being put in order and used as a Royal Palace, to the deep satisfaction of the Scottish people. It was the first occasion, in modern times, when the King's son and his wife had accompanied the Sovereign to the Palace of Holyroodhouse. Throughout the week the Duke and Duchess of York took part in ceremonies, but there was more free time at their disposal then than there would be today, to go sightseeing quietly and by themselves to some of the historic places of the city, and on expeditions to the countryside round Edinburgh.

The King's relationship with his daughter-in-law was a very happy one. The Duchess of York came from a family with a high sense of duty. She appreciated and understood the foundation of the Sovereign's life, its background of history, the King's desire for decency and orderliness, the unbroken thread of duty that made up the dedicated lives of King George V and Queen Mary. 'I miss him dreadfully,' the Duchess of York wrote to his doctor, Lord Dawson of Penn, after King George V's death. 'Unlike his own children, I was never afraid of him, and in all his twelve years of having me as a daughter-in-law he never spoke one unkind or abrupt word to me, and was always ready to listen and give advice on one's own silly little affairs. He was so kind and so *dependable*. And when he was in the mood, he could be deliciously funny too! Don't you think so?'

Queen Mary was very kind to her daughter-in-law, the more so because she had often been thoughtlessly wounded by her mother-in-law, Queen Alexandra. She was thankful to see her son Bertie so happy, and she marvelled at her daughter-in-law's gift of lively conversation, and at her ability to be at ease in any surroundings and to speak in public.

The day-to-day life of the Court was conducted quietly, soberly and with extreme precision. As the Duke of Windsor wrote in *A King's Story*:

'My father's life was a masterpiece in the art of well-ordered, unostentatious, elegant living. No matter the place, no matter the occasion, perfection pervaded every detail.'

The Court was regulated with the precision of a chronometer. Punctuality was absolute. Sir Frederick Ponsonby, afterwards Lord Ponsonby, Keeper of the Privy Purse, commented in *Recollections of Three Reigns* on the impossibility of being late:

'When I say late, the ordinary meaning of the word hardly conveyed the wonderful punctuality of the King and Queen. One was late if the clock sounded when one was on the stairs, even in a small house like York Cottage.'

The sound of the Prince of Wales's car, driven furiously up the Long Walk from Fort Belvedere to Windsor Castle, when he was in danger of being late for dinner, remains in the memory of more than one member of the Household.

The Duchess of York had come from a very different world, where a much more elastic idea of time prevailed. Nothing more clearly underlined the King's affection for his daughter-in-law than the way in which he even excused her occasional unpunctuality. Sir John Wheeler-Bennett recorded:

'To no-one else would he have said—as he did, when his son and daughter-in-law arrived two minutes late for dinner and she apologised, "You are not late, my dear. I think we must have sat down two minutes too early." '

A senior Member of the Household remembers an occasion when someone slightly unkindly mentioned to the King that the Duchess of York was sometimes unpunctual. 'Ah, but if she weren't late, she would be perfect, and how horrible that would be,' replied the King.

The Court may well have seemed a little stiff to a girl of twenty-two, coming straight from the jolly, family-party atmosphere of Glamis.

Dress was formal. At Buckingham Palace the King, and of course male Members of his Household, wore frock-coats by day: so did visitors. The morning coat was only just tolerated, and the short black jacket and striped trousers worn today by the Household of Queen Elizabeth II was unheard of.

At Windsor, the Ladies of the Household during the day wore tailored clothes, and at all times wore or carried gloves. Dress in the evening was always very formal. When the King and Queen dined alone at Buckingham Palace, without even their Household, he wore tails, she full evening dress with tiara.

Among the most formal of private occasions were the dinners held at Windsor Castle during Ascot week. Before dinner, which was held at 8.30, the guests gathered in the Green Drawing Room, so called from the walls covered with green damask and gilded furniture upholstered in green silk. The ladies assembled on one side of the room, the men on the other. In the corridor outside the Royal family gathered, awaiting the arrival of the King and Queen.

The King, his sons, and the senior members of the Royal Household wore the Windsor uniform, worn only at Windsor Castle, and consisting of a dark-blue evening dress coat with collar and cuffs of scarlet, worn with knee-breeches. Princess Marie-Louise told the author that it owed its origin to being a colour becoming to one of King George IV's mistresses. The buttons on the coat are gilt, and show the Garter Star within the Garter, surmounted by the Imperial crown. Other men present wore black evening dress coats with knee-breeches.

The Ladies wore long gloves with their full evening dress, and were expected not to pop their hands out through the convenient buttoned wrists, but if they wished to remove their gloves, to do so completely. The table was laid with the Grand Service of silver-gilt, decorated with boar, stag and foxhunting scenes, made for George IV, and the forks were laid prong-downwards, in the original manner, so that the wrist ruffles of the Georgian men would not catch in the points. Dinner was served by pages in blue and footmen in scarlet livery. Soft music was played by a string band of one of the Regiments of Guards behind a gauze wall, which was painted to look solid. At the end of the meal, the long side cloths were rolled back by the footmen, leaving the clean undercloth for dessert. When the ladies withdrew, each faced the King and dropped a deep curtsey.

In the drawing room after dinner, Queen Mary had her special settee to which one or two guests to whom she wished to speak were brought, while the other ladies chatted somewhat stiffly among themselves. When the men returned from the dining room, they would linger among the ladies for only a few minutes until the King disengaged himself and went on, the men following to a further room where they smoked their cigars and talked.

Even at Sandringham the men wore knee-breeches at dinner during King George V's reign, and when the widowed Queen Mary entertained at Marlborough House, right up to the outbreak of war in 1939, all the men invariably wore knee-breeches.

There was little mixing or general conversation after dinner. People generally stood about in little groups, talking quietly, although in the later years of George V's reign, bridge or mahjong were sometimes played.

The Duchess of York achieved a good deal in warming the atmosphere, bringing joy and warmth into the lives of King George and Queen Mary. She had then, as now, that gift of drawing people out and making them talk easily. Queen Mary greatly admired her for it. She would sit down at the piano and play and sing, as she had done at Glamis, and the others would gather round and join in.

The Duchess of York could almost always break the ice, and dispel shyness or moodiness or resentment. But not quite always. Once, during a Windsor house-party after King George VI had come to the throne, the guests were playing charades, but Mr. Winston Churchill remained withdrawn and apart. The Queen, as she was then, made a series of appeals to him for his help and guidance, but she succeeded only partly in mollifying him, and Mr. Churchill never really entered into the spirit of that particular game.

Weddings and christenings brought together the Royal family, as in other families, and during the Duchess of York's first year of marriage she attended three Royal weddings and one christening, which provided her with early opportunities of getting to know her husband's kin in the closely interlinked circles of European royalty.

A somewhat formidable initiation into Royal life was a double occasion celebrated in Belgrade in October, 1923. This was the christening of the infant son and heir of King Alexander of the Kingdom of the Serbs, Croats, and Slovenes, soon to be known as Yugoslavia; and, on the following day, the wedding of King Alexander's cousin Prince Paul to Princess Olga of Greece. The Duke and Duchess of York had been invited to be *Koom* (God-father) and *Koomitsa* (Godmother), but had not contemplated attending the ceremony itself, until it suddenly became politically desirable. So, at short notice, they found themselves at Victoria station bound for Yugoslavia.

They were met at the frontier by a representative of King Alexander, and their special train proceeded by way of Liubliana and Zagreb down the valley of the Sala to Belgrade, where, at 7.30 of a chilly evening, they were met by the King; his widowed sister Princess John Constantinovitch of Russia; the bridegroom's father, Prince Arsène Kakageorgević brother of King Peter I of Serbia; and the bridegroom Prince Paul. Dominant was the exuberant and pro-British Queen Marie of Roumania, 'Cousin Missy' to the Royal family, who was extremely proud of her descent from Queen Victoria—she was the daughter of the Duke of Edinburgh, Queen Victoria's second son—who 'stole' the wedding, magnificent in a richly embroidered dress in the style of a Russian boyarina. Queen Marie took an immediate and characteristically enthusiastic liking to the Duke of York's Scottish bride.

The christening was a picturesque ceremony. While the *Koom* had a leading part to play in the ceremony, the Duchess of York as *Koomitsa* had only to stand beside him. The Duke carried the child on a cushion into the church and held him until his grand-mother, Queen Marie of Roumania, and his aunt, Princess John, had unswathed him, after which the Duke of York handed him to the venerable Patriarch of Serbia, Mgr. Dimitriye, for total immersion according to the rites of the Greek Orthodox Church. Unfortunately the Patriarch lost his grip and the infant slipped into the font, but was 'landed' dexterously by the Duke of York. After this the baby understandably yelled loudly and continuous-ly, but the noise was drowned by the singing of the choir, as Queen Marie placed a cross round his neck and the child was anointed. After this the Duke of York carried the infant on a cushion three times round the altar, before the child was sprinkled with holy water and a lock of his hair was cut off. It was a considerable ordeal for the baby, and not entirely plain sailing for the *Koom*.

The Duke gave the traditional gold coin to the baby, and received the equally traditional set of handmade embroidered underwear from the baby's parents, while the *Koomitsa* gave the baby a set of clothing, and received a length of beautiful handwoven white silk, with a gold thread running through it.

Unfortunately, Queen Marie of Yugoslavia was not well enough to attend her son's christening, but the rest of the Royal party, together with the baby, appeared on the balcony. According to Serbian custom, the baby had been named immediately after the birth, but his original name of Stephen had been changed at the christening for Petar (Peter), after his grandfather, first King of the United Serbs, Croats and Slovenes, who had died in June 1922. By an oversight no announcement of his name had been made. A peasant in the crowd shouted '*Kako mu ime?*' (What's his name?) and the announcement was immediately made. There was a great burst of cheering and calls of '*Zhivio Petar!*' (Long live Peter).

This baby came to the throne only eleven years later, when his father, King Alexander I, was assassinated while riding in a State procession through the streets of Marseilles. His *Koom* and *Koomitsa* undertook their responsibilities as his god-parents seriously, but it could hardly have been realised at the christening just how important his god-parents would prove to be for him, when they were King and Queen of England, and King Peter was an exile from his country, occupied by the Germans. A silver cigarette case which King Peter gave them in gratitude is still in Queen Elizabeth the Queen Mother's possession.

The future would also bind the Duke and Duchess of York closer with the bride Princess Olga, eldest daughter of Prince Nicholas of Greece, third son of King George I of Greece and of the Grand Duchess Helen Vladimirovna of Russia, and the bridegroom, Prince Paul, whose wedding they attended on the following day, October 22. Eleven years later the bride's sister, Princess Marina of Greece, married the Duke of York's young brother, Prince George.

The Duchess of York took the visit in her stride: the strangeness, the picturesque customs, the considerable discomfort inside the overcrowded Palace, and meeting the armies of clannish, interrelated Royalties, most of them known by nicknames; Sir John Wheeler-Bennett tells how the reserved Duke of York wrote to his father, almost with surprise as well as pride:

'They were all enchanted with Elizabeth especially Cousin Missy. She was wonderful with all of them & they were all strangers except two, Paul & Olga.'

In due course the engagement was announced of Gustaf the Crown Prince of Sweden (son of King Gustaf V of Sweden) and Lady Louise Mountbatten, daughter of the Marquess of Milford Haven (Prince Louis of Battenburg, who had dropped his Royal title and changed his name during the Great War). They became King Gustaf VI and Queen Louise of Sweden. The wedding took place on Saturday, November 3, 1923, in the Chapel Royal at St. James's; the Prince of Wales and the Duke and Duchess of York lunched with King George V and Queen Mary at Buckingham Palace, and went on together to the wedding. Lady Louise wore a wedding dress of Indian silver gauze, the gift of her uncle, the Grand Duke of Hesse, and a lace veil which had been given by Queen Victoria to Princess Alice of Hesse, who was Queen Victoria's second daughter and the bride's grandmother. She was given away by her brother, Lord Louis Mountbatten. The bridesmaids were the bride's four nieces, the four sisters of Prince Philip, now Duke of Edinburgh. Prince Philip, who was then a child just over two years old, was not present.

Only a few days later, on November 12, 1923, Princess Maud, daughter of the Princess Royal by her marriage with the Duke of Fife, and granddaughter of King Edward VII, married Lord Carnegie. Like the Duchess of York, the bridegroom belonged to an old Scottish family. The name and title of Carnegie had been granted to John de Balinhard by David II, only son of King Robert the Bruce, in the fourteenth century. This time there was a family luncheon, given beforehand by the Princess Royal in Portman Square. The marriage took place in the Guards' Chapel, which was destroyed with tragic loss of life in the Second World War.

In 1924 Princess Mary, as she was expecting her second child, and living quietly in Yorkshire lent the Duke and Duchess of York the Lascelles' London house for the Season. This was Chesterfield House (now demolished for a block of flats), which stood on the corner of South Audley and Curzon Streets, on ground belonging to the Curzon family. It was built for the famous fourth Earl of Chesterfield, the connoisseur, statesman, gambler and satirist, by Isaac Ware.

For several years the Duke and Duchess of York took a furnished London house for the Season, they leased Curzon House for a time, they took 40 Grosvenor Square in the spring of 1926, and they also took over 17 Bruton Street, the London home of the Strathmores.

It was in 1924 that the Duchess of York attended her first Courts as a member of the Royal family. The Royal family assembled in the Royal Closet at Buckingham Palace, and when all was ready moved in procession through the White Drawing Room, Music Room and Blue Drawing Room of Buckingham Palace, preceded by the Lord Chamberlain (walking backwards), while the guests, held back behind red cordons to leave a wide lane free, bowed or curtseyed deeply as the King passed. The Duchess of York took her place behind Their Majesties on the dais, as those to be presented came forward and made their curtseys.

The ladies attending the Court wore low-cut evening dresses (not necessarily white) with Court trains not more than two yards in length falling from the shoulders, and on their heads veils with three small white feathers mounted as a Prince of Wales plume. The men wore black silk velvet Court Dress with white silk velvet breeches with white silk hose and buckles at the knee and on the shoe. That year, the concession of wearing an ordinary black evening coat with black knee breeches and silk stockings (which had been temporarily granted in 1920 when Evening Courts were resumed after the war) was confirmed, but few took advantage of it.

The Duchess of York's first Court Ball, another splendid and magnificent occasion (and the Duchess of York enjoyed a grand occasion) was the State Ball for the King and Queen of Roumania at Buckingham Palace on May 15, 1924. All the State Rooms were in use, and supper was served in five supper rooms.

But the Royal occasion in 1924 which was to have the greatest future significance took place at Wembley on April 23, the Opening of the British Empire Exhibition. For the first time, the voice of the Sovereign was broadcast.

King George V did not ignore the developments of science, and took this opportunity to be the first King of England to speak to all his peoples at one and the same time. The Prince of Wales, who had been closely connected with the Exhibition, received the King and Queen on their arrival. In the first carriage were the King and Queen and their sons the Duke of York and Prince Henry. The Duchess of York was in the third carriage with Prince George, the Duchess of Devonshire, who was Mistress of the Robes, and the Home Secretary, Mr. Arthur Henderson.

The technical difficulties connected with the broadcast were considerable. The B.B.C. had set up a large Marconi polarised moving coil microphone on each side of the Royal Dais and about five feet from the King. In all, they used four microphones and four amplifiers. The cumbersome accumulator-driven equipment was housed in a B.B.C. kiosk from which three private Post Office lines ran to headquarters at 2 Savoy Hill.

Something went wrong with the first few minutes of the broadcast, and the introductory sentences of the Prince of Wales as he asked his father, the King, to open the Exhibition, were lost. Then the King rose to speak, and this time all was well.

'There were no chatterings nor scufflings among the children now. There was not a whisper, scarce even a stifled cough (and we are still in April and this is England) in all the great assembly. So great was the silence that a creaking door and an echo . . . were the only sounds that crossed in the smallest degree His Majesty's clear, rich tones.'

When the King spoke the words, 'I declare this Exhibition open', the message was flashed round the world by cable in Morse code, and completed the circuit in one minute and twenty seconds.

'A very few moments after the King had spoken the words, a telegraph boy entered the arena with a large white envelope. He was not in a hurry: he did not run. He walked briskly with the assurance of one who has a happy duty to perform and plenty of time to do it in . . . he bowed low and handed to the King the news that had come round the world—the news that His Majesty had declared the Exhibition open.' (*The Times*.)

Only Britain could actually hear the King's voice, but all over the country, wherever there was a wireless set, people gathered round it, often sharing parted head-phones. The blind soldiers in St. Dunstan's were listening. Twenty thousand people gathered in Princes Street Gardens, where a loud-speaker broadcast the speech. In the Mansion House Court an electrical and wireless manufacturer had been summoned before Alderman Sir John Baddeley for an obstruction in St. Paul's Churchyard where, it was alleged, he had used a portable wireless and loudspeaker. The wireless expert mentioned that his set required no aerial, and that he had it with him in Court. The Alderman thereupon suggested that they might listen to the King; the portable was put into action; and the closing passages of the King's speech were clearly heard. It seems only fair that the pioneer was found guilty of a technical offence only, and that no conviction was recorded against him!

It is estimated by the British Broadcasting Corporation that about seven per cent of the population of the British Isles heard the King's broadcast, which was relayed by transmitters in London, Birmingham, Manchester (which also served Northern Ireland), Cardiff, Glasgow and Aberdeen, with booster stations at Liverpool, Sheffield, Dundee and Swansea. It was a foretaste of changes to come.

The pace of life was much slower then. The Royal family lived a life apart from the rest of the country, and their contacts even with the nobility were somewhat formal. The Duchess of York experienced some losses of friendship and freedom upon her entry into the Royal family. In one way, she felt it less than another girl might have done. The Bowes-Lyon family had such a wonderful and close inter-relationship that they hardly felt the need for many intimate friends outside the family. Those friends who had become a part of the life of Glamis and St. Paul's Walden remained unchanged. But she was cut off from her outer circle of friends, and from this time on it was not easy for her to make new intimate friends outside the Royal circle. The effect was not immediate, but cumulative. While her husband and her brothers and sisters lived, they filled her life; now death has thinned their number and for all her multitude of acquaintances, she has fewer intimate contemporaries than she might otherwise have had.

After her marriage the Duchess of York could still enjoy many pleasures of ordinary life. She could go shopping; lunch or dine in hotels or restaurants; visit art exhibitions and other places of interest without hindrance either from protocol or from excessive public interest. But she no longer used public transport.

However, at that time, there were so many things that an unmarried girl was not expected to do, unless she belonged to a very 'modern' set—which Lady Elizabeth Bowes-Lyon had never done—that the many freedoms gained as a married woman could be set against those lost as a private person.

One pleasure which the Duchess of York enjoyed was that she had much more money at her disposal than before, and she would have been less than human if she had not enjoyed it. She bought presents to delight those dear to her—how she enjoyed getting a little car for her brother David, which was the apple of his eye.

Above all, there was the joy of her marriage. It would be impossible to exaggerate what his wife did for the Duke of York. He was an introspective and highly-strung man who had always been severely handicapped by nervousness. A man who knew him at this time recalls, 'When I met the Duke of York first, before he was married, I think he was not a happy man. He was greatly cut off by his stammer. He did not thrive in the admirable but somewhat serious atmosphere which his parents thought best for their family, and he was completely overshadowed by and appeared rather in awe of his elder brother. Underneath, the Duke of York was always a sterling character, but then it was not easy, on a slight acquaintance, to get to know the real man.'

Those who knew the Duke of York well always appreciated

him. During his active service with the Royal Navy the Duke had liked and been liked by the men in his ship, particularly by the men in his own gun-turret, who were under fire beside him. James Moffatt, who served with Prince Albert in H.M.S. *Collingwood*, wrote, after King George VI had become a much-loved King:

'Just as, when a midshipman, he had gradually won his way into the hearts of the men amongst whom he worked, and earned not only their liking but their respect, so in the far more difficult task of gaining his people's love and respect, he has succeeded in a most remarkable manner.' (*King George Was My Shipmate*.)

Already, before his marriage, the Duke of York had begun to show evidence of his individual thinking and strong personal convictions. He was much before his time in his outlook on industrial relationships. He concerned himself to find ways to bridge or fill the deep cleavages that existed between classes, and which were harder to cross then than they are today. The Duke of York was convinced that if people knew each other better, they would like each other better, and that they would work better together. The Duke of York's camps, where public school boy met and played in the same team as factory boy, were pathfinders for today's adventure courses and Outward Bound schools, so vigorously encouraged by his son-in-law, the Duke of Edinburgh.

The Duke of York's concern with industrial relationships and the welfare of young people was far more than just a conscientiously executed duty. It was part of his life. Everyone connected with him heard about his camps and his boys' clubs. When Queen Mary visited a boys' club in the East End of London, she asked to see what became of the magazines the Duke of York was always collecting for his Club boys, when he lived at Buckingham Palace. When the Duke revisited the Homes for Little Boys at Farningham and Swaley (now the Farningham House for Boys) of which he was President, he spoke with obvious sincerity about the excellent cabinet the boys had made for him, and about 'a beautiful little table, which is greatly valued by my wife and myself'. The Duke of York's friends and acquaintances were left in no doubt that they would greatly please him if they showed real interest in helping boys' clubs and in improving industrial relationship.

Yet before his marriage, the Duke of York had often found difficulty in expressing his ideas. He needed a warm and abiding love: this he found in the remarkable woman he married, and he found more—gaiety and a radiance which made the daily round of life delightful. His home life was an enchantment and revelation to him: he knew himself to be 'the most fortunate of men', as he once expressed it, and his love and delight in his wife never waned.

His young wife had recognised in him, before they were clearly visible, the qualities that would be known across the world by the end of his life. She did not plant those qualities there, but she nurtured them as no one else did or could have done. She gave him confidence and faith in himself. She actively encouraged her husband in his work, not only because she would always help him but because she believed in it. Without the love and devotion of his wife, it is extremely improbable that the Duke of York could ever have risen to his full stature as a greatly-loved King of England and the Commonwealth, a part which no one then knew, of course, that he would be called on to bear.

Now that the Duchess of York was part of the Royal family, on national occasions she would take her place in the second rank; and she must also learn to 'fly solo' when the senior members of the Royal family were not present. The King and Queen showed consideration and understanding for their daughter-in-law, and she was allowed time 'to find her feet'.

The strength of the Royal family is like that of a rope; each and every strand, however different, contributes to its strength, and the rope is far stronger than even its most powerful strand. The public duties of the British Royal family are constantly evolving and changing to meet the changing conditions of life. Apparently inflexible, the British monarchy is in fact a delicately adjusted instrument, giving both unifying strength and stability to the people it serves. It is always progressing, always modifying to meet the feeling of the times, yet based on the constant truths of family, home, faith and duty. We can see in the Royal family a reproduction, under at once more favoured and more searching conditions, of our history and of our own family.

The Royal family was then as short of women to undertake public duties as it was to be short of men a generation later. The King's only daughter, Princess Mary, lived mostly in Yorkshire with her husband and young family, while the Duke of York was the first, and so far the only one, of the King's sons to marry. The Duchess of York, by undertaking even a limited share of the Royal duties, would be helpful to the King.

Up to the time of her marriage she had done rather more than the average young girl's share of public work; she was a Commissioner in the local Girl Guides; she had helped her mother in church and other local work; but like most of her contemporaries she did not know a great deal about poor people in the towns, or about industrial problems.

Quickly she widened her interests, her key always her avid interest in people. No formal sphere of influence was allocated to her: and her earliest public interests were in many cases like Topsy's—'they just growed'. Some of her early engagements were connected with Richmond, where she now lived; others were with her old home counties of Forfarshire (now Angus), and Hertfordshire; or with Yorkshire from which her title stemmed; or because friends had engaged her support for their special charity. Her first national Presidencies and Patronages were those left vacant by the death of Princess Christian. Among the earliest were the North Islington Infant Welfare Centre and Wards; the Young Women's Christian Association; the Mothercraft Training Society; and the National Society for the Prevention of Cruelty to Children.

She remains interested in the Royal Hospital and Home for Incurables at Putney of which she succeeded Princess Christian as Patron in 1923. When admission to the Home was regulated by the votes of the subscribers, she always exercised her vote. The Hospital was the concept of Andrew Reed, an enthusiastic but temperamental clergyman, who wrote in 1845, 'It would be a blessed thing if we had a provision in the land to give shelter to the despairing incurables.' There are about two hundred and fifty men and women patients in the Hospital who are suffering from rheumatoid arthritis, multiple sclerosis, polio and similar lifelong but not quickly killing diseases. She has gently remonstrated about its chilling name, but the patients themselves voted for it to continue. In spite of their disabilities, the patients follow a wide range of interests from their wheel-chairs or beds.

Elderly patients in the Hospital recall every one of her visits, but it is the Garden Party which she attended as Queen Elizabeth the Queen Mother in 1957 which is most vividly remembered. 'Everyone sparked up, patrons as well as patients,' said the Matron, 'and every patient felt that Queen Elizabeth had spoken directly to them.'

That first summer of her marriage, the Duchess of York went to see one thousand poor children from the East End of London enjoying their first sight of the country, when they spent a day on the outskirts of Epping Forest. At a coconut shy the Duchess of York won a coconut, which was sold for the fund to a by-stander for £2.

Just before Christmas, 1923, the Duke and Duchess of York went to the 'Banquet for Little Londoners and a distribution of Hampers to Crippled Children', arranged by Miss Florence Treloar, after the pattern set by her father, Sir Frederick Treloar, at the Guildhall. The children had a dinner of roast beef, potatoes and milk, while an orchestra played. Afterwards there was an entertainment, and vigorous singing of the choruses of well-known songs, while the Duke and Duchess of York watched from the gallery. Later they talked to the children, who had each been given a packet of food, to which the Duke and Duchess had contributed biscuits. The Duchess of York handed waybills to all the van-drivers, who clattered off to distribute four thousand hampers to crippled children unable to leave home.

Visits to hospitals for the war wounded were a sad but recurring part of the Duchess of York's early duties. Through the twenties and for long years afterwards, the war-wounded lingered in hospital. Nearly twenty-five thousand soldiers were in hospital in the United Kingdom at the end of the First World War—and five years later, at the time of the Duchess's wedding, there were still nearly nineteen thousand soldiers in hospital. Only just over seven thousand soldiers remained in hospital five years after the end of the Second World War.

Throughout her life Queen Elizabeth has given support and thought to schemes by which the disabled could become partly or wholly independent. In her own words:

'We all owe a special debt to those who have been disabled in war. We cannot discharge it better than by doing everything in our power to enable those who have fought our battles to recapture their longed-for independence and thereby once more to take their place among their fellow men to lead again a useful and contented life.'

Some battles have had better outcome: tuberculosis is not today the dreaded disease that it was in the early days of the Duchess of York's marriage, when she paid a visit to the Papworth Village Settlement and remarked 'upon the bright and cheerful aspect of the men, who carry on the work in spite of being afflicted in varying degrees with the scourge of consumption'.

The Duchess's consideration for others shone through the formality of her early engagements. On an extremely hot day, she noticed that a very old lady who was to be presented was lingering as long as possible in the shade, although at some little distance: she walked over to her, and then returned to her original sun-baked position, from which she could best be seen.

A soldier, meeting her before one of her first military occasions, had at once to conduct her through a particularly dank and dirty passenger subway; he remembered nearly forty years later 'how she laughed and was so sympathetic and nice that it put you at your ease, and made you feel it was a shared adventure'.

The Duchess of York soon made acquaintance with the perennial Royal occasions, the laying of foundation stones, the opening of new buildings, attendance at centenary celebrations and so forth, which sympathisers (and pseudo-sympathisers) with the Royal family so often suggest are boring and tedious.

Yet the formal ceremony has its definite purpose. Walter Bagehot, the nineteenth-century constitutional writer who has had such influence upon our ways of Government, divided Government into two parts:

'First, those that excite and preserve the reverence of the population—the *dignified* parts . . . and next the *efficient* parts —those by which it, in fact, works and rules . . . The dignified parts of government are those which bring it force—which attract its motive power. The efficient parts only employ that power. The comely parts of a government *have* need, for they are those upon which its vital strength depends. They may not do anything definite that a simpler policy would not do better; but they are the preliminaries, the needful prerequisites of *all* work . . .'

Maintaining the dignified and comely part of the Government is one, but only one, of the Sovereign's duties; it is, however, a most important part of the duty of other members of the Royal family.

Fortunately for the Government and the nation, the Duchess of York had a special gift for public and ceremonial duties. She always appeared to be enjoying herself, whatever she was doing. This was deftly described in an article in *The Times* on the day of her Coronation:

'She lays a foundation stone as though she has just discovered a new and delightful way of spending an afternoon.'

The Duchess of York has always enjoyed individuals. She has always sympathetically supported solo efforts by one man or one woman, or by a small group of men and women. She has gaily but stubbornly refused to give up helping little individual efforts of goodwill, even when some people have suggested that they might be below the dignity of official encouragement from a member of the Royal family, and especially from a Queen. Queen Elizabeth has kept up her interest in even the very small charities she took on as Duchess of York. She has gradually developed and improved the knack she has for picking out interesting people to speak to, as well as those selected for presentation. She has eyes that pierce through three ranks of people and pick out a friend.

The Duchess attended horse shows; started heats in regattas; patronised fêtes, visited bazaars and sales of work which were even more numerous then than today; attended concerts; visited working men's clubs; boys' clubs; hospitals and Lord Mayor Treloar's Cripples Hospital and College at Alton; took charge of a stall of old china, linen, silver, glass and petit-point stools at a sale of work at the Royal School of Needlework ('she looked charming in a dress of ecru lace and georgette with a rose-coloured crinoline hat'); watched the King's birthday parade; went to the Royal Tournament; and in short lived a busy and useful life in the context and at the tempo of the Royal family's public duties of the period.

She travelled about in Britain to undertake her duties. At Queen's Belfast, she received her first honorary degree as Doctor of Laws—only the second woman to receive a degree there. In Glasgow, wearing a fur cloak over a blue dress trimmed with ostrich feathers, she declared open a flower show and attended the annual gala of the Girls' Guild of which she was President. (The Duke of York, on independent duties, kicked off for a football match, served the first ball on a lawn-tennis court and bowled the first ball on a bowling green, all in one afternoon!) She danced an eightsome reel at the Forfar County Ball in the Masonic Hall, Forfar, where she was greeted by rousing cheers. In Manchester she received a cheque subscribed to Manchester hospitals through the Lord Mayor's Million Shillings Fund. She visited Hove and Brighton, wearing a rust-red velour coat and skirt with a skunk collar and a black hat with rust-red hanging ostrich fronds. She was delighted with a masque written by Thomas Campion in 1607, which she saw performed at Hatfield. She opened a new wing of the Royal Surrey County Hospital at Guildford. She even, in October, 1924, saw a baseball match at Stamford Bridge between the New York Giants and the Chicago White Sox, played before a very small and ignorant crowd who were, nevertheless, impressed by the magnificent catching—which *The Times* correspondent noted with a certain condescension 'was better than in many county cricket matches'.

Public speaking holds no horror for her. The voice of a Royal lady was seldom heard in those days. Queen Mary remained so shy throughout her public life that she found it almost impossible to speak in public, and did so only very occasionally. From the first, the Duchess of York spoke naturally and well, and Queen Mary once remarked to her Household how much she wished this gift had come naturally to her own shy family.

At the Francis Holland School, Clarence Gate, she inspected a guard of honour from the school troop of Girl Guides, and made a neat little speech, in which, referring to the variety of prizes which she had presented, she wondered if there was any subject that they did not study, and spoke of the 'triple alliance' of teachers, parents and children. The importance of the parent in every system of education is a theme to which she was to refer on many occasions.

At home the Duchess of York did a certain amount of quiet entertaining. She gave several garden parties at the White Lodge during the first summer after their marriage, and sometimes entertained at Chesterfield House in London. On several occasions she was hostess at Claridges at a small dinner party, which often included the Prince of Wales.

A journalist remembers her as a slightly nervous young hostess waiting for the guest of honour at a charity committee meeting. She was not tall enough to see out of the high windows of the hall, and she appealed to this young Pressman, 'Would *you* be kind enough to look out of this window and see if the Countess has arrived yet?' in a way which made him feel an integral part of the proceedings.

The Duke and Duchess went away quite often at week-ends, either to the Royal family or to members of her family, and also to such old friends as Lord and Lady Plunket, whose tragic deaths in an air crash some ten years later were to be a sad blow; to Lord Derby; to the Earl and Countess of Ancaster, with whom they also stayed in Scotland; to Lord and Lady Annaly; Colonel and Mrs. Brinton; Mrs. James; Mrs. Gilmour; Lady Amy Coates; Commander and Lady Doris Vyner; and Lady Eldon.

Lady Katharine Hamilton, afterwards Lady Katharine Seymour—her childhood friend and bridesmaid—later became her Lady-in-Waiting. All her Ladies-in-Waiting were and are personal friends, and none more so than Lady Helen Graham. She succeeded Lady Katharine Meade, the first Lady-in-Waiting to the Duchess of York, in July 1926, and throughout the remainder of her life was a close friend and stalwart support.

The Duke of York's close friend from wartime days, Wing-Commander Louis Greig, had been succeeded as Comptroller in 1923 by Captain Basil Brooke, R.N., who held the post until the time of the Duke of York's accession to the Throne. Lieutenant Colin Buist, R.N., was an Equerry from 1923 until 1928. Mr. Patrick Kirkham Hodgson, C.M.G., O.B.E., was appointed private secretary to the Duke of York in February 1926.

The Duchess of York had to accustom herself to a quite new relationship with her Household. Men and women who had been her equals before her marriage were now serving her—a perfectly straightforward position to play according to the rules in public, but in private requiring a delicate balance between frank friendship and sustained dignity. A Member of the early Household, who continued to serve them for many years, commented, 'Their idea was to have a nice Staff, made up of people whom you like immensely . . . they believed you could be Staff and a very dear personal friend at the same time.' It was the wish of the Duke and Duchess of York entirely to drop the formality of public occasions when they were at home with their Household, and indeed they did so. Any sense of distance that remained was due to the circumspection of the Members of the Household, who had a deep respect for the Royal family, and who feared that if, for instance, they became on reciprocal Christian name terms they might at some time let the name slip in public. So the Duke and Duchess of York, like the present Queen and Duke of Edinburgh today, always called their Household by their Christian names, while the Household occasionally addressed them as 'Your Royal Highness' or later as 'Your Majesty', but more generally said 'Sir' or 'Ma'am'.

Although the Duchess of York encouraged her husband in his outdoor activities, she did not go in much for sports after her marriage. He was a very good and keen shot, if not so outstanding with driven game as his father the King. The Duke of York was also fond of fox-hunting. He rode well and he enjoyed going out with the Pytchley and Whaddon Chase packs. For a time he leased a hunting lodge at Guilsborough in Northamptonshire. The Duchess of York never hunted, but went to meets and followed by car.

In the summer, the Duke of York's favourite sport was lawn tennis. He had the tennis court improved at the White Lodge, where the Duchess sometimes played with him, and where the Duke used to practise hard with leading players. He played left-handed, and had a specially strong service and excellent concentration. He was a good doubles player and with his friend and Equerry, Wing-Commander Louis Greig, played in Inter-Service Championship doubles, winning a number of them. He also often played with the Swedish international, Herr S. Malmström.

An unfortunate incident afterwards took much of the Duke of York's pleasure out of tennis; he had been playing well, and entered with Wing-Commander Greig for the men's doubles at Wimbledon. It is said that he requested to play on one of the minor courts, but that in a misplaced courtesy his wishes were disregarded and they were put on a prominent court, to face Mr. A. W. Gore and Mr. H. Roper-Barrett, the former Wimbledon doubles champions. In these very public surroundings the Duke's game went to pieces and they were soundly trounced. To the Duke of York, who was a perfectionist, it was a public humiliation, and he was very upset. 'I shall never forget the Duchess's wonderful gentleness with him in the car afterwards,' said her Lady-in-Waiting.

During the first winter of her marriage, the Duchess of York suffered from bronchitis, and so for part of the second winter, the Duke of York wished to take his wife to East Africa, but for this the King's permission was necessary. It was impossible for a son of the Sovereign to go overseas without specific and by no means inevitable permission, but it was immediately granted on this occasion.

The Duke and Duchess of York planned a visit to Kenya, Uganda and the Sudan, to include some official duties in each country, and also big-game shooting. This was the Duchess of York's first visit to a continent which she loved instantly, and has altogether visited eight times. They took with them Captain

Basil Brooke (later Admiral Sir Basil Brooke), Lady Annaly and Lt.-Commander Colin Buist.

They travelled out through Paris, where they spent a few days, overland to Marseilles and there joined the two-year-old British India steamer *Mulbera*, of nine thousand gross tons (Captain Walter Steadman), and sailed, by way of Port Said and Aden— crossing the Equator with appropriate ceremony—to Mombasa.

On December 22, the Duke and Duchess stepped ashore on to the landing stage at Kilindini, Mombasa, beneath a flag inscribed 'Welcome to Kenya'. Thousands of Europeans, Africans, Arabs, Somalis and Indians were assembled to greet them, and that first African evening was spent at a great *ngoma* or dance festival at which five thousand dancers from tribes in Kenya, Tanganyika, Uganda, Nyasaland and the Belgian Congo danced in their honour to compulsive rhythms from drum and conch-shell, among them Kikuyu stilt-walkers, wearing gilt crowns set with flaming candles. The Duke and Duchess of York were presented with a gold coin on a red ribbon 'from all the Mombasa dancers'. It was an evening they would never forget.

Nor would they forget their train journey from Mombasa to Nairobi. There were then many wild animals to be seen on the journey, even before reaching the Game Reserve on the flat Athi Plains. Here, to get the best possible view of the wild game, they transferred to a kind of garden seat which had been fixed to the buffers of the engine, and where they were secured by straps from any possible fall.

Christmas was spent at Government House, Nairobi, as the guests of the Governor of Kenya, Sir Robert Coryndon, who was born in Cape Colony and had been an associate of Rhodes: he was a man who deeply loved Africa and was held in high regard in the Colony, where he worked hard for all the people under his jurisdiction, and both the Duke and the Duchess greatly liked him. A few days after Christmas they went on their first safari. The Governor accompanied them for part of the way; his car was badly damaged when it ran into a swamp.

This first safari was to the north of Kenya, and took them on both sides of Mount Kenya. They spent a fortnight going up-stream along the broad river Uaso Nyero, crossing the river at

Archer's Post, where the expedition's one car was manhandled across the water by a long line of bearers. Then they made another sortie into lion country, north into the Masai reserve. The tsetse flies were bad, and the Duke and Duchess and their small party mostly walked, although they occasionally rode mules, which stood up to the tsetse fly better than horses.

Safari was then very primitive. It was an extremely tough affair, in terrific heat, and they did the whole thing by foot. The Duchess of York wore slacks, with a belted bush-shirt, a scarf knotted round her neck and a big felt bush-hat, a practical garb which greatly suited her. The atmosphere was gay and happy. The life was exciting, they were young and newly married and very much in love.

They ate in the open, at a card-table, sitting on camp chairs. At night they slept in tents: two cottage tents were pitched close together for the Duke and Duchess of York. They carried little luggage, although they always had at least one reasonably formal outfit for use on more official occasions. In Kenya their expedition was led by Captain Keith Caldwell (who also went on to Uganda), Mr. G. H. Anderson and Mr. Pat Ayre, who had a saw-mill in Kenya and was a keen hunter in his spare time.

They had come off safari for a few days, and were staying on the Kenyan farm of Lord and Lady Francis Scott, when suddenly, on February 10, the news was received that the Governor of Kenya, Sir Robert Coryndon, after a few days' illness, had been operated on for nephritis and had suddenly died: Lady Coryndon and their family were on their way home by boat on leave. Immediately the Duke of York cancelled the remainder of his safari in Kenya, and returned to Nairobi for the funeral.

Nor was news from England free from anxiety. The King was suffering from a severe attack of bronchitis, following influenza. It is strange how often visits of members of the Royal family to Africa have coincided with illness of the Sovereign at home. In December 1928 the Prince of Wales had to abandon safari in Tanganyika and hurry home when the King was desperately ill. King George VI himself died while his daughter was in Kenya.

A few days later the Duke and Duchess of York left Kenya with regret. Already they loved the country, and their appreciation touched off much affection in the Colony. The people of Kenya even offered them a farm, but neither the King at home nor the Colonial Office favoured its acceptance.

However, the visit to Africa was not at an end. The party travelled by road and rail to Kisumu on the Kavirondo Gulf, and on February 15 crossed the northern waters of Lake Victoria, and incidentally re-crossed the Equator, to Entebbe on the north-west of the lake.

There followed two days of official ceremonies in Kampala, where the acting Governor was Mr. E. B. Jarvis, C.M.G. There the Duke invested with the K.C.M.G. his contemporary, the young Kabaka of Buganda, Daudi Chwa, who had been on the throne since childhood. The Kabaka's gift to the Duke and Duchess of York was a pair of magnificent elephant tusks.

The Royal party then travelled by motor-car west to Fort Portal, in the shadow of Ruwenzori, where the official visit to Uganda ended, the 'tidy' clothes were packed away, and they began their Uganda safari. The camp at Fort Portal was actually a quite elaborate affair, with a concourse of thatched mud huts decorated with fine carving 'which seemed like the Ritz Hotel, in contrast with the other camps', said a member of the expedition.

They then set out on a forty-mile march down the Semiliki Valley to Lake Albert. They still had the one car with them, an 'L-type' Ford, which was loaded with gear. Monowheels were produced—vehicles made from the back wheels of bicycles, fitted with seat and canopy and hauled richskaw fashion, but they were more a gimmick than a practical conveyance, although the Duke and Duchess of York were both photographed aboard them.

The Uganda safari was led by Captain R. J. D. Salmon, a very well-known hunter nicknamed *Sumaki*, which means 'fish', and Mr. Pete Pearson; they were the Chief and Assistant Game Wardens of Uganda. They were assisted by a well-known Portuguese white hunter, who was known by his nickname of *The Hoot*, and who always wore a black shirt. During a visit to Nyasaland in 1960 Queen Elizabeth instantly recognised him, and was delighted to see him again.

On the march down the Semiliki Valley the chief native cook got an attack of malaria, and had to be carried most of the way by four bearers on a makeshift stretcher slung on two poles. It was a strenuous march, and as the cook did not look particularly ill, there were those who whispered his illness was strategic. He was not, however, the only member of the party to suffer from fever.

Elephants were hunted during the Uganda safari. This was at the end of the great days of elephant hunting. In the early days poaching was a dangerous but lucrative business. Ivory was worth about 21s. 6d. a pound, and no one shot an elephant with tusks weighing less than forty pounds a side. Thus the old-time hunters could easily earn £100 with a single shot. The Duke of York's expedition did, in fact, see at Nimule a Wanderobo African hunter with two tusks weighing 210 and 203 pounds, worth close on £500.

The Duke of York always hunted elephants on foot, at close range—'feet rather than yards', said a member of his party—and with little cover. He killed one elephant with a difficult shot, and with only a few reeds for cover: the tusks were later mounted and stood in the hall at 145 Piccadilly. He was a fine shot, and soon proved himself expert with a rifle in Africa. The Duchess of York also shot, with an 0·275 Rigby rifle.

The whole party carried cameras, and the Duke of York and other members of the party took photographs of wild life, including a splendid shot of six elephants, led by the bull and accompanied by their attendant white egrets, on the move through the bush, taken, of course, without telescopic lens and at a very short distance. But the art of photographing big game was then in its infancy.

When they reached Lake Albert, they embarked in the small paddle-steamer *Samuel Baker* for passage down the Lake and into the Southern Nile, leaving the ship for an expedition along the Katengri River. They stopped at Rhino Camp, where they were rejoined by the acting Governor, Mr. Jarvis, who had come to bid them official farewell from Uganda, and they exchanged their Ugandan Game Wardens for Captain Philip Brocklehurst, Game Warden of the Sudan, and his assistant, Major Walsh.

At Nimuli they disembarked from the *Samuel Baker* as rapids made the Nile unnavigable at this point, and motored ninety miles to Rejaf near Juba, where they rejoined the White Nile and went on board the Nile gunboat *Nasir* (Captain Flett): this had an absolutely vertical funnel. The expedition's cars, now numbering four or five, were shipped on board a flat which the *Nasir* pushed in front of her, and there followed a slow, and in spite of the mosquitoes, fascinating passage down the Upper Nile valley, watching the quantities of game which had been driven close to the river by drought. They were particularly thrilled to see a herd of elephant swimming the Nile.

When they reached Mongalla Talodi they made an expedition of some eighty miles by car to see a Nuba and Shilluk gathering, where famed Nubian wrestlers competed. They were impressed by the Nubian spear-throwers, where the spear was caught at close range, with great skill and courage, on the defender's shield.

They turned aside to sail up Lake No and made a short trip up the Bahr el Gazal, and then returned to the Blue Nile and sailed down to Sennar and Khartoum, where they visited the battlefield of Omdurman—on which young Winston Churchill had taken part in a cavalry charge which had contributed to the defeat by Kitchener's British and Egyptian forces of the Army of the Khalifa. There they resumed some official duties, including the laying of the foundation stone of the Makwar Dam, when the 'L-type' Ford sported an unaccustomed Standard.

Thence the Duke and Duchess of York went by train to Port Sudan on the Red Sea, where they took passage in the P. & O. liner *Maloja* (Captain S. C. Warner). They were delayed in the Red Sea for four hours by a sand-storm so severe that the vessel had to anchor. On April 17, reluctantly dressed in formal clothes after months of carefree travel, they disembarked at Marseilles, and travelled overland in the special boat-train by which the five days' steaming from Marseilles to London could be avoided. They always looked back on their safari in Africa with particular pleasure; it widened their horizons and fanned their interest in the Empire.

Almost exactly a year later, on April 21, 1926, the London papers carried the following announcement:

'Her Royal Highness the Duchess of York was safely delivered of a Princess at 2.40 this morning. Both mother and daughter are doing well.'

The child was born at 17 Bruton Street; King George V had readily agreed to the Duchess's return to her parents' home for the birth of his first grandchild in the male line. During the hours preceding the birth the Duke of York restlessly wandered about the house. He saw to the comfort of the Home Secretary, Sir William Joynson-Hicks, who had been summoned in accordance with the decree that the Home Secretary should be present in the house when a child was born in the Royal Succession, following the rumours (almost certainly false) that a baby had been substituted in a warming pan for a dead child or in a simulated confinement to Queen Mary of Modena, second wife of King James II. This custom, which King George VI later called 'archaic', he abolished before the birth of *his* first grandchild after it had been temporarily in abeyance during the war. The Duke of York also went in to see waiting reporters, and saw to it that they were provided with coffee and sandwiches.

The news was at once telephoned to Windsor, where King George and Queen Mary were wakened between 3 and 4 a.m. to learn of the birth of their first grand-daughter. The Home Secretary sent a special message to the Lord Mayor of London. The first news to the Press came as a 'flash' through the Press Association, and it was not until 10 a.m. that the first signed bulletin was issued:

'The Duchess of York has had some rest since the arrival of her daughter. Her Royal Highness and the infant Princess are making satisfactory progress.'

Henry Simson
Walter Jagger

There was no disappointment that the child, third in succession to the Throne, was a girl. The newspapers showed polite and friendly interest; there was a small crowd in the street outside Bruton Street, who cheered when the King and Queen arrived from Windsor to see their grand-daughter; there were many other callers, and many florists' messengers and telegraph boys.

The Times pointed out:

'The birth of the little Princess of Great Britain and Ireland who, as soon as she has a Christian name, will be "of York", for according to custom the children of a Royal Duke who is a son of the Sovereign are known by courtesy as Princes or Princesses of the place from which he takes his title—as, for example, Queen Victoria, who was known as Princess Victoria of Kent—affects the position of her uncles, Prince Henry and Prince George, in the succession to the Throne.'

A lesser authority might well have forgotten to bring that sentence to its successful conclusion! No one had the second sight to prophesy that this was the birth of a future Sovereign Queen.

The baby Princess was only thirteen days old when the General Strike broke out on May 4 and lasted until May 12. It was a particularly trying time for the Duke of York, who knew so much more than most people about industrial relationships, and who was unable to do anything at all about it, because of his constitutional position. It took all the Duke's joy in his new daughter, and all the tact of his wife, to alleviate his frustration.

One task on hand was to choose the names for the baby and to submit them for the approval of the King. The Duke and Duchess of York decided upon Elizabeth after her mother; Alexandra after Queen Alexandra, her great-grandmother who had recently died; and Mary after her grandmother, Queen Mary. The Duchess's own initials, E. A. M., were thus ingeniously repeated. Again, no one could foresee the day, many years ahead, when both mother and daughter would be Queen Elizabeth.

The christening was held on May 29 in the private Chapel at Buckingham Palace, which was afterwards destroyed by bombing. The Archbishop of York was assisted by Prebendary Percival, and the baby Princess—who cried—was christened in water specially brought from the River Jordan. The choristers of the Chapel Royal, St. James's, sang. Only about twenty close relatives and friends, together with a few of the older servants of the King and Queen, were present. At the christening the old Duke of Connaught, seventh child of Queen Victoria, who had been born in 1850, turned to Lady Elphinstone, the baby's aunt, who was one of the godmothers and said sadly, 'You'll see her grow up: I shan't.' The life span of the older generation of the Royal family was growing to a close.

The reign of King George V was entering its last decade—a rewarding decade, when he would realise the great love his people held for him. The years of fulfilment and parenthood which lay immediately ahead of the Duke and Duchess of York were to be the happiest of their lives together.

CHAPTER FIVE

THE WORLD TOUR TOGETHER

Daughter of an Honoured House, welcome, welcome . . . Is it a woman's peace you bring? Woman's hands and woman's tears have soothed the wounds of a warring world . . . Come, then with the Empire's call to all your kind, to cement its foundation in seriousness, with patience and forbearance

Maori welcome by Sir Maui Paomare to the Duke and Duchess of York, in Rotorua

THE Duke and Duchess of York were given little time to enjoy the delights of their daughter. The baby was only a few weeks old when, one morning in Buckingham Palace, King George V suddenly told the Duke of York that he was sending him to Australia, to represent the Sovereign at the first meeting in Canberra, the new Federal capital, of the Parliament of the Commonwealth of Australia, which was to take place on May 9, 1927.

The King's decision was not only a complete surprise to the Duke and Duchess of York, it was something of a shock. Before the birth of Princess Elizabeth they would have liked nothing better than such a long and interesting journey, but it was very different now that they had a new and engrossing daughter. The Duchess of York especially looked forward with dismay to a six months' separation from her baby.

There could, however, be no question of refusal. Inexorably, a world tour was planned round the Opening of the Australian Federal Parliament in Canberra. The official announcement was made simultaneously in London and Melbourne (which was then the capital of Australia) in July 1926.

The 1927 tour was the Duke and Duchess of York's first really big assignment on their own. Up till then they had been comparatively little known. Indeed, in Australia and New Zealand, the news that King George had chosen the Yorks to visit them was received with polite acquiescence in the King's wishes rather than with enthusiasm. The Prince of Wales had created devotion close to adulation and had drawn fantastic crowds when he had toured Australia and New Zealand in 1920, and it was *his* return which had been desired. The Duke and Duchess of York had as yet no public image, no drawing power to match that of the fabulous Prince of Wales, while rumours of the Duke's speech difficulties had lost nothing in re-telling. In Australian and New Zealand official circles it was anticipated that the Duke and Duchess of York would receive a polite but rather luke-warm reception in the Dominions.

The Duke of York was still greatly handicapped by his stutter. Always a perfectionist, he was frustrated and depressed when he failed to measure up to his own ideals. While he struggled through his speeches, the Duchess of York sat by, smiling and apparently entirely at her ease, gloved hands quietly folded in her lap, head high, 'listening to every word. When he paused, and the pause grew longer and longer, the sympathy that gripped his audience might have turned to embarrassment if it had not been for that quiet, apparently confident figure sitting on the platform beside his empty chair. She created calm and an atmosphere of imperturbable serenity. A close relative said, 'She must have gone through some awful moments when the Duke was speaking in those early days, yet I have never heard her say a word about her husband's speech difficulties.'

Perhaps the true quality of the Duke of York first became apparent to the people as a whole through these public battles with his disability, because no one present could fail to recognise and to salute the dogged courage of the man.

Skilled help was at hand, however. Lionel Logue, the Australian speech therapist, was recommended to the Duke of York by Patrick Hodgson, the Duke's private secretary. The Duke of York was sick and tired of the many differing forms of treatment he had tried in vain, and he was at first reluctant to see Mr. Logue, but the Duchess urged her husband 'to give him a try'. At the first consultation Mr. Logue caught the Duke of York's interest, and he quickly managed to gain the Duke's confidence and to release his ability to express himself, although many years of hard effort still lay ahead. The treatment involved considerable daily work for the Duke of York, as he had to develop a new use of the diaphragm and a new method of breathing. Mr. Logue emphasised to the Duchess of York that much would depend upon her help with his practice work, which involved much reading aloud. Even more depended on her general encouragement and support.

Throughout the summer and autumn of 1926, the Duke and Duchess of York prepared for their tour. The whole complex pattern of a Royal tour was being cut. In those days there was much less 'know-how' about planning tours. This would be only the fourth royal visit to Australia and New Zealand, following the tours of Prince Alfred, Duke of Edinburgh, son of Queen Victoria, in 1869–71; King George V and Queen Mary, when themselves Duke and Duchess of York in 1901; and the Prince of Wales in 1920.

The Duke and Duchess of York spent a quiet but busy autumn. Bruton Street was a very simple home, and they led a very simple and quiet life. They did hardly any entertaining, they were too busy making preparations to go to Australia. They went away most week-ends, often to St. Paul's Walden. Although some of the Duke and Duchess of York's possessions were still at the White Lodge they never went there.

There were a hundred and one things to do. Plans were made and re-made. A succession of dressmakers and tailors came to Bruton Street, as clothes were selected and fitted. The Duchess took great care about her clothes, seeing that all the details were right. Presents were bought.

The Household of eight persons was chosen, not without last-minute changes and problems. General the Earl of Cavan, who was to be Chief of Staff, broke his ankle out hunting, but he decided to carry on although he was laid up for weeks on board during the early stages of the voyage. Lady Cavan and Mrs. John Little-Gilmour, who was not only a close personal friend but very efficient, were the Duchess of York's Ladies-in-Waiting. Patrick Hodgson was the Duke's private secretary, and Harry Batterbee was Political Secretary. Two men who had been at Dartmouth with the Duke of York, Surgeon-Commander H. E. Y. White and Lieutenant-Commander Colin Buist, R.N., were Medical Adviser and Naval Equerry respectively. Major T. E. G. Nugent of the Irish Guards (later Lord Nugent, and for many years Comptroller of the Lord Chamberlain's Office) was Military Equerry. They proved a well-knit and happy party.

Most important of all to the young Duchess were the plans which had to be made for the care, in her absence, of Princess Elizabeth. She was leaving the infant in very capable hands: Queen Mary and Lady Strathmore were alternately in charge of the baby, and her Nannie was 'the wonderful Clara Knight' in the words of the late Sir David Bowes-Lyon, who was brought up by her. 'Allah'—as she was called because one of her young charges could not pronounce Clara—was a remarkable woman, the daughter of a farmer in Whitwell, Hertfordshire, a member of a very well-brought-up family with deep Christian principles. Her brother Harold farms at St. Paul's Walden; and the red-brick farmhouse on the top of the hill was the goal of many family walks for the present Queen and Princess Margaret.

Allah had come to the family of the Earl and Countess of Strathmore as a girl of seventeen, when their youngest child David was one day old; she continued in the service of Lady Strathmore and her family for the rest of her life. When the eldest daughter of Lady Strathmore married Lord Elphinstone and had children of her own, Allah went to look after them, often returning to St. Paul's Walden and Glamis with the Elphinstone family. When Princess Elizabeth was born to the Duchess of York, Lady Elphinstone was reluctant to let Allah leave them to look after the Duchess's baby, but the Duchess of York persuaded her, saying 'she was mine first'.

In appearance Allah was above middle-height and well-built, with brown hair which later went almost completely white, and dark-brown eyes. She had a quiet voice and was not a great talker, and she was always discreet and always loyal. Allah was one of the old-type nannies who were used to being left to cope with everything, and who seldom took a holiday or even a day off. She was strict—'No more of that nonsense, that will do now', was her brisk way of dealing with nursery tantrums—but she was absolutely fair. She was utterly reliable: her children were her life, and she brought them up in her own high principles. When her children grew up, they continued to migrate in the late evening to the nursery, where Allah presided over the tea-pot and a select circle of her children and their favourite friends.

Allah died suddenly at Sandringham House on January 2, 1946. The funeral was held at St. Paul's Walden on a bitterly cold January day, and was attended by most of her surviving 'family', including the Duchess of York, then Queen, whose wreath of violets bore the handwritten message, 'In loving and thankful memory—Elizabeth R.' She said sadly to Allah's sister, 'She mothered us all.'

The Duchess of York knew that, from the physical point of view, Princess Elizabeth was as safe while she was overseas as the baby would have been in her own hands, but this could not prevent the wrench of leaving her at the time of her most rapid development. Everything possible was arranged to keep the Duchess of York in touch with her daughter. A cable in code, giving all the news of Princess Elizabeth, was sent to her every week—the radio telephone was still a thing of the future. Long letters were despatched to every port. Photographs of Princess Elizabeth were taken every month by Marcus Adams, the child photographer, so that the Duchess of York could follow her daughter's every stage.

But it was a terrible strain to say goodbye; when they were all ready to go the Duchess of York was standing in the front hall, holding her little daughter for all she was worth. Even after she handed Princess Elizabeth over to Allah she came back twice to kiss her again.

When she got into the car in Bruton Street to drive to Victoria Station she was so much affected by the parting that the car had to be driven twice round Grosvenor Gardens, to give her time to regain her composure before she felt able to face the friendly crowds and the official farewells at the station.

Princess Elizabeth was seven and a half months old when her parents left: she was over fourteen months old when they returned.

The Duke and Duchess of York travelled in H.M.S. *Renown* (Captain N. A. Sulivan), in which the Prince of Wales had voyaged extensively. The King had originally wished that the Duke and Duchess should travel out to Australia on an ordinary liner in service (the cost of chartering a liner being prohibitively high), but, as it was politically desirable to stress the importance of the tour, it was decided for prestige purposes to use the naval vessel. *Renown* was a battle cruiser of 32,000 tons, completed in 1916: designed as a fast, shallow-draught cruiser, during her career she underwent many refits, which considerably altered her appearance; she was sunk by Japanese aircraft in the Gulf of Siam in December 1941.

Renown sailed from Portsmouth on January 6, 1927. The Duchess of York had a severe initiation into travel in a naval vessel. *Renown* encountered a high wind and cross sea as soon as she cleared the land. After the wind dropped, a heavy swell continued; this was long before the days of stabilisers, and *Renown* rolled so heavily that at times the quarter-deck was inaccessible.

On the first morning the Duke of York sent off a cable to his parents, which read, 'All on deck and cheerful.' 'It was a good thing he did it so soon,' remarked one of his Staff drily, 'it would not have been accurate much longer.' The tossing, added to the after-effects of her typhoid inoculations, tried the Duchess hard, but she did manage to remain on her feet, which was more than could be said of many on board.

The Duchess of York was, and is, an excellent traveller on almost all occasions. One of her Ladies-in-Waiting remarked recently, 'I have never known her upset by a train, a car, a boat or an aeroplane: she's impervious. One can hardly imagine a more useful quality for royalty.'

On January 10, the high peak of Teneriffe in the Canary Islands was sighted above the sea-mist, and that afternoon *Renown* anchored off Las Palmas for a two-day visit, in order to refuel.

A nasty swell was running, and it was only with difficulty that the Duchess managed to get ashore in the tossing Royal barge, where she was given a rousing reception by the islanders and by the small British community. On the second day, which was rougher still, the Duchess was discouraged from going ashore, although her sailor husband managed to land. Some intrepid Spanish visitors managed to make *Renown*, but unfortunately their interpreter did not, which complicated hospitality. The heavy weather persisted to the end of the visit, and the Las Palmas tugs were shipping water over their bows as they escorted *Renown* out to sea, their sirens sounding continuously so that they drowned the music of the band of Royal Marines playing on *Renown*'s quarter-deck.

After that, better weather prevailed, and life on board gradually settled down into a pleasant routine.

At dawn on January 20, Jamaica was abeam. The Duke and Duchess of York came on deck to watch through their glasses the richly green tropical valleys running inland and up the towering flanks of the Blue Mountains, which were crowned with purple thundercloud, and as they steamed closer they could distinguish the sugar plantations and mills and the little shacks of the workers. The scene changed to the long, low-lying spit of sand and jungle which formed Kingston Harbour. The Duke of York had been there before in the Navy, but it was exciting and entirely new to the Duchess.

The Royal couple managed to spend one night up-country in an hotel during the three-day visit, and altogether much enjoyed the sunshine, the warm welcome and the wide smiles after winter in England and a fortnight at sea.

Renown passed through the Panama Canal on January 25, welcomed to the American continent by an aerial escort from the United States air service 'of close upon thirty machines'. In Panama they attended a lively and crowded ball.

The long voyage across the Pacific was punctuated by the customary ceremony of initiating the landlubbers into the 'Kingdom of Neptune on Crossing the Line'. The Duke and Duchess of York good-naturedly ignored their previous crossings of the Equator in the Indian Ocean and Africa. The Duke of York was boisterously initiated by midshipmen into 'The Order of the Old Sea Dog', or, as he more formally referred to it in his reply, 'The Order of the Hound, Marine and Ancient', while the Duchess was more gently invested with 'the Order of the Freedom of the Seas' which had been ingeniously made on board: the main-brace was duly spliced.

Such innocent capers did not please everyone: a cable was

received on board from one of the more repressive groups of religionists, deploring that the Duke and Duchess of York 'had sanctioned a burlesque of baptism'.

The next interlude was a two-day visit to Nuku Hiva in the Marquesas, where they had a rendezvous with the fleet tanker *Delphinula*. *Renown* arrived one day ahead of schedule and the visit was the more pleasant because the island's official strength consisted of the Governor and one gendarme, and ceremony was perforce cut out.

This is the island described by Herman Melville in *Typee*. The jagged high mountains, the wonderful deep, wooded valleys, the gorges and the high waterfalls remained as he saw it, but the teeming life in the valleys that Melville knew had died away.

In the biggest village of Taiohae the Polynesians, the girls wearing calf-length flame-coloured chiffon dresses, with the traditional flowers in their hair, danced the bowdlerised version of their traditional dances at that time insisted upon by the missionaries. The most impressive was the Pig Dance, in which the old hog sought out a mate. An old man, who as a boy had eaten human flesh, described to the Duke and Duchess of York the etiquette of cannibalism, which was a ritual ceremony. A man who had survived an attack by a shark showed them his mauled arm.

This leisurely voyage of *Renown* in 1927, altering course so that the Duke and Duchess could see the green Samoan Islands and, later, the coral atoll of Wailangilala, affords a striking contrast with the second journey to the Antipodes which the Duchess of York, as Queen Elizabeth the Queen Mother, was to make in 1958. It is an apt illustration of the way in which life has speeded up, and how stresses have increased upon members of the Royal family, as upon many other travellers. In 1927 it took the Duke and Duchess of York twenty-two days to sail from England to Auckland in New Zealand. In 1958 it took Queen Elizabeth the Queen Mother only ninety-one hours to make the same journey by air to Auckland, with a flying time of forty-nine and a quarter hours.

On February 17, *Renown* entered the harbour of Suva, the capital of Fiji, with an impressive escort of the famous swift-sailing Fijian canoes. Unfortunately the islanders were in the throes of a virulent infection of measles, a killer disease in the South Seas, and so crowds were not encouraged to gather; many ceremonies were cancelled or curtailed.

The serious business of the tour began with the arrival of *Renown* in New Zealand on February 22. The weather was atrocious:

> '. . . Just as *Renown* was about to drop anchor a rainstorm of extraordinary intensity broke over the city and came sweeping across the water towards the battlecruiser. White sails and red roofs, black cranes and warehouses, the green, cone-shaped hills in the background—all were blotted from sight by the dense white curtain of rain.' (*The Royal Embassy.*)

The rain had fortunately stopped by the time the Duke and Duchess received the Governor-General, Sir Charles Fergusson (whose son, Sir Bernard Fergusson, became Governor in 1962), and the Prime Minister, Mr. J. G. Coates, and his Cabinet on board. The New Zealand officials soon left to be on shore to greet the Royal party when they landed.

The Duke and Duchess of York then embarked in the Royal Barge to make the short passage to the quayside. They had only covered a few yards from the ship's side when the Royal Salute crashed out. Everyone on board the Royal barge came to attention, and the barge had to be allowed to drift amid an enthusiastic crush of sailing boats to port, launches to starboard, even a rowing 'four', all crowding in upon the Royal Barge for an unexpectedly long view of the motionless Duke and Duchess of York, in what a reporter in the *New Zealand Star* described optimistically as a 'delightful air of go-as-you-please'.

The personality of the Duchess of York took hold of the crowd from the first moment of the landing; the New Zealanders liked

> '. . . the way the Little Duchess waved to the daring and soaked boys on the top of the wharf buildings.' (*Auckland Star.*)
> 'Her lovely colouring, the swift, upward, smiling glance, the steady eyes, blue as the forget-me-nots in her little blue hat' (*New Zealand Herald.*)

They noticed:

'Never once during the formality of the morning functions did her face lose the look of alert interest.'

and ended:

'She smiled her way straight into the hearts of the people.'

The tour was a most important step for the Duke and Duchess of York. 'It was a very big job for them. The Duke had never done anything like it before: he had never been robust enough. At the beginning of the tour, a great deal fell upon the Duchess, who was simply wonderful. She had this terrific personality and ability to get along with everyone; she carried him along. But what was most noticeable to all the Royal party upon that tour was the way in which the Duke of York developed, gained confidence, independence and stature,' said one of the party.

A Royal lady had not visited New Zealand for twenty years, and the Duchess's clothes were a great topic of interest among New Zealand women. Men who attended Royal functions without their wives were expected to bring back detailed descriptions, and what they had probably failed to grasp was recounted in every newspaper. These reports from the *Auckland Star* are typical of hundreds:

'The Duchess of York . . . was in periwinkle blue flowered georgette, draped on one side, worn under a beautiful wrap shot in blue and gold, with a heavy collar of squirrel fur lined with blue velvet in the same tone and a small hat turned up from the face in periwinkle blue . . .'

and again

'. . . The Duchess of York was lovely in palest pink ninon encrusted with diamanté and with a draping of tule from the shoulder caught with a diamond and emerald pendant with ropes of pearls, and carried a feather fan shaded in pink and a bouquet of pale pink roses.'

The Duke and Duchess of York enjoyed everything, and the

New Zealanders, who had put out their best for them, were delighted with their guests.

They first met the Maoris at a reception in Auckland Town Hall.

'The stage was delightful, being arranged as a glade in the New Zealand bush with a stream of water trickling down from the heights through the mossy grown banks, between stones and native plants. All the stage was carpeted with mosses, and ferns grew in every crevice, where a *whare* (native house) stood in the background with a camp-fire burning before it . . . with a pretty Maori girl in native garb weaving flax outside. Many an envious eye was cast on the dusky maiden sitting there so cool and aloof from the heat and dense crowding of the body of the hall, but she went on plaiting, calmly indifferent to all darting glances of admiration or envy.'

This was a foretaste of their reception by the Maoris at Rotorua, which deeply impressed them; two thousand Maoris welcomed them with traditional ceremony and dances and song. The Duke of York unveiled a memorial to the Maoris who had fallen in the war. Later, in Wellington, the Duchess spent a whole afternoon listening spell-bound while Sir Maui Pomare, Minister of Native Affairs, recounted to her the legends of his people.

Both the Duke and Duchess of York were much impressed by the fine physique of the New Zealanders, and they admired especially the healthy, lively children they saw everywhere. In Auckland eighty thousand children stopped their car by sheer weight of numbers, and engulfed the Household, who were on foot, to the amusement of the Duke. They were touched when Maori and Pakeha children knelt at the side of the road, near Lake Tapa, holding streamers across their path for the car to break. They were touched, too, by the spontaneous and sympathetic cheers frequently given for 'Baby Elizabeth'. It was a posy of wild flowers with a scrawled note 'God Bless the wee Baby Princess', tossed into the car by a child at the roadside, that the Duchess carried, in preference to the official bouquet, at one civic welcome.

Although the tour was crowded with official engagements, the New Zealanders had made arrangements for their visitors to have some time to themselves. Two fishing trips were arranged, one for deep-sea sport in the Bay of Islanders and the other for trout fishing.

By the time the tour had reached Wellington, the capital, the New Zealanders had awakened to the discovery that they had new and very popular Royal personalities among them. The cheering, not particularly evident in Auckland, became a roar of welcome as the tour proceeded; the crowds were everywhere enormous.

The tour of the North Island was triumphantly completed, that of the South Island just begun when there was a serious setback. On March 10, 1927, the Duke and Duchess of York landed from *Renown* at Picton, went by train to Blenheim and then drove ninety miles by dusty roads in an open car to Nelson. The Duchess of York, although she had said nothing about it, had not been feeling well for several days, and after this long and tiring day she had to go straight to her room in her Nelson hotel, hoping that she would feel better after a night's rest. But she had developed tonsillitis with a temperature of 102° F., and in the morning it was obvious that it was out of the question for her to go on.

At first it appeared as though the Duke of York would find it impossible to continue the tour alone. He had been delighted by the warmth of their reception during the first part of the tour, but he gave the whole credit to his wife. Once, during the early part of the tour, when he had driven out without the Duchess, he had not been recognised and consequently no one cheered: this had confirmed him in this fixed belief, and he insisted to his Staff: 'It is my wife they want to see, not me.'

The Duchess eventually persuaded the Duke to carry on the rest of the tour alone. To begin with there *was* great public disappointment. Wistful dismay among the New Zealanders still to be visited took the place of excitement; sales of tickets to Charity functions which the Duke and Duchess had promised to attend died away.

Before long, the unexpected happened. The Duke, his feet on the firm ground of his recent successes, took up the tour, at first diffidently, but with growing confidence and success. During his visit to Westland he heard on all sides sincere regrets for his wife's illness and (as Mr. Taylor Darbyshire wrote):

> 'This sympathy was noticed and appreciated by the Duke during his day at Westport, and had the tendency to bind him even closer to the people of this district.'

The Duke's confidence showed in the vigorous way he handled little incidents. At Hokitiki he heard that a soldier's Victoria Cross was missing and set in motion steps to try to trace it. He held up the Royal train at a wayside stop, to watch a tall red pine-top being sawn through; went out of his way to accept a sprig of rara from a child in Otira; drove an electric train with verve through the dripping darkness of the Arthur's Pass tunnel. He was among friendly and well-wishing people, and they liked him. He was actually enjoying himself . . .

The climax came during his visit to Christchurch where the Duke of York received a rapturous welcome:

> 'The fervour with which the people of Christchurch wel-comed the Duke on his arrival was typical of the wonderful reception he had during the entire four days he was in the city. Cheering throngs packed the wide, well-paved streets, and the spacious Cathedral Square, in which was situated the hotel at which the Duke was to stay, was a solid mass of wildly excited humanity. The bells of the cathedral pealed joyously and competed with the tumultuous applause of the populace in making the most noise.'

> 'Christchurch went absolutely mad,' wrote one of those who accompanied the Duke of York on his tour of the South Island; 'in my view it was the arrival in Christchurch and the reception there and in Dunedin which opened the Duke of York's eyes to his popularity. I really believe that in his humble way he thought no one would bother to turn out to see him alone, and when the streets were crowded with enthusiastic, happy people throwing streamers and obviously delighted to see him, he was quite over-whelmed and from that moment grew in confidence and stature.'

There came a 'Diggers' smoking concert in Christchurch. The

returned soldiers were of all ranks from the Commander-in-Chief to private and they were 'all on an equality, not only of rank but of affection for their guest'. Halfway through the evening, to the utter astonishment and consternation of his Household, the Duke climbed through the ropes into the boxing ring and gave an impromptu speech. When it was good-humouredly heckled, he took the sallies in his stride and made excellent ripostes. There was hardly a hesitation throughout the whole speech, and it was cheered to the echo: it was perhaps the turning-point of his whole public life.

Meanwhile the Duchess of York had left the Commercial Hotel in Nelson, where she had been anxiously nursed, in order to convalesce at Government House, Wellington. A week later she was able to leave and go on board *Renown*. It was 10 o'clock on a blustery and wet night.

'Several thousand Wellingtonians braved a drenching rain to wave and cheer God-speed . . . the extent to which the Duchess of York had captured the popular imagination received its best attestation last night.' (*The Dominion*.)

After a rough passage down the east coast of the South Island of New Zealand, *Renown* anchored off the Bluff in the exposed Foveaux Straits between South Island and Stewart Island. There the Duchess of York waited while her husband completed his solo tour.

When they left New Zealand it was realised that their visit had been an outstanding success, far beyond anything anticipated by the King, the New Zealand Government, the people of New Zealand or by the Duke and Duchess of York themselves.

The visit to Australia began on March 26, 1927.

The principal event of the Australian tour was the first opening in Canberra of the Commonwealth Parliament, but much of the touring of Australia took place before this. The Duke and Duchess of York visited New South Wales; then went north to Queensland; passed south to Sydney again where they embarked in *Renown* to sail to Tasmania; returned to the main continent for their visit to Victoria; then to South Australia; and then and only then entrained for Canberra. After their visit to Canberra they returned by train to Melbourne, where they took ship for Western Australia, the last of the States to be visited.

Each and every State had its strenuous and often basically repetitive programme, yet each was different according to its character, climate and condition.

Sydney opened the ball with a vociferous welcome. Mr. Ian Lucas wrote:

'It is difficult to imagine a more perfect setting for the ceremonial entry of royalty into a country than that provided by Farm Cove and the people of Sydney on that sunny autumn morning. The blue of the sea and sky, the green of the trees, the red, white and blue of the landing stage, the bright uniforms and the many-hued summer clothes of the attendant crowds provided a picture which one could never forget.

'The ensuing progress of the Duke and Duchess through the streets was a veritable ride of triumph. The Duke wore the uniform of a naval post-captain, with cocked hat, while the Duchess was looking lovelier than ever in a pretty dress of pink georgette with a flowing cloak, of which the collar was trimmed with ostrich feathers. Despite the hot sun they rode in an open car so that all might see them. A finely mounted military escort with lances and flying pennons trotted ahead of the royal car . . . The crowds were ten deep in places, and every window and balcony of the high flanking buildings held its quota of sightseers. The whole length of the route to Government House, about four miles in all, was kept by smart citizen forces and returned soldiers, while twenty bands distributed at intervals made martial music.'

There were, however, complaints and counter-complaints. The procession, said the people of Sydney, had gone too fast, 'fairly whizzed through the city'. The responsible authorities contended that the scheduled speed of six miles an hour was adhered to. Be that as it may, the enthusiasm of the Sydney crowds for their Royal visitors was unquestioned. Some of the most uninhibited enthusiasm in the experience of long-serving Members of the Household took place at the public reception (after the pattern set by the Prince of Wales) held in Sydney Town Hall, at the

Garden Party and at the Ball, at which one Member of the Household had his dress-suit studs crushed flat against his chest in the press of the crowds.

In Queensland the Duke and Duchess of York saw boomerang and woomerah throwing at a corroboree by aborigines at Beaudesert, where they attended a bushman's carnival. They saw the rich black soil of the fertile Darling Downs and the red soil round Toowoomba, and the inroads of prickly pear which was devouring many square miles of pasture. They went through the sugar-cane-growing districts along the Tweed River, and returned to Sydney in order to board *Renown*. They were sung out of Sydney Harbour by twelve hundred children on board a ferry steamer, singing 'Sydney, I Love you' and 'Will Ye No Come Back Again?' oblivious of the heavy rain.

The Duke and Duchess of York arrived by sea at Melbourne, then the Commonwealth capital as well as the capital of Victoria. The Royal barge traversed extremely rough water from *Renown*'s side to the quay. Silence fell. Faces turned whiter. 'We were landed just in time,' recalls an official.

There followed a formal drive in procession into the heart of Melbourne. The Duke and Duchess of York were loudly cheered by large crowds: Members of the Household were in full-dress uniform and thought they looked rather smart, until one member of the Staff, driving along in his carriage, heard a Melbourne woman tell her child, 'Come along home now, Harry—these is only the fish'eads.'

A magnificent State Ball was held in Victoria, at which the Duchess of York's first partner was the Governor General, Lord Stonehaven; her second Mr. Bruce, the Prime Minister; and her third a young civilian from the floor of the hall. He was one of the Australian officers who had convalesced at Glamis; the Duchess of York had asked him to come to Government House so that she could talk over old times. At the ball she sent an A.D.C. to fetch him to the dais, to be presented to her husband and to dance with her.

The deep bond between Australia and Britain was made visible two days later, on Anzac Day, when the traditional parade took place.

'A magnificent parade of 25,000 returned sailors and soldiers led by Lt. General John Monash, commander of the Australian forces in France, and including 40 holders of the Victoria Cross from all parts of Australia, marched past the replica of the Whitehall Cenotaph erected for the occasion in front of the Federal Parliament house. The Duke, accompanied by the Duchess, dressed in black, took the salute. The significance of the occasion was deeply impressed on the minds of the unprecedented crowds by a procession of motor-cars containing 700 blind, disabled and invalid soldiers who preceded the main parade. 43 bands were included in the procession and the pride of place was given to the band of H.M.S. *Renown*.' (*The Times*.)

The Duke and Duchess of York travelled by train to Adelaide, where they lived in Government House in the centre of that well-planned city for five days. Among the many functions they attended was a great rally of Boy Scouts and Girl Guides, at which they appeared in Scout and Guide uniform—the first time that the Duchess of York had put on uniform during the tour, and the last occasion on which she ever wore Girl Guide uniform.

The Duke and Duchess of York left Adelaide by train on May 5, on the long journey to Canberra. Their railway carriage was almost hidden by flowers, and people turned out to see them pass all the way to Tailem Bend, three hours' run from Adelaide, where they left the train for a two-day holiday on the shores of Lake Alexandrina.

On Sunday, May 8, the Duke and Duchess of York arrived at Canberra, the main objective of their whole tour. This new capital of Australia had been discovered by a number of senators on a fishing trip, and had eventually been preferred to innumerable other rival sites. It was still pretty much as the Prince of Wales had succinctly described it, 'a city of hope and foundation stones'.

Considerable thought had been given to this opening of the Commonwealth Parliament. Constitutionally, the ceremony had to be held in the Senate, but this was so small that it could only hold the Senators and Cabinet Ministers, together with their wives, who were insistent that they should be present. There was no room for the other Members of Parliament, nor for leading Australians representing civil branches of Government, the military forces, sciences, social services and the arts, as well as the distinguished representatives of many other countries.

As the Prime Minister said, 'The opening was going to be a pretty drab affair for a great many people.' It was therefore proposed that, for the benefit of those who could not be placed in the Senate, another ceremony should be contrived outside, at which the Prime Minister should invite the Duke of York to open the door of the House, in view of the distinguished persons who could not be in the Senate, but who could be accommodated on stands.

Further, to augment this simple ceremony the Proclamation would be read, by which, for that one day only, the Duke of York became the King's representative and displaced and took precedence over the Governor-General. Throughout the tour, except on this one occasion, the Duke of York, ranking as a Royal Duke and the King's son, was yet junior to the Governor-General, who was the King's representative. (The protocol laid down was exact: for example, the Duke of York was entitled to the playing of six bars of the National Anthem, but not to the full Anthem.) It was not proposed that the Duke of York should reply outside the Senate: he would, however, read the King's Speech inside the Senate at the Opening of Parliament. When the reasons for the additional ceremony were explained to the Duke, he at once agreed to the suggestions, and added, 'Don't you think I should say a few words?' This showed the confidence which had come to him in New Zealand.

When the day came, the ceremony outside went with great dignity. Dame Nellie Melba sang the first verse of the National Anthem. The Prime Minister of Australia made a moving oration, to which the Duke of York replied with a simple and sincere speech, spoken perfectly. 'I have never heard him speak better,' said an Australian official who was present. 'There was not a hesitancy. It went frightfully well with the multitude, and did a power of good.'

At the second ceremony inside the Senate, things did not go so well. It had been arranged that the historic scene in the Senate should be filmed. When the Duke of York heard this, something of his old nervousness returned, and he was most reluctant that the Speech itself should be filmed. It was only when the Prime Minister promised that the moment the Duke rose to speak 'he would have a gentleman with a meat-axe standing behind each cameraman to see the speech was not filmed' that the Duke of York would permit cameras to operate inside the Senate House.

When the time came, possibly because the Duke of York was wondering whether in fact the cameras had been stilled or perhaps because of the intense heat in the overcrowded Chamber, he lost some of his confidence, and suffered a partial return of speech hesitancy, but it soon passed.

When the ceremony was completed, the Duke and Duchess of York were vastly relieved. 'Those happy young people were like children let out of school,' said one of the Australian Ministers. The Duke of York had undertaken an imperial occasion of the first order, and he had carried it off with conspicuous success. The Duke and Duchess were filled with high spirits and gaiety, sharing an adventure which had turned into a triumph.

There is a spirit of loyal friendliness about the Antipodes which was 'made' for the more reserved members of the Royal family, somehow establishing their confidence in themselves. 'We in Australia don't only take credit for the Yorks,' said a leading Australian. 'Queen Mary once told me, "Australia also made King George and me, when we went out as Duke and Duchess of York to open the first Parliament."' Later, her first Australasian tour did much to establish the confidence of Queen Elizabeth II.

The Duchess of York continued to play a major part in helping and encouraging her husband. The Duchess was quite remarkable in the way she always managed to switch the limelight back to the Duke. The first impact was always for her; she instantly became the centre of the picture. She always found some way to shift the interest to him. She would begin an animated conversation, and when it was well under way and he was taking part, withdraw and leave it to him.

After a train journey from Canberra, frequently interrupted by both scheduled and unscheduled stops at which they were greeted with immense enthusiasm, the Duke and Duchess of York returned to Melbourne, and early in the morning of May 12, they sailed on board *Renown* for Western Australia.

Storms at sea fortunately occur rather less frequently than the tales of returned travellers would have one believe, but on this world tour *Renown* had more than her share of rough weather. The heaviest weather of the round voyage occurred on the passage across the exposed Australian Bight to Fremantle:

'Much damage was caused to picket-boats and cutters, seats on the decks were smashed to matchwood, furniture was flung about cabins, and mess-decks were flooded. A massive ladder fetched away and crashed on the deck outside the royal apartments . . . *Renown* experienced one of the worst buffetings she has received during the whole of her career. Though speed was reduced . . . she groaned and shivered from stem to stern as, hit by mountainous green walls of water and despite her thirty-two thousand tons, she was tossed about almost like a cork . . . all the dead lights were down, so that inside the ship one lived by artificial light and in an atmosphere of which the description foetid is hopelessly inadequate.

'A number of minor casualties was caused among the members of the ship's company by falls owing to the violent lurching of the ship, and one seaman sustained a fractured rib. Despite the vessel's liveliness the Duke and Duchess were quite unaffected by sea-sickness, and during the wild time the Duchess made several trips up to the bridge with Captain Sulivan, to watch the waves breaking their fury on the fo'c'sle and the watery sun forming countless rainbows in the foam.' (Ian F. M. Lucas.)

Fremantle, on a perfect Australian winter's day, was a welcome landfall. During their few days in Perth the Duke and Duchess saw as much as they could of the immigration schemes in progress. In particular the Child Emigration Society's Farm School, founded by the late Kingsley Fairbridge at Pinjarra, delighted them. They saw sturdy and happy children, who had been living under very different conditions in the slums of East London. The Duke of York made an appeal on his return to England, to send poor orphaned or probationer children by means of this and similar schemes, to settle in Australia.

The last engagement of all was to visit sixty wounded ex-servicemen in a local hospital. Here the Duke and Duchess considerably overstayed their time. Their return to the ship was further delayed by stopping for many farewell bouquets, so that they were well behind schedule when farewells had been said, and *Renown* finally put to sea.

The Duke of York sent this message to the Governor-General:

'With very great and genuine regret the Duchess of York and I must now say "Goodbye" to Australia. I find it difficult to express in words our gratitude to the Government and people of the Commonwealth for the wonderful welcome everywhere accorded to us, and the countless kindnesses we have received.

'The demonstrations of loyalty and wholehearted affection and devotion to the Throne have far surpassed anything we have imagined and have most deeply moved us . . .'

Shortly afterwards, an experienced political observer had occasion to make a tour of Australia which roughly followed the route of the Duke and Duchess of York. 'I made a special point,' he said, 'of finding out how the Duke of York had gone down. The Prince of Wales had been phenomenally fêted and popular, yet almost everywhere people had liked the Duke of York better. This was not the opinion I had expected, so that I cross-questioned them closely on this. "This fellow's trying to do his job better than the other," was the reply.'

The voyage home started on Monday, May 23, 1927. Three days later the Duchess of York experienced that most unpleasant emergency—fire at sea. *Renown* was sailing without an escort westwards across the Indian Ocean, one thousand miles from land. The weather was fine, with a light northerly breeze and slight easterly swell. It was Queen Mary's birthday, and that morning the ship was dressed with flags and a salute of twenty-one guns was fired in her honour.

At 13.25, while the Duke and Duchess of York sat at lunch, fire broke out in 'D' boiler-room. It was caused by a human error; a stoker had turned the wrong valve and tried to top up a tank which was already full; the oil had overflowed and then caught fire. The situation was immediately serious, because the fire was in an inaccessible part of the stokehold and close to the small-arms arsenal. If there were an explosion, or if fire spread to the oil-fuel tanks, it might be impossible to extinguish or contain the fire.

Plans were made to abandon ship, but some of the boats damaged by the storm in the Australian Bight were still unserviceable. A naval officer who was on board commented afterwards, 'If we had had to abandon ship it would have been several days before anyone could have got there—and it was not so easy to find people in open boats at that time.'

The fire quickly gained control of the boiler-room which had to be abandoned. The Captain had a difficult decision: the usual course of fire-fighting would be to withdraw air from the compartment affected, and let the fire burn itself out. But inside the burning boiler-room a powerful in-draught fan was still working. It was possible to cut off this fan by shutting off all the steam at the main controls, but then steam would also be lost for fire-fighting. Speed was first reduced and then all eight boilers were shut down.

'The Engineer Commander and his staff made superhuman efforts to reach the controls of the fan through the inferno of smoke and gas fumes and terrifying heat welling up from the flaming oil floating on top of the water ten feet or so below the gratings . . . dash after dash was made along the gratings, to give the control gear one twitch or two and dash back before completely exhausted. At last it was done and the boiler-room sealed off.' (Ian F. M. Lucas.)

The fire was within a few feet of the main oil-tanks by the time all vents around the fire were closed off, but it was then possible to re-start the engines. Even after the boiler-room had been sealed off, there remained hours of anxious waiting. Preparations were made to flood the magazines if the temperature rose above the danger mark. The deck above the bulkheads around the fire was red-hot; water poured on the deck of the boys' messdeck over the fire turned to steam, and there was one small outbreak of fire in an adjacent boiler-room; this was quickly put out.

The Duke of York went down close to the seat of the fire, to watch and encourage the work of the firefighters: the Duchess of York gave no sign whatever of noticing that anything was amiss. Those not engaged in firefighting carried on with their work as usual, with an occasional surreptitious glance at the heavy oil smoke belching from the after funnel. Meals were served.

It was not until 22.00 that the fire was reported to be out. 'D' boiler-room had been burnt out, there was no electric light, and four men were in hospital with burns and scalds, but the ship was safe.

A few days later Captain Sulivan said to the Duchess of York, 'Did you ever realise, ma'am, that at one time it was pretty bad?'

'Yes, I did,' she said; 'every hour someone came and told me that it was nothing to worry about, so I knew there was real trouble.'

On June 1, *Renown* arrived at the Island of Mauritius and entered the harbour of Port Louis, under the shadow of the volcanic peaks of Pieter Botte and La Pouce. The island had last been visited by Royalty when King George V and Queen Mary called on their world tour.

Renown's next call was at the barren, desolate, volcanic rocks of the Great Hanish Islands, desert islands of bare red and black lava Just within the entrance to the Red Sea, where *Renown* refuelled from a fleet tanker, and the ship was painted before entering the home stretch. The temperature was officially recorded at 95° F. in the shade, but felt higher.

As the relationship between Britain and Egypt was uneasy, *Renown* steamed through the Suez Canal without stopping. On June 17, *Renown* came into sight of Malta, upon which the Duke of York would one day confer the Cross bearing his name. The nine destroyers of the First Flotilla came out of harbour to escort her in, and sea and land planes flew overhead.

There was a break from the round of official duties on the Sunday of their visit, and after attending the morning service they went picnicking with Lord Louis Mountbatten in his yacht *Shrimp*, which anchored in St. Paul's Bay. The anchor became fouled but was cleared by two Maltese Boy Scouts who happened to be there and volunteered their services. Each received a note in the Duchess's handwriting, 'Thank you for helping with our anchor', signed by both the Duke and Duchess.

On the last evening of the visit a splendid water carnival was staged:

> 'Against the background of Malta harbour, the warships and other vessels were illuminated with electric lights, and the boats in the guise of swans, dragons, argosies and galleys glided over the water.
>
> 'The Duke and Duchess took part in the procession in the *Shrimp* and passed in midstream through hundreds of Maltese gdhaisas, while showers of rockets shot up from every direction, sirens shrieked, bands played, the multitude cheered, clapped and sang and the searchlights illuminated the sky.' (*The Times*.)

The last port of call before reaching England was Gibraltar, where *Renown* was brought safely alongside despite a thick fog. Among the decorations in the streets, and the shawls hung from the windows, were banners reading 'Mercy to Duffield', in reference to Lieutenant Duffield of the East Surrey Regiment, who was in prison in the colony, under sentence of death for the murder of his commanding officer. It had been expected that a direct appeal on his behalf would be made to the Duke of York, but none was, in fact, received, nor could the Duke of York have done other than forward such an appeal to the authorities. Later Lieutenant Duffield was, in fact, reprieved and was brought back to Britain to serve his sentence.

In the Bay of Biscay, *Renown* crossed her own outward track, and the Duchess of York, her Ladies-in-Waiting and maids, became the first women ever to have sailed right round the world on board a ship of the Royal Navy.

The long voyage of thirty thousand miles ended on the morning of June 27, when *Renown* entered her home port of Portsmouth, escorted by five bombers. The Prince of Wales, Prince Henry and Prince George waved to their brother and sister-in-law from the quay. The Duke and Duchess of York had returned home.

CHAPTER SIX

FAMILY CIRCLE

I always liked the term 'family circle'. It sounds so close, and safe
and happy

*Queen Elizabeth, when Consort, opening a new block of flats for
St Marylebone's Housing Association, March 1949*

THE Duchess of York was re-united with Princess Elizabeth in
Buckingham Palace. Her daughter was now fourteen months old,
an enthusiastic and swift crawler, just beginning to poise peri-
lously on her feet: she could say quite a number of words, among
which Allah had made sure was 'Mummy'. She was dressed in a
frilly white frock. Queen Mary lifted her in her arms and pointed
to the Duchess of York, saying 'There's *Mummy*.' There was a
heart-stopping moment of uncertainty. Then Princess Elizabeth
smiled and held out her arms to her mother. The separation was
over: all was well.

The Duke and Duchess of York with Princess Elizabeth drove
to their new home at 145 Piccadilly, where Princess Elizabeth
had already been living for a few days. At last they had a convenient London home, after some years of living at White Lodge,
Richmond, and spending the busy Season in other people's
London houses, which they had been lent or had taken furnished.

Number 145 Piccadilly was Crown property, a four-storey,
stone-faced house in a terrace of similar houses. It was solid,
dignified and unremarkable, with a first-floor balustrade, little
stone balconies to the second-floor bedroom windows, and
topped by another balustrade, which concealed the roof. Its only
unusual attribute was a flagstaff. This was to be the Duke and
Duchess of York's London home for nine and a half years.

When 145 Piccadilly had become available for re-letting in
October 1921, an advertisement in the *Financial News* described
it as:

'This important mansion, situate at Hyde Park Corner . . . The Mansion, which is approached by a carriage drive used jointly with No. 144 Piccadilly, contains spacious and well-lighted accommodation, including entrance hall, principal staircase hall, a secondary staircase with electric passenger-lift, drawing-room, dining-room, ballroom, study, library, about 25 bedrooms, conservatory etc. . . .'

But no one wanted the house—'there appears no prospect of obtaining a tenant', ran one official letter in 1923, and its only useful function for the next few years was when it was lent for 'The Health and Empire Christmas Bazaar' in 1922, and for 'The Poppy Day Display' in 1924. A proposal to turn it into flats was considered by the Crown Estate Commissioners, but that fell through. Meanwhile, the Duke and Duchess of York were searching for a London house. They rather wanted one in Carlton House Terrace, but no suitable house became vacant there. They considered Norfolk House in Norfolk Street, Mayfair and then finally, 'after long protracted negotiations', arrangements were concluded between the Crown Estates Office, the private secretary at Buckingham Palace and the Duke of York's Comptroller, that the Duke should lease 145 Piccadilly on a yearly tenancy. The house would be termed a 'grace and favour residence' although the Duke would pay rent for it, the Crown Estates Office would get the fabric into order, but the Duke would pay for the installation of an extra bedroom. A fire escape was added to the nursery floor, and various necessary and overdue repairs were carried out.

Although the Duke and Duchess of York had made plans for the decoration of 145 Piccadilly before they went overseas on their world tour, again they were not on hand to supervise the decoration and furnishing of their home. They regretted this very much, as both had a strongly developed sense of home-making. Pastel shades, which were just coming in, were chosen for the house.

Under Captain Basil Brooke, the Duke's Comptroller, the Staff worked with a will, headed by Mr. Ainslie the butler, Mrs. Macdonald the cook and Mrs. Evans the housekeeper. Queen

Mary was indefatigable in her help, and often drove over from Buckingham Palace immediately after luncheon to inspect progress. When all was ready, both the King and Queen Mary came to inspect and approve.

The house was entered through double, black-painted doors. The hall was short and wide, with pale green pillars and a moleskin-brown carpet. In the hall, the Duchess of York placed some of the cages containing parrots and budgerigars she had been given during the world tour, others were in the dining room (which was to the left of the front door). Chief among these birds, by force of character, was a white parrot called *Jimmie*, who had been given to her by members of a working men's club in Western Australia. Jimmie had a repertoire of unconventional phrases including, 'Hullo, Jimmie, have a drink.' He was devoted to the Duchess, but fierce with most other people. For a time, there were some small animals, too, to the joy of the children, but eventually they went to the zoo.

At the back of the hall three low, wide, steps led to the morning room door which was flanked by the tusks of the elephant shot by the Duke of York in Uganda.

The morning room was the most-used room in the house. It was a large room, opening through a door-window onto Hamilton Gardens. At first it was used by the Duke of York as his study, while the Duchess of York had a sitting room upstairs, but she took a great liking to it, and so a smaller room next door, also looking onto Hamilton Gardens, was made into a new study for the Duke.

This sitting room of the Duchess of York's was very much the centre of family life. The furniture included a beautiful scarlet lacquer cabinet and the Duchess's large desk, at which she sat with her back to the window. The bookcase was filled with modern novels, biographies, histories and children's books. Framed photographs stood on the little tables of Princess Elizabeth (and later of Princess Margaret) and of the Duchess of York and her brother David as small children.

Always, there were many massed flowers. There was also an aquarium with tropical fish, a gramophone and a wireless, and generally some of Princess Elizabeth's toys.

The drawing room was on the first floor, but it was a somewhat bleakly formal room, and little used. The cheerful, old-fashioned, comfortable nurseries with red carpets and brass-topped fire-guards were at the top of the house. On the landing outside stood the children's precious collection of toy horses. The day nursery overlooked the bustling traffic of Hyde Park Corner, and the night nursery faced Hyde Park.

Here the family settled down to a happy, self-sufficient and contented home life.

The Duchess of York's object in life was to make her husband's life happy. She worked for this with all her love, but also with her intelligence, devising for him a way of life which released tensions and reinforced his confidence.

The measure of her success was the Duke of York's steady emergence as a strong and steadfast personality, who became a universally respected king. As the Duke of York strengthened, a change took place in this partnership of husband and wife. His wife changed imperceptibly from being the supporting pillar, and in turn relied more and more upon him. 'That was the measure of her greatness as a woman,' said an intimate friend of both the Duke and Duchess of York. 'She drew him out, and made him a man so strong that she could lean upon him.'

The Duchess of York enjoyed running her home, down to planning and supervising all the menus—she has always kept a particularly good table. She has a wonderful collection of recipes, many of them handed down in the Bowes-Lyon family.

She took a great interest in the well-being of her Staff, and knew each by name and nature. It was a sizeable establishment. The butler was in command of an under butler, two footmen, an odd man and a steward's room boy; under the housekeeper were three housemaids, and under the cook three kitchenmaids. Mrs. Knight—'Allah'—had an assistant, Miss Margaret Macdonald, now the Queen's Dresser. The Duchess of York's Dresser was Miss Catharine McLean. The Duke of York had a valet. There was an R.A.F. orderly and a night-watchman. A Boy Scout, who had come in to help during the reconstruction, stayed to become the telephone operator. In all, the Staff numbered a couple of dozen, all of whom slept in, in newly constructed staff quarters, with the exception of the telephone operator and the R.A.F. orderly.

The routine of the days was quiet and orderly. Princess Elizabeth and later Princess Margaret always went down to see their parents early in the morning before returning to the nursery or later to the schoolroom. The Duchess's mornings were generally occupied with routine desk work and general household decisions. The Duke and Duchess lunched together, and when the children were very small and began to toddle and walk, they used to be brought down by 'Allah' to join them when they were finishing dessert. Then there was a great cry from the Princesses for the coffee sugar.

In the afternoons the Duke and Duchess often went out on public duties, or the Duchess would go shopping or visit her friends. Practically every day, unless the weather was very bad, there was a stir and bustle inside and outside 145 Piccadilly around 2.15 or 2.30. Then a royal carriage, drawn by a pair of nice bay horses and with a coachman and footman on the box, arrived from the Mews to take the Princesses with their nurses for an afternoon drive through Hyde Park or to Battersea Park, which lasted about two hours.

When the Princesses were old enough to have dancing lessons, the well-known dancing teacher Madame Vacani used to hold a class in the drawing room. The time of the dancing lessons was changed at the Duke of York's request, so that he would more often be in, and be able to come and watch. One of Madame Vacani's assistants at that time said, 'The Duke of York was absolutely delightful with the little girls. The Duchess was so gay and such fun. The atmosphere in the house was so happy and homelike that it was a delight to go there.'

The Duke and Duchess did not entertain on a big scale: their privacy and their home life were too precious to them. They had small luncheon parties from time to time for about eight, at which the Duchess's brothers Colonel Michael and Mr. David Bowes-Lyon and their wives, and their old friends Lord and Lady Plunket were often among the guests. Very occasional dinner parties for twenty-four, and once for thirty-six guests were held. Then the morning room had to be turned into a dining room, as the dining room would only hold about twelve. Once Mr. Ramsay MacDonald and Miss Ishbel MacDonald and the Marquess and Marchioness of Salisbury were among the guests.

Occasionally the Duke and Duchess of York entertained people connected with their public duties. The Duchess of York received teachers and student members of an Indian Women's Education tour. In February 1928 the Waratahs, the members of the touring New South Wales rugby team, came to tea.

'During their visit Princess Elizabeth was carried into the dining room by her nurse, and smiled a welcome to the men, who stood up to receive her. The little Princess waved her hand and chuckled, and she shook hands with three or four who could get near enough.'

Even when visitors were present, the children were not isolated in their top-floor nursery. The Duchess of York, as Colonel-in-Chief of the King's Own Yorkshire Light Infantry, used to invite the officers and their wives to an annual tea-party at No. 145. The little Princesses were always present, and the centre of an admiring throng. Princess Elizabeth was very much the little hostess and enjoyed it all thoroughly.

There used to be great excitement as the birthday of Princess Elizabeth approached. The birthday party was eagerly looked forward to. A day or so before, a magnificent, huge, square cake used to arrive from McVitie and Price. Four men were needed to carry it upstairs to the drawing room, where it was set out on its own table. About twenty to thirty children came to the party.

The Duke and Duchess of York went to Sandringham for Christmas, but they gave Christmas presents to their staff before they left London. They were anxious that everyone should get what they wanted, and when lists had been made out and approved, the presents were bought by the housekeeper and sent up to the Duke and Duchess of York for inspection and approval. Then the Staff all went up to the drawing room to be given them individually.

It was still possible then for Members of the Royal family to retain a certain degree of privacy, with the possible exception of the Prince of Wales, who was mobbed almost everywhere he went. A smiling picture of the Prince of Wales was pinned up in millions of homes, and often beside it was a picture of the fair-haired little Princess Elizabeth. Although a few bystanders would wait outside 145 Piccadilly to see Princess Elizabeth taken for her afternoon drive in an open horse-drawn landau, the Duke and Duchess of York and other members of the family could go in and out of the house without hindrance, and could pursue a comparatively quiet private life when they were not specifically undertaking public duties.

Today, the division of private from public life has become an almost insoluble problem for the members of the Royal family. The image of the Royal *family*—father, mother, children, grand-children and grandmother—living a secure and happy life is one of the most powerful influences for unity throughout the Commonwealth. It is no longer possible to drop an impenetrable curtain upon the lives of the Royal family at home: but for the sake of their stability and health, and for the sake of their personal happiness, members of the Royal family must be able to relax in safety away from prying eyes and prattling tongues.

Shortly after the Duchess of York returned from Australia, King George V appointed her a Grand Dame of the Order of the British Empire. Her public duties were gradually stepped up in importance. To each she brought that serene personal touch which had become more clearly recognised as a result of the world tour.

In August 1927, the King approved the appointment of the Duchess of York as Colonel-in-Chief of the King's Own York-shire Light Infantry. That this was her first Regiment was due to the enterprise of the Colonel, who approached the King through an Equerry, adding in support of his request that there was a precedent, as Princess Mary was Colonel-in-Chief of the Royal Scots, while the Duchess's title of 'York' seemed a particularly appropriate association for a Yorkshire Regiment—indeed the only Yorkshire Regiment bearing a Royal prefix. The famous K.O.Y.L.I., now part of the Light Infantry Regiment, prided itself on being the only infantry Regiment entirely Yorkshire in its history. The first Battalion was raised in Leeds in 1755, and was only four years old when it took part in the battle fought in a rose garden at Minden on August 1, 1759: the Second Battalion was formerly the old 105th. Officers wore a black sword-knot in place of the usual brown leather sword knot, in memory of Sir John Moore.

The Duchess of York soon visited her Regiment. She was presented with a brooch with the Regimental crest, a French hunting horn curved round a white rose, surmounted by a crown: she always wears it when visiting the Regiment. On several occasions she has distributed the Minden roses; she has attended the Minden dinner; and has taken part in a number of Regimental occasions. Every year since her appointment she sent the Regiment a large Christmas pudding. When the Regiment was serving in the Ruhr at the end of the Second World War, it weighed six and a half hundredweight, and was reckoned the biggest Christmas pudding in the world!

Later, the Duchess of York was appointed Colonel-in-Chief of other Regiments, and throughout the years she has maintained the same lively interest in them all. She receives the Colonels and Lieutenant Colonels on appointment and retirement; presents Colours on behalf of the Sovereign; visits the battalions; attends receptions and keeps in touch through reading annual and half-annual reports, Regimental journals and through talks with those who are or were serving with her Regiment. She takes a great interest in Commonwealth Regiments allied with the United Kingdom Regiments—during the war she made a special visit to the Saskatoon Light Infantry, the Canadian Regiment allied to the K.O.Y.L.I. Nor has she neglected the territorial battalions, for which she has a great admiration. In 1985 visits to 'her' Regiments feature strongly.

The Duke and Duchess of York continued their informed and concerned interest in social conditions and their work to improve them. They wanted material standards raised for those who were badly off. When, in September 1927, the Duchess of York was made a Burgess of the City of Glasgow—a city battling against particularly extensive slum problems—the Duke of York replied to the Lord Provost's address of welcome:

'Your kind words regarding the interest which is taken by my wife in movements for social and educational advancement are especially gratifying, for no one knows better than I do how great is the help which she has given me in my public duties. The exhibition which is to be opened by her this afternoon is concerned with subjects [Health and Housing] in which we are both intensely interested. I am glad to learn that houses are now being built in Scotland at a rate which far exceeds anything yet accomplished, and that the schemes for reconstructing the poorer districts, which your Corporation has been so active in promoting, are making good headway.'

They also wanted greater access to the arts to be generally available. This letter from the Duke's Private Secretary was written after the Duke and Duchess of York had paid a private visit to see the Lena Ashwell Players in *A Message from Mars* in the Century Theatre in Notting Hill in December 1927:

'Dear Miss Ashwell,

'The Duke and Duchess of York have frequently heard of the work you have been doing during the past eight years in giving to the poorer people of Greater London the best dramatic entertainment at prices which they can afford.

'In order to obtain first-hand knowledge their Royal Highnesses went, as you know, last night to the Century Theatre, Notting Hill (the headquarters of the movement), and saw *A Message from Mars*, which they keenly enjoyed. The Duke and Duchess were amazed to find that it is possible to present players of such quality with such excellent acting, and charge the public so little. They are convinced that this work is of the greatest possible social and artistic value, and they warmly commend it to all who are interested in social progress of any kind.

'It is the earnest wish of their Royal Highnesses that this movement may be developed in such a way as to make it possible in every district, for people to enjoy the best entertainment which can be provided. Meanwhile, I am to express to yourself and the other ladies and gentlemen concerned the sincere gratitude of the Duke and Duchess for having provided them with such a delightful evening.'

Everywhere the Duchess of York went, her hosts asked after Princess Elizabeth, and often gave her small gifts to take home to her daughter, a china mug from Pudsey, Yorkshire, a posy of flowers from St. Martin-in-the-Fields High School at Tulse Hill; a box of linen handkerchiefs, each embroidered 'Betty', from Dunfermline; and a Noah's ark containing hand-carved animals from the Princess Mary maternity home. When the Duchess of York visited a tobacco factory in Bristol, a sixteen-year-old boy, Thomas Preen, from the nearby Dockyard Settlement, asked her to accept for Princess Elizabeth a painting of a caterpillar playing leapfrog with a rabbit and a mouse.

But generally the gifts were dolls—a doll dressed in white fur presented at the Christmas festival of the Sunshine Guild in Paddington; a doll in a wicker chair from the Streatham Hospital for Incurables; a doll in the uniform of a junior nurse, presented by the smallest and youngest nurse on the staff of the Bradford Infirmary. Princess Elizabeth (though she was fonder of animals) had a fine collection of dolls in the immense cabinet with glass doors, crowded with souvenirs and presents from all over the Empire, which dominated her nursery. Pride of place was held by a coster doll, which was presented at a lively Carnival of Coster-mongers in January 1928. This was one of the gayest functions the Duke and Duchess of York ever attended:

'The Duke and Duchess of York were delightedly welcomed at the annual carnival ball of costermongers belonging to the National Association of Street Traders, held at the Finsbury Town Hall last night. Indeed, after their arrival there was less dancing than carnival excitement and it was only with difficulty that a strong body of stewards could clear even a small space in the middle of the room.

'Most of the guests wore fancy dress or headgear and some the famous "Pearly" costumes, once so familiar and now so rarely seen, either on Hampstead Heath or in East End streets. The devices on these costumes generally proclaimed their wearers to be "King" and "Queen" of some London borough, and in some cases as many as 17,000 buttons went to a single costume. There were also a number of burlesque "Kings and Queens", small children who, if they were queens, walked with difficulty under enormous hats weighted with feathers.

'The Duke of York was wearing a Garter sash and the Duchess wore a rope of pearls over a shell pink georgette dress. A cordon of "pearly Kings" kept open a way to the dais through the throng of dancers waiting to welcome the Royal party, and so unbounded was the enthusiasm of the costermongers' greeting that one woman succeeded in crowning the Duchess with a paper hat as she passed. The Mayor of Finsbury extended a more formal welcome to the Duke and Duchess, and the Duke briefly replied.

'Almost immediately the Duke and Duchess took part in a set of lancers, the costermongers, with linked arms, keeping back a ring of onlookers, and many onlookers beating time to the music with their hands and heels. When the Royal party had returned to the stage a "pearly" doll for Princess Elizabeth was presented to the Duchess by Frank Lawrence, whose father has had a stall in Farringdon-street for 20 years. In response to a clamorous appeal, the Duke and Duchess danced a foxtrot together, and after the fancy dress parade the Duchess of York presented prizes to the successful entrants.' (*The Times.*)

In November 1928, King George V became very ill with pleurisy, from which he nearly died. Under great strain the members of the Royal family continued their public duties, but the Duchess of York herself caught influenza in the early months of 1929, and for a time bulletins of her progress was posted at 145 Piccadilly, and reported in the newspapers beside the bulletins about the King.

The Duchess recovered in time to go with her husband to Norway to represent the British Royal family at the marriage of Crown Prince Olav (now King Olav), the only child of King Haakon and Queen Maud, daughter of King Edward VII, to Princess Märtha of Sweden. The Duke and Duchess travelled through Denmark and across the ferry to Skåne, the rich, flat southern province of Sweden. There they visited Torup, one of the most beautiful of the castles of Skåne, which was owned by Friherrinnan Henriette Coyet, nicknamed 'the uncrowned Queen of Skåne'. They went on by train to Oslo, where they attended a gala performance in the National Theatre on the night before the wedding. A Swedish journalist recalls 'her little fringe, which was so modern then, her intensely blue eyes, and her friendly smile, which seemed to light up the whole row'.

The wedding of Crown Prince Olav of Norway and Princess Märtha of Sweden took place on March 21, 1929.

'To the notes of Mendelssohn's wedding march, the bridegroom proceeded up the centre aisle, escorted by his "best man" the Duke of York—two stately and manly young princes . . . The Duchess of York wore a diamond diadem and a cape of gold patterned in dark green and red.' (Translated from *Svenska Dagbladet*.)

Later in 1929 the Duke and Duchess of York first saw for themselves the new invention which was transforming the cinema, the 'talkie', when they went to the Elstree studios of British International pictures to see four films on the floor, including *The Vagabond Queen* with Miss Betty Balfour. They watched a rehearsal of the first British International 'talkie' film *Blackmail*.

'Expressing a desire to see and hear a scene taken, the Duchess went into the camera booth with the director, Mr. Alfred Hitchcock, and listened with a pair of earphones while the Duke went to a recording booth where he heard the scene enacted through a loudspeaker.' (*The Times*.)

In May, the Duke and Duchess of York went to Edinburgh on a more than usually important occasion. It was the six-hundredth anniversary of the granting of the City Charter to Edinburgh by King Robert the Bruce, their mutual ancestor. It was also 'the Year of Reunion' between the Church of Scotland and the United Free Church of Scotland, which would be formally agreed at the General Assembly of the Church of Scotland. To mark the occasion the Duke of York had been appointed High Commissioner (to represent his father the King) to the General Assembly. This was the first time a Member of the Royal family had been appointed Lord High Commissioner since 1679.

On the day of the opening of the Assembly:

'Sunshine and cheers were blended in the great welcome which Edinburgh gave her Royal visitors when they rode through the streets in the State procession from the Palace to St. Giles . . . The air was still, the sun shone through a slight haze; it was morning that touched the broken skyline in Edinburgh's Old Town with romance, a glint of sunlight on some spire or turret, the mist that ever suggests the glamour of its bygone story . . .

'The Duke and Duchess had an ovation infused with an extraordinary interest and enthusiasm. The association of the King's son and the little Duchess who had become the popular darling of the people transformed the routine welcome into rapture . . .

'. . . The Duke's salute was naturally the more formal acceptance of the great welcome, the smile of the Duchess was to her hosts of admirers the more intimate and less official expression. Her Royal Highness waved freely to the crowds, took special notice of the children, of whom there were many, and did not forget to bestow frequent acknowledgement to spectators in high windows.' (*The Scotsman.*)

A second daughter was born to the Duke and Duchess of York on the evening of Thursday, August 21, 1930, and so the family became complete. The baby was born at Glamis, not in the Duchess of York's apartments, nor in the old nurseries, but in Lady Strathmore's pleasant bedroom, which overlooked the small private garden.

There had been a protracted period of waiting before the birth. Mr. J. R. Clynes, Home Secretary in Mr. Ramsay MacDonald's second Government, who had to be present in an adjoining room, had been put up at Cortachy, the home of the Earl of Airlie (Mr. Angus Ogilvy's father) for no less than sixteen days, whence the affairs of State were conducted with some difficulty, while his entertainment was beginning to tax the ingenuity of the Bowes-Lyon and Ogilvy families.

The little princess was the first Member of the Royal family to be born in Scotland since Prince Robert, Duke of Kintyre, younger brother of King Charles I, was born at Dunfermline in

1602. The patriotic Scots were jubilant at the birth of their princess, and took pride in the fact that an all-Scottish team of doctors had been chosen, who slipped into one of their bulletins the homely Scottish expression, 'The infant Princess is doing fine', which was primly amended in the Court Circular next day to 'doing perfectly well'.

'The Glamis pipe band, in full dress, piped the villagers to the top of Hunter's Hill, two miles from the Castle, for the lighting of the beacon which had been built to celebrate the event. At the summit two large barrels of beer had been taken up to enable the foresters, ploughmen and others to drink the health of the infant Princess.

'Three village girls from Glamis lit the beacon with torches used to light similar beacons when the Duke and Duchess of York were married. The pile burned fiercely and could be seen by watchers in six counties. Hundreds of Scottish folk joined hands, danced round the beacon and burst into cheers. The bagpipes played "Highland Lassie" and a piece specially composed for the occasion, "The Duke of York's welcome".

'In the Castle grounds the Duke of York and Lord and Lady Strathmore stood in a little group with Sir Henry Simson and Dr. Reynolds (two of the doctors) watching the beacon signal, and from a high window of the Castle Princess Elizabeth (who had seen her little sister during the day) was allowed to catch a glimpse of the fire.' (*The Times.*)

The baby was christened Margaret Rose.

The following years were perhaps the happiest of all for the Duke and Duchess of York; they were young, they were together, and they had two lovely children. They had won through to fill their junior but important niche in the Royal family. Their public duties were considerable, but did not occupy the whole of their time, nor had the burden of crushing responsibility laid its weight upon them.

Yet the sky was darkening: the economic depression already raging in the United States struck Britain, a trade depression so widespread and so terrible for millions that the new generations today have little idea of its effect upon the country.

In 1926, after the General Strike, there was considerable concern in Britain about the number of unemployed, which was not far short of one and a half million, and the figure, though fluctuating, remained much the same for some years. Then in 1930, the number suddenly shot up to just under two million, and moved in the following year to two million six hundred and fifty thousand, rising still further in 1932 to the peak figure of two million seven hundred and forty-five thousand unemployed. Thereafter, general unemployment in the country decreased fairly steadily, although there remained pockets of misery which were named the 'Depressed Areas'.

Figures give little idea of the suffering involved. Families were without a breadwinner, existing on inadequate relief. Grave human problems sprang up. Fathers lost their self-respect; officials could invade the privacy of the home; a daughter might be the only one in a family bringing home a wage, doling out a shilling a week to her idle brothers. Self-sacrifice (many mothers never took their share of the meagre food) and stoicism walked hand in hand with bitterness and ruthlessness. Extreme policies, both communist and fascist, found unexpected adherents.

The hunger, the poverty, the hopelessness of the workless and their families bit deep into the minds of the Duke and Duchess of York, who knew personally some of the people involved, through their visits to many of the worse-hit areas.

The Duchess of York, in a speech written in her own hand, made in February 1933, at the fifth Festival of Toc H, said:

'Tonight we are thinking of the dark places that exist in all parts of the country just now, dark patches where unemployment and poverty exist. A new problem for the civilised world has arisen suddenly—the problem of enforced leisure. Leisure has been called the growing time of the spirit, but at the present time, looking round at the misery of thwarted energy, it is anything but that. In certain places, however, by sympathy, brains and the craftsmen's lead, enforced idleness has been transferred into well-directed leisure. These circles of light have shown what can be done to pierce the gloom, and we know that our League of Women Helpers has its contribution to make in lightening their darkness. Specialized work, must, of course, have first place in all

Glamis Castle

St Paul's Walden Bury

Lady Elizabeth and the Hon David
Bowes-Lyon

As bridesmaid to Princess Mary

The Duke and Duchess of York

The wedding day, April 26, 1923

The newly married Duchess in Belgrade for the wedding of Prince Paul and Princess Olga

A family group at Liverpool Street Station, including King George V, Queen Mary, the Duke and Duchess of York and Prince George, afterwards Duke of Kent

The opening of the Federal Parliament of Australia in 1927

On the moors at Glamis with the Prince of Wales

The Duke and Duchess of York with Princess Elizabeth just after their return from Australia

A family group at Windsor in June 1936

Queen Elizabeth seated in state after her coronation as Queen Consort

The Royal Family on the balcony of Buckingham Palace, May 12, 1937

From the top: Windsor Castle, Balmoral and Sandringham

such activities, but casual work, in the form of the innumerable small friendly jobs that are always there to be done, is of great value.

'As an optimist has said, "The trying time is the time to try", and I feel sure that all of you who are present tonight, when you return to your homes, will throw your minds and energies into helping to transform the black patches in our country wherever possible, into circles of Light and Friendship.'

The King wished to share in the economies the nation was called upon to make; immediately after the formation of a National Government in August 1931, the Keeper of the Privy Purse was instructed to inform the Prime Minister that His Majesty had decided that, while the emergency lasted, he would reduce the Civil List by £50,000 per annum. At the same time, the Prince of Wales donated £50,000 to the National Exchequer.

This involved economies all round in the Royal family; the Duke of York decided to sell his horses and give up hunting. This was a minor sacrifice compared with the grim existence of the workless, but none the less he enjoyed his hunting, and he was very fond of his six horses. 'They are looking very well, too,' he wrote in a letter to his Equerry, Commander Colin Buist, quoted in Sir John Wheeler-Bennett's biography. Typically, the Duke of York went himself to the Leicester repository to see his horses sold.

Just at this moment a new interest—one which was to give the Duke and Duchess of York the greatest happiness—came into their lives. The Prince of Wales had been given Fort Belvedere near Virginia Water as a grace and favour residence in 1929, and he was much enjoying the pleasures of a country home and the joys of making a woodland garden. His enthusiasm was contagious, and fired his young brother with similar ambitions. As a result, in September 1931, King George V drove out with the Duke and Duchess of York from Windsor Castle to The Royal Lodge in Windsor Great Park, which was also a grace and favour residence, and which was to be so important to them.

Although generally called Royal Lodge, the King wished it to be known always as The Royal Lodge, saying, 'There can be any number of Royal Lodges, but only one known as 'The Royal Lodge,' and the Duke of York, too, always preferred it to be so called.

Small houses have been built from time to time inside most of the Royal parks, some the retreats of members of the Royal family, some the homes of courtiers, and some to house estate workers. Capricious in origin, and built for a special, often fleeting purpose, these 'cottages' and lodges are often exotic in design, and mirror their age even more clearly than the Palaces and Castles which were intended to last for centuries and to impress posterity. The Royal Lodge is one such house, and has in turn fulfilled various rôles. It lies halfway between Windsor Castle and Virginia Water, towards the eastern side of Windsor Great Park, a little to the south of the statue of King George III commonly (though not correctly) known as 'The Copper Horse'. Bishop's Gate is the nearest Park entrance.

The first house recorded on the site was built in the eighteenth century, a small trim pinky-red house with a red tile roof, a white porch and white window frames and green shutters. It was known as Lower Lodge, to distinguish it from the nearby Great Lodge. The Great Lodge was afterwards called Cumberland Lodge after the Duke of Cumberland, son of George II, who lived there and whose horses, including probably the great *Eclipse*, were exercised on nearby Smith's Lawn, named after the Duke of Cumberland's horsemaster.

Lower Lodge was occupied for many years by Thomas Sandby, Deputy Ranger of Windsor Great Park. The headquarters of the Windsor Park estate were then at Lower Lodge, and the Estate Yard, with its stores of timber for fencing and house repairs, lay beside the house. Thomas Sandby had been Secretary to the Duke of Cumberland during the 1745–6 campaign in the Highlands, which culminated in the tragic Battle of Culloden, of which the only happy thing that can be said is that it was the last battle to take place between Britons on the soil of Britain. When the Duke of Cumberland was made Ranger of Windsor Great Park in 1726, Thomas Sandby became his Deputy Ranger. He was the brother of Paul Sandby, the artist, and was a considerable artist in his own right: it is from the Sandby brothers' drawings and paintings that we know of the appearance of the Lower Lodge and its surroundings.

One delightful watercolour of Lower Lodge painted by Paul Sandby in 1798 shows women and children of the Sandby families in front of the house. It was sold at Christie's in 1959, in an important sale of Sandby paintings and drawings. When the sale was announced Queen Elizabeth was naturally eager to obtain the painting, but was told that her daughter the Queen, who has a fine collection of Sandby drawings at Windsor, would be bidding through an agent. The Queen Mother therefore did not bid for the picture. The following Christmas, among the presents from the Queen to her mother was the watercolour: it now hangs in the dining-room of The Royal Lodge.

When George III, during his second period of insanity, was confined in Windsor Castle, the Prince Regent decided to have his own residence at Windsor, and to enlarge Cumberland Lodge for that purpose. While the alterations were going on, he lived at the Lower Lodge nearby. When the Regent succeeded his father in 1820, characteristically—he suffered from building mania—he then decided that Lower Lodge, in its turn, should be pulled down and rebuilt on a grand scale.

The plans for this new building, which was given the name of The Royal Lodge, still exist, and show an imposing structure stretching away east of the present house, and boasting three libraries, a great dining room, a gothic passage, a breakfast room, and so on. Fifty yards away from the present front door of The Royal Lodge a fine cedar is growing: this is supposed to mark the eastern end of George IV's house. A good deal of building of The Royal Lodge did take place, although it is not clear if it was ever completed. A contemporary print shows that this house was cream-coloured, with chalet-type roofs covered with slates (in some accounts it is said to be thatched), and with a deep verandah running almost the whole way round it. Pheasants are shown coming up to be fed on the grassy slope in front of the building.

The diarist Greville gives a picture of the ailing, querulous George IV in The Royal Lodge in 1829, the year before his death:

'He leads a most extraordinary life—never gets up till six in the afternoon. They come to him and open his window curtains at six or seven o'clock in the morning; he breakfasts in bed, does whatever business he can be brought to transact in bed too, he reads every newspaper quite through, dozes three or four hours, gets up in time for dinner, and goes to bed between ten and eleven. He sleeps very ill, and rings his bell forty times in the night; if he wants to know the hour, though a watch hangs close to him, he will have his *valet de chambre* down rather than turn his head to look at it. The same thing if he wants a glass of water; he won't stretch out his hand to get it. His valets are nearly destroyed.'

King George IV died in 1830, leaving half-built Palaces all over the place: his successor William IV, who was a bluff man of simple tastes, hard-pressed by the debts of his extravagant brother, was left with the problem of what to do with them all. He tried to dispose of Buckingham Palace, then an incomplete white elephant intended to replace Carlton House, to Parliament for use as the Houses of Parliament and then to the Secretary of State for War to use as a barracks, but no one wanted it. (Eventually, of course, Buckingham Palace was inherited and at once occupied by his niece Queen Victoria.)

William IV pulled down Cranbourne House and a number of other houses and lodges in Windsor Great Park. He pulled down part of The Royal Lodge, too, leaving only the great Saloon and possibly—the records are obscure—the octagonal Tent Room and the passage connecting them, although the Tent Room may have been built for Queen Victoria. Queen Victoria liked to drive out in the afternoon, and she liked an objective to her drive. She sometimes took tea in The Royal Lodge, as she did in the other towers and lodges in the Great Park and its neighbourhood.

After Queen Victoria's death, The Royal Lodge was given as a grace and favour residence to Major-General Sir Arthur Ellis, who was Comptroller to the Lord Chamberlain in the reign of Edward VII. To accommodate a family and provide more rooms, the great George IV Saloon was partitioned into five narrow rooms, which were almost as high as they were large. It was an awful thing to do from the architectural point of view, but it would otherwise have been impossible to use as a family home.

In January 1926 Major F. H. W. Fetherstonhaugh, racing manager to Edward VII, was given the house as a grace and favour residence. Two or three bedrooms were built over the Saloon for him, in a modest style which did not blend happily with the Georgian Gothic Saloon. It was after the death of Major Fetherstonhaugh in 1931 that the Duke of York asked his father if he might have the house.

When George V drove out with the Duke and Duchess of York to inspect it The Royal Lodge looked far from attractive; it was in shabby condition and besides it was small for its intended purpose. However, the Duchess of York was immediately fired with enthusiasm for what might be made of it, and the Duke too —although to a lesser degree at first—saw its possibilities. So the King granted them The Royal Lodge as a grace and favour residence.

The Duke and Duchess's first plans for the house were modest. The partitions were removed from the Saloon, and to compensate for the number of rooms thus lost, a small ground-floor wing was built to provide bedrooms, to the east of the octagonal Tent Room, on the site of the George IV conservatory. A bathroom or two were added. The plans, as they so often do, gained momentum, and in the later 'thirties there were two further additions to The Royal Lodge, the first to provide nursery and guest accommodation, and the second to enlarge the garage and build a servants' wing on top of it.

The present house has unusual proportions. It is dominated by the Saloon which is forty-eight feet long, twenty-nine feet wide and twenty feet high; suitably palatial proportions for a Regency extravaganza. To it are wedded the modern additions, which are small country-house proportions.

The repairs and decoration took over a year, and during this time the Duke and Duchess, who had felt 'bottled up' in their Piccadilly house, with its overlooked garden, used to go down to The Royal Lodge every Saturday or Sunday, taking a cold lunch, and get down to work in the overgrown grounds.

Immediately after lunch the Duke of York changed into overalls and trundled a barrow containing his tools down to the part of the grounds where he was working, helped by the Duchess of York, his daughters and some of the staff—a police officer perhaps, the Duke's valet, the two chauffeurs, all working voluntarily together.

One afternoon the King and Queen drove out to The Royal Lodge unexpectedly, and went down into the grounds to find the Duke of York. They found the Duchess raking leaves and Princess Elizabeth pushing a barrow full of leaves down to dump on a fire tended by the chauffeur. 'But where is the Duke?' asked the King. 'There he is, grandpa,' said Princess Elizabeth, pointing to her father's feet. He was lying at full length under a mass of tangled rhododendrons, hacking away at the branches. Queen Mary lined them all up, with their blackened faces, and photographed them.

The Duke and Duchess of York began their gardening by clearing and planting a strip of wood close to the house, adjoining the lawn that rolls down to the front of the house. Clearings were made in the large thickets of ponticum rhododendrons, and the sheltered areas provided were planted with new rhododendrons and camellias. Fine trees were freed from the undergrowth to stand out alone, including a magnificent sycamore, a tree of remarkable size and shape. New trees were planted, among them a *davida involuncrata* or 'handkerchief tree', so called from the whitish bracts which hang from its branches when in flower. There are many fine and rare trees at The Royal Lodge—the maples are as good as any in the country—but everywhere the individual plant or tree is blended with the whole.

The Duke of York then embarked on what was probably his greatest gardening feat, the creation from the well-named 'Wilderness', a solid mass of overgrown rhododendrons banked below old trees, of a beautiful quiet glade. It was a long, arduous and dirty job. Everyone was pressed into service, and even those who came dressed tidily for tea found themselves lugging grimy branches to the bonfires.

In the Wilderness, vistas entice you onward. By clever use of the comparatively limited ground, the path wanders, sometimes through a narrow passage from one glade to the next, sometimes through wide and tranquil avenues, seemingly cut off in the depths of a limitless and mysterious wood. The green paths are bordered by a mossy sward. A creeper grows on a great tree, and below it is a tempting seat. There is a sunken garden of azaleas.

The Royal Lodge gardens are created for enjoyment at all seasons, but their special glory is the spring, when the woodland is alight with daffodils and every shade of rhododendron and azalea, white and cream, pink and red, even blue.

At the very limit of the Wilderness wood, which rises slightly at this point, there is a statue of a mother bending protectively over her three children, which was copied as a gift from a friend from the original statue, much-loved by the Duchess of York, which stands in the grounds of St. Paul's Walden.

Turning here, you see, framed down a long glade and across the wide and undulating lawn, King George IV's Banqueting Saloon.

It is colour-washed in a charming strawberries-with-cream pink, which the Duchess of York substituted for the former white, because she liked the colour of the Duke of Devonshire's Compton Place, near Eastbourne, where she stayed when convalescing after a bad attack of influenza. She has therefore restored The Royal Lodge (knowingly or not) to almost the shade of the original Lower Lodge.

The gardens of The Royal Lodge consist essentially of woodland and lawns. The only formal garden at The Royal Lodge is close to the house: just outside the ground-floor main bedrooms there is a small sunk garden, and against its western hedge, a herbaceous border.

The little Welsh house, a miniature two-storey cottage, which was presented to Princess Elizabeth on her sixth birthday by the people of Wales, stands hidden from The Royal Lodge behind a pocket-sized garden with a central sundial and plots edged with box hedges. Cream-walled and thatched, it is a little house exactly tailored to delight young children: when it was first built, Queen Mary insisted on inspecting the little Welsh house from kitchen to bedroom in her usual thorough manner, and although it was a tight squeeze, she achieved it.

There is also an open-air swimming pool, which was built in

1938: the soil used in the excavation has been piled into a protective grassy bank which gives additional shelter.

Just outside the garden hedges of The Royal Lodge, and well within the perimeter fence, is the Royal Chapel, where the Royal family worships every Sunday when they are at Windsor, excepting only such special festivals as Easter Sunday, when they go to St. George's Chapel, Windsor.

This homely little church was built by George IV, and given a vaguely 'Scottish kirk' air by Queen Victoria. It is made of blocks of the same greystone from Bagshot Heath as Windsor Castle and roofed with red tiles, and has an open belfry for two bells, surmounted by a Celtic cross. There are flowering trees in the churchyard, and rambling roses trained along the wires of the fence which surrounds it.

Inside, it is like a Victorian hamlet church, but has been partly redecorated recently by Sir Edward Maufe, the architect of Guildford Cathedral. The varnish has been stripped from the original pitch-pine timbers supporting the roof of the nave. The chancel roof has been painted blue-green and decorated with the stars and badges of various Orders.

The Royal family sit on separate, green-covered chairs in a box pew in the chancel. The Royal pew is out of sight of the rest of the congregation, made up principally of those who live and work on the Windsor estate, who sit in the nave. King George VI liked to see who was in church, and he had the pillar of the chancel arch cut back so that he could, by leaning forward, see the congregation.

The Royal Lodge gave the Duke and Duchess of York great happiness. 'The gardens are the inspiration and the work of the Duke and Duchess of York themselves,' said Sir Eric Savill, former Deputy Ranger of Windsor Great Park to whose genius in landscape gardening Windsor Great Park owed so much. 'I can picture them now, walking there, stopping at every plant and discussing its habits. How was it doing? What to do to buck it up? What about next winter? Where should we extend the garden? Do you think that branch should come off?—talking about all the things that keen gardeners are always discussing. They were so close together, that they thought alike.'

A member of the Royal Household wrote, 'I was extra-Equerry when they moved into The Royal Lodge, and they used, most kindly, to put me into waiting for Ascot week, when I stayed with them there. It was the most charming, comfortable and simple home you can imagine. I can honestly say that never in my whole life have I seen a family so happy.'

When the Duke and Duchess of York entertained for Ascot, the guests would come down for breakfast at 9 a.m., and afterwards they would all go out riding—the Duke's hacks and the Princesses' ponies were stabled at Cumberland Lodge—and come back to lunch at The Royal Lodge. Afterwards they went off to the races, and returned about 4.30, and if the weather was fine, the party had tea in the sunken gardens. Dinner was always at 8.30.

At The Royal Lodge the Duke and Duchess of York enjoyed their happiest times. The family was very close. Both father and mother saw much more of their children than most parents who employ nannies: Princess Elizabeth and Princess Margaret never lived a nursery life completely apart from the main stream of the house, as many children did at that time.

Princess Elizabeth and Princess Margaret learned their very real faith from their mother, who taught them to say their prayers and read them Bible stories. The Duchess of York always emphasised the spirit rather than any sectarian doctrine in religion, and she formed in them the same trusting faith on which she and her husband founded their lives.

The Duchess of York taught Princess Elizabeth to read, and did her early lessons with her. Both the Duke and Duchess of York played every sort of game with their children, hide-and-seek, ball games, riotous card games. There were splashing water games in the bathroom and stories read aloud, or better still, the Duchess of York told them about her childhood. Life was a family thing, shared and enjoyed by all.

The Duke and Duchess of York made haste very slowly with their daughters in their formative years. They were determined that their children should be happy, without the pressure of too exacting a curriculum.

The Duchess of York believes that a good life can be founded only upon the simple strength of good character. Given the choice *between* higher education and good character training, she would make her choice without a second's hesitation. If both could be achieved, so much the better.

When Princess Elizabeth was seven, plans for her education were reviewed. Both the Duke and Duchess of York wished to send Princess Elizabeth to school, believing that it would be good for her to have the normal experience and discipline of a school-girl. But the King was adamant: Princess Elizabeth was third in the line of succession, it had always been traditional that the heir to the throne should be privately educated, and he wished his grand-daughter to be privately educated too.

Even though the succession of Princess Elizabeth to the Throne seemed most unlikely, the Princesses were the grand-daughters of the Sovereign and their up-bringing was more than normally important.

The little girls were young, pretty and photogenic and they were regarded with sentimental affection by the nation. Even when they were young, they had to comport themselves in public with a high degree of decorum.

Princess Elizabeth and Princess Margaret had to meet many eminent people and they had to know how to address them correctly. The Duchess of York typically made the acquisition of this special knowledge into a game. She would sweep into the room saying, 'Now I am the Archbishop of Canterbury . . . now I'm Grannie . . . now I'm the Prime Minister,' taking rôle after rôle, so that the children learnt by play exactly how to meet each different personage. 'She was so good at getting on with her children,' remarked a close friend. 'She made fun out of nothing —and she taught them by example.'

The Duchess of York also introduced her husband to the pleasure of owning a house dog. There had always been gun dogs at Sandringham and Balmoral, but Queen Mary did not like house dogs and there were none in Buckingham Palace, perhaps a reaction from the very large number of dogs which Queen Alexandra effortlessly collected. (Queen Alexandra was a natural succourer of all animals—when she sailed up the Nile a floppy-eared Egyptian sheep, destined for dinner, was brought along to amuse her, whereupon she insisted on having it shipped to England to live to a happy old age at Sandringham.)

The Duchess of York had always been accustomed to dogs around her in her home, and when, in the summer of 1933, her daughters fell in love with a corgi puppy belonging to some friends they had little difficulty in persuading her that they should have a puppy too. Mrs. Thelma Gray, a well-known breeder of corgies, was asked to bring a selection of puppies to 145 Piccadilly, from which the Duke and Duchess of York chose a short-tailed Pembroke corgi called *Rozavel Golden Eagle* who speedily became an important member of the family under the nickname of *Dookie* (a contraction of 'The Duke of York's puppy'). Later they acquired another corgi, *Rozavel Lady Jane*, known as *Jane*.

Soon afterwards Princess Elizabeth was photographed leading a puppy across Ballater railway bridge; public interest at once became focused upon the Welsh corgi, and especially upon the short-tailed Pembroke corgi. The name is derived from *Gi* or *Ci* a dog and *Cor* a dwarf. At that time these intelligent cattle dogs from West Wales were little known. Only ten Welsh corgis were registered with the Kennel Club in 1925, but in 1938 the number had risen to nine hundred and nineteen, and twenty years later, when the Royal family still remained faithful to the descendants of their original corgi, their number had risen to eight thousand five hundred and eighty, and the corgi had become the second most popular of all breeds of dog in England. While the corgi would probably have become better-known in any case, its amazing growth in popularity is obviously in large measure due to its association with the Royal family.

The choice of a corgi was made by the Royal family, and any popularity that the breed enjoys as a result is perfectly fair; but it is an example of the way in which popularity—and consequently financial gain—follows Royal patronage. Most of the gifts offered to the Royal family stem from loyalty and affection, but others may be offered in the hope of publicity and consequent profits. There was a great incentive to manufacturers, distributors and other financially interested parties to induce, if they can, members of the Royal family to favour a particular ware. This applies not only to possessions, but to plays, artists to whom they sit, or whose work they admire publicly, in fact anything that may be associated with their name and so receive recognition. The Royal family are perfectly well aware of this, and they do not therefore (except on rare occasions such as the wedding of Princess Elizabeth) accept presents from persons unknown to them. By the seventies the Pembroke corgi was slipping back, and in 1973 was only nineteenth in popularity, while the number of registered corgis had dropped to about half.

Though they fully recognise the part they can and must play in the promotion of British trade, they will not have their names used merely for publicity purposes. Hence the strict regulations laid down for the Royal Warrant Holders, who are pledged not to misuse their valued recognition.

Soon the Duke and Duchess of York had other dogs too. The Duke of York had golden labradors, *Mimsy*, which was particularly devoted to him, and her sons *Stiffy* and *Scrummy*. A Tibetan lion dog, who was named *Choo Choo* after the panting noise he made, was equally devoted to the Duchess. *Choo Choo*'s temper became a little uncertain with age, and during the war he was evacuated to St. Paul's Walden which had been turned into a convalescent home, and where there was less bombing. When she paid a visit there, *Choo Choo* greeted her with almost hysterical delight. The Queen (as she was then) forgot all about the duties that awaited her as she sat down beside her faithful old dog.

The Duchess of York was not sentimental about her dogs, but she did and does derive great pleasure from their companionship. Her dogs are her constant companions and know that they are welcome not only when she is in country tweeds, ready for a walk, but when she is in full evening dress. She believes that children should be brought up with animals and that they will learn tolerance and responsibility by looking after living creatures dependent upon them. She taught her daughters to look after their dogs themselves, to feed and groom them, and to this day Queen Elizabeth II keeps a dog brush in her desk and brushes her dog herself.

It must be admitted that the temper of the corgis was not always of the best. *Dookie*, in particular, was 'quick on the draw', and there were few of the Household who had not suffered a quick snap. A Member of the Household has stood, his bleeding hand held behind his back, talking amiably with the Princesses and concealing from them the damage their pet had wrought upon him. He also remembers, not without a certain relish, an occasion when *Dookie* was not well and the Queen (as the Duchess of York had become) very charmingly asked him if he would be kind enough, as *Dookie* knew him so well, to go with the dog to the vet? So he took *Dookie* to a very distinguished veterinary surgeon indeed, and *Dookie* was placed on the examination table. The Member of the Household said to the distinguished veterinary surgeon, 'Would you like me to hold him for you?' The lofty reply was, 'I need not remind you that I have had some little experience with dogs.' In a flash *Dookie* had the expert by the hand.

*　*　*

In 1934, Prince George, Duke of Kent, youngest surviving brother of the Duke of York, married Princess Marina of Greece and Denmark in Westminster Abbey, and Princess Elizabeth was one of the bridesmaids. In 1935, Prince Henry, Duke of Gloucester, followed the Duke of York's example and married the daughter of a Scottish peer, Lady Alice Montagu-Douglas-Scott, daughter of the seventh Duke of Buccleugh. The Duchess of York was now one of three daughters-in-law of the Sovereign, but the heir to the Throne was still unmarried.

In 1935, also, King George V celebrated his Silver Jubilee, acclaimed by his people in a great outpouring of love and loyalty, which deeply touched him. Yet imperceptibly the old regime was drawing to a close. The King had rallied from his severe illnesses of 1928–29 and 1931, but they had greatly weakened him. His health was precarious, and indeed he had only a few months to live.

In the middle of January 1936, King George V contracted a chill, and his condition almost at once caused anxiety to his doctor. On January 16, a telephone message from Sandringham House to The Royal Lodge informed the Duke of York of his father's illness: he left at once for Sandringham. On the following day the Prince of Wales also returned there. The first bulletin to the public, announcing 'some disquiet', was issued late that evening.

On Saturday, two bulletins were issued on the King's health, and three on Sunday: by Monday January 20, 1936, the last day of his life, the whole world realised how desperately ill he was. The hours dragged slowly away: during the evening the words of the last bulletin were given over the wireless: 'The King's life is moving peacefully to its close.'

Life would never be quite the same again for the Duke and Duchess of York nor for their daughters.

CHAPTER SEVEN

WIFE OF THE HEIR PRESUMPTIVE

He has one matchless blessing, enjoyed by so many of you and not
bestowed on me, a happy home with his wife and children

Prince Edward of Windsor in his Abdication Broadcast

KING GEORGE died a few minutes before midnight on January 20,
1936.

On Wednesday, January 22, the Duchess of York travelled to
Sandringham to take her part in the harrowing and long-drawn-
out funeral ceremonies of a King. On the same day she returned
to London, riding with Queen Mary and Princess Royal in the
first closed carriage, behind the coffin of the King, from Sandringham House to Wolferton station. The bare-headed bystanders
could only glimpse dimly three figures swathed in black draperies,
a blessed obscurity not yet penetrated by the telephoto lens. The
train was before time at King's Cross station in London: Queen
Mary, with the Royal Duchesses (of York, Gloucester and Kent)
standing close to her, spent a seemingly endless ten minutes on the
platform, so that the procession could leave the railway station at
precisely the right time.

The body of King George V lay in state in Westminster Hall
from January 23 until January 28 while the Royal and official
mourners assembled. The coffin was then carried through the
streets of London to Paddington station and thence by train to
Windsor. The Duchess of York rode with her back to the horses
in the Glass Coach with Queen Mary, Queen Maud of Norway
(who was King George V's sister), and the Princess Royal. All
were wearing the heavy black veils of royal mourning, consisting
of short veils about eighteen inches long which conceal the face,
and second veils about one and a half yards long which fall down
the back.

Princess Elizabeth was waiting forlornly with her governess at

Paddington station; the Duchess of York put out her hand to her, and the little girl went quickly to her and remained beside her through the rest of that exacting day. The delays amounted to forty minutes by the time the King's coffin was carried into the choir of St. George's Chapel, where mother and daughter stood together with the other Members of the Royal family. Princess Elizabeth held her mother's hand during the moving committal of the King's body to the vault below.

As the mourners were dispersing from St. George's Chapel, Lady Helen Graham, the wise and understanding woman who was lady-in-waiting to the Duchess of York, turned to a Member of the Household beside her, and looking at the solitary figure of King Edward VIII, who stood a little apart from the others, she said, 'I feel so sorry for him. *He* is not going home to a wife behind the tea-pot and a warm fire, with his children making toast for him.'

The reign began with enormous goodwill at the disposal of the new King. The prestige of the monarchy stood high. King George V had steadied the nation and Empire, had guided his peoples through the shifting currents of the post-war world: he had been universally respected and loved; he was deeply mourned.

For the period of change which lay ahead, it was felt by the ordinary man and woman that no one could better bridge the gulf between the generations and between the classes than the Prince of Wales. Everyone expected that his reign would be attuned to the outlook of ex-servicemen. The Commonwealth, which he knew so well, looked to him for leadership at once as steadfast and true as that of his father, but also more flexible and modern.

The new King was welcomed also by the leaders of the great political parties. Mr. Stanley Baldwin, Prime Minister, speaking in the House of Commons after the death of King George V, said of King Edward VIII:

'He brings to the altar of national service a personality richly endowed with experience in public affairs, he has the secret of youth in the prime of age; he has a wider and more intimate knowledge of all classes of his subjects, not only at home, but throughout the Dominions and India, than any of his predecessors . . . We look forward with confidence and assurance to the new reign, believing that under God's Providence he will establish the throne more firmly than ever on its surest and only foundation, the hearts of the people.'

Mr. Attlee, who was leader of the Opposition, said:

'We offer our loyal service and congratulations to King Edward the Eighth, who as Prince of Wales has endeared himself to all hearts. He is continuing in a higher sphere and with greater responsibilities the work which he has been doing so well for this country. Like the late King, he showed sympathy with and knowledge of all classes of his subjects, both at home and overseas. He has earned the affection and confidence of all. We know that he will bring to the service of the nation the same great qualities of the mind and heart which his father displayed. May he be spared the same anxieties. The wish of us all is that his reign may be long and prosperous and peaceful.'

His family looked forward to serving him with the same devotion with which they had served his father. The loyalty and unstinted service of the Duke and Duchess of York were his to command.

At the same time there was considerable sympathy with the new King, because it was widely recognised that his life would be lonely, and that much of his formal work would be uncongenial to him. He was loved not least for the sacrifices he must make of his private life, his inevitable loss of informality.

There had always been a great contrast between the brothers. The boyish Prince of Wales, with his infectious charm and ability to get on with all kinds of people, his nervous energy and physical daring, had from his youth stood out in sharp relief against his shy, more serious younger brother. The Prince of Wales had entered man's estate quickly, and had made an outstanding success of his rôle as 'Britain's Best Ambassador', as he was frequently called. The Duke of York had been a slow starter; but with marriage, maturity had come to him. He was a happy family man, his private life was not merely contented, but actively filled with joy. The Duke's public duties, though more limited than those of the Prince of Wales, were interesting and challenging, and he was deeply and sincerely interested in them. He was steadily gaining mastery over his stammer.

On the other hand, perennial restlessness seemed to have seized his elder brother, together with a growing distaste for criticism. This caused him to lean heavily upon those who might be expected to give the answer 'Yes', and sometimes to turn from those who had so deeply loved him, and who now braved his anger to give him advice they knew would not be welcome.

The two brothers had always been close friends, although it had always been the Prince of Wales who led, and the Duke of York who had admiringly, diffidently followed. The Prince of Wales had been a frequent visitor to White Lodge and 145 Piccadilly, and when the Duke of York acquired The Royal Lodge, the brothers shared an additional and engrossing interest in landscape gardening. The Prince of Wales was fond of his nieces, and he was their much loved 'Uncle David'.

Gradually, King Edward VIII withdrew, even from his brother, and became almost inaccessible to many of those formerly close to him. There is such a burden of continual work and responsibility upon the shoulders of the Sovereign that inevitably he cannot see as much of his family and friends as he did before he succeeded to the Throne. There is also the distance maintained even between the King and his family, because of the respect and awe in which the Sovereign is regarded. This was clearly shown by Queen Mary's first act of widowhood, when she took and kissed the hand of her eldest son, in acknowledgement that he was now her Sovereign. Yet the withdrawal of the new King from intimate contacts with his family was greater than they or those around them had anticipated.

The accession of her brother-in-law brought a change in the status of the Duchess of York. She was now the wife of the Heir Presumptive, and as the King was unmarried, and until Queen Mary emerged from mourning to take up whatever part of her public work she decided to resume, the Duchess of York was virtually first lady in the land.

By Order in Council, the words 'Our Gracious Queen Mary, the Duke of York and the Duchess of York' were inserted into prayers, liturgies and collects for the Sovereign and the Royal family. The Loyal Toasts were given a new form: the first toast was, 'The King', the second, 'Queen Mary, the Duke and Duchess of York and other members of the Royal family'. Ambassadors now paid their respects to the Duke and Duchess of York at 145 Piccadilly, after they had presented their credentials to the King. The new King, in a pleasant gesture to his Scottish sister-in-law, appointed Lord Elphinstone (her brother-in-law), Captain-General of the Royal Company of Archers, the King's Bodyguard in Scotland.

When the Civil List was announced in April 1936 (in which a clause provided £40,000 a year for a Queen Consort if the King should marry, to be increased to £70,000 if she survived the King) the finances of the Heir Presumptive, the Duke of York, were reviewed. As had been anticipated in informed circles, the King would provide for the Duke of York as Heir Presumptive from the incomes of the Duchy of Cornwall, but it was stipulated that if these should fall below £25,000 a year, then an annuity making his income up to that sum would be paid from the Civil List to the Duke. Should the Duke of York die while Heir Presumptive, then the annuity would continue in trust for the Duchess of York and the surviving children, so long as there was no Heir Apparent.

There were other changes. The new King was cutting with tradition in many details. King Edward VIII received the Privileged Bodies (those who by tradition have the privilege of presenting an Address to the Sovereign on his Accession, and who include the Lord Mayor of London and the Dean of Westminster Abbey) all together instead of individually as had been the custom. Similarly he received the Ambassadors together instead of separately. He decided that the Royal Standard would not be flown over the house where he was in residence, but always over Buckingham Palace, whether he was there or not. He decided that the Ribands of Orders should not be worn in the open air, and would therefore not be worn at the King's Birthday Parade. He ordered that the Field Marshal's baton made for him should bear only the inscription 'His Majesty King Edward VIII, Field Marshal, January 21st, 1936' in place of the full titles with which it had always previously been inscribed. He decided to have King George V's racing yacht *Britannia*, famous since her Clyde launch in 1893, broken up—which, though not unexpected, would, *The Times* commented, 'bring a sharp sense of deprivation . . . to all lovers of ships'.

He made considerable changes among his Household, and more changes, involving some dismissals, on the private estates of Sandringham and Balmoral. Although some of the matters were trivial, their cumulative effect disappointed many people.

The new reign opened with a period of six months' full mourning and three months' half mourning. This was less than previously, and was one change welcomed by the whole of the Royal family, not least by Queen Mary, who had a deep dislike for the formal trappings of mourning. (After the death of King George VI in 1952 the period was further shortened to four months' full mourning.)

During this time the public duties of the Royal family were curtailed, which enabled the Duke of York to spend more time than usual with his family. The Duchess of York would, in any case, have been unable to undertake any public duties at this time. She was much pulled down by an attack of pneumonia the previous winter, and required a period of convalescence to rebuild her strength. After resting quietly at 145 Piccadilly or at The Royal Lodge for some time, it was recommended that she should complete her convalescence by the sea. On March 4, the Duke and Duchess of York and their daughters left London by car for Compton Place, Eastbourne, belonging to the Duke of Devonshire, where they spent a month, returning to London on April 1, and almost at once going to The Royal Lodge for Easter.

The Princess Royal was Queen Mary's closest companion during the months following the death of King George V, and then, unfortunately, the Princess Royal caught measles. Queen Mary therefore came to The Royal Lodge to spend Easter with the Duke and Duchess of York and stayed for almost a month, during which time her daughter-in-law did everything, in her thoughtful way, to make life less unhappy for the widowed Queen. She accompanied Queen Mary on her favourite motor drives round the countryside and to visit friends. Queen Mary joined in the party for Princess Elizabeth's tenth birthday, at which their neighbours from Cumberland Lodge, Princess Marie Louise and Princess Helena Victoria, the daughters of Princess Christian and grand-daughters of Queen Victoria were also present. Queen Mary was also a guest at a luncheon party at The Royal Lodge on Sunday, April 26, to celebrate—one day early—the thirteenth wedding anniversary of the Duke and Duchess of York.

Towards the end of May many members of the Royal family, including Queen Mary, the Duke and Duchess of York and Princess Elizabeth, went to Southampton to inspect the new liner *Queen Mary*. The *Queen Mary* was more than the largest ship in the world, she had become a symbol of the depression as she lay unnamed, a stranded Leviathan towering on the stocks above the narrow Clyde in John Brown's shipyard at Clydebank for twenty-eight frustrating months: work had stopped on her on December 12, 1931, and had not re-started until April 7, 1934. So her completion was also a symbol of the approaching return of prosperity. All the Royal family were still wearing mourning, with the exception of the young Princess Elizabeth, who wore a grey coat with a blue hat. The visitors assiduously toured the giant liner. The Cunard officials had expected that Princess Elizabeth would like best the elaborately equipped nurseries, but it was the vast, white-washed engineroom which most fascinated her: her party, which included the Duke and Duchess of Kent, lingered there for nearly an hour.

Again, the Royal family were together at the Chelsea Flower Show, and the Duchess of York gave permission for a gloxinia to be named after her. The King ordered thirty-six tons of stone to be delivered at Fort Belvedere, for his new rock garden—hardly the action of a man contemplating exile!

The Duchess of York's first public engagement after the death of George V was to attend the annual national conference of the Women's Section of the British Legion on April 29. With the end of Court Mourning on July 21 the increase of work and prominence falling upon the Duchess became apparent. Queen Mary had naturally withdrawn completely from public life at this time. The Princess Royal, only daughter of the late King, was much occupied with her family life, although she did much valuable public work in Yorkshire, her adopted county. The Duke of Kent had married Princess Marina of Greece and Denmark in November 1934, but the births of Prince Edward in October 1935 and Princess Alexandra in December 1936 curtailed the amount of public work she was able to undertake. The Duchess of Gloucester was just finding her feet in her first royal duties.

On the day on which mourning ended an Afternoon Garden Reception, which took the place of a Court, was held at Buckingham Palace. The King sat in a throne chair under the Shamiana, a table at his elbow holding his top hat. Behind him sat the Duke and Duchess of Kent, the Duke and Duchess of York and the Princess Royal. A strip of carpet had been laid on the camomile lawn for the débutantes to walk on, and they were marshalled past, each for her single curtsey. After only half an hour drizzle began to fall, which soon changed to heavy rain, and the King, after inspecting the clouds to windward, decided to break off proceedings, though some waiting débutantes would rather have been soaked!

Among the Duchess of York's increasing engagements was a second visit to the Girls' Heritage for Crippled Children to open a wing which on her first visit there she had urged should be built.

One date to which she had looked forward, but which she could not keep because of toothache (the Duke of York went instead) was to open Margaret McMillan House, a new and happy form of nursery school, at Wrotham in Kent. At the Princess Elizabeth of York Hospital for Children at Barnstead the Duchess laid a foundation stone with a difference. Because of a heavy rainstorm the outside ceremony was cancelled, and instead she placed a miniature foundation stone upon a model of the hospital. She deputised for Queen Mary at the opening of Coram's Field and Harmsworth Memorial playground at Guildford Street, in the City of London, by which the site of the Foundling Hospital was saved 'for the use and enjoyment of the children of London for all time to come'.

At the opening of the Imperial War Museum in the old Bethlehem Hospital, which gave its name to Bedlam, the Duchess showed much interest in a Short seaplane which flew on a reconnaissance of the Germans at Jutland, the sea battle in which her husband had taken part. This aircraft was damaged by bombing during the Second World War: now only the cockpit section survives.

There were a fine crop of agricultural shows to attend that summer, not always in the best of weather. During the five-hour tour of the Royal Show at Bristol the Duchess of York bought a pair of willow-calf clogs with sycamore soles at one of the stands, and immediately put them on.

Apart from the weather, outwardly all was set fair. The date for King Edward VIII's Coronation was fixed for May 12, 1937, and the Duke of York was appointed a Commissioner of the Coronation Council. Many of the multitude of decisions for a new reign had been taken. Some of the new postage stamps came out on September 6.

Yet behind the scenes there was a lack of contact in the relationship between the King and those who had previously been close to him. Some turned to the Duke of York and asked him to speak for them. His was a difficult position; even if he felt inclined to urge the case of the person asking his help, he had the obligation of obedience to the wishes of his Sovereign. If he did intervene, he found his brother somewhat difficult to approach.

On May 28, 1936, King Edward VIII gave a dinner party at which Mr. Stanley Baldwin, the Prime Minister, met both Mr. and Mrs. Simpson. The other guests were Lord and Lady Louis Mountbatten, Lord Wigram, Major and Lady Diana Duff Cooper, Lady Cunard, Lord and Lady Chatfield and Mr. and Mrs. Charles Lindbergh.

In July first mention was made in the Press of the King's forthcoming holiday in the Balkans, on board the chartered yacht *Nahlin*. The King boarded the yacht at Sibenik in Yugoslavia.

Soon photographs were being sent from the ports of the Dalmatian coast and the Greek islands in the Aegean, which emphasised that Mrs. Simpson was one of the guests on board. The newspapers abroad began to whisper and then to shout the name of Mrs. Simpson in connection with the King. Even though the newspapers of this country maintained what appears today to have been an almost incredible self-control in avoiding any reference to the subject, many people concerned for the King's prestige wrote to Queen Mary at Marlborough House, and to others in positions of influence and authority in Britain.

The Duke and Duchess of York were deeply worried and saddened by these rumours. Their sense of the monarch's duty was such that they saw only one solution to the problem, which they felt would only grow harder the longer it was postponed. But they did not under-estimate what such a decision would mean for the King, and they were deeply sorry for him. They saw their own duty to lie in showing a serene and confident face in public, and in going ahead, doing each job as it came to hand as well as possible. Queen Mary, though she was bitterly hurt, showed great courage. Their demeanour had a stabilising effect and did much to reassure the ever increasing number of people in Britain who were bewildered and deeply concerned by the rumours which had reached them.

The Duke and Duchess of York lived through growing strain during these months of tension. As they had planned, at the end of July the Duke and Duchess went with their children to the wedding of the Duchess's niece, the Hon. Jean Elphinstone, to Mr. John Lycett Wills at St. Margaret's Westminster. Then they went north, to stay at Lumley Castle with Captain Roger Lumley (afterwards Lord Scarbrough and later Lord Chamberlain) and to visit Newcastle-on-Tyne. The Duchess of York opened at Hebburn-on-Tyne a coal staithe, which was capable of loading ships of up to fifteen thousand tons deadweight at the rate of five hundred tons of coal an hour. It had a special interest for the Duchess of York as John Bowes and Partners, the coalowners, was a family business of which her nephew, Lord Glamis, was chairman. Afterwards, the Duke and Duchess of York went down one of John Bowes's new pits, Kibblesworth Colliery: they inspected a coalface underground and both tried to hack out coal with picks. Afterwards they visited the homes of miners. The Duchess took the opportunity to go to the old family home of Gibside Hall, near Rowlands Gill, and to visit the vault of the Bowes family.

They went on to stay with the Duke of Northumberland at Alnwick Castle. The Duke of York then returned south for what was always one of the most important engagements of his year, his Boys' Camp, while the Duchess celebrated her birthday at Alnwick. The Duchess of York with Princess Elizabeth and Princess Margaret Rose then went north to Gannochy, where they were the guests of Mr. J. P. Morgan. They were joined there by the Duke of York, and afterwards they relaxed in the peace of Glamis on their eagerly anticipated annual holiday.

They arrived at Birkhall near Balmoral Castle at the end of August. The King brought a house party to Balmoral Castle in the early days of September: Mrs. Simpson was a member of the party. The tempo of life was very different from what it had been in the measured days of King George V.

As the autumn advanced, the pace of the crisis quickened. The nation entered into 'that nightmarish time', in the words of a Member of the Household of King Edward VIII. Mrs. Simpson received a decree nisi at Ipswich on October 27. Talk mounted. The Government was seriously alarmed. With the Prime Minister's knowledge, Major Alexander Hardinge, who was the King's Private Secretary, wrote a letter to King Edward VIII which he received, not inappropriately, on Friday, 13 November. This letter clarified the views of the Government and of the United Kingdom and the independent Commonwealth countries and of the Church, and strongly underlined the possibility of the Government resigning and the House going to the country on the subject of the King's private affairs. It urged the withdrawal abroad of Mrs. Simpson. The letter was not very tactfully worded and it showed, perhaps, a limited understanding and sympathy for the feelings of the King, but it was written by a loyal and desperate man. Everyone around the King expected that the advice given in this letter would, sooner or later, be followed.

On Monday, November 16, the King acted unexpectedly. He summoned Mr. Stanley Baldwin to Buckingham Palace, and he told him what had never yet been put into words, that he intended to marry Mrs. Simpson. If he could do so as King, so much the better. Otherwise he was prepared to abdicate.

That night the King went to dine with Queen Mary at Marlborough House. Present were the Princess Royal and the Duchess of Gloucester, 'a newcomer, almost a stranger to the family', as King Edward VIII expressed it in his memoirs. After dinner, the Duchess of Gloucester withdrew as soon as possible. Both Queen Mary and her daughter, who had always been so loving and close a companion to her brother, were obviously deeply sympathetic at the outset of the meeting because they anticipated, and did not under-estimate, a renunciation. With growing consternation they found that the King was determined to marry Mrs. Simpson, even if it meant abdication.

It was only next day, on November 17, that the King informed the man whose life would be changed forever by his contemplated action—his Heir Presumptive, the Duke of York. The Duke of Windsor wrote in his memoirs:

'Bertie was so taken aback by my news that in his shy way he could not bring himself to express his innermost feelings at the time. This, after all, was not surprising, for next to myself Bertie had most at stake: it was he who would have to wear the crown if I left, and his genuine concern for me was mixed up with the dread of having to assume the responsibilities of kingship.

'He waited a few days before confiding his thoughts to a letter. He wrote that he longed for me to be happy, adding that he of all people should be able to understand my feelings: he was sure that whatever I decided would be in the best interests of the country and the Empire.'

The shock for the Duke of York was appalling, he had never anticipated this sudden turn of events. He was thrown into what he afterwards recalled as 'a life of conjecture'.

On November 18 and November 19 the King was in Wales, where he toured the depressed mining areas and was greeted, as always, with loud acclamation by the men to whom he had come to mean so much. But behind the scenes great activity was under way, as the proposal of morganatic marriage, which the King had put forward as a preferable alternative to abdication, was put to the self-governing countries of the Empire and decisively rejected.

The rest of the Royal family waited; Queen Mary was the rock round which they gathered. 'She was a person who suffered unbelievably at this time,' said one in close contact with her. 'She

lived for Royalty, yet this crisis brought out her humanity.'
Queen Mary herself was heartened by the sturdy trenchant attitude of her brother, the Earl of Athlone, and by the consoling
company of his wife, Princess Alice, who went to stay with her at
Marlborough House. The Duke of York frequently went to see
his mother, sometimes accompanied by his wife, more often
alone.

The Duchess of York regarded the increasing possibility that
her husband would succeed to the throne with grave apprehension, for its effect upon him, their children and herself. She
wished most strongly to remain as she was. But she faced the
future with courage. 'The Duke, as a man, minded his accession
even more than she did,' said a member of the Duchess's family.
'A woman can take it better; a woman is more adaptable.' The
Duchess of York was wonderfully calm: she had immense self-
control. She was greatly concerned that such a thing could
happen, but she did not mention the future, nor was she
bitter.

The Duke of York, wrestling with the imponderables of the
future, needed all the comfort and strength which the Duchess
could give him. By Wednesday, November 25, he could write to
Sir Godfrey Thomas in the following words:

'If the worst happens and I have to take over, you can be
assured that I will do my best to clear up the inevitable mess, if
the whole fabric does not crumble under the shock and strain
of it all.'

On the night of Sunday, November 29, the Duke and Duchess
of York left London for Edinburgh, where the Duke was to be
installed Grand Master Mason of Scotland; they were given a
tremendous welcome, and carried through a full programme
without outward sign of stress.

It was on Tuesday, December 1, that Dr. Walter Blunt,
Bishop of Bradford, addressed his Diocesan Conference in terms
which were taken to mean a censure on the King, and which
released a torrent of Press comment upon the King's relationship
with Mrs. Simpson. The dam had burst.

The Duke and Duchess of York travelled from Edinburgh

overnight on Wednesday, December 2, to be greeted at Euston station on the Thursday morning with newsbills boldly lettered THE KING'S MARRIAGE. On the day of his return the Duke of York drove to see his mother at Marlborough House. The King was there, and told Queen Mary in the Duke of York's presence that he could not live alone as King and must marry Mrs. Simpson. The King asked his Heir Presumptive to come and see him on the following day at Fort Belvedere. The King then left London and went to the Fort.

During the days that followed the general public went through the successive emotions which the Royal family had already been experiencing—stupefaction and shock, followed by incredulous horror. Such high hopes had been centred on King Edward VIII that it seemed impossible that it should all end in nothing. 'Kings of England do not abdicate,' was repeated, at first arrogantly, then doggedly, as it slowly became conceivable to the world at large, as it was already apparent to those around the King, that abdication was indeed possible. Yet many of those closest to the King felt, as did many millions of his subjects, that at the very brink of abdication he would withdraw.

There followed what must have been a terrible week-end for both the Duke and Duchess of York. All through that interminable Friday and Saturday and Sunday and Monday, the Duke of York waited and waited with his wife at The Royal Lodge for the summons from his brother which never came. At last, on Monday, December 7, 1936, in the Duke of York's own words quoted by Sir John Wheeler-Bennett, 'My brother rang me at ten minutes to seven p.m., to say, "Come and see me after dinner." I said, "No, I will come and see you at once." I was with him at seven o'clock p.m. The awful and ghastly suspense of waiting was over.'

The point of no return had been reached: King Edward VIII would abdicate. The Duke and Duchess of York immediately drove back to London. There the Duchess of York, who had not faltered under the intense strain of the past weeks, had to retire to bed with influenza.

The Duke of York now had an immense amount of work to

cope with, and at high pressure. This was, however, easier to take than the period of frustrated conjecture which had preceded the King's decision to abdicate. Edward VIII left almost everything in the hands of his brother and successor: only very occasionally did he make some order, which the Duke of York at once obeyed. Hither and thither he travelled, to Fort Belvedere; to The Royal Lodge, where he intended to take a short break but found that without his wife it was impossible to relax; to Buckingham Palace; to Marlborough House; back to 145 Piccadilly. He never knew where he would sleep, so he carried his luggage about in the car. Twice he drove in the car belonging to his Private Secretary, Sir Eric Miéville (who had been appointed in July of that year) to 10 Downing Street, once entering through the garden entrance and another time through the Home Office, which had a connecting door with the Prime Minister's residence. These visits went unrecognised and unrecorded.

The Duchess of York, ill in bed, had all too much time alone in which to think of her changed future.

On Wednesday, December 9, when the Duke of York, with his Private Secretary at his side, drove back to 145 Piccadilly very late in the evening, they saw with some surprise and apprehension that a large crowd had collected outside. But when the car drew up the crowd cheered—in both senses of the word—their next King.

At last it came to an end: at 10 a.m. on Thursday, December 10, 1936, in the drawing room of Fort Belvedere, the Duke of York witnessed his brother's act of abdication.

On Friday, December 11, 1936, at 1.52 p.m., the last act of the reign of King Edward VIII took place in the Chamber of the House of Lords. The Clerk of the Crown turned and faced the Royal Assent Commissioners, seated on a bench in front of the Throne, and read the name of the last bill of the reign: 'His Majesty's Declaration of Abdication Bill'. The Peers present were assembled on both sides of the House, facing inwards. The Speaker and grave-faced Ministers and Members of the Lower House stood at the Bar of the Chamber. The Clerk of the Parliaments spoke in Norman-French the last and significant words of the reign of King Edward VIII, '*Le Roy le veult*'—The King wishes it.

All that Friday there was a crowd outside 145 Piccadilly, where, in sight of the house, stands had been going up for the Coronation of the King who would never be crowned.

'The most persistent crowd was that which tried to see the comings and goings at the house of the Prince who began the day as Duke of York and by two o'clock in the afternoon had succeeded to the Throne. At one period during which the callers included Prince and Princess Arthur of Connaught, the people were persuaded by the police officers on duty to keep moving in order to avoid congestion but later a gathering on the pavement was permitted if a passage for pedestrian movement was kept clear. This meant that only about three hundred persons were able to take up positions which gave a view of the entrance and others who halted soon passed on again.' (*The Times.*)

Inside 145 Piccadilly, the anxiety of the past weeks had been succeeded by a more cheerful reaction. Uncertainty was past, and nothing could be as bad again. When a King dies, at the exact moment of his death his heir becomes King. But in Accession upon abdication there was no such clear-cut moment of succession. The King—or was it the Duke of York?—was at luncheon, at which his wife was sufficiently recovered to be present, when Sir Eric Miéville received a telephone call from Sir Maurice Hankey (afterwards Lord Hankey) from the Houses of Parliament; Sir Maurice said: 'Will you tell His Majesty that he has just been proclaimed King?' Sir Eric took the message to the King, who was with the Queen and the Princesses at table.

King George VI looked round the luncheon table and said, 'Now if someone comes through on the telephone, *who* shall I say I am?'

The Royal Standard was not hoisted above 145 Piccadilly, although there was an available flagstaff. In accordance with the innovation established by Edward VIII, who had flown his Royal Standard at Buckingham Palace even when he was not actually in residence, the flag of the new King flew at Buckingham Palace, within sight of the nursery window of 145 Piccadilly.

By a sequence of unforeseen and unprecedented events, Lady Elizabeth Bowes-Lyon, at the age of thirty-six, and after thirteen and a half years of marriage, was Queen.

CHAPTER EIGHT

QUEEN CONSORT

No more than the King does Her Majesty the Queen stand in need of any introduction to the people's love. Her name evokes great memories in the people's history, and both by her gift of charm and simple goodness of heart she has already won for herself a secure and distinctive place in their affections

Lord Halifax, Lord Privy Seal, moving a Humble Address in the House of Lords, December 14, 1936

KING GEORGE VI came to the Throne on Friday, December 11, 1936. Public confidence had been badly shaken. Restoration of the fabric of the monarchy was of greater urgency than innovation, and the King's first actions were to turn back to the ways of life of his father.

As a result, most people have a false idea of the 'modern outlook' of one brother against the 'conventionality' of the other, forgetting that both had seen active service in the First World War; both were pilots; both were widely travelled (although few men could equal King Edward VIII's record of travel); both grappled with modern problems and worked hard to break down class barriers; both were keenly interested in youth and industrial problems.

We shall never know what King George VI might have added to the pattern of modern kingship if he had had a conventional Accession and a peaceful reign: by the time the abdication crisis had been surmounted war was imminent, and war brought its own violent and lasting changes.

In those last weeks of 1936 the King was plunged at once into the business of State. From the very moment of his Accession Council, life was completely changed for both of them. Breakfast for the King was at 9 sharp and immediately afterwards he left for Buckingham Palace, often not returning until 7 in the evening.

The Queen was busy rearranging the Household, breaking up their home at 145 Piccadilly and arranging the move into Buckingham Palace. The new King's first task was to choose the name by which he would be known. This is a matter for the Sovereign's own wishes. Queen Victoria was christened (after a font-side proposal of Georgina after King George IV) Alexandrina Victoria, and as a little girl was sometimes called Drina. Edward VII was christened Albert Edward and Queen Victoria wrote to 'Uncle Leopold' of the Belgians on the evening of his christening 'what a pleasure that he has that dearest name': he signed 'Albert' until his Accession. George V was always known as George (and to his Mother Georgie); Edward VIII, named Edward Albert Christian George Andrew Patrick David, had always been known to his family as David.

The Duke of York, who had been christened Albert Frederick Arthur George, was, like his grandfather, known to his family as Bertie. Now it was strongly urged that he should emphasise the link with his father by choosing King George VI for his title. Momentarily, he resisted. 'But I can't do that!' he exclaimed to one of his Household. 'Why not, Sir?' The new King scribbled 'George' and placed it close to a signature of his father's; the two signatures were almost identical. 'Look,' he said, 'I should always be confused with my father!' The signature of Queen Elizabeth II is almost indistinguishable from that of her mother.

The King and Queen had many decisions to make about the removal from 145 Piccadilly to Buckingham Palace; about the Coronation (which was fixed to take place on May 12, 1937, the same day on which Edward VIII would have been crowned); about the New Year's Honours (which were deferred by one month); about the usual Christmas broadcast (which was cancelled, but the King broadcast a message of dedication at the New Year); about stamps (some bearing Edward VIII's head had already been issued); about coinage (the designs for King Edward's head had been chosen, but were never issued); about changes in the Royal Household; about the private estates of Sandringham and Balmoral where additional complications were caused by the terms of George V's will; even about the future of the Royal stud and racehorses.

Meanwhile the Queen was still confined to the house at 145 Piccadilly. Queen Mary visited her on the day following King George VI's Accession: the King remained with her in London over the week-end.

Monday, December 14, was King George VI's forty-first birthday—although he requested that it should not be celebrated publicly in any way—and he chose the day to pay the first of many tributes to his Consort, conferring upon her the dignity and title of a Lady of the Most Noble Order of the Garter.

By Wednesday of that busy week, one or two decisions taken could be announced. The Royal family would go to Sandringham as usual. Lord Wigram, who had been Private Secretary to King George V until 1935, was recalled from retirement to act as the King's Private Secretary for three months and to be Permanent Lord-in-Waiting. Major Alexander Hardinge, who had been Private Secretary to Edward VIII and had been under such strain during the past months, was appointed Private Secretary to the new King but would take three months' leave of absence.

Where there had been gloom at the death of King George V, now there was confusion. Confusion grows where different conclusions are drawn from the same event, witness these accounts of the first public appearance of the King after his Accession—his journey with his family from London to Sandringham for Christmas.

Mr. Warren Bradley Wells (London Staff Correspondent of the *New York Herald Tribune*) in *Why Edward Went*, an anti-British Government book published in the United States in November 1937, wrote:

'The Royal party's departure had been announced beforehand in the newspapers. But there were a mere handful of people in the station . . . King George VI, hat in hand, bowed right and left automatically as he drove up. Scarcely a hat was raised in reply . . .

'Behind two lines of police drawn up across it [the departure platform], on either side of the Royal Saloon, was a little throng of people, perhaps six deep. There was not long to wait for the appearance of the Royal party; but the little throng dwindled.'

'King George VI and his family walked bowing across the platform to his saloon. Perhaps half the men in the throng raised their hats. There was a subdued murmur, which might have been a suppressed cheer—or might not.

'In short, on his first public appearance after succeeding to his brother King George VI was given an extremely cold reception.'

But a different account was given by *The Times*:

'. . . The Royal train left King's Cross a few minutes before one o'clock and its departure was watched by a crowd of several hundred people at the station. The Queen was dressed in black with a spray of white flowers on her left shoulder, and smilingly acknowledged the cheers of the people as she walked along the red carpeted platform.'

At Sandringham the new King and Queen took stock of their position. Christmas 1936 was very different from Christmas 1935, over which King George V and Queen Mary had presided. Now King George V was dead; his eldest son in exile. Every person present at Sandringham was suffering in some degree from the aftermath of the crisis through which they had just passed.

For the King himself the worst was over. He was surprised to find his task in some ways easier than he had imagined it. He said at this time, 'It's much easier now that I have a definite job to do—I've always had to do what my father and elder brother didn't want to do.'

King George VI and Queen Elizabeth were not short of advisers: they were surrounded by their family, and also by the Households of King George V, King Edward VIII and those who had served them when they were Duke and Duchess of York. As a naval member of the Household put it succinctly, 'Three ships' companies were manning one ship.'

Queen Mary's presence emphasised the human tragedy that lay behind the constitutional crisis. Her devotion to the Monarchy and her deep love for her first-born had been closely interwoven:

now they were torn apart. She was heart-broken, but she struggled to conceal it and she gave all her support to her second son and his wife.

Queen Mary had taken the unusual step of issuing a moving public appeal both for the good name of her eldest son and for the nation's support for her second son and his wife. She wrote:

'I need not speak to you of the distress which fills a mother's heart when I think that my dear son had deemed it to be his duty to lay down his charge and that the reign which had begun with so much hope and promise has so suddenly ended.

'I know that you will realise what it cost him to come to this decision, and that remembering the years in which he tried so eagerly to serve and help his country and Empire you will ever keep a grateful remembrance of him in your hearts.

'I commend to you his brother, summoned so unexpectedly and in circumstances so painful, to take his place.

'. . . With him I commend my dear daughter-in-law who will be his Queen. May she receive the same unfailing affection and trust which you have given me for six-and-twenty years . . .'

In this house of men and women in a state of shock, the new Queen set to work, with all her tact and sympathy, to relax some of the passionate tensions of the past months and to create a harmonious atmosphere. She showed great gentleness and imaginative understanding, especially towards Queen Mary. The almost inevitable little hurts to a widow whose daughter-in-law has succeeded her were avoided wherever they could be anticipated. Everyone around the Queen, whether of the old or the new regime, was made to feel wanted and of value.

Many of the dismissals and changes which had been ordered at Sandringham by Edward VIII, who found it old-fashioned and too lavishly run, were cancelled. But there was no return to 'Sandringham time'—the Sandringham clock had been kept half an hour fast since the reign of Edward VII, to give more daylight for shooting.

It was obvious from the first that there were going to be great changes, and it was also obvious that changes of personnel and in material things would be effected with the least possible hurt to other people. In particular, Queen Mary's wishes were always consulted and respected.

When a King dies, there is a period of mourning, of withdrawal from the public eye, in which his successor can make adjustments. There was no such respite for King George VI, although the fact that the Abdication in early December was quickly followed by Christmas was a lucky chance: as the nation's thoughts were turned from political to personal affairs, it made possible the Royal family's much needed break at Sandringham.

When the King and Queen returned to London early in February to take up their new lives they drove straight to Buckingham Palace, which had been hurriedly prepared for them. There had been no time to redecorate the Palace according to the personal tastes of the new Queen, and the formal dignity of the surroundings underlined the new formality of their future. The chilly atmosphere damped the spirits of the young Household, and possibly also the spirits of Queen Elizabeth, but that was something she did not let others see. Buckingham Palace could never be as homely as 145, but both establishments were very happy households.

Public reactions to the King were awaited with some anxiety. One of the Queen's Ladies-in-Waiting, kept indoors by a cold, remembers standing at an upstairs window with her maid watching King George VI drive out to take the first Levée of his reign at St. James's Palace. There was only a little handful of somewhat listless spectators at the gate. 'Not many of them, are there, my Lady?' commented her maid with tactless candour.

The tangled emotions of the badly-jarred country and Commonwealth over the abdication defy classification. Reactions were subjective and individual, and personal memories have become fused with national events in a way which happens only when personal emotions are closely involved.

Opinions differ as to the time at which public confidence in the Monarchy was restored. Some believe it happened at once, others set the Coronation, the visit to Canada, or even the war as the date of stabilisation; but whatever the actual time, the ultimate fact is not disputed.

The Sovereign is a vital link in the chain of Government. Any interruption of his work, from whatever cause, brings immediate and multiplying problems. During the last months of Edward VIII's reign the Household had found it increasingly difficult to work on the level of ordinary, necessary daily routine while the Abdication itself had completely disrupted work. The business of the State had been held up. Upon his Accession King George VI at once tackled the backlog, and the paperwork was quickly reduced to normal proportions.

The Royal Household immediately welcomed the new King and Queen; they felt relieved and happy, and were not in the least worried about the new reign.

The friends of King George V and Queen Mary, and the older members of their Household, some of whom had been retired by Edward VIII, hastened to support the new King. 'The new code is hush-hush and rally round the new King,' one foreigner commented acidly.

George VI's task was made easier by the good wishes of his abdicating brother, who had made public his allegiance to his successor in his historic and moving broadcast from Windsor Castle on his last evening in England.

'And now we all have a new King. I wish him and you, his people, happiness and prosperity with all my heart. God save the King.'

It is not, however, painless to switch a loyalty, and public reaction differed. Edward VIII had been greatly loved. So much had been expected of his reign. Many saw King Edward's proposed marriage as the excuse to escape a rôle found unbearably uncongenial, rather than as the real reason for abdication. Some believed that political reactionaries had forced the King to abdicate because of his too openly expressed sympathy with the unemployed. Churchmen, holding marriage to be indissoluble, and that the Sovereign must give a moral lead, welcomed a return to the tenets of their faith. Many women, who had been half in love with the Prince of Wales for years, thought it wonderful of him to give up all for love. Many men failed to understand how a woman could so influence the King. Some ex-Servicemen, whose hope and ideal had been the Prince of Wales, clung to their former King, others reacted immediately in favour of his younger brother. Strangely, many serving officers and men in the forces, formerly strongest in their support for King Edward VIII, appeared to react sharply against the abdicating King, holding that the loyalty unto death for their King and country, which was expected of them as their duty, had not been reciprocated.

The fact that the Duke of York was so obviously not a man to intrigue against others, but a simple man who had never thrust himself forward, and who was courageously undertaking a rôle he had never sought or wanted, was liked by the British public. The ordinary people knew that the King was taking on a thankless task 'and in a funny way, without saying anything, they showed that they did appreciate it very much,' said a man who served him. The very reserve and shyness of King George VI helped him with the public.

Public recognition of Queen Elizabeth as Queen Consort was retarded because of the overwhelming regard of the British public for Queen Mary. Queen Mary's ramrod carriage; her intricately curled hair-style; her piercing yet kindly blue eyes; her individual way of dressing (which the French admired for its *chic*, the British just because it was Queen Mary's own); her boundless curiosity and energy; her relentless search for and acquisition of beautiful objects; above all her uprightness, her unchanging dependability, made her the very epitome of regality. The staunch figure of the dowager Queen immeasurably strengthened the Monarchy in the eyes of the people, and her support for King George VI was a big factor in quickly stabilising his position.

A generation later this feeling that loyalty must not be too lightly transferred was repeated when the gay, warm humanity of Queen Elizabeth the Queen Mother was so widely loved that it took time for the British public fully to realise the remarkable qualities of her daughter, Queen Elizabeth II. Possibly this identification of loyalty with an individual is the reason why so many people insist upon analysing and placing in order their relative affections for different members of the Royal family, something they would never think of doing with any other family. It was widely felt that *it would have been quite impossible for the Duke of York to take on the kingship without his wife.*

Perhaps the greatest of all debts the Commonwealth owes to Queen Elizabeth the Queen Mother stems from just these months, when the second son of King George V 'was suddenly bounced onto the Throne'.

The story of these times is part of our history; but it is also the story of a husband and wife who, with little preparation or warning, armed only with love, faith and an unflinching sense of duty, set themselves the tremendous task of restoring the equilibrium of an Empire.

'They were so particularly together: they both leant so much on the other,' said Queen Elizabeth's eldest sister, the late Lady Elphinstone.

Those closest to them felt that they were together far more than most married people, 'yet their marriage never had the staleness so often found among those who are seldom away from each other. It was Queen Elizabeth's gift to be able to reward and encourage the King with a look or a smile. He could never take his eyes from her.'

The King was a perfectionist, and he was highly strung. If he failed to live up to the standards he set himself—and they were inordinately high—his temper sometimes flared up. If someone near him did something slovenly, or the gremlins got into the arrangements, out it would flash, a legacy of the frustrations of which his speech difficulties had been an outward expression. A missed putt at golf or a mistaken order on an official occasion, a delay on the road, a breach of discipline, any of these might suddenly irritate the King beyond the bounds of endurance. Yet he always responded quickly to his wife. When the King 'blew up', the Queen had only to smile and say, 'Now, Bertie', and his outburst would subside without a trace.

It was his wife who had been the first to recognise the qualities of the Duke of York, and it was within the happiness of his marriage that they had been able to develop. 'The Duke of York had no confidence at all until he entered this most wonderful relationship upon marriage,' said one who had known them both since childhood.

But when he became King, a change took place; the strength that had always been there, pent up within him, was released, and he became 'a totally different man'. King George VI once said to a friend, 'It became much easier when I was King. Then I could make up my own mind, instead of trying to do what other people told me to do.' Gradually he was to gain an authority that few who had known him only as an immature young man would have believed possible.

Gradually, imperceptibly even to those constantly with them, the relationship between husband and wife changed. For King George the centre of his life and joy continued to be his wife, but, as the King gained confidence, so Queen Elizabeth leant on him more and more. They became completely inter-dependent. In big things, the King made the decisions. 'The King was a rock to her, indeed to all of us,' said Rose, Lady Granville, the Queen's sister. 'In fundamental things she leant on him: I have always felt how much the Queen was sustained by the King.'

One would have thought that the Queen was absolutely the mainstay of the family, but behind her was always the strength of the King. 'In a really big crisis he was the only quiet person, and would come out with an answer and decision so wise, so sound that one could only marvel,' said one of the Household. The Queen gave him the greatest moral support, and helped him in every way. But the person who was the head of the family was the King.

This development took place over years: it was not the sudden result of kingship. Indeed a remarkable diffidence lingered in the King. 'He had at first a feeling of inadequacy,' said a relative. 'He was the least self-pleased person in the world. I remember being touched when the King, in the first summer of his reign, was arranging his guest list for Balmoral. I remember him saying rather doubtfully, "Do you think they will really want to come?"'

The Sovereign is set apart from all his people, and divided by a wide gulf even from the rest of the Royal family. One immediate result of becoming Queen was that Queen Elizabeth saw considerably less of her husband. This was no new problem for a Queen Consort: when George V came to the throne, Queen Mary had felt deeply the new loneliness. It is felt the more strongly because, although the Queen Consort does not share his constitutional work with her husband, she does share much of the isolation and so, at the same time that she saw less of her husband, Queen Elizabeth found herself set at a distance from those around her.

The King and Queen were now apart for hours of every day. The King put in a full day's work at his desk, the Queen was fully occupied all morning at her desk, doing her correspondence with her Ladies-in-Waiting and Private Secretary. Yet no King was ever more constantly in the company of his wife. The Royal couple always lunched together, and they practically always dined together, sitting opposite each other across the table. They very rarely slept under different roofs. When they were parted, almost always because the King had to be away on official duty, they made long telephone calls to each other every evening, talking sometimes for an hour or more over a 'scrambled' line. Their week-ends remained the same when they escaped to The Royal Lodge, where everything was kept unchanged.

The constitutional work which falls upon the Sovereign is full of responsibility, and it requires hard, slogging desk-work, day in and day out. A continual stream of despatch-boxes, containing official papers of the most complex and exacting kind, 'head-aches' in every sense of the word, as well as a mass of routine paper work, come to the Sovereign's desk.

Edward VIII, who had been Heir Apparent for over twenty-five years, observed in his memoirs:

'... the ceremonial façade that provides the public with a romantic illusion of the higher satisfactions of kingship actually disguises an occupation of considerable drudgery.

'This fact was hardly a discovery to me. From long observation of my father's activities, I knew only too well what I was in for. The picture of him "doing his boxes", to use his own phrase, had long represented for me the relentless grind of the King's daily round.'

Even when on holiday in Scotland, King George VI could no

longer go out on the moors all day, but worked at his boxes until 11.30 or 12, before joining the guns on the hill. When he came back at tea-time, instead of sitting down and chatting to the Queen and his guests, he had to slip off 'to do his boxes', while in Buckingham Palace they occupied a considerable proportion of each day.

The King's Household never knew to what extent he discussed his constitutional affairs with Queen Elizabeth, but they took for granted that she knew everything. Without a doubt Queen Elizabeth knew far more of affairs of state than did Queen Alexandra or Queen Mary, but she never by word or sign indicated her knowledge.

Time and time again the King would be given certain papers, and he would take them away, presumably to show them to the Queen, before he would give an answer. He would show the Queen drafts of his speeches. 'Sometimes he would say, "I have talked to the Queen about that, and I shall do such and such." Generally the conclusions the King and Queen had reached were very good, but sometimes, because they were human, you had to say, "Are you quite sure, Sir?" Then they would think again. Their joint advice was extremely sound,' said a senior member of the Household. Although the King often asked the Queen's advice, his staff soon found out that it was not the slightest use trying to short-circuit the King by approaching the Queen direct. She invariably referred any such attempt to the King.

When the Private Secretaries were with the King, Queen Elizabeth would sometimes come into the room, generally towards the end of a session. She would not stay long, and she did not involve herself in the subject under discussion, but it was something that Queen Mary would not have felt able to do. 'When a tour was being planned,' said one of the Private Secretaries, 'the King and Queen sat round a table with us and worked it out, and the Queen was extremely helpful. We always sat down: the Queen was always very good about telling one to sit down, she thought about that sort of thing more than the King did.'

The Queen Consort's rôle is a curious anomaly. The Queen Consort is crowned by ancient custom although not by right (the male consort of a Sovereign Queen has only a very small part in the Coronation ceremony, when he takes an oath of allegiance to his Sovereign and wife).

The Queen Consort is part of the recognised pattern of Monarchy. Her position is secured in the Constitution, again unlike that of the husband of a Queen Regnant. By a statute of King Edward III 'It is equally high treason to compass the death of our lady the King's companion as of the King himself'. In Anson's *Law and Custom of the Constitution* the position of the Queen Consort is thus defined:

> 'The Queen Consort is a subject, though privileged in certain ways. Her life and chastity is protected by the law of treason. She has always been regarded as free from the disabilities of married women in matters of property, contract, and procedure. She could and can acquire and deal with property, incur rights and liabilities under contract, sue and be sued, as though she were *feme sole*. She has her separate officers and legal advisers. But in all other respects she is a subject, and amenable to the law of the land save in respect of some small privileges which are not in use. At one time she had a revenue from the demesne land of the Crown, and a portion of any sum paid to the King in return for a grant of any office or franchise. This was *arum reginae* or queen-gold. Provision is now made by statute for the maintenance of a Queen Consort.'

This provision is part of the annuities payable to the Sovereign and some other members of the Royal family, known as the Civil List, which is granted by Parliament upon the recommendation of a Select Committee. Queen Elizabeth's income was fixed at £40,000 per annum, subject to tax. Should she become a widow she was to receive an annuity of £70,000 per annum (subject to tax), the same as Queen Mary.

Queen Elizabeth now had the title of 'Her Majesty', the form of address used to a Queen and to an Empress. She was the last Empress of India, but she has never visited that continent, although the King and Queen planned to go there before the war.

After her Coronation, she would be entitled to wear that 'cincture or covering for the head worn by a King as mark of sovereignty, by a Queen regnant and by a Queen Consort'. She took precedence over every other lady in the Empire, including the dowager Queen Mary; and her elder daughter Princess Elizabeth, the Heiress Presumptive.

Queen Elizabeth had her own coat-of-arms, in which the canting or punning arms of the Bowes-Lyon family were impaled with the Royal Arms. In the quartered coat, the first and fourth quarters had a blue lion rampant with the double tressure flory counterflory on a white ground of Lyon, in the second and third quarter the three bows 'proper' on an ermine field of Bowes.

Queen Elizabeth's Standard was flown for the first time when she inspected The Queen's Bays at Aldershot on July 24, 1937. It was flown over Buckingham Palace for the first time when the King made a short visit to Sandringham in November 1937. Her Standard was flown over Buckingham Palace whenever the Queen was there without the King, but, following custom, not over any other Royal Palace, except at her express desire.

Her pages wore very dark blue livery, like the livery of the King's pages. The footmen wore scarlet livery.

On her birthday, scarlet robes were worn by the Judges of the King's Bench division, and the Union flag was hoisted over Government buildings; the Union flag was also hoisted on the anniversary of her marriage. Her birthday was a 'Collar Day', when the Knights of any British Order, when attending a Court levée or other Court ceremony in daytime—the collar was never worn after sunset—wore the collar of their senior British Order. When the Queen was present at evening dress functions, the men wore their Orders, miniature decorations and medals.

In the official toast list, the second Loyal toast was now, 'The Queen, Queen Mary and other members of the Royal Family', received standing and followed by the National Anthem.

At the State Opening of Parliament, Queen Elizabeth's throne, an exact replica of the Sovereign's, was placed level with that of the King. Up until the reign of Edward VII the throne for the Queen Consort had always been placed a little behind that of the King, but Edward VII had Queen Alexandra's throne drawn level with his own (Queen Victoria required the Prince Consort to *stand* behind her throne). Queen Elizabeth was the last Queen to ride in the State Coach to the opening of Parliament: the less elaborate Irish State Coach is now used instead.

In King George VI's Regency Act of 1937, Queen Elizabeth was the first Queen Consort to be named as eligible to be a Counsellor of State. There is no actual Council of State: the important papers which require the signature of the Sovereign (with certain major exceptions) are, if he is overseas or incapacitated by illness, signed by a quorum of two of his Counsellors of State, acting on his behalf.

During the first few years of King George VI's reign the Queen had no occasion to act as a Counsellor of State, as on the King's visit to Canada she accompanied him. But during the war, when he visited British forces in North Africa and Italy, and again in France and Belgium, and later still during his illnesses, Queen Elizabeth acted as a Counsellor of State. Then the papers, which are always taken individually to the Counsellors, were always taken first to Queen Elizabeth. When King George VI died his widow ceased to be eligible as a Counsellor of State but her daughter Queen Elizabeth II so worded her Regency Act of 1953 that Queen Elizabeth the Queen Mother is still eligible as a Counsellor of State, and so acts when the Queen is overseas.

Now the Queen had to appoint her own Household. While she was Duchess of York she had required only one Lady-in-Waiting; she had now to appoint a considerable establishment, including a Lord Chamberlain and a Mistress of the Robes. She chose men and women she knew and trusted.

Her Lord Chamberlain was the Earl of Airlie, K.C.V.O., M.C., a neighbour at Cortachy, which lies not so very far from Glamis, whom she had known since childhood, while his mother Mabell, Countess of Airlie, was for many years Lady-in-Waiting and close friend of Queen Mary.

Rear-Admiral Sir Basil Brooke, K.C.V.O., formerly Comptroller to the Duke of York and a popular member of the Household at 145, was appointed her Treasurer.

The Duchess of Northumberland, whom Queen Elizabeth appointed her Mistress of the Robes, held her appointment until shortly before her death. The Mistress of the Robes is the Queen's senior lady, and has special duties at a Coronation, and attends the

Queen on state occasions. She is responsible for the roster of Ladies-in-Waiting.

The Ladies of the Bedchamber were the Countess Spencer, the Viscountess Halifax, the Viscountess Hambleden and the Lady Nunburnholme. Ladies of the Bedchamber are always Peeresses, and one must be in attendance upon the Queen Consort on every public occasion at which the Sovereign is present, while they always attend the Queen Consort at Courts and other ceremonies.

The Women of the Bedchamber were Lady Helen Graham; Lady Katharine Seymour; Lady Hyde and Hon. Mrs. Geoffrey Bowlby. Lady Victoria Wemyss was Extra Woman of the Bedchamber. One of these Ladies was Extra Lady of the Bedchamber to Queen Mary, who was asked if she would release her. This she did most graciously, writing to her, 'I am glad you are going to the Queen, who needs you so much.' Twenty-five years later, Lady Helen Graham had died, but the other four ladies were still serving as extra Women of the Bedchamber.

Until the time of Queen Charlotte, wife of King George III, the Women of the Bedchamber had always to be present at the toilet of the Queen. Today one of the Women of the Bedchamber is always in waiting, in daily attendance on the Queen, her constant companion and acting as her secretary in many official and private matters. Both the Ladies of the Bedchamber and the Women of the Bedchamber are generally known as Ladies-in-Waiting.

Queen Elizabeth turned for advice particularly to Lady Helen Graham. Lady Helen was a tall woman, with almost white hair and very blue eyes. She was charming, intelligent, authoritative and a great social worker. Like the Queen, 'She welcomed you as though you were the one person in the world she wanted to talk to.' Lady Helen was closely in touch with many sides of life, and although she was not a person on whom one would presume, she got on well with all sorts of people. She had a great sense of fun, and a deep love for the open air and for her native Scotland.

To the young Household of the new Queen, Lady Helen was 'a wonderful support—we could never have got through it without her.' She was an able and methodical worker with high standards for herself and others, and she was good at delegating work. She was very wise, wonderfully encouraging, and she knew how to give a criticism when it was necessary. Lady Helen deeply loved the Queen and the Queen always could, and did, turn to her for advice. Her death in 1945 was not only the loss of a close personal friend but of a valued counsellor.

The work which the Queen would do was not clearly defined. A Queen Consort had no constitutional duties of her own, although she had some dual engagements with the King, such as the Opening of Parliament. Her work was mainly in support of the King, and she had also an area of duty and influence which was almost her own, particularly with regard to the social services benefiting women and young children, and the promotion of British and Empire trade through using and wearing British and Empire products.

For the most part the Queen Consort organises her own public work, through her own Household. If, however, Queen Elizabeth was accompanying the King on a public engagement, it was the duty of his Household to see that she was fully informed about the timetable—and especially the time of starting. Although Queen Elizabeth has a better sense of time than the extremely unpunctual Queen Alexandra, she is hardly as precise a timekeeper as was Queen Mary. The Master of the Household, who writes the Court Circular, had to be informed about the public engagements of the Queen Consort, so that they were correctly recorded.

In the intimate atmosphere of 145 Piccadilly, the small Staff consisting of the Comptroller and the Private Secretary to the Duke and the Lady-in-Waiting to the Duchess of York had been so closely in contact with them, and with each other, that everyone knew everything that was being planned. In the honeycomb of Buckingham Palace this was no longer possible. The King's Household and the Queen's Household were two separate entities and the Queen's plans, although always dovetailed with those of the King, were carried through independently.

The Queen's desk work had greatly increased. Queen Elizabeth has never been an over-methodical worker. Not for her the accountant's mind in which everything is reduced neatly and irrevocably to its proper little pigeon-hole. Queen Elizabeth is inflexible in matters of principle, but in details she may be moved by mood and impulse. She liked to put aside matters about which she felt disinclined to decide, and these would sometimes lie on one side for some time. Consequently the daily harvest of paper sheafed upon her desk tended to pile up. She had a little notice on her desk which read 'DO IT NOW', about which she once remarked, with a chuckle, 'I don't know why I have that there—I never *do*, you know.' When matters became pressing the Member of the Household who was responsible would come and tactfully re-introduce the subject. Queen Elizabeth would then search among the papers, saying disarmingly, 'Oh yes, of course you will want to know about that, won't you?'

Queen Elizabeth discovered, as Queen Mary had found earlier, that during the first months of the reign the Queen Consort has to deal with

> 'An enormous number of problems connected with the Royal palaces, the Household, hospital and other charitable patronage, and the preparations for the Coronation.' (*Queen Mary*: James Pope-Hennessy.)

The matter of Patronages was quite tricky. Queen Mary wished to retain a number of her Patronages, and of course did so. Others were specially associated with the Queen Consort and were taken on by Queen Elizabeth. In general, a Queen Consort gives her Patronage only to nationally important charities and organisations. Where she has been President of an association, she will often become the Patron. She usually gives up most of her more localised connections.

But this did not meet with Queen Elizabeth's approval at all. She was determined to maintain her connection with as many as possible of the little societies in which she took such a personal interest.

Among the new Patronages was that of Queen's College, Cambridge, thus renewing an association with the Queen of England which began in the first century of its existence. The Queen also carried on certain interests of former Queens Consort. At Sandringham, she gave the traditional Queen's Prize to a pupil from the King's Lynn High School for services to the school.

*   *   *

The Queen had also to give up many personal things. Some were trifling, but they meant a loss of informality, and withdrawal from the everyday world in which she had grown up.

From this time forward, Queen Elizabeth would always have to plan her movements and to inform those about her of even her least important arrangements. Even within the privacy of her home, she would continually have to think of the many others who would be affected by even her minor decisions.

As Duchess of York she had lunched and dined with friends in restaurants: she has never done so since she became Queen. The Duke and Duchess of York used to go out dancing, which they both enjoyed, often at the Four Hundred Club: after King George VI's Accession they only danced at home or—very occasionally—at a private ball. When they went to stay with friends, it could no longer be an informal, entirely private stay, and because of Private Secretaries, Ladies-in-Waiting, dressers and detectives, they were limited to staying in large houses where there were plenty of servants.

Possibly Queen Elizabeth missed moving freely less than many other women would have done. Her life was centred upon her husband and her children, and because her husband had always valued his home, and much preferred his wife's company to that of anyone else, the Duke and Duchess of York had been used to spend most of their leisure quietly.

The Accession of the King affected their daughters' lives also. 'Nothing in the Abdication cut so deep as the changed future for their children—it was hardest of all for their sake,' said Queen Elizabeth's brother, Sir David Bowes-Lyon. The King and Queen took great care from the time they entered the Palace not to let Buckingham Palace life come between them and their children. They had fixed times daily to go and see them, just as Queen Elizabeth II has now. But it was very different from the free and easy life at 145. Only at week-ends at The Royal Lodge was it just the same as it had always been.

How could they prepare Princess Elizabeth for the Crown without ruining her girlhood? How not to bring up the heir to the Throne was blue-printed in the well-meaning yet appallingly restrictive plans of Queen Victoria and Prince Albert for their eldest son: indeed our most successful Kings, among them George V and George VI, have often been second sons, who have escaped the earnest striving for perfection imposed upon the Heir Apparent.

Now Princess Elizabeth was Heiress Presumptive, and had to be brought up as the future Sovereign. Her parents had excellent material with which to work; Princess Elizabeth, now ten and a half years old, was straightforward, affectionate and happy. She had inherited the sense of duty of both parents, and while she had something of her father's shyness, it was much less than that which plagued his youth. At this time she was completely engrossed (when her lessons and other interruptions would permit) in country life. She has always loved dogs and horses. She was happy with her parents, met their friends with open courtesy, and was much loved by those around her.

To bring Princess Elizabeth up to be a normal, well-adjusted and happy woman had presented no great problem, but her future years would be mortgaged to her position. Her adult life would be spent in heavy and responsible duties. Her character and way of life would be held in a searchlight, her qualities an example to millions; her least foible dissected and exaggerated.

The King and Queen together worked out their plans, founded primarily on the building of character. For a modern constitutional Monarch, stability of character is far more important than brilliance, indeed flawed brilliance might be the most dangerous of all attributes.

Queen Elizabeth regards a wise person as much more than just a well-educated man or woman. Over and over again, in speeches which spring from her beliefs, she emphasises that education is of little value unless it is founded upon sound character. At Cambridge University, speaking to an academic audience, she said:

'In the breathless pursuit of technical mastery, we must not lose sight of something even more precious—the true purpose of education which is, surely, the making of human beings, by the training of the three aspects of man—body, mind and character.

'Human progress does not rest wholly upon what may be revealed by marvels of applied science—it depends also on what men see in life and what they choose to value in it . . . Do not, therefore, in today's tumult, lose sight of the ancient virtues of service, truth and vision.'

Queen Elizabeth has never doubted where character is formed —in the home. She has said (in New Zealand in 1958):

'I would like to say a special word to parents, especially to the young parents. In their hands lies the whole future of this Dominion. The pattern of their homes will be the pattern of the country.'

In her own home Queen Elizabeth led by example, she did not drive by threat. She never believed in a catalogue of 'don'ts'. For her, discipline is more subtle and is self-imposed. Queen Elizabeth's sense of duty and her obedience to the demands of duty are almost overdeveloped. Her acceptance of the demands of duty is so complete that there are none of the outward signs of conflict. It is a paradox—the good things of life are there, but you must discipline yourself against over-indulgence. Always duties must be fulfilled.

Queen Elizabeth has never subscribed to the view that there is any special merit in being uncomfortable, and certainly not in being unhappy. To be happy means to her to be good, and she does not believe that selfishness can lead to happiness.

Queen Elizabeth is a very wise woman and she has a very sure touch with her children. The two girls had a very happy upbringing.

When they moved into Buckingham Palace, to give Princess Elizabeth companionship and a sense of continuity Miss Margaret Macdonald, a Highland farmer's daughter who was assistant nannie at 145 Piccadilly, was asked to sleep in Princess Elizabeth's bedroom at the Palace; so began the long, valuable and happy friendship with Queen Elizabeth II which continues today.

King George VI and Queen Elizabeth planned together their daughter's formal education. An article in *The Times*, published shortly after the Accession, detailed Princess Elizabeth's course of study:

'It covers not only the normal school subjects, but many others, such as economics, upon which, as possible future Queen, she must be more than usually well informed. It is, indeed, a little frightening to contemplate the curriculum that confronts the heir to a modern Throne, languages, history, economics, deportment—these subjects and many others have to be studied more deeply than by ordinary school children. Princess Elizabeth is already making progress with French and German, Latin of course is essential for anyone who wishes to understand fully the working of British law and constitution, for many of the vital documents are in this "dead language".

'The King and Queen have helped her in her languages by speaking to her, and "French lunch" was quite an institution at "145".

'Queen Mary helps with deportment and bearing instruction and the Princess already shows signs of being exceptionally graceful in her bearing. Riding lessons, dancing lessons and music lessons have all helped to prevent Princess Elizabeth's education from becoming too "stodgy". She has regular hours of study like any school child and only the most exceptional event is allowed to interfere with them.'

When Queen Elizabeth was looking for a way to bring her daughter more into contact with other girls of her age, she naturally thought of the Girl Guide movement in which she had worked herself. She had already, before the Accession, planned that Princess Elizabeth should become a Guide.

Princess Elizabeth was enrolled in June 1937. Princess Margaret and another six-year-old became Brownies, attached to a special Buckingham Palace Company. The Princess Royal took the enrolment (she was to enrol Princess Anne a generation later) in the summer house in the grounds of Buckingham Palace. The King and Queen watched through the half-open door, but signalled that they did not want to show themselves. Later, the King's Piper played country music on his pipes, and the Princess Royal joined in 'The Dashing White Sergeant'. Then the Guides scattered into the grounds—one girl knocking into the Queen, who had stayed unobserved to watch the dancing. She laughed and waved her on.

Princess Elizabeth asked the Commissioner whether they would have to wear long stockings with their uniform, adding 'because

Mummy says we needn't'. This was something of a poser, as the Girl Guide authorities were at that time insisting upon stockings being worn with uniform: a compromise was reached by allowing the Princess to wear knee-length stockings.

The Buckingham Palace Company closed down at the outbreak of war, but was restarted as an evacuee company with the same leader at Windsor in 1942, with children from the Royal school in the Home Park and from a Hammersmith school evacuated to Windsor, together with a few girls from the Castle, and of course, Princess Elizabeth and Princess Margaret. The Guides met in winter in the Waterloo Chamber; in summer under the Castle walls.

King George VI and Queen Elizabeth continued to take a keen interest in their activities. When the Guides went into camp, they were unexpectedly visited by the King and Queen. The King's car was piled with cushions and chairs which he had thoughtfully brought out to the camp. Queen Elizabeth's contribution was a splendid meal sent down by horse brake: as she said they were engaged in so many activities that they would not have time for cooking.

When Princess Elizabeth was sixteen she became a Sea Ranger.

Princess Elizabeth later also received special tutoring in Constitutional History from Sir Henry Marten, the Vice-Provost of Eton College, and later still her father spoke to her often and seriously of his work as King, which would be her work as Queen Regnant. The war, which imposed the overriding consideration of the Princess's safety, set a more restricted pattern upon Princess Elizabeth's education than might otherwise have been the case.

After the Abdication, it was wished to stress the family life of King George VI, and in the early months of the reign Princess Elizabeth and Princess Margaret took a greater part in Court life than the children of Queen Elizabeth II and the Duke of Edinburgh do today.

'My first waiting,' recalls a Lady of the Bedchamber, 'was on March 16, 1937, at an afternoon party at Buckingham Palace, which was held from 4 to 6. I remember Princess Elizabeth and Princess Margaret were present—real little girls. It was all rather alarming and strange for them, but the Princesses were quite composed, if a little shy.'

Sometimes arrangements were made so that the Princesses could be present: the Coronation party for badly disabled soldiers, sailors and airmen, held by the 'Not Forgotten' Association in the grounds of Buckingham Palace, was specially arranged on an afternoon when the Princesses could come with the King and Queen, and the Princesses cut the special Coronation cakes.

When the reign became more firmly established and the demands of the schoolroom were more pressing, the Princesses were seen less in public.

Naturally Queen Elizabeth wanted to make changes. She was also most anxious to avoid hurting Queen Mary, and so changes were introduced gradually and gently. It was obvious Queen Elizabeth was making the office much more homely.

She managed to bring private affections into public life, yet she never gave away any of the essential dignity.

Queen Elizabeth set aside the protocol by which the King and Queen alone could introduce a fresh subject of conversation. She is interested in a wide range of subjects, and if any new topic is unsuitable for political or other reasons, she can adroitly turn the conversation into less controversial channels.

The private apartments at Buckingham Palace became less formal. The Queen's four-poster bed was brought from 145 Piccadilly. Her kidney-shaped dressing table with triple mirrors had satin skirts. A comfortable sofa was placed beside the fire. Books in their dust-jackets, magazines and gramophone records appeared on the big oval table in her bedroom, which was filled in the daytime with flowers.

Windsor Castle was only used on the more formal occasions of Easter and Ascot. The Queen had some of the private apartments redecorated and made some minor changes directed towards the greater comfort of her family, Household and guests. More bathrooms were installed with running hot and cold water: no longer did housemaids interminably carry burnished copper hot-water cans to every bedroom.

King George V had dined at 8.30 p.m., now dinner was served

at 9 p.m., and it was often the early hours of the morning before the Queen, and of course the Household and guests, retired. The King and Queen were both very fond of dancing, and they and their guests would dance in the Crimson Drawing Room, the largest of the Regency State Rooms. The King particularly enjoyed the Waterloo dinner, held on June 18, anniversary of the battle, in the Waterloo Chamber at Windsor. It was one of the first events he revived after the war.

Dress at Court was formal, even when dining in private. Black knee-breeches were worn with evening dress. At Windsor Castle, men of the Royal family and of the Household wore the Windsor uniform, which consisted of a dark-blue evening-dress coat with scarlet lapels and cuffs worn with knee-breeches. Even at Sandringham men wore evening dress and decorations for dinner every night until the outbreak of the Second World War.

Most of the old ceremonies and entertainments continued right up to that time. From the beginning of King George VI's reign, until the declaration of war with Germany in 1939, there were held fourteen Courts, two Court Balls and two Evening Presentation Parties. The last Court was held on July 13, 1939. After the war, the King and Queen held only one Evening Presentation Party, for the Diplomatic Corps, which took place in 1951. Levées at St. James's Palace continued until the war.

These occasions required a great deal of preparation. The guest list and invitations and the general form of the occasion were the province of the Lord Chamberlain and his staff at St. James's Palace. The actual preparation and carrying-out of the function was in the control of the Master of the Household. The Orders for a State Visit looked like Battle Orders, a thick sheaf of papers, amended and typed out freshly every time. From them each Member of the Staff knew exactly where he should be and what he should do.

The male indoor Staff at the beginning of King George VI's reign numbered seventy-two, all under the control of the Palace Steward. His second-in-command and deputy was the Yeoman of the Gold and Silver. Other heads of departments, each responsible for his own section, were the Yeoman of the Glass and China, the Yeoman of the Cellars and the Page of the

Chambers. The Sergeant Footman and the Deputy Sergeant Footman worked in close co-operation with the Palace Steward. The Housekeeper looked after the maids.

For an Evening Court all the drawing rooms were opened up, and buffets laid out in the Ball Supper Room, the Green Drawing Room and the Throne Room. On the buffets silver-gilt candelabras and plate were placed on the white cloths and the buffet suppers prepared.

On the evening, the servants wore livery. The senior servants wore black, heavily gold-braided uniforms with white breeches, white stockings and black silver-buckled shoes. The footmen wore scarlet livery decorated with gold braid, scarlet plush knee-breeches, white stockings and black silver-buckled shoes. The footmen wore their hair powdered. Ordinary wheat flour and very fine rice flour, procured from the chemist, were heated in a tin in the oven, then mixed with water and plastered on the hair, where it dried hard. It looked very fine, but was messy and disagreeable and often gave the footmen bad colds. Footmen went into powder again for the Coronation of Queen Elizabeth II, but since then the practice has been stopped, by the Queen's order.

The Queen's Page before the war wore a magnificent dark livery trimmed with gold braid and lined with white silk, creamy white breeches, a white waistcoat with broad gold braid, gold garters on white stockings, and black, silver-buckled shoes.

When everything was ready the Queen, and often the King too, when he could get away, came round and inspected the rooms. The Queen was quick to see any detail which should be bettered, and quick too to recognise and remark on good work which had been done.

All the entrances to Buckingham Palace were opened up, the Grand Entrance, the Privy Purse Door (used by the Household), the Visitors' Door, the Ambassadors' Entrance and the Garden Entrance (used by Members of the Royal family).

For a Presentation Party the Royal family proceeded from the private apartments, through the White Drawing Room, the Music Room, and the Blue Drawing Room to the Ballroom, where the King and Queen and all about them stood during the

Presentation of the Diplomatic Corps, which took some time. The King and Queen then seated themselves in the Throne Chairs, with the other members of the Royal family drawn up in a semi-circle behind them on the dais, the Lord Chamberlain standing at a lectern reading the names; first of the lady making the presentation, and then of the débutante, and the débutantes each came forward to make two deep curtseys, first to the Queen and then to the King, before passing through to the reception rooms.

For a State Ball, the Royal family similarly made their stately way to the Ballroom. The State Ball had always been opened with a State Quadrille, but by 1937 few people knew how to do it. The King and Queen therefore decided instead to have a good modern dance-band to play for modern dancing. When a well-known dance-band was engaged, the Court official concerned was asked, 'Do you want the full band?' 'Yes, of course,' was the reply, which resulted in the surprising but brief appearance in the orchestral gallery of the Ballroom of a glamorous and lightly-clad girl crooner! No one enjoyed their Ball more than the King and Queen, who danced until 5 in the morning.

Clothes play an important part in the life of a Queen Consort. Queen Elizabeth likes clothes and will take trouble with them. Sketches are submitted by her couturier, and from them she selects the dresses she wishes. Even to this matter-of-fact process Queen Elizabeth brings her individuality and consideration for others. Her couturier once made about twenty designs for her, and was later summoned to discuss them with her. His sketches were lying in two piles in front of Queen Elizabeth. First of all she went through the pile of discarded sketches, one by one, commenting on each. Then she laid them down reluctantly saying, 'They are absolutely charming—but I think *these* are even more delightful,' and she took up the sketches of the dresses which she had selected. 'If only other women would realise,' said her couturier, 'the effect of even a fraction of the charm and interest of Her Majesty, they would always have *service de luxe.*'

The necessary fittings can be tedious for both fitted and fitter, but Queen Elizabeth maintains an unusual level of freshness. 'We didn't get at all tired fitting the Queen Mother, very different from fitting some so-called grand women,' wrote Mme. Ginette Spanier in her book *It Isn't All Mink*.

The Queen knows what suits her, and has always liked for herself the feminine rather than the strict. She likes subtle colours and often wears different materials dyed to one exactly matching shade. She has always worn a lot of blue. When in public she often chooses pastel colours including lilac, dusty pink and pale blue, which can easily be seen at a distance and which, during the war, had the advantage that they did not show the all-pervading blitz dust as much as darker clothes. She also wears rich reds and blues.

Although Queen Elizabeth looks extremely handsome in black and had a favourite and beautiful black velvet evening dress, she seldom wears black. Queen Elizabeth likes full evening dress, and will wear it with tiara and necklace *en suite*, when attending a semi-private function. She always wears high heels; even her country shoes, which are thick brogues with tackets in the soles, are specially made for her with half-heels. A rare concession to age—is that recently she has worn lower heels.

Although she has, of course, a considerable and changing wardrobe of dresses, there are some old possessions of which she is very fond. There is a story that a former Dresser, when Queen Elizabeth visited her in retirement, exclaimed as she rose from her curtsey, 'Not still that old handbag, your Majesty!'

Queen Elizabeth has a rather old-fashioned black umbrella with a gold pencil fitted into the handle. In Australia in 1958 her Lady-in-Waiting picked up the wrong umbrella after watching a cricket match in unseasonable weather. When the right umbrella was returned to her, Queen Elizabeth remarked that she was delighted to get it back, as she had had it since her marriage and was very fond of it.

King George VI took great interest in Queen Elizabeth's clothes. He delighted in the Queen's beauty and it was he who suggested perhaps her most effective dresses, the evening dresses based on the Winterhalter portraits in Buckingham Palace which the King himself pointed out to Mr. Norman Hartnell. Once the King thought that a sketch submitted to Queen Elizabeth looked as if it were being modelled by the Queen herself, although the sketched figures were always kept deliberately anonymous. 'Is this meant to be the Queen?' he asked in an icy voice, at which Queen Elizabeth quickly intervened, saying, 'Oh no, dear. I only wish I were as beautiful as that.'

Queen Elizabeth dresses for a great occasion with the intuitive skill of a great artist. She has an eye for the colour or detail which will stand out in a group. Every movement is graceful and effective: she imposes an effect of composition upon the most casual group to which she is speaking. 'When Queen Elizabeth comes in, you have eyes for no one else,' remarked a man who is by no means easily bowled over. 'I thought she was the most beautiful woman I have ever seen.' Joyce Mather conveyed this quality in the *Yorkshire Post* when she wrote of Queen Elizabeth at Ascot:

> 'The Queen was an unforgettable picture under the sun-dappled trees. She swung her little, feathery cape in one hand. The chiffon panels of her dress floated in the wind. The sun struck rose lights out of the diamonds pinned on the softly folded corsage of her dress. She bowed to the curtseying women . . . she is lovelier far than I thought . . .

On April 13, 1937, the Crown jewels, which had remained in the possession of Queen Mary during King Edward VIII's reign, as he had no Queen to wear them, were made available to Queen Elizabeth. This is the jewellery which belongs to the Sovereign, and is at the disposal of his Consort, but is not a personal possession. It is a large collection of jewellery, varying from fabulously valuable and historic jewels to a quantity of pieces of only sentimental importance, such as mourning rings for forgotten Royal Dukes and Princes of the eighteenth and nineteenth centuries.

Important jewellery suits Queen Elizabeth. Her great, creamy pearls, among the finest in the world, glow against her skin. The diamonds in her brooch and on her wrist sparkle as she moves. Jewellery, when she wears it, does not seem cold and hard, but shimmering and alive with the reflection of the colours she is wearing.

Some of the most important decisions facing Queen Elizabeth at the beginning of King George VI's reign concerned the Coronation. Because of the decision to keep the date arranged for the Coronation of Edward VIII there were only five months instead of, as was usual, and desirable, more than a year in which to prepare everything. (It took sixteen months to make ready for the Coronation of Queen Elizabeth II.) Five months may seem plenty of time, but actually it imposed a great strain upon the jewellers, robemakers and couturiers who undertook delicate and time-consuming work in preparing the crowns, making and embroidering the robes, and making the Coronation dress, and the dresses for the attendants.

Queen Mary had gifted the crown made for her to her successors, but she took an active and able part in the plans for the Coronation, and she had decided to break the unwritten but ancient tradition that a dowager Queen never attended the Coronation of her successor. Queen Mary's natural wish to attend the Coronation ceremony was warmly welcomed, but it did mean that a new crown had to be made in haste for Queen Elizabeth.

There could be no delay: in January 1937, the Crown Jeweller was summoned to Sandringham for preliminary discussions. Designs for the crown were sketched and submitted for the consideration of the King and Queen and the most likely were mocked up in painted metal models. Some had eight arches like Queen Mary's crown; some had four arches, like the Imperial State crown. They were fitted with purple velvet caps turned up with imitation ermine, so that the Queen could try them on her head. So difficult was the choice, that for a time during the winter and early spring King George VI and Queen Elizabeth saw the Crown Jeweller at 5 o'clock on most evenings. Eventually a design with four rather square-shaped arches was chosen.

The stones for the circlet base of the Queen's crown came from the Regal circlet of 1858 made of diamonds supplied by Queen Victoria: this regal circlet had consisted of four fleurs-de-lys and four cross pattées. The base had contained sixteen large diamonds and sixteen quatre-foils, and also four Greek honeysuckle ornaments, one of which was adapted to take the Koh-i-Noor, which could be detached and worn separately. The circlet had been slightly altered for Queen Alexandra in 1901 and later the Koh-i-Noor had been removed for Queen Mary's crown. When the jewels were removed, the gold and silver mount of the Regal circlet was lent for exhibition in the London Museum.

The Koh-i-Noor was now removed from Queen Mary's crown (where it was replaced with a brooch containing the heart-shaped fifth part of the Star of Africa) and set in the new crown. Still more diamonds were required for the arches, the monde and the cross pattée, and these were supplied by the Crown Jewellers, with the exception of one stone. This is the drop-shaped diamond in the top cross pattée, a fine stone from the treasury of Lahore presented to Queen Victoria in 1851.

Queen Elizabeth has worn this new circlet several times since her Coronation; she wore it when she attended the ceremonial Openings of Parliament, and she followed the custom of Queen Mary in wearing the circlet at the first Evening Court of each sessions; she also wore it at her daughter's Coronation.

A few Crown Jewels were also altered or re-set for Queen Elizabeth.

King George was secretly preparing a magnificent present for his Queen. In spite of the great store of Crown and personal Royal jewellery, like all collections, however large, it has certain weaknesses. There was, for instance, only one jewelled Thistle Badge and Star. The King joked, 'We have only one Thistle—I wear it one night, the Queen the next.' So he had made for his wife a superb Thistle Badge and Star, of very fine South African diamonds, which he gave to her just after the Coronation.

Meanwhile there were discussions about the Coronation robe. Queen Elizabeth chose a robe similar in pattern to that of Queen Alexandra, with a combined cape and train. The white ermine cape was worn over the arms. (In 1953 Queen Elizabeth II's cape was cut away to come under the arms.) It was fastened on the shoulders with white satin bows, and with gold cord and tassels.

The train was made of fine Royal purple velvet forty-four inches (two widths of the velvet) wide, and eighteen feet long. The yarn was 'thrown' (twisted preparatory to dyeing and weaving) by James Pearsal and Company, from silk spun by Lady Hart Dyke's silkworms in Kent, and woven by Warner Brothers at Braintree in Essex. It was then richly embroidered at the Royal School of Needlework with the emblems of the ten countries of the British Empire. Three rows of gold galloon lace ran round the train. The train was lined and faced with ermine.

After the Coronation, when the robe had been exhibited at St. James's Palace, it was also sent to the London Museum for exhibition, but first the fine ermine lining, though not the facing of the train, was removed for further use, and mock ermine substituted.

Queen Elizabeth required other robes. At the Opening of Parliament she wore a Royal robe of crimson velvet with a train six yards long, with a large ermine cape decorated with two rows of two-inch gold lace with three-quarter-inch scalloped lace in between. It was not, however, made specially for her, as the Royal family always uses existing family mantles and robes when they are available. Queen Elizabeth wore Queen Alexandra's Garter mantle, which was refurbished for her, but a dark green Thistle mantle was now made, and later, in 1939, the dark blue mantle of the Royal Victorian Order.

Her Coronation dress was made by Messrs. Handley Seymour of New Bond Street, and was cut in a princess style with square décolleté and slashed sleeves flounced with old lace. It was embroidered in gold and diamanté with emblems of the British Isles and the Dominions.

Queen Elizabeth also had to approve the designs for the dresses, robes and circlets worn by her daughters. Princess Elizabeth and Princess Margaret Rose were given Princesses' Coronation robes of purple velvet, lined and edged for two inches with ermine, but without tails, with three rows of gold lace on the train next to the ermine edging: little ermine capes, gold cords and tassels tied them on each shoulder; and light gilt circlets. She decided, after consultation with those concerned, the dresses of the Mistress of the Robes; of the Queen's trainbearers, who wore Hartnell dresses of stiff white Duchess satin, with embroidered garlands in pearls, diamanté and crystal in a wheat-ear motif; for the four Duchesses, dressed by Molyneux in heavy white and gold faille brocade in a rose design (wearing red velvet kirtles and trains, trimmed with ermine), who held the canopy over her at the moment of crowning.

As the day of the Coronation approached the pace quickened. There were many family and official gatherings. Queen Mary gave special presents to the King and Queen, including a diamond and tortoiseshell fan which had belonged to Queen Alexandra. King George conferred his Family Order on his closest women relatives and bestowed other Orders on those around him. He conferred an earldom of the United Kingdom upon the Earl of Strathmore, his wife's father, whose earldom was Scottish.

Queen Elizabeth gave her badge to her Ladies-in-Waiting. This consists of a monogram 'E' in diamonds, which is worn on official occasions, such as garden parties, so that the Lady-in-Waiting can be easily recognised.

At last it was May 12, 1937, the day of the Coronation. The King and Queen had been awakened very early by the noises of loudspeaker testing, bands playing, troops marching and the sounds of the patient yet wonderfully cheerful crowds outside—who stood for as much as eighteen hours in chilly showery weather to see the King and Queen pass to and from Westminster Abbey.

The hours of dressing and waiting before it was time to leave the Palace were the most trying of the day, but at last, at 10.30 a.m., the golden Coronation coach, drawn by eight grey horses, rolled out of the central gateway of the Palace, the cumulation of a long and magnificent Coronation procession which King George VI and Queen Elizabeth never saw. Their view of their own procession was confined to the three Indian Maharajahs who rode just ahead of the coach as honorary Indian aides-de-camp to the King, and beyond, part of the Sovereign's escort of Household Cavalry, led by the massed bands of the Household Cavalry, whose martial music was overwhelmed by the cheers of the crowds on either hand. On one side of the coach, as Field-Marshal commanding the troops, rode an old friend, Field-Marshal the Earl of Cavan, who had gone with them on their 1927 tour to Australia and New Zealand; on the other the Master of the Horse, the Duke of Beaufort, who had married one of Queen Elizabeth's bridesmaids. The coach drove at walking pace by way of the Mall, Admiralty Arch and Whitehall, arriving at Westminster Abbey just before 11 a.m.

There King George and Queen Elizabeth entered the annexe always built for a Coronation in front of the west door of

Westminster Abbey, which was constructed of concrete, with doors of elmwood in a curious grey colour made from the foundations of the old Waterloo Bridge, which had recently been demolished. The interior was hung with tapestries, and here, in a large hall, the processions slowly formed.

'They were very, very nervous in the Annexe before the ceremony,' said an eye-witness. They felt deeply the significance of the Coronation. At last, the processions formed. The Queen's procession began to move first into Westminster Abbey, where a distinguished congregation of seven thousand people waited. Then there was a further delay when one of the Presbyterian chaplains fainted.

This was not only a long, complex and extremely tiring ceremony through which they must pass perfectly, it was also the taking of a most solemn oath of service, a dedication to their life of duty. Sincerely and simply religious, as they both were, it was of the utmost importance to them.

One of their office bearers recalls, 'I think that her Coronation Day was the first time I recognised this unusual quality which Queen Elizabeth has for drawing all eyes to her, so that you do not notice that other people are present at all. The Duchess of Northumberland [the Queen's Mistress of the Robes, who followed closely behind Queen Elizabeth in her procession] is a fine-looking woman, yet we never looked at her. Queen Mary looked so majestic that when she entered I feared she would completely overshadow the younger woman, yet that was not so.'

The long service began. For the whole of the first part of the ceremony only the King took active part. Queen Elizabeth, bareheaded with her brown hair centre parted (her daughter wore a diadem until the time of crowning, her husband wore a purple velvet Cap of Maintenance) sat, stood or knelt at her Chair of Estate, immediately in front of the Royal box. Queen Elizabeth's daughters and her parents were in the front row of the box, in company with Queen Mary, who wore magnificent cloth of gold embroidered with crystals and diamanté in a cascading design of roses and fuchsias; Queen Maud of Norway; the Duchess of Gloucester; the Duchess of Kent; and the Princess Royal, sitting beside Princess Margaret, the youngest person in the Abbey. The

Princesses were wearing princess-style long dresses of ivory lace over satin, trimmed with gold bows and sash, with robes of Coronation purple velvet with narrow bands of ermine, and on their heads specially light coronets.

For the first time, the ceremony of Coronation was broadcast.

Only after King George VI had been crowned and had been led to the throne-chair in the centre of the theatre and there received homage from his brother and the senior peers of each rank, did the Archbishop of Canterbury leave the King on his throne to go to the altar for the crowning of the Queen Consort, a rite going back to Saxon days. With a Bishop on either side of her Queen Elizabeth rose, and left her Chair of Estate; as she moved forward to the steps of the altar she stole a look at her daughters in the Royal box.

She knelt while the Archbishop prayed (in the words of the Order of Service):

'Almighty God, the fountain of all goodness: give ear we beseech thee to our prayers, and multiply thy blessing upon thy servant ELIZABETH, whom in thy Name, with all humble devotion, we consecrate our Queen; defend her evermore from all dangers, ghostly and bodily; make her a great example of virtue and piety, and a blessing to the kingdom; through Jesus Christ our Lord, who liveth and reigneth with thee, O father, in the unity of the Holy Spirit, world without end. Amen.

'*This prayer being ended, the Queen shall arise and come to the place of her anointing; which is to be at the faldstool set for that purpose before the Altar, between the steps and King Edward's Chair. There shall she kneel down, and four Peeresses, appointed for that service, holding a rich pall of cloth of gold over her, the Archbishop shall pour the Holy Oil upon the crown of her head saying these words:*

'In the name of the Father, and of the Son, and of the Holy Ghost: let the anointing with this Oil increase your honour and the grace of God's Holy Spirit establish you, for ever and ever. Amen.'

The four Duchesses, of Norfolk, Rutland, Roxburghe and Buccleuch, held over her the same canopy of cloth of gold with four silver staves that had been held over the King. Queen Elizabeth was anointed with oil upon the head only, whereas the King was anointed on the palms of both hands, on the breast and on the crown of the head.

> '*Then shall the Archbishop receive from the Keeper of the Jewel House the Queen's Ring, and put it upon the fourth finger of her right hand saying:*
> 'Receive this ring, the seal of a sincere faith; and God, to whom belongeth all power and dignity, prosper you in this your honour, and grant you herein long to continue, fearing him always, and always doing such things as shall please him, through Jesus Christ our Lord. Amen.'

The Queen's ring, worn previously by Queen Adelaide, Queen Alexandra and Queen Mary, is a ruby surrounded by brilliants, with smaller rubies set round the outset of the ring: it was placed on the fourth finger of the right hand, which used, before the Reformation, to be the 'wedding ring' finger in this country, as it still is in some Continental countries. Queen Elizabeth wore it for the rest of that day.

> '*Then the Archbishop shall take the Crown from off the Altar into his hands, and reverently set it upon the Queen's head, saying:*
> 'Receive the Crown of glory, honour and Joy: And God, the crown of the faithful, who by our Episcopal hands (though unworthy) doth this day set a crown of pure gold upon your head, enrich your royal heart with his abundant grace, and crown you with all princely virtues in this life, and with everlasting gladness in the life that is to come, through Jesus Christ our Lord. Amen.
> '*The Queen being crowned, all the Peeresses shall put on their coronets.*'

Many thought this moment the most beautiful of the whole day.

> '*Then shall the Archbishop put the Sceptre into the Queen's right hand, and the Ivory Rod with the Dove into her left hand, and say this prayer:*

'O Lord, the giver of all perfection: Grant unto this thy servant ELIZABETH our Queen, that by the powerful and mild influence of her piety and virtue, she may adorn the high dignity which she hath obtained through Jesus Christ our Lord. Amen.'

The Queen's sceptre was made for Queen Mary of Modena, wife of King James II. Two feet ten inches in length it is made of gold ornamented with diamonds. The ivory rod with dove was also made for Mary of Modena. Three feet one and a half inches in length, it is made of three slim pieces of ivory joined by bosses of chased gold. It has a white enamelled dove with closed wings (in contrast to the King's sceptre with dove which has spread wings) perched on a monde, decorated with enamel emblems of thistles, roses and fleurs de lys in colour.

'The Queen being thus anointed, and crowned, and having received all her ornaments, shall arise and go from the Altar, supported by two Bishops, and so up to the Throne. And as she passeth by the King on his throne, she shall bow herself reverently to his Majesty, and then be conducted to her own throne, and without any further ceremony, take her place in it.'

The Queen's throne, on the left of that of the King, and of the same design, was on a dais three steps above the floor, whereas the King's was two steps higher.

The newly crowned King and Queen, removing their crowns, received Communion, and afterwards the King put on the Imperial State Crown in place of the heavier St. Edward's Crown, and the Queen replaced her Crown for the formal procession from the Abbey. Then, after a delay of half an hour, the Procession re-formed for the longer return route to Buckingham Palace, by way of Parliament Square, the Victoria Embankment (packed with children), Northumberland Avenue, Trafalgar Square, Pall Mall, St. James's Street, Piccadilly, Regent Street, Oxford Street, Park Lane, Hyde Park Corner, Constitution Hill and home to Buckingham Palace.

At Hyde Park Corner television cameras were waiting for the procession, to make the first outside television broadcast in the world. The visual signals from these cameras were carried to

Alexandra Palace over a special type of cable installed by the Post Office.

The crowds were dense and enthusiastic, in spite of heavy rain which coincided with the return procession, and great crowds massed outside Buckingham Palace that evening, calling for the King and Queen, who appeared five times upon the balcony.

The Coronation was over. Only five months had gone past since the confused days of the abdication, yet the tentative days of apprenticeship were past, and King George VI and Queen Elizabeth entered with growing confidence into their reign. 'The Queen and I,' said King George VI in his broadcast on the evening of their Coronation day, 'will always keep in our hearts the inspiration of this day.'

CHAPTER NINE

THE EBB OF PEACE

They reigned for such a short time before the war

One of Queen Elizabeth's Household

AFTER the Coronation there are traditional celebrations—State drives in London, an inspection of the Fleet at Spithead, and tours to Scotland, Wales and Northern Ireland.

In 1937, the tour of Northern Ireland was the last of these, and took place in July. Serious I.R.A. violence was forecast, and caused apprehension. On the first day of the visit, continental newspapers actually carried an 'account' of the attempted assassination of King George VI and Queen Elizabeth. In the event, there was minor disturbance only, a Customs post was burnt down, some railway trucks were mined, and a land-mine went off in Belfast, causing no particular damage.

The welcome was considerably noisier. It began in Belfast Lough itself, when hundreds of men and women, young and old, took off their shoes and stockings and waded for half a mile through shallow water to the Holyhead sandbank close to the dredged channel, and cheered loudly as the Royal yacht *Victoria and Albert* steamed past.

The King and Queen stepped ashore in Belfast to a bedlam of cheering, which hardly stopped during the nine-hour day. At Lisburn it was only the second time a King passed through—the first being William III on his way to the Battle of the Boyne. The Queen, to give the dense crowds a chance to see her, unexpectedly accompanied the King when he was inspecting a guard of ex-servicemen. A nod from a member of the official party was optimistically interpreted by the crowd as a signal to come closer, whereupon:

'The enthusiasm of the crowd became absolutely uncontrollable . . . hundreds surged over the barriers and gathered round their Majesties, who were obviously delighted with such a tremendous reception' (*The Northern Whig and Belfast Post*).

Perhaps the most testing moment in the visit to Northern Ireland was King George VI's speech in the Council Chamber at Belfast, after he had received the Loyal Address. Rumours about his speech difficulties had preceded him and had caused concern in Northern Ireland, as elsewhere. *The Northern Whig and Belfast Post* wrote:

'Would the King speak? It was a question which everyone asked and the delight of the company when His Majesty stepped a short pace forward on the dais was obvious in the hush of expectancy.

'His voice, reminiscent of his father's in the depth of its tone, but free from the huskiness that was characteristic of King George V's, halted a little at first, but as he came to recall his former visit in 1924, and to speak of his pleasure at being once again with the loyal people of Northern Ireland, he gathered confidence, and except that a pause here and there was prolonged a little, there was only the faintest trace of the nervous disturbance which makes public speaking a task for him . . .

'His speech finished, the King turned to the Queen with a slight smile, to receive in return a quick smile of encouragement that captured the sympathy of everyone who noticed it.'

After the visit had ended, the same paper summed up the feeling in Northern Ireland:

'Those who were privileged to see His Majesty in Ulster noted with the greatest satisfaction the evidence both of physical vigour and of that strength of character which enabled him, with calm courage, to assume the Sovereign's rank in compliance with the will of his people . . .

'At his side was the smiling and radiant Queen, whose grace and charm, added to splendid qualities of mind and heart, have enthroned her in the affections of the whole Empire. Their Majesties have now completed their round of Coronation visits, by means of which they have not merely heightened their personal popularity, but have made the Throne even more securely founded upon the solid basis of constitutional usage and popular assent.'

The King and Queen had been pitchforked into the jungle of international politics at an alarming moment. During the period of twenty-eight months between the Coronation of King George VI and September 3, 1939, when war was declared with Germany, it sometimes seemed in Britain as though two musical scores were being played at once. Against the calm melody of peaceful things at home there broke in ever more loudly a cacophony of violence from Nazi Germany.

The responsibility of the Sovereign must always be a heavy burden, but the despatch boxes in those years made particularly grim reading for King George VI. He faced the future courageously, but the strain was often intense. More than ever he needed the calm atmosphere which his wife created for him. The Queen threw herself into making the best of each day as it came, and she kept her forebodings about the future to herself. Meanwhile there were public duties to perform. Queen Elizabeth particularly interested herself in better housing. She made a series of unofficial visits to many of the poorer parts of London, to see slum conditions and what was being done to relieve them—not only new housing schemes, but the reconditioning of damp basements and poor old houses. Her calls were unheralded—sometimes the tenants were out. She liked to see everything, especially the kitchen: 'and she chatted to me as though she was my neighbour from over the fence', as one housewife put it. Occasionally she was told 'the kettle's on the boil', and if there was time she stayed for a cup of tea.

Whatever public duty the King and Queen were undertaking, time was almost always found for a visit to a local housing scheme. From personal observation, they could compare the merits of the trim three-roomed houses designed for a rental of £15 a year in Lanarkshire; the four-bedroomed houses with a fine view of the hills of Durham, for which the tenants paid 9/3d. a week; houses in Birmingham built of 'screened concrete resembling brick', which, for very poor families, were furnished with gifted furniture. The Queen saw the badly water-logged, rotting slums of Gateshead which were being pulled down, and then visited a family in Victoria Road re-housed in a modern four-room brick house; she commented that even its modest rental of 10/9d. a week was heavy for the men of the house, who, in two and a half years, had only three weeks' work.

King George and Queen Elizabeth gradually built up a considerable knowledge of what was being done. When they went north to open the Empire Exhibition in Glasgow in 1938, they spent four hours at the exhibition itself and two days going round industrial plant, welfare clubs, and housing schemes in Renfrewshire and Lanarkshire, which remained badly hit areas of unemployment at a time when recovery of trade was making life easier in many parts of Britain. Twenty per cent of all insured persons were unemployed in Lanarkshire—24·7 per cent in Hamilton, 28 per cent in Airdrie.

The King and Queen took a keen interest in various Ministry of Labour training schemes, to enable workers to switch into another industry where there was a better chance of employment, and to train young men and women who had never had regular employment since leaving school.

Home industries were set up by public and private organisations so that wives could earn a bit and tide things over while their men were out of work, and these the Queen encouraged both by attending exhibitions of work and by making generous personal purchases, to which publicity was given to encourage others to do the same: for instance, from an exhibition of hand-quilting by miners from the hard hit areas of Durham and South Wales, she ordered quilts and dressing-gowns to be made for her and for the Princesses.

Abroad things were blacker still. Hitler's threats, backed by vigorous re-arming, were making it painfully clear to those in authority that our defence, which had run down almost to a stop, would have to be hastily wound up again.

The people of Britain were slow to interest themselves in grim and costly preparations for the war they hoped would never come. The King, assisted by Queen Elizabeth, spent much time in stressing the imperative need for national defence. Preparations for some protection against the threat of air attack had to be made. The King and Queen—and through them the general public—were shown their first Air Raid Protection centre in Leeds in October 1937.

'A small party of the new air raid wardens was on parade, wearing steel helmets and respirators over civilian clothing,' commented *The Times* in a very long account, typical of the coverage given by the Press in general. The Royal party examined different types of gas-mask, which contained finely powdered charcoal. The King showed the Princess Royal (they were staying with her at Harewood House) a gas-mask from the Great War and how it pinched the nostrils together, making it almost impossible to speak. Lord Harewood and Mr. Alan Lascelles, the King's Private Secretary, put on the new gas-masks and demonstrated that they could still talk. They saw a 'Home Office Gas Van' through which volunteers were passing, and decontamination plans.

The King, often alone, sometimes accompanied by the Queen, made many inspections of troops and of army living conditions. ARP exercises were put on at Windsor Castle. Much was made of both 'modern methods of warfare' and 'what is being done to house the modern soldier in comfort'.

When the Territorial Army was being expanded, the King and Queen accepted the 'T.A.' Badges, Number One and Number Two—the badges were all numbered to increase the sense of personal service. A unit of the Territorial Army for the first time mounted the King's Guard at Buckingham Palace: it was drawn from the Honourable Artillery Company and attracted considerable notice, as the men were wearing khaki uniforms.

During this time, Queen Elizabeth was anxious about the health of her mother. At one time of crisis, when Lady Strathmore was in a London nursing home, the Queen, who had a houseful of important political guests, motored every day from Windsor to see her mother, returning to be the imperturbable and gracious hostess.

Lady Strathmore was an exceptional person, a constant source of strength and joy to her close-knit family. To the last she maintained a lively interest in all her loved ones, and her fading strength deeply distressed them. The Queen continued steadily with her public duties and even on the last day of her mother's life, when she paid her fourth visit to the Mothercraft Training Society at Cromwell House, Highgate, she showed no signs of strain, though she afterwards hurried to her mother's bedside.

At 2 a.m. on the morning of Tuesday, June 23, 1938, the Countess of Strathmore died in her London home, in the presence of her husband and children, and the King who was her son-in-law. She was seventy-five years old. It is impossible to convey what Lady Strathmore meant to her family. She was the pillar by which a whole idyllically happy way of life had been supported, a guide and counsellor in all kinds of trouble, and a gay and bubbling personality, even in old age, in whose presence life always seemed so very much worth living.

Lady Strathmore was profoundly missed by her friends, who were of all ages. Those now living who knew her speak of her with quite a special affection. Tributes to her at the time included the following, in *The Times*:

'She possessed a genius for family life—a most rare and priceless gift. She had a great power of loving, which always brings pain, and the loss of her four children, especially that of her eldest girl, a child of eleven, left wounds which never healed, but these sorrows gave her an unusual power of sympathy and a rare understanding of other people.

'Lady Strathmore called forth an exceptional feeling of admiration and love from all who came into contact with her.

'It was once said of her by an older woman that she was perfect in all her relationships of life and when one thinks of her as daughter, wife and mother, one realises that it was true and she had friends in every walk of life.

'She was beautiful to the end, and had great fascination and charm, and her manner to young and old was perfection. She had a great enjoyment of anything that amused her, and an enchanting laugh . . . She possessed great courage . . . and a power of endurance which never allowed her to give in or feel self-pity. She had great wisdom and her advice was always of value. It was said by a member of her family that she never asked them questions and therefore was told everything.'

The Archbishop of Canterbury, the Most Rev. Cosmo Gordon Lang, speaking at Lady Strathmore's memorial service, said:

'She raised a Queen in her own home, simply, by trust and love, and as a return the Queen has won widespread love.

'Her charm and graciousness were not due to any conscious effort but the simple outflow of her spirit. Her many thoughts, words and acts of kindness flowed from the deep sense of charity within her heart.'

Lady Strathmore's death occurred only five days before the King and Queen were due to leave for France on the first State Visit of their reign, a State Visit of particular importance because of the urgent need to find a closer *rapport* with the French in the deteriorating European situation. The Queen was resolved to go, if only the visit could be put off for a short time; and M. Lebrun, President of France, at once suggested the visit should be postponed for three weeks.

The funeral of Lady Strathmore took place at Glamis, on a day of torrential rain. After a private service in the Chapel in Glamis Castle, the coffin was borne by a farm-cart through the rain to the burial ground over a half a mile away, followed by a long column of mourners, among them the King, bareheaded. When the cortège arrived at the graveside, the rain, which had been pounding down steadily for some days, increased to cloudburst force, smashing the flower wreaths and soaking everyone present.

The King prevailed upon the Queen and the Earl of Strathmore to remain in their car, while he and other principal mourners helped to carry the many wreaths to the graveside, he himself carrying the cross of white carnations and blue irises from Princess Elizabeth and Princess Margaret. He then returned to escort his wife and father-in-law to the graveside, for the service of committal held by the Bishop of St. Andrews, whose voice could scarcely be heard above the noise of the rain.

The King and Queen then went to Birkhall, on Deeside, for a

few days before returning to London. They observed family mourning, but Court mourning was not declared out of consideration for the many plans made for the London season, which was at its height.

On July 19, King George VI and Queen Elizabeth, who was wearing black, embarked in the Escort Vessel *Enchantress*, which did duty as Admiralty yacht. They crossed the Channel on a day of thick mist, escorted by eight 'E'-class destroyers of the Fifth Flotilla,—*Electra*, *Escort*, *Express*, *Esk*, *Escapade*, *Eclipse*, *Echo*, and *Encounter*—and an air escort of eighteen Anson machines from Bircham Newton aerodrome. In mid-Channel they were received by a French escort of seven destroyers, all flying the Union flag at the masthead in honour of their visitors.

This was the King and Queen's third official visit to Paris; in July 1930 they had been on a four-day visit to the French Colonial Exhibition, and in November 1935 to the St. Andrew's Night Ball in aid of the British Hospital in Paris. They had also visited Paris privately on their way to and from East Africa in 1924–25.

It was their first visit abroad since King George VI's Accession, and it was the first British State Visit to Paris since 1914.

The Parisians had prepared a great welcome for them. As the King and Queen alighted from the blue train which had brought them to the specially re-opened ceremonial railway station in the Bois de Boulogne, they were greeted by enormous cheering crowds and a salute of one hundred and one guns; thousands of white doves were released: and a huge Union Jack measuring one thousand five hundred square yards and believed the largest flag ever made, was flown from the Eiffel Tower.

The Queen had changed into a white two-piece dress and coat, edged with a wide border of silver fox. From the Parisians' first view of the King and Queen, bowing and waving as they drove in state along the Champs Élysées, escorted by the Republican Guard and Moroccan Spahis, the visit proved an outstanding success. Paris was one maze of colour and roaring, cheering crowds. The French royally entertained their guests with banquets, gala performances and receptions, organised with true French distinction. They were delighted by the King and Queen's obvious appreciation of all that was done for them. There was no trace of her grief in Queen Elizabeth's manner, and her pretty, fluent French contributed to her personal success.

The Queen's wardrobe of white clothes—even her furs were white or silver—captivated the French. The question of mourning had been adroitly solved. Black is not usually worn at Court, traditionally because the wearing of mourning might show a lack of sympathy with the régime. Yet the Queen did not wish to wear colours so shortly after the death of her mother. With all possible haste, the five principal dresses designed for the visit had been copied in white.

The French Press hailed Queen Elizabeth as 'the best-dressed Queen to visit the world's fashion centre', and recorded, 'The Queen's grace and charm have captivated Paris; she is a picture by Winterhalter.' After the visit, Mme. Lebrun, wife of the President, wrote to the Queen, 'I wish to assure your Majesty that she has won the heart of the whole of Paris.'

Yet throughout the State Visit there were undertones of war.

At Villar-Bretonneux the King unveiled the war memorial to the 10,982 Australians with no known grave who died in the Battles of the Somme, Arras and 'the hundred days', and the 731 buried in the attached cemetery. The appalling number of Australian casualties was 215,585 out of 331,781 embarkations, or nearly 65 per cent. After the King had laid his official wreath, Queen Elizabeth spontaneously walked forward and laid down an armful of red poppies picked in the neighbouring fields that morning which had been given her by a schoolboy.

The might of the French Army was paraded before them, when King George VI reviewed fifty thousand of France's best troops at Versailles.

*　　*　　*

A few days after the King and Queen returned from Paris, the Queen and the Princesses embarked at Portsmouth in the Royal yacht *Victoria and Albert*. For the first time the Queen's Standard was flown afloat: when next it was flown afloat it was in a naval barge manned by Wrens, in badly bombed Plymouth in 1940. Two days later, on July 28, the King joined them on board, and the family enjoyed a picnic in the New Forest and attended Cowes regatta.

Then *Victoria and Albert* steamed east through the Channel and into the North Sea. On August 2 *Victoria and Albert* and her escorting destroyer anchored off Southwold in Suffolk and the King—while the Queen and Princesses remained on board—was rowed ashore in a small open boat manned by two elderly fishermen to visit his Boys' Camp, which had been successfully held there for the past seven years. The sea was blue but choppy, and the fishermen were impeded by a swimming escort of boys from the Camp. However, the King got safely ashore and spent a relaxed and happy day with his boys, although on the return journey the King himself had to help pull in one of the old fishermen, who had left jumping aboard a bit late and was up to his waist in water.

At last the Royal family was back on Deeside; the King went out daily on the hill; the Queen relaxed; the Princesses rediscovered old haunts. Visitors came to stay, among them the King and Queen of Bulgaria, who came for a week-end.

King Boris, who was then forty-four years old, had come to the throne of Bulgaria, in succession to his father King Ferdinand, amid the confusion following the Great War. Twice he had nearly been assassinated, but had shown himself merciful to his would-be killers, and had achieved considerable popularity. He was half-Italian, and had married an Italian, Princess Giovanna of Savoy, third daughter of the King of Italy.

That year, King Boris had achieved a diplomatic triumph when he had managed to free Bulgaria from the Treaty of Neuilly, signed at Lausanne in 1923, under which Bulgaria's military strength had been held to a minimum. On July 31, 1938 his Prime Minister had added Bulgaria's signature to the Four-Pact Balkan treaty which had been signed by Greece, Rumania, Turkey and Yugoslavia in Athens four years earlier: there had been in consequence a definite lightening of Balkan tension and increase in Bulgarian status.

The British Government was eager to woo Bulgaria, and indeed King Boris was anxious to retain neutrality for his country, but gradually he yielded to Axis pressure and two and a half years after his visit to Balmoral he was to sign a pact with Germany and Italy and open his frontiers to her troops, soon afterwards declaring war on Britain and the United States. He died in mysterious circumstances during the war.

On September 14, the day after the departure of the King and Queen of Bulgaria, the King left for London, to attend at Windsor the funeral of Prince Arthur of Connaught, his first cousin once removed. It was not only the funeral that brought him south: only that day he had received from his Prime Minister, Neville Chamberlain, a grave letter about the German threat of invasion to Czechoslovakia, timed, it was believed, to take place that very month. Mr. Chamberlain proposed, as a desperate measure to maintain peace, to fly to see Herr Hitler the German Chancellor—in a postscript the Prime Minister added that the visit must take place on the following day.

The Queen remained at Balmoral and with Princess Elizabeth attended a memorial service for Prince Arthur at Crathie Church, but the crisis kept the King in London, and on September 21 she went south to join him. Queen Mary and the Duke and Duchess of Kent had also gathered in London—the Duke and Duchess of Gloucester were overseas on a visit to Kenya. The days crawled by in a succession of crises, cabinet meetings and rumours.

The Prime Minister's first visit to Germany had produced no helpful effect, except that Hitler had agreed to extend until October 1 the date by which he insisted that the Sudetenland, which had a considerable population of German origin, 'must be evacuated by the Czechoslovakian forces'.

The King and Queen did not even go to The Royal Lodge for that anxiety-laden week-end. The Queen had meant to make only a brief stay in London and to return north to her children on September 23, but she twice postponed her departure.

On September 27, the Queen was to launch the world's largest liner, the *Queen Elizabeth*. The King was to accompany her and make a speech, but the crisis was so grave that he could not leave London. She left London by train on the evening of September 26. On that day thousands of children, with labels tied to their clothes, were evacuated from the cities into the country. Slit trenches were dug in the London Parks; gas-masks were being fitted (the King and Queen had been fitted for theirs); and a few anti-aircraft guns had been set out at strategic points in London.

Queen Elizabeth was joined at Ibrox station in Glasgow by Princess Elizabeth and Princess Margaret, who arrived by train from Ballater half an hour after she arrived from London. The morning was spent in the Princesses' long-anticipated tour of the Empire Exhibition, which was achieved in a remarkably normal atmosphere, imposed by the imperturbable manner of the Queen.

'A great multitude of people gave them a welcome which the tension of the moment seemed to charge with a deeper and more personal feeling than would have coloured enthusiasm at a less critical time.' (*The Times.*)

The Royal party then crossed the Clyde to Clydebank.

The great liner lay in John Brown's shipyard; one thousand and thirty-two feet long, and not yet fitted with funnel and masts, the great hull looking more like a long city block than a movable, floatable object.

An elaborate launching platform with a glazed bow window to give shelter from the weather had been built below the bows; two thousand four hundred tons of drag-chains, which would run out and check the impetus the liner would gain in her giant slide to the water, were coiled down in pairs, eighteen of them on either side of the vessel.

The launch was timed for 3·15 p.m., an hour before high-water. The Royal party came onto the launching platform well before time, and the Queen almost immediately made her broadcast speech. It was the first time she had deputised for the Sovereign. In a clear voice she said:

'I have a message for you from the King. He bids the people of this country to be of good cheer, in spite of the dark clouds hanging over them, and indeed over the whole world. He knows well that, as ever before in critical times, they will keep cool heads and brave hearts; he knows too, that they will place entire confidence in their leaders who, under God's providence, are striving their utmost to find a just and peaceful solution to the grave problems which confront them.'

While the last props were being removed there was a pause. To the people on the ground these minutes seemed to fly, but I understand that to the party on the platform time seemed to drag. Queen Elizabeth looked at a book showing photographs of the ship at all stages of construction, while the Princesses examined two models of the ship.

Suddenly there was a cracking of wood, and a universal cry of 'She's off!' The Queen looked up startled, and quickly moved forward to say, 'I name this ship *Queen Elizabeth* and wish success to her and all who sail in her.' She released the decorated bottle of champagne, which broke against the liner's stem.

Only after the ship was already moving down the slipway did the bell ring, to announce the moment of launching. The liner slid steadily down to the Clyde; as her stern touched the water there was a deafening roar of steam-whistles which almost drowned the thundering rattle of the drag-chains, as they roared out, pair by pair, while the rising cloud of red iron-dust almost hid the ship and river from the Royal party.

This was the launch of the biggest ship the world had ever known, yet the imminence of the war caused *The Times* (which had planned a special issue for the occasion, published some time later) to relegate the news to a quarter column on their main page, whose headlines ran:

FLEET TO MOBILISE
PRIME MINISTER ON THE ISSUES 'IF WE HAVE TO FIGHT'
FRANCE WAITING: CALM BUT ANXIOUS
GENERAL FRANCO'S ATTITUDE: 'WE DESIRE TO BE NEUTRAL'

and only then

LARGEST SHIP LAUNCHED: THE KING'S MESSAGE TO HIS PEOPLE
'BE OF GOOD CHEER'

The Queen returned with the Princesses to Balmoral, but international tension continued to rise and on the following day, Wednesday, September 28—the day on which Mr. Chamberlain flew for the second time to Germany—she returned to London to be at her husband's side.

Agreement was reached at Munich at 1.30 a.m. on Friday, September 30, 1938. In the overwhelming relief of the moment even the bitter price to be paid by the bewildered Czechs seemed to most Britons to be small in comparison with a general war.

Queen Elizabeth shared this sense of relief with her husband and with the country as a whole, and she felt profound gratitude to Mr. Chamberlain for his efforts for peace. Mr. and Mrs. Neville Chamberlain, flanked by the King and Queen, appeared on the balcony of Buckingham Palace, to receive the cheers of a vast, excited crowd.

Personal plans could be made again. The King and Queen returned to Scotland, to spend a quiet fortnight on Deeside with their daughters. But now there was a basic difference to their outlook. They, like their people, were coming to realise that it was impossible to parley with Hitler, and that war was virtually inevitable.

In February 1939, the King and Queen travelled north to Tyneside, where, in the Walker Naval Yard, the King launched the battleship *King George V*. The battleship, still a major weapon in British armament, was to be of thirty-five thousand tons displacement and to have ten fourteen-inch guns and a secondary armament of sixteen 5·25-inch guns in twin turrets, as well as numerous smaller guns and aircraft to be accommodated in hangars and flown off by catapult. The shipyard directors announced at the launch an order for a battleship in the 1938 naval programme, and two more large ships in the 1939 programme. The King and Queen visited the Elswick works of Vickers Armstrong, and saw tanks, tracked vehicles, naval gun mountings, bombs, guns and aircraft components.

Many visits were paid to see the secret plans of the 'backroom boys', the scientists. They visited army depôts and heavy industries—even at the British Industries Fair they were shown anti-aircraft guns and gunfire predictors.

Plans went forward for the care of civilians and the evacuation of hospital patients and children in the event of war. Queen Elizabeth went to the House of Commons to hear a debate on a

Government bill to provide fifty large camps, to be used by school children if peace continued, and by refugees from the cities in the event of war.

There was a sudden increase of tension when Italy invaded Albania at Easter in 1939. King George immediately motored up from Windsor Castle to see Mr. Chamberlain, and the newspapers carried an ominously phrased reassurance:

> 'It is understood that there has been no change in the plans for the visit of the King and Queen to Canada and the United States. They will leave Portsmouth in H.M.S. *Repulse* on May 6, as already arranged.'

The guests at Windsor Castle assembled for Easter rather later than usual and the entertainment provided was unusual: on April 16 King George and Queen Elizabeth took their guests (who included Mr. Kennedy, the American Ambassador) to No. 2 Balloon Centre, Hook, Surrey: Mr. Kennedy came in with them to see secret equipment in a separate building. Immediately, the visit was followed by an Air Ministry announcement that 'Balloon squadrons are now being formed' and giving full particulars about qualifications required and how to join. The balloon was about to go up.

The visit of King George VI and Queen Elizabeth to Canada had been proposed by the Canadian Prime Minister, Mr. Mackenzie King, at the time of the Coronation, and was linked with a subsequent invitation by President Roosevelt to visit the United States. This tour of Canada was the first made by the Sovereign to one of his overseas Dominions and it was the first time the Sovereign crossed the Atlantic.

The visit had been fixed for the early summer of 1939. As the day approached the King was increasingly reluctant to leave London at a time of such anxiety, nor did he want to deprive the Fleet of the battle cruiser *Repulse*, in which he was to travel. It was at his suggestion that the Canadian Pacific liner *Empress of Australia* had been tentatively chartered for the outward voyage, and so was able to be substituted, at the last moment, for the battleship.

King George VI and the Queen embarked at Southampton on

May 5, 1939. With them travelled their staff, who included Lady Nunburnholme and Lady Katharine Seymour as the Queen's Ladies-in-Waiting, and the Earl of Airlie as Lord Chamberlain to the Queen. The possibility of a Nazi coup against the King and Queen had been considered, but in fact the very real dangers of the voyage were due to marine causes. That year the icefields were lying far south across the shipping routes, and, as so often happens, were shrouded by fog. The *Empress of Australia* found herself in dense fog, and surrounded by icebergs.

The report of the Commander of the *Empress of Australia* for those critical days was:

'*Thursday May 11th*. 6.26 a.m. Weather becoming hazy, reduced speed to 10 knots. 6.34 a.m. Thick fog, stopped engines. R.A. approved. Thick fog continued throughout the day and night.

'*Friday May 12th*. 1.36 a.m. Proceeded at 10 knots, weather clearing, speeds according to visibility. H.M.S. *Southampton* stationed 10 cables and burning searchlights. Overcast and clear. 2.05 a.m. Dense fog—stopped engines. 6.19 a.m. Weather clearing, proceeded at various speeds. 5.36 p.m. weather cleared, full speed, passing berg and growlers. 6.28 p.m. Reduced speed as fog became thick and stopped. During the night fog very thick and patchy, proceeded as visibility permitted.

'*Saturday May 13th*. 4.50 a.m. Weather fog, smooth sea and low swell proceeding as visibility permitted. 12.29 p.m. Sighted large berg and growlers in ice field. 1.02 p.m. stopped engines, dense fog. 12.15 p.m. H.M.S. *Glasgow*'s whaler alongside (port) and debarked Surgeon Captain Maxwell, R.N., and Surgeon Captain White, R.N. 2.20 p.m. whaler left and proceeded back to H.M.S. *Glasgow*. Weather foggy. Surgeon Captain Maxwell, R.N. and Surgeon Captain White R.N. returned on whaler at 5.36 p.m. Proceeded at 5 knots when visibility permitted. (Fog very dense skirting ice fields.)

'*Sunday May 14th*. Proceeding through ice fields and fog at various speeds and courses. 11.00 a.m. Held Divine Service in Main Dining Saloon. Their Majesties attended. Purser Armour officiated and second Purser Philpott read the lesson. Hymns were selected by Her Majesty the Queen. 2.50 p.m. Cleared field ice. Weather clearing, increased engines to 21,000 H.P. 4.07 p.m. Reduced speed, fog very patchy. 4.34 p.m. Increased to full speed 21,000 S.H.P. 8.00 p.m. Slight sea, fine and clear.

'*Monday May 15th.* Weather fine, cloudy and clear, slight swell. 9.15 a.m. Gallantry Head. 9.54 a.m. Plate Pt.L. House. 4.55 p.m. Cape Ray Lt. House distance 7 miles. 5.30 p.m. H.M.C.S. destroyers *Skeena* and *Saguenay* joined Squadron and cheered ship, weather fine and clear, smooth sea. 8.23 p.m. Bird Rock Lt. distance 11 miles.'

In tense situations human beings take heart from strange details—in this case the laying of an egg by the First Officer's canary was decided to be a good omen!

Queen Elizabeth wrote, in a letter to Queen Mary quoted by Sir John Wheeler-Bennett:

'For three and a half days we only moved a few miles. The fog was so thick that it was like a white cloud around the ship and the foghorn blew incessantly. Its melancholy blasts were echoed back by the icebergs like the twang of a piece of wire. Incredibly eery, and really very alarming, knowing that we were surrounded by ice and unable to see a foot either way.

'We nearly hit a berg the day before yesterday, and the poor Captain was nearly demented because some kind cheerful people kept on reminding him that it was about here the *Titanic* was struck, and just about the same date!'

The reactions of the Queen are typical: too intelligent not to realise the danger, she retained sympathy for those in authority.

The King's reactions were in much the same vein: he commented to his mother:

'The whole incident has been a most interesting experience . . . As a matter of fact I have been able to have a good rest on the voyage and the two extra days are all to the good for me, but I should not have chosen an ice field surrounded by dense fog in which to have a holiday, but it does seem to be the only place for me to rest in nowadays!!'

The ship had had some time in hand, but two days could not be made up. The carefully prepared plans for the tour had to be curtailed, which of course involved work for both the Canadian authorities and for the King's Household: the Canadian Prime Minister proved a voluminous telegrapher.

The Governor General (who was Lord Tweedsmuir, better known as the historian and novelist John Buchan) and his wife were present at the arrival and at the departure of the King and Queen. Lord and Lady Tweedsmuir were the King and Queen's hosts at Government House in Ottawa: but for the rest of the time the Governor General kept quietly in the background, continuing to perform routine constitutional work, which would otherwise have complicated and overloaded the King's programme.

The King's visit was intended to demonstrate that the Dominions of the British Commonwealth were equal partners; this raised the question of which country would provide the Minister in Attendance upon the Sovereign.

The King was accompanied throughout Canada by a Canadian Cabinet Minister, and indeed the Prime Minister of Canada, Mr. Mackenzie King, himself accompanied the King wherever possible. No Minister of the Crown from the United Kingdom or from any other Dominion accompanied the King: visible proof of the complete independence of Canada. Such procedure seems self-evident today, but it was new in 1939.

The day-to-day conduct of the tour raised its own practical problems. Certain clear rules had to be laid down and kept, or the many people inevitably disappointed in their wish to entertain or to meet the King and Queen might feel there had been personal discrimination against them.

Originally, the Government of Canada had expected that the King and Queen might only visit the Dominion capital: it was the King who proposed that the trip be extended to include every province of Canada.

King George and Queen Elizabeth were deluged with invitations from Canadians, but because the people of Canada as a whole were considered to be their hosts the King and Queen decided to accept no invitations from individuals. The King and

Queen also asked that there should be no gifts from individuals, organisations or public bodies. As the people of Canada would be represented by their duly elected or officially appointed representatives, special groups, who were vigorously lobbying for inclusion in the programme, were warned that special favours and concessions could not be expected, whether on account of political, social, religious or any other special affiliations.

Because time was short, it was decided that Honorary degrees could not be accepted, nor would there be visits to educational nor charitable organisations nor to industrial plants. To save the strain upon the King and Queen, it was requested that the number of addresses of welcome should be cut down, and that double-stops at provincial legislatures and city hall buildings should be arranged in commonsense order. Only one official luncheon or dinner was to be planned for each day, with the exception of the days spent in Ottawa and Quebec.

It was difficult, before the tour began, to predict the reactions of Canadians. King Edward VIII, enormously popular in Canada, had endeared himself to the Canadian people by buying a ranch in Alberta, while the Duke of York, although he had visited Canada briefly in 1913 when he was a naval cadet on board the cruiser *Cumberland*, was less well known. 'It was thought that, particularly in the French-speaking province of Quebec, where the tour opened, the reaction might be somewhat half-hearted, but the welcome there 'was absolutely terrific and set the tone for the whole enormously successful tour,' said an official in the party.

The tour was a strenuous one; King George and Queen Elizabeth covered 4,281 miles over Canadian National Railways, and eight miles in the Canadian Pacific steamer *Princess Marguerite* and the Canadian National steamer *Prince Robert*.

The Queen loved Canada. She found the scenery splendid, and compared it with Italy, which she had visited as a girl with her maternal grandmother, Mrs. Scott. She was deeply impressed by their train journey through the Rockies. They had a brief period of rest at Banff where they watched beaver at work on a dam, and saw chipmunks, bear, moose, elk, wapiti, mountain goats and mule deer. Jasper, where they spent another brief recess in wonderful weather, appealed to them greatly, and the whole party left there with reluctance.

Most of all the King and Queen were delighted by the Canadians themselves, and by their obvious good health and prosperity. Everywhere, tremendous assemblies of people waited. At Unity in Saskatchewan, which had a normal population of under seven hundred, a crowd of twenty thousand assembled to greet the King and Queen.

At Winnipeg the train had to go dead slow for some miles, because of the vast crowds pressing onto the track.

At Windsor, close to the States border, stands had been built and were crammed with people for a stretch of five miles alongside the track. American citizens poured over the border from Detroit at the rate of twenty thousand an hour, and the crowds were estimated at anything up to half a million people. When the King and Queen walked over to speak to a group of ex-Servicemen, the crowd broke through the barrier and the engine of the Royal train, which had been coaling and watering, was unable to force a passage back to the carriages. That was a particularly worrying occasion for the security men, as members of the Irish Republican Army were known to be present.

'I have never seen such crowds as those in Canada,' said a member of the party. 'As we proceeded, they grew and grew. The word of the King and Queen's tremendous success spread ahead of us, so that the build-up was terrific.'

At one small stop there were thousands and thousands of people and hardly any town at all. The Queen looked at them with tears in her eyes.

The tour was strenuous, but there were opportunities for relaxation no longer possible in the heavy schedules of today. On the journey across country the Royal train would be stopped, and the King and Queen would get out and walk along the side of the track. From time to time they would come across small groups of people, waiting for the Royal train to pass.

'One morning I was walking with Lord Eldon ahead of the King and Queen,' said a Lady-in-Waiting, 'when we passed two men standing by a water tower. They were covered in dirt and dust. We said, "Good morning." They said, "Where is our

King?" We told them, "Stand just there and you will see him, he is coming along now." They said, "He couldn't . . . we mustn't," and we had to persuade them that it would be all right. When the King and Queen came past—a fresh-faced young couple in country dress, the King was wearing shorts—the two men fell down on their knees. They were White Russians. It made us realise the difference between Royalty in different countries and how comprehensive is the Commonwealth.'

The tour saw the first beginnings of spontaneous contacts and informal conversation between the King and Queen and members of the public. In a record made from day to day by a member of the Royal party, preserved at Buckingham Palace, there is an account of talk between the Queen and a tousled small boy, who met the King and Queen near a farm one Saturday afternoon when they had driven into the country. The Queen said 'Hello.' Boy, 'Hello.' There followed a talk about the boy's dog. The Queen said, pointing to the King, 'Do you know who that is?' Boy, 'No.' Queen, 'It is your King.' The boy made noises of disbelief. Queen. 'But it is your King.' Lord Airlie also said 'But it is the King,' and induced the boy to take the rakish cap off his head. The Queen then talked about school and family to the boy, and finally moved on, after which the lad saw the Mounted Police and realised that he had really seen the King and Queen.

In Regina the Queen met Miss Hazell, the guiding spirit in the Canadian Sunday School Caravan Mission, and was immediately impressed by her enthusiasm and resolve. Every year since then Queen Elizabeth has sent Miss Hazell a donation and a few words of encouragement.

For the greater part of the tour the King and Queen were together, but there were occasions when the Queen undertook an engagement of her own. In Toronto the Queen presented Colours to the Toronto Scottish Regiment on the Campus of the University, while the King was fulfilling a duty in another part of the Campus.

One of the rare occasions when a Queen Consort took the leading rôle in the presence of the Sovereign took place on May 20, 1939, in Ottawa, when the Queen laid the foundation stone of the new Supreme Court building. Her speech, partly in French, was broadcast and contained a happy allusion to her own double heritage:

'Au Canada, comme en Grande-Bretagne, la justice s'administre selon deux legislations diffèrentes. Dans mon pays natal, en Écosse, nous avons un Droit basé sur le Droit Romain; il provient de la même source que votre Droit Civil dans la vieille province de Quebec. En Angleterre, comme dans les autres provinces du Canada, le Droit Coutumier l'emporte. A Ottawa, comme à Westminster, les deux sont administrés par la Cour Suprême de Justice. Cela est, à mes yeux, d'un très heureux augure.

'Voir vos deux grandes races avec leurs legislations, leurs croyances et leurs traditions diffèrentes, s'unir liens d'affection, de respect, et d'un idéal commun; tel est mon désir le plus cher.'

Everywhere they went in Canada they met Scots. The King once remarked, when advised for the umpteenth time that at the train's next halting place a group of people emanating from Kirriemuir would be assembled, that Canada seemed to be entirely peopled by the men of Angus.

On May 18 at Montreal men from The Black Watch (The Royal Highland Regiment) of Canada, of which the Queen was Colonel-in-Chief, formed a composite guard of honour with Les Fusiliers Mont-Royal. Every Highlander was over five foot nine inches, much taller when wearing full ceremonial dress, including feather bonnet. It was the King who inspected the Guard of Honour, but Queen Elizabeth sent for the Commanding Officer and asked him many questions. Driving past the troops the Queen smiled and waved at them with such enthusiasm that officers and men were hard put to it not to wave and cheer back.

That evening the King and Queen appeared on the balcony of the Windsor hotel, where a banquet had been held, to a huge crowd in Dominion Square. Queen Elizabeth gave a special wave to her Regiment, drawn up below her, which was answered by a mighty yell. She was seen to wipe tears from her eyes. 'To a man, the Regiment has fallen in love with their Colonel-in-Chief,' said one of the Canadian Black Watch, writing to the parent Regiment in Scotland. 'You, with us, are particularly honoured in having her for our Colonel-in-Chief—a Queen and a Lady.'

It is amusing to record two minor incidents: in one Canadian city the King, always interested in uniform or regalia, asked the Mayor's wife if her husband did not have a chain of office, as he was not wearing once. 'Oh yes,' she replied, 'but he only wears it on important occasions.'

The name—but not the gender—has been changed in the following incident. A man, overcome with emotion, ran out of the crowd after the Royal train, calling, 'Wonderful, wonderful! My mother was John Jones of Leeds!' A surprising statement at which the King and Queen were much amused.

The success of the tour owed much to the thoughtfulness and care of detail with which it had been planned, a difficult task because of the distance to be covered, the limited time available and lack of precedents.

One of the big successes of the tour was the escort of the four Canadian Mounties specially assigned to the King and Queen. They were magnificent men, six feet three or four inches tall and broad in proportion, who could handle a fair-sized crowd on their own, and who became great favourites with everyone. They accompanied the King and Queen throughout the visit to Canada, but they had to leave them when they crossed into the United States.

The visit to the United States was extremely important. It was on June 7, 1939, that the King and Queen crossed that 'significantly unfortified frontier', of which President Roosevelt was to speak in his welcome to the King

As the train rushed through Buffalo station King George performed his first act on American soil: he knighted his Private Secretary, Sir Alan Lascelles, whose knighthood had been announced in the Birthday Honours List, but who had not yet received the accolade. This was the first time that any man had had been knighted on the soil of the United States.

King George VI was not the first Crowned Head to visit Washington, nor the first member of the British Royal family to enter the United States, but this was the first visit of the King of

England to Washington and the feelings of the American Revolution still lingered in some quarters. Washington itself had been burnt down by the Redcoats in 1814, and that was the original reason why the White House is white; it had been whitewashed to hide the smoke stains that disfigured the walls after the fires. It was thought that resentment might be shown to King George because his brother had abdicated to marry an American lady, as some Americans believed the obstacle to recognition had been her nationality and not her previous marriages. In addition, there was considerable political support for the Germans, and more for neutrality.

Nevertheless, President Roosevelt knew that, however acid the bickering between the United States and Britain might be, there was an underlying sense of partnership between the two English-speaking powers. He saw that in the approaching war, the United States would almost inevitably be forced eventually into the war on the side of the Allies. It was to bring the two nations closer together that he had invited the King and Queen to Washington.

The visit to the United States took place in a heat-wave so humid and so enervating that it is an inescapable memory to all who endured it. In the record of the visit which was made by His Majesty's Household, the chronicler noted that the temperature was 95° F; this has afterwards been altered firmly by another hand to '97° F. in the shade': the humidity made it feel much higher.

The heat was worst for King George and his Staff, as they had to bear the discomfort of full-dress uniform, but Queen Elizabeth has always suffered in the heat, and although no one would have realised it from her imperturbable manner, she felt giddy at the garden party for British residents in Washington. Although this garden party was held in the early hours of the day the heat was so intense that one Embassy official had to send his daughter, who was waiting to present the bouquet, post-haste home for a fresh collar to replace the one wilting round his neck.

The warmth of Washington's welcome matched the warmth of the weather. A great many people turned out to see and cheer the King and Queen on every possible occasion from their first drive into Washington until the end of the visit.

On the second day, their Majesties visited the Rotunda in Washington, where they shook hands with four hundred Congressmen and women. Extremely hot and trying lights had been fitted up in order to film the scene. These lights were causing the King and Queen discomfort, and the Speaker, noticing this, made an order for the lights to be extinguished, which was not immediately obeyed. He then said to the American naval aide to the King, Admiral Richardson, 'Can you get your boys to put out these lights?' Admiral Richardson turned to the Marine Guard and said, 'The Speaker will judge the efficiency of the Marines by the rapidity with which those lights are extinguished.'

The lights went out almost instantly.

One Senator, a well-known isolationist, had a long chat with Queen Elizabeth, after which he spontaneously congratulated King George 'on being a very good Queen-picker'.

On the following day, the King and Queen having sailed from Mount Vernon to Sandy Hook on board the U.S.S. *Potomac*, the President's yacht (which flew the Royal Standard at the foremast and the Presidential Standard at the mainmast) transferred to the U.S.S. destroyer *Warrington* to enter New York harbour. Unfortunately the day was overcast, and the heat mist almost wiped out the famous skyline, but they were given the traditional and impressive New York welcome from firefloats, ferries and small craft. For part of the passage their unofficial escort included Mr. J. P. Morgan in his fine yacht *Corsair*.

The King and Queen drove through the City of New York with an unfamiliar motor-cycle escort, to the World Fair where they visited the Court of Peace—a peace which lad less than three months to run. It was an exhausting day, and an unexpected addition to the programme was an unscheduled line-up for presentation of about five hundred extra people. After two hundred or so had been presented, the programme was running so much behind time that the King and Queen had to abandon shaking hands with everyone, and walked slowly along the line of those still waiting, speaking to a few people as they passed.

At last King George and Queen Elizabeth could leave the Fair, and motor to Hyde Park, the country home of President and Mrs. Roosevelt, where they arrived an hour and a half behind time.

The delayed dinner provided Mrs. Roosevelt with a domestic crisis and there were some spectacular crashes of dishes, but in the relaxed and easy atmosphere prevailing between them, these only provoked a lighthearted reaction. Queen Elizabeth found the large, friendly, outspoken family gathered there reminiscent of her own family tradition, and Hyde Park had much the atmosphere of an English country house. 'I admired both of them and found the Queen a warm and positive personality,' wrote Mrs. Roosevelt afterwards.

Ending this long day, King George VI and President Roosevelt had an important talk, in which the President outlined many of the aids which he hoped America, in the event of a war, would make to Britain, and which he later implemented: but at that time were well in advance of American public opinion, which had yet to harden against the Axis powers.

On the following day, Sunday, June 11, the King and Queen attended divine service with their hosts in the Church of St. James, and afterwards the President gave a picnic luncheon (at which hot dogs were served) to some two hundred people.

That night the King and Queen returned to Canada. Mrs. Roosevelt wrote:

'I shall never forget the day they left Hyde Park to go back to London at a time when the threat of tragic events in Europe already weighed heavily on all of us. Franklin and I went with them to the Hyde Park railroad station, where their special train was waiting. Nobody had arranged any ceremony, but, of course, the public knew the time of their departure and crowds had gathered. The steep little banks rising on the side of the river were covered with spectators who waited, rather silently, until our good-byes were said. But, as the train pulled out, somebody began singing "Auld Lang Syne" and then everyone was singing, and it seemed to me that there was something of our friendship and our sadness and something of the uncertainty of our futures in that song that could not have been said in any other words. I think the King and Queen, standing on the rear platform of the train as it pulled slowly away, were deeply moved. I know I was.'

The last three days of the Canadian visit had come: the Canadians vied with one another to make them particularly happy for the King and Queen.

By this stage of the thirty-day-long tour of Canada and the States, Queen Elizabeth had almost drained herself of vitality and energy, although those who saw her in public could not have realised it. Throughout, she had given of her warm and friendly personality to all around her, and she had supported her husband in public and in private. 'The Queen was really exhausted by the time we left for home. But she would never say she found anything tiring, and she always brushed off any reference to her fatigue,' said her Lady-in-Waiting.

Canada impressed the King and Queen profoundly. Their hearts were filled with love for and gratitude to the Canadians. The Queen was moved by the warmth of their reception, by the sense of unity with the Canadians in the dark days on the brink of war. She gained an inner strength from the tour upon which she drew during the years ahead.

In the Queen's broadcast to the women of Canada, she said of her visit to 'this great and friendly continent':

'Seeing this great country, with all its varied beauty and interest, has been a real delight to me, but what has warmed my heart in a way I cannot express is the proof that you have given us everywhere that you were glad to see us. And in return I want particularly to tell the women and children of Canada how glad I am to have seen so many of them.

'This wonderful tour of ours has given me memories that the passage of time will never dim . . .'

On the evening of Thursday, June 15, 1939, in Government House, Halifax, which was decorated in a froth of white flowers and the great branches of apple blossom from the Annapolis Valley; the King and Queen thanked, gave presents and bade farewell to all the Canadian staff who had personally served them during the Royal visit.

At 8.20 a.m. the *Empress of Britain*, flying the Royal Standard, the Lord High Admiral's flag, and the Red Ensign, let go her moorings and began slowly to move into the fairway. Great crowds cheered and sang. H.M. ships *Southampton* and *Glasgow* and H.M.C. ships *Skeena* and *Saguenay* escorted the liner out of the harbour.

'We went to see them leave harbour,' wrote Lady Tweeds-muir, 'and stood on a balcony while the wildly cheering crowds watched the *Empress* move slowly away, the King's and Queen's figures getting smaller and more distant and then being lost to sight.

'The line from *Antony and Cleopatra* came into my mind. I tried to push the thought away, but it kept coming back: "The bright day is gone, and we are for the dark." '

CHAPTER TEN

WAR

... The destruction is so awful and the people so *wonderful*—they *deserve* a better world

> *Queen Elizabeth in a letter to Queen Mary (quoted in 'King George VI' by John Wheeler-Bennett)*

WHEN King George VI and Queen Elizabeth returned to Britain from Canada and the United States, they went to Balmoral, but the holiday was soon interrupted when the King reviewed the Reserve Fleet at Weymouth on August 8. He had not long returned to Deeside when, on August 23, the increasing gravity of the situation brought him south again. The Queen followed him to London on August 28, while the Princesses remained at Balmoral.

On September 1, the last flicker of hope was extinguished; German troops crossed into Poland, German aircraft bombed Warsaw. An ultimatum was delivered to Germany. The Privy Council met, at which the King formally declared that 'a state of great emergency' existed, and signed proclamations mobilising the Navy, and calling up the Army and R.A.F. reserves. The Queen returned to Balmoral, where she explained gently and clearly to her daughters, Princess Elizabeth (who was thirteen), and Princess Margaret (who celebrated her ninth birthday on August 21), that war had come, why it had come, and how they must face the future. She then hurried back to London to be at the King's side. 'I have never seen the Queen more closely resemble her mother, Lady Strathmore, than she did in those first days of the war,' said an old friend, 'She was a tower of strength.'

At 11 o'clock on Sunday, September 3, the ultimatum to Germany expired and a state of war was deemed to exist between Britain and Germany. Within the next few days each Dominion, with the exception of Eire, separately declared war on Germany.

At once, the Queen began the endless round of inspecting and visiting, encouraging and heartening the people of Britain, which was to occupy most of her time for the coming years. Her first engagement was to accompany the King on a tour of the defence workers of London; she inspected barrage balloons (and was told landing a balloon was just like playing a fish), sandbagged shelters, A.R.P. posts and casualty centres.

The London Scottish regimental *Gazette* of October 1939 gives an account of one of the Queen's military visits:

'Headquarters were honoured on September 6 by a surprise visit from our Honorary Colonel, Her Majesty the Queen.

'Attended only by her Lady-in-Waiting, Her Majesty was received by Captain Bishop, M.C., Commanding the National Defence Company, Lieut. Clapham, O.C. Rear Guard Party and Company Commander Miss MacTaggart of the Auxiliary Territorial Service.

'Her Majesty inspected the Orderly Room and Quarter-master's Stores, and talked with the A.T.S. (Women Territorials) working there and was most interested in the new battle dress being issued to the National Defence Company and inspected Pte. Millmaker, who was one of the first to wear it.

'Her Majesty next visited the Canteen, where the Rear Party was having dinner, and spoke to several of the men there. On leaving the cheers made the roof ring, and caused a crowd to gather outside the Hall.

'While passing through the Drill Hall, Her Majesty stopped and spoke to C.S.M. Bill Ball, D.C.M., M.M., of the Defence Company about his dog, and asked if there was a gas mask for him. Through having been patted by Her Majesty, he has now been re-christened Royal Bob.

'. . . Company Commander Miss MacTaggart received from Buckingham Palace later the A.T.S. Visitors Book signed by Her Majesty . . .'

Queen Elizabeth went with the King round London Docks, in the Port of London Authority's launch *St. Katharine*, where they saw a merchant ship painted battleship grey; an American freighter which had the neutral Stars and Stripes painted large on her side; and ships still discharging cargoes which had come into port just before the outbreak of war. The King and Queen went on board a cargo ship which had come in from the River Plate with four thousand tons of grain; at the King's wish unloading went on without interruption. During the first month of war the King and Queen went to the headquarters in London of Canada, Australia, and New Zealand, and South Africa, the Dominions which had chosen to fight beside Britain.

At the outbreak of war, many Members of the King and Queen's Households and of the Staff had rejoined their Regiments. Duties were telescoped and combined. Formerly there had been six Lords-in-Waiting and four Grooms-in-Waiting: now there were none. The four Equerries were reduced to two. The Queen's Private Secretary had rejoined his Corps. The Queen's Treasurer, Sir Arthur Penn, was working as Adjutant of his Regiment, yet still found time to carry on much of the urgent work for the Queen. A great deal of extra work fell on the Women of the Bedchamber, who found themselves coping with organisation, paperwork and letters in ever-increasing quantities.

Buckingham Palace was hurriedly prepared for war. Display cases were emptied of porcelain, pictures were taken down and stored in places of greater safety. The carriage horses were sent to Windsor Mews, where they worked on the farms. Servants not recalled to the forces and not urgently required were evacuated, many going to Windsor with their wives and families. A Home Guard was formed among the men who remained and others close to Buckingham Palace.

The Queen saw and heard much of the problems of evacuees, from the point of view of mothers and children. Although the country was a place of delight to her, she could appreciate the up-rooted feeling of town dwellers carried away from the cheerful life of the towns to some remote place. Her understanding of the difficulties of sharing a home and a kitchen with strangers made her the more appreciative of the large numbers of foster parents who made evacuees welcome; she decided to send a message to each foster parent:

'I wish to mark, by this personal message, my appreciation of the service you have rendered to your country in 1939.

'In the early days of the war you opened your door to strangers who were in need of shelter, and offered to share your home with them.

'I know that to this unselfish task you have sacrificed much of your own comfort, and that it could not have been achieved without the loyal co-operation of all in your household.

'By your sympathy you have earned the gratitude of those to whom you have shown hospitality, and by your readiness to serve you have helped the State in a work of great value.'

Elizabeth R.

The uncanny lull continued: King George and Queen Elizabeth spent Christmas at Sandringham House, which was closed shortly afterwards. For the rest of the war when they managed to go to Norfolk they stayed at Appleton House, the home of Queen Maud of Norway. From Norfolk, in his second Christmas broadcast, the King quoted the words of an allegory upon which he happened by chance in a newspaper:

'I said to the man who stood at the gate of the Year, "Give me a light that I may tread safely into the unknown" and he replied, "Go out into the darkness, and put your hand into the hand of God. That shall be to you better than light, and safer than a known way."'

*　　*　　*

The year 1940 opened quietly. The King, with the Queen, went north to Clydeside to launch the battleship *Duke of York* at John Brown's yard, and to visit armament factories, a Royal Naval torpedo factory and A.R.P. organisations. It was a bitter winter, and a Lady-in-Waiting remembers almost collapsing with cold during a long, leisurely inspection of battle-ready troops, during which Her Majesty spoke to almost every man on parade, while the snow lay on the ground and the winter wind blew.

On April 9, 1940, Hitler invaded Denmark and Norway. Little Denmark was smothered as she slept, and the disastrous German advance through Norway was quickly followed by even more incredible disasters in Holland, in Belgium, Luxembourg and in France.

'There was an appalling feeling of apprehension in the Palace,' said a Lady-in-Waiting: 'And the most wonderful comradeship. The Queen was perfectly wonderful. News, all of it bad, came to the Palace all the time, but we never asked anyone anything. Sometimes we heard scraps of information and sometimes we picked up things wrongly and imagined it was even worse than it was. The Queen was tremendously reserved, she carried on steadfastly with the daily things that had to be done, and she was always giving out help to people, but she seldom said anything about what she was thinking. Once, I heard her say she was so thankful that her mother was not there to have to go through a war all over again.

'One time I was driving with her to visit some hospital. The news was awful. Newsbills were still allowed, and on one I saw "The Germans reached so-and-so" and I pointed it out to her.

' "Yes they've reached there," she said, but she made no further comment.'

As Hitler engulfed Europe at frightening speed, Royal refugees arrived at Buckingham Palace, badly shaken, and without personal possessions.

On May 13, 1940, came Princess Juliana, Heiress to the throne of the Netherlands, her husband Prince Bernhard and their daughters Princess Beatrix, aged two, and Princess Irene, who was only nine months old. Prince Bernhard, having seen his family to safety, at once returned to Holland.

There the situation had deteriorated so fast that Queen Wilhelmina herself arrived at Harwich later on May 13, brought by a British destroyer, having tried in vain to find a Dutch port at which to land. Although she wished to return to Holland, she was persuaded that she could not do so and went on by train to London, where she was met at Liverpool Street station by the King.

The unhappy visitors behaved with great courage and self-control. Not only had their country been overwhelmed, their homes lost, their peoples suffering terribly, but unexpected traitors had been found in high places. Prince Bernhard barely managed to escape for a second time from the Germans. Exhausted and battle-stained he returned from disastrous defeat to Buckingham Palace, where he was met on the steps by Members of the Household and by the Royal servants. Prince Bernhard immediately turned to a page, whom he had met during his first arrival in London, and who had mentioned that his wife was ill. Prince Bernhard asked, 'How is your wife now!', a sign of consideration and control which much impressed those who witnessed it.

Queen Wilhelmina and those of her Household and Government who had escaped were afterwards found suitable accommodation in London, while Princess Juliana and her children were taken to greater safety in Canada.

Only three weeks later, King Haakon VII and the Crown Prince Olav of Norway arrived at Buckingham Palace. King Haakon's ordeal had been protracted: for two months he had been hunted by land and air through Norway by the German troops, but refused to leave while there was any part of his kingdom free from Germans. At last, on June 7, at Tromsö in the arctic north, King Haakon had to take ship in H.M.S. *Devonshire*. Three days later he was met by King George VI on his arrival in London at Euston station.

The Royal refugees and their Staffs were received by Queen Elizabeth with the kindest consideration. The refugees had *nothing*—no change of clothes, no sleeping clothes, not even a toothbrush. The men had no shaving kit, no spare shirt. All were supplied with everything they needed. Everything they asked for was procured for them, often with some difficulty. The Ladies-in-Waiting went out shopping for the Dutch Royal ladies and children. Not only was everything practical done for them; it was done with great perception and gentleness. Things were left about for them, so that they were not put to the continual embarrassment of asking for small necessities.

Queen Elizabeth came to Princess Juliana's aid in a very personal way. The christening of Princess Juliana's baby should have taken place in Holland during the summer: she suggested that it should, instead, take place in the private Chapel at Buckingham Palace before Princess Juliana left for Canada. Queen Elizabeth was godmother to the baby, who was christened Irene Emma Elizabeth on May 31, 1940.

This was the last christening to take place in the old Chapel, which was shortly afterwards destroyed by bombs.

The Royal refugees always dined and spent much of their time with King George and Queen Elizabeth; both Queen Wilhelmina and King Haakon showed intrepid courage, as did their families, but their tragic and horrifying experiences, their urgent warnings that the same quick overthrow was possible, and indeed probable, in Britain, made constant demands upon the fortitude of the King and Queen.

When Belgium shared the fate of the Netherlands, and was overrun, and the King of the Belgians decided to remain under Nazi domination with his people, there was bitter condemnation of his action, but in this King George and Queen Elizabeth did not join.

Shortly afterwards the exiled King Zog and Queen Geraldine of Albania, forced to flee for a second time within a year, appealed to the King from France, and were immediately promised sanctuary in Britain.

Nor were Royal refugees from the Second World War alone in gratitude to King George and Queen Elizabeth. The Grand Duchess Xenia of Russia, sister of the murdered Tsar Nicholas II of Russia, had been saved from the Crimea by British warships at the time of the Russian Revolution at the instigation of King George V, and had lived for the rest of her life in houses lent her by King George V and his successors, first at Frogmore Cottage in Windsor Great Park and later in Wilderness of Craiggowan, near Balmoral on Deeside. Queen Elizabeth showed such a special consideration for her and kindness to her that on one occasion at Balmoral Castle, when the elderly Princess was talking about Queen Elizabeth's sympathy to one of the Household, she burst into tears of gratitude.

Meanwhile events in France were moving from bad to worse. France fell, and on June 3 *Operation Dynamo* was completed: three hundred thousand troops—ten times the estimated maximum—were saved from the beaches of Dunkirk.

Three British Generals, together with a French admiral who had been awarded the Croix de Guerre and then a bar to his

Croix de Guerre, both within the preceding week, came to Buckingham Palace to give a first-hand account of the battle to King George and Queen Elizabeth, who were deeply moved.

There was now constant personal danger to the King and Queen and their children. It was known to be part of the Nazi pattern of invasion to capture the Royal family and hold them hostage for the good behaviour of their peoples. Security was tightened. The King travelled in a bullet-proof car, carried a steel helmet and service gas-mask, and had a sten-gun, which he knew how to use, hidden in a despatch case. The Queen, who was already a good shot, and other ladies in the Royal household learnt to use a rifle and revolver. The Queen had a steel helmet, although she was never known to put it on, and a service respirator, which she later disguised in a sort of outsize dorothy-bag.

In spite of the danger the King and Queen decided to keep their daughters in Britain. Windsor Castle was put to its intended original use as a fortress (although considering its long history it has seen little action) and during the months of greatest danger of a German paratroop 'snatch', Princess Elizabeth and Princess Margaret were never allowed far from its protective walls.

In September 1940 the blitz on London began. The King and Queen stayed at Buckingham Palace. The arrangements made for their security there, while fully living up to the great British tradition of unpreparedness, were almost ludicrously inadequate. The shelters were useless against modern bombs. The King and Queen's shelter was a cream-walled basement room which had been a housekeeper's room. The ceiling had been reinforced with some steel girders; the window, which was at ceiling height, was protected by steel shutters. It was incongruously furnished with gilt chairs, a regency settee and a large Victorian mahogany table, surrealistically surrounded by emergency steps to reach the window, axes on the wall with which to hack one's way out, oil lamps, electric torches, a bottle of smelling salts and a supply of glossy magazines. Next door, the room used by the Household was also supplied with a piano, though the attempts of a Member of a refugee monarch's Household to enliven the nocturnal hours with a rousing sing-song were not appreciated by the King. The Dressers were allocated another nearby room into which a number of extremely valuable clocks from the Palace collection formed by King George IV had been put for safety; their energetic ticking causing a distracting background of sound. There was a threat of rats, which some women confessed frightened them more than the bombs.

'The King did not minds bombs, he was as brave as a lion, it was only little irritations that could upset him, and the Queen was magnificent, she was without physical fear. And she utterly ignored the possibility that anyone else might feel less brave,' said one of the wartime Household.

I am indebted to one of Her Majesty's Ladies-in-Waiting for the following account of the Royal family taking shelter at Buckingham Palace during an early air-raid alert.

'There was a Purple Warning and I saved myself with such alacrity from the top floor that I was the first down, and then hung about on the ground floor, ashamed to be the first to go down to the shelters.

'Along came the Duchess of Kent, looking as lovely as though she had had all the time in the world to get ready.

'Then came the King and the Queen. He was carrying a corgi, and she was carrying a small case, perhaps containing her jewels. They had a brief consultation in the hall, and he gave her the corgi to hold. Then the King darted back upstairs to find the other corgi. Eventually he returned with the missing dog, and they went down to shelter together.'

On September 10 the first bomb damaged Buckingham Palace; it was a delayed action bomb which had fallen on the previous day, just outside the north wing of the Palace and which had not been regarded as dangerous. By good fortune no one was injured in the explosion, but the windows of the Royal apartments were broken and the King and Queen moved to rooms overlooking the courtyard.

On September 13, they had just returned after spending the week-end at Windsor when a stick of six bombs was dropped right across the Palace: two bombs falling and exploding in the courtyard in sight of the King, and a third falling just beyond them at the side of the wing in which they were standing, destroying the

Chapel and filling the Palace passages with tons of debris. The King and Queen had extremely narrow escapes, but they said nothing about it. Even the Prime Minister, Winston Churchill, only heard how close they had been to the bombs after the war, although he with them inspected the damage done. 'The King was not the least upset. He was laughing about his escape afterwards; the Queen, of course, was marvellous, quite unruffled.'

Queen Elizabeth immediately accompanied the King on a visit to the damaged parts of the Palace; they lunched with their Household in the shelter, and afterwards, as they had planned, went down to the East End to see the bombed areas there and to visit the bombed-out. The Lady-in-Waiting on duty commented, 'When we saw the devastation there, we were ashamed even of the glass of sherry we had had after the bang.'

Queen Elizabeth said, 'I'm glad we've been bombed. It makes me feel I can look the East End in the face.'

Two days later—although the King and Queen were not in the Palace at the time—another bomb fell through the Queen's apartments into the Belgian suite, but did not explode. In all Buckingham Palace was hit by bombs, flying bombs and rockets on no fewer than nine occasions. Queen Elizabeth herself was bombed six times, as she told Mr. Walter Nash and Mr. Holyoake at a Government lunch in Wellington during her 1958 tour. But the mention was made casually; she was talking mainly of her memories of the courage of those who had been bombed-out, seen in visits to blitzed towns.

Once she had promised to visit an exhibition of work by war-disabled ex-servicemen, but an air-raid was actually in progress when the Queen was due. She came, driving to and from the exhibition in an armoured car.

The Queen had another narrow escape; one night, early in the war, she was dressing for dinner at Windsor. The King had gone downstairs to take the dogs out. The page, who generally sits in the corridor outside the Royal apartments, was tidying up the sitting room. The Queen went into her bedroom. Suddenly a man sprang out at her from behind a curtain. He flung himself at her, seized her round the ankles. The Queen said afterwards, 'For a moment my heart stood absolutely still.' She realised that the man was half-demented, and that if she screamed he might attack her. She said in her normal voice, 'Tell me about it.' Then she moved quietly across the room and rang the bell. The man poured out his story to her: he was a deserter, whose family had all been killed in the raids.

'Poor man, I felt so sorry for him,' she said later. 'I realised quickly that he did not mean any harm.'

The man proved to be a workman employed by a firm doing work in the Castle, who had obtained the post through false credentials. He had planned his moves carefully and he had been lucky. He had clocked out, and then said he had forgotten something. Carrying a light bulb in his hand, he had gone along the corridors until he had met someone, who happened to be a young and inexperienced housemaid, whom he had asked for the Queen's apartments as he had to change a bulb there. She unthinkingly showed him the way.

Queen Elizabeth never spoke about the possibility of death, but she once said to Dame Leslie Whateley, who was then Director of the A.T.S., that she had written letters for her daughters which would be given to them if anything happened to her.

Only very rarely did she show any signs of nervousness and it was never for herself. Once she spoke of her fear, which must have been ever present, that Princess Elizabeth and Princess Margaret might be captured and held as hostages. Once, during the flying bomb period, the Princesses paid one of their rare visits to London to the dentist. While they were away, and Queen Elizabeth was out of London on public duty, there were reports of bombing with heavy casualties on the Princesses' route. Queen Elizabeth carried through her programme, but she was in torment until she had news that the Princesses had returned safely to Windsor Castle.

Whatever the strain upon her, Queen Elizabeth showed a perfect courage to the world. In wartime her support was taken for granted, as a matter of course: it never failed. To the King she contributed affection and moral support. 'She did not write his letters nor his speeches, but she was his sheet anchor. She literally kept him going. If she had ever made a fuss or lost her temper, of course, it would have been noticed and remembered. But she always did her job, she was always ready to give support and help. It is a great tribute to her.'

'Not only did the Queen have all the courage in the world,' said one of her Ladies-in-Waiting, 'she had the power to transfer it to you. When London was being heavily bombed and one had all sorts of problems to contend with at home, I used to arrive feeling more or less battered, at the Palace to go into waiting, and then I would have to take over all the current problems there. Altogether, life was rather a strain. Yet, once I had seen the Queen, I felt absolutely all right, and able to face anything.'

During the times of heavy bombing, the King and Queen went to the badly bombed areas as soon as, and often before, it was safe to do so. Crowds gathered wherever they went, and most movingly the bereaved and the homeless would give them an amazing welcome. 'The King wanted to go, as King and man, as much as she did. But it was she who had that gift that, though her heart was breaking, she could turn to a woman who had lost everything and find something kind and loving to say. Sometimes even Chief Constables wept, but she never broke down,' said a Lady-in-Waiting.

During the war, during the tours in the train which lasted ten days to a fortnight, it was extremely exhausting for both the King and Queen. They were not heartless. Those who were brought to them were those who had suffered most, who had lost their families, their all. They were bewildered, exhausted and on the point of collapse. It was agonising. People did break down sometimes—yet the King and Queen had to keep their terrible self-control. They were trained never to show their emotion, but they were even more tired from having kept it all in.

'It was amazing what comfort the King and Queen used to give to these bereaved people. They used to look after them, calling, "God bless you!" All the people loved her being there, and for looking smiling and serene. They used to say that cliché continually, "Isn't she lovely?"'

In Portsmouth there had been a very heavy raid just before their visit. The Mayor, who was a retired Sergeant of Marines, told Queen Elizabeth that he knew of a woman who was now in her third home, having been bombed out of the other two. 'Does she live near here? Could we go and see her?' asked the Queen.

Immediately the route was altered and the Royal car turned down a side street and drew up without warning outside the house. The King and Queen got out, the detective knocked at the door, and the mother came to it, holding a baby, with another clinging to her skirt.

Queen Elizabeth said, 'We heard of your misfortune. May we come in and talk to you?' The mother stood uncertainly, too surprised to speak.

The Queen said gently, 'The King and I would so much like to bring you such comfort as we can, and to hear your story.'

The mother said, 'Oh, do come in,' although she was still unsure of the identity of her visitors, and they all went into the little parlour, where Queen Elizabeth and she talked as woman to woman about her ordeal and her family.

King George, who was listening, then said, 'We understand this is your third home?'

'That's right,' said the Portsmouth woman, 'he burned us out of one and he flooded us out of another, but'—with a defiant toss of the baby in her arms—'he will never get us out of here.'

When King George and Queen Elizabeth visited South Wales they drove through district after district where the factories and little homes had dissolved in penetrating, choking dust and tawdry fragments. Groups of half-stunned people uncomplainingly told their stories of losses and narrow escapes. Once the King turned to the Queen and said, 'This is the fourth man I have met this afternoon who has told me of people being saved by sheltering under the stairs. I think half Cardiff must have been under the stairs that night.'

The Queen spoke in Swansea to Mrs. S. A. Williams, who rocked her baby in a shawl, and had an older girl standing beside her. She and five others had been dug out of the coal shed, and she had just learnt that her husband was a prisoner-of-war. Alderman P. Morris of Swansea, who took the Queen round the ruins, had just had his wife, his sister-in-law and brother-in-law killed in the raid.

Often, soon after the King and Queen had returned from a

visit to a blitzed city, they would hear that it had again been bombed. While they were visiting Plymouth an enemy aircraft, obviously on reconnaissance, had been buzzing about at intervals all day. That evening, when the Royal train was on its way back to London, Plymouth was bombed again. 'We got the news in the train,' recalls her Lady-in-Waiting. 'I remember the Queen's great, great unhappiness that night.' While the Queen was shocked by the suffering, she was also saddened by the material losses. 'Almost daily during the war,' she said when she re-laid the foundation stone of St. Columba's Church of Scotland, Pont Street, which had been destroyed in 1941, 'we mourned the destruction of more than one precious building.'

A Lady-in-Waiting remembers: 'On the day after the very heavy fire blitz on London when St. Paul's Cathedral had been ringed by fire, the Queen telephoned me and asked if I would go to the City with her saying that, "after the burning I think the Dean will be very unhappy and worried about the Cathedral". So we went down that afternoon, and there she met many of the faithful clergy and lay workers, many of them elderly men, who slept each night on iron bedsteads in the side chapels, and who had fought firebombs on the steeply pitched lead roofs of the Cathedral, regardless of their lives. As she left one of the staff said to the Dean, "You know, Sir, you feel you would go through hell for her."'

When Queen Elizabeth was given the Freedom of the City of London tribute was paid that 'during the full weight of the enemy attack on London, the Queen became the shining symbol of her sex. Wherever the bombs fell thickest, there she was to be found bringing comfort and encouragement to the homeless.'

Queen Elizabeth was the first Queen of this country to broadcast to other countries. Just before the Fall of France, she broadcast to the women of France in French. André Maurois helped her with the correct phrasing.

Later the Queen broadcast to the women of the United States, and this time her message was heard by millions, who helped towards better understanding of life in Britain: President Roosevelt congratulated her on it, saying that it was 'really perfect in every way'.

The King and Queen travelled round the country in wartime in the Royal train, which they used as their headquarters. The King travelled well over half a million miles by train during the war, accompanied by the Queen on most occasions.

The Royal train consisted of three L.M.S. coaches—one for the King, one for the Queen, and one for the Staff. Each was sixty-nine feet in length and weighed fifty-three tons, probably the heaviest passenger vehicles in the country. The Queen's car contained a lounge furnished with a comfortable sofa, three armchairs and some small tables; a bedroom and bathroom; and a small compartment for her Dresser. At the end of each coach were special vestibules, with just enough space for the Royal party to assemble. Double doors were fitted, and also folding steps.

The King's coach was similar in design. A private telephone system with a twenty-five line automatic telephone was fitted in the auxiliary car, which contained a baggage compartment and sleeping accommodation for the Household and Staff, as well as a special power unit.

When on tour, the King and Queen would leave the train after breakfast and get back to it generally around 5 o'clock, for a welcome cup of tea. At night, the train was shunted into a siding, blacked out and the lights dimmed—the Royal party adopted the railwaymen's term of 'stabling'. The King and Queen had dinner with their staff, and then went to their sitting room. The train was always on the telephone and the flow of despatch boxes arrived for the King as usual. Queen Elizabeth saw a great deal, although not as much as the King, of the Armed Forces in readiness or training in Britain.

The Queen took a keen interest in everything happening in the women's services, and she never forgot the family commitments and anxieties of the women serving in the Forces. Dame Leslie Whateley, Director of the A.T.S. in succession to Dame Helen Gwynne-Vaughan, wrote in *As Thoughts Survive*:

'The Queen showed a really sincere interest in my private life. She asked if I had anyone to cook my meals and look after me in my flat; whether my husband was still engaged in

At Royal Lodge, Windsor, during the war

A Cecil Beaton photograph showing pre-war Buckingham Palace

The Palace in war-time: making Red Cross dressings

The Queen visiting a bombed area in the East End of London

The end of the war and victory celebrations in the streets

Princess Elizabeth, Queen Elizabeth, Winston Churchill, the King and Princess Margaret on the balcony of Buckingham Palace as victory is celebrated

One of the King's last portraits: with the Queen, Prince Charles and Princess Anne

The christening of Prince Henry of Wales, younger son of the Prince and Princess of Wales, on 21st December 1984. From left to right, HM Queen Elizabeth the Queen Mother; HM the Queen; Prince William (born 21st June 1982); and the Prince and Princess of Wales.

A country walk on Deeside with her eldest grandson, Prince Charles

A sixteensome reel at the Royal Caledonian Ball in London

At the Clydebank launching of the *British Queen* in 1959

Wearing some of her superb jewellery on the way to a dinner for statesmen attending the Commonwealth Prime Ministers' Conference in 1962

A visit to the site of the National Theatre on the South Bank

Fishing during a visit to New Zealand

A private photograph of a picnic on Deeside

The Queen Mother unexpectedly rose early to greet territorials of the Black Watch, of which she is Colonel-in-Chief, in the hills above Balmoral

secret work; and if my son had recovered from his long illness in India. It is that personal interest in everyday life which puts everyone so much at ease when talking to Her Majesty, and must in part account for the feeling of encouragement which remains with one after being in her presence.'

★ ★ ★

Later the Queen found herself in a new rôle in connection with the A.T.S. As she said at the fortieth birthday celebration of the Women's Services at the Seymour Hall in 1957: 'During the war I came to have an even closer interest in the Auxiliary Territorial Service as the mother of one of its officers. From that vantage point I learnt something of the hopes and anxieties, of the achievements and disappointments, but most of all the loyalty and enthusiasm of those who were serving at that time. I think I learnt, too, a little of the measure of forbearance and patience which is demanded and which is so loyally given by the parents of those in your Service.'

The Queen appreciates the loyalty of the Servicewoman in her own service. Once, when visiting a Wren depot, she asked a girl in 'civvies', 'Have you just joined the Service?' only to receive the indignant reply, 'Oh NO, Ma'am, I'm a second-weeker.'

During the war Queen Elizabeth visited many R.A.F. stations on which W.A.A.F. officers and airwomen were serving, and saw the work of the airwomen servicing the aircraft, working in air traffic control, or in less glamorous jobs in the cook houses, account sections, hospitals and sick quarters and she asked the Director of the W.A.A.F. to send her reports especially about welfare facilities.

She always made it quite clear that she regarded women in uniform as women, and not as substitute-men. Both the King and Queen were anxious that all femininity should not be swept aside, in the effort to maintain absolute equality with the men: efficiency could and should be combined with grace.

The Queen considers that becoming dress plays an important part in self-respect, and so maintaining morale. During her many visits to the Soldiers', Sailors' and Airmen's Families Association during the war, she was fully in agreement with the care taken to select clothes of good quality and correct fit for the bombed-out families who were being re-equipped.

The late Dame Vera Laughton Matthews, Director of the Wrens, recalls in *Blue Tapestry* that the Queen took a dislike to the first Wren hat, which, although it was allegedly a copy of a Bond Street yachting hat, closely resembled the pudding basin after which it was nicknamed. The First Lord of the Admiralty, backed by the Admirals, insisted on a change.

Dame Vera seems to have cherished some affection for the hat, and was twice summoned to the Palace to discuss it, once with both the King and Queen, and again with the Queen alone who 'made no secret of the fact that she had tried on the cap herself and had been greeted by "the children" in a manner representative of the best family tradition'.

When the Women's Land Army was formed in June 1939, the Queen became its Patron. On the fourth birthday of the Land Army in July 1943, three hundred land-girls from all over Britain were brought together in London without knowing why. They were then told that the Queen had invited them to have tea with her at Buckingham Palace. The party was planned at first to take place in the gardens, but the Queen reversed the decision, saying with characteristic imagination, 'Land-girls see quite enough of gardens and out-of-doors. I am sure that the inside of a Palace, which isn't so much part of their daily lives, would interest them much more.'

The King changed into uniform at the outbreak of war, and invariably wore uniform in public for the duration. The Queen never wore uniform. During the war, whatever the circumstances, Queen Elizabeth always dressed carefully and beautifully. Her couturiers said: 'Her Majesty wished to convey the most comforting, encouraging and sympathetic note possible.' During the war Queen Elizabeth never wore green, which some think an unlucky colour, nor did she wear black. The Queen certainly did not believe that wearing drab clothes would help to raise morale, and she took particular care to look her best when visiting war factories and bombed areas. Yet she did not wear anything too frivolous. She said once, as she went to change her hat after an official luncheon before visiting the homeless, 'I don't think this hat strikes a very sympathetic note.'

Queen Elizabeth wore mostly clothes made for the tour of Canada and the United States in 1939, which did yeoman service. Her few new clothes were extremely practical or made out of fabrics found in the Palace storerooms; old dresses were often re-modelled.

One of the greatest tests of the Queen's considerable stamina was the inspection of factories, which always involved walking for miles over concrete floors. Worst of all were the munition factories, where special rubber-soled footwear, which did not always fit too well, was provided to avoid the risk of sparks. Endless factories blurred into a general memory of vast draughty spaces, sometimes hot and stuffy, sometimes chilly, often noisy, of rows and rows of overalled and dust-capped women engaging in the indispensable, hard, monotonous work of producing weapons and necessities. Women continued at their machines during the Queen's visit, while she walked slowly past them speaking to as many as possible. Production always dropped on the day of her visit—and then soared up.

The Queen could always find something to talk about to the men and women she met. When the conditions were terrible and those round her were overtired and overwrought, the Queen just sailed gently on, taking her time about everything, with a word and smile for everyone, imposing her own serene tempo.

She visited many hospitals, not all of which contained war victims. In one maternity ward Royal comment was made on a very red-faced patient who did not seem quite well: the Lady-in-Waiting made enquiries and was told by Matron, 'She's in advanced labour, but she will *not* go into the labour ward until she has seen the Queen.'

Whenever possible the Queen still visited charities not directly connected with the war, which were struggling along with great difficulty. At an old people's home, when the word got around that the Queen was coming, one old lady was seen by Matron down on her knees touching up the seams of her old red carpet with red ink on a toothbrush. The Queen was told, and as she went into the old lady's room and shut the door behind her she was heard to say, 'What a *lovely* red carpet.'

At this same home a very lame gardener was working, his help much valued in the great shortage of labour. He was presented to the Queen, and when he bowed, it looked as if he would never be able to straighten up again. A year later Queen Elizabeth re-met an official from the home, and immediately asked after the gardener.

The King and Queen visited Ulster in June 1942—it was supposed to be a close secret, but they were escorted through the Northern Ireland countryside by American light tanks, their sirens sounding and their pennants fluttering, while at every cross-road and corner there were groups of people waiting who raised a cheer as they passed, and Union Jacks fluttered from houses and trees.

They visited a United States base, where they watched a display of American tanks—advancing at high speed over sandhills, pitching and rolling, jumping a bank, charging a dry-stone wall and climaxing in a couple of tanks charging through and demolishing a wooden house. For the first time they saw a jeep—so new that it was reported as a 'peep'. They lunched with the Americans, and enjoyed a pear and lettuce salad with their roast beef. Herbert Morrison, who was the Minister in attendance, was heard to remark afterwards ruefully that only too late had he learnt that somewhere on the table there was *white* bread.

The Queen spoke to many of the G.I.s. One, asked about it afterwards, said, 'We talked about my old man's stomach-ache . . . You'd never guess how interested Her Majesty was in my old man's ulcer.' Commented an American Sergeant, 'The Queen is a swell-looking gel.'

One moving moment during that visit took place at Harland and Wolff's, in a large and gloomy shipyard-shop. When the King and Queen passed through the shed every vantage point had been manned by tiers of men in their working clothes.

'With a spontaneity for which there is no accounting thousands of voices, in a single instant, broke into song . . . in the presence of their Majesties, men were singing, "God Save the King".' (*Northern Whig.*)

King George and Queen Elizabeth saw many secrets of the war. Sometimes—in Wales and again in Derby and elsewhere—they visited plants where weapons were being forged so secret that only the King and Queen, after signing their passes, were able to enter: even their Staff were left outside.

On August 25, 1942, the King's youngest surviving brother, the Duke of Kent, was killed when his aircraft crashed in Scotland on its way to Iceland, where the Duke was to inspect R.A.F. bases. The body was found, by a sad coincidence, by a shepherd whose son was a servant at Buckingham Palace. The King and Queen were spending a few days at Balmoral, after inspecting the Fleet at Invergordon, and the Duke of Kent had stayed with them only a few days earlier. It was a crushing blow to the King, always fond of his younger brother and increasingly close to him during the last years. It was a terrible tragedy for the Duchess of Kent, whose youngest child Prince Michael was only seven weeks old.

When King George VI was going to visit troops in North Africa the plans were kept secret from all but the Staff most intimately involved. The Queen went with him in the car to the airport, waiting with him there through the hours of tension preceding take-off. (King George used the incognito of 'Mr. Lion'.)

Queen Elizabeth never deterred the King from going into danger, but she naturally suffered on such occasions. Sir John Wheeler-Bennett quotes her letter to Queen Mary, written at this time: 'I had an anxious few hours, because at 8.15 I heard that the plane had been heard near Gibraltar, and that it would soon be landing. Then after an hour and a half I heard that there was a thick fog at Gib. and they were going on to Africa. Then complete silence till a few minutes ago, when a message came that they had landed in Africa, and taken off again. Of course I imagined every sort of horror and walked up and down my room staring at the telephone.'

On the day on which it had been announced that the King was

in North Africa, Queen Elizabeth was in the East End of London. It was a most moving experience. She was greeted with overwhelming enthusiasm. The cheering crowds brought the Royal car to a halt, and swarmed all over it.

While the King was overseas the Queen acted as a Counsellor of State and undertook some of his duties, including the holding of an Investiture at which she decorated two hundred and fifty-five officers and men.

Alastair Philips in the *Glasgow Herald* Editorial Diary wrote:

'On that day a long line of men and women in uniform, headed by the late Wing Commander Guy Gibson and his dam-busting colleagues, overflowed from the investiture room through a corridor and into a large ante-room.

'At the tail-end of the line were low-ranking officers of the R.A.F.—the junior service. A colleague who was among them recalls that they moved forward at a snail's pace. Indeed he and those with him were still in the ante-room more than two hours after they first arrived in it, and they were thankful that a considerable number of chairs were available.

'At that time they did not realise that there was anything unusual in all this, until they noticed one of the palace flunkeys glancing impatiently at his watch. From this they gathered that this particular investiture was taking much longer than usual, "because the Queen is speaking to everyone being decorated".

'Although the Investiture began quite early in the morning it was long past one o'clock when those at the end of the line came to a spot where they could see the Queen, and they were able to note that she was indeed talking to everyone in turn and showing no signs of tiring from the long session.

'When our colleague at last came before her and his answer to her first question announced his Scottish accent the Queen seemed pleasured, and she did not let him go until she had extracted from him a potted autobiography.

'He left the dais feeling elated, though he confessed that the last few minutes of waiting to ascend the dais were far more nerve-wracking than any of his pre-operational "jitters" on bomber raids over Germany.'

The Queen's Lady-in-Waiting remembers standing behind her at this investiture, and how the Queen turned immediately afterwards to the elderly Lord Clarendon, who was Lord Chamberlain, and said, 'I do hope you are not tired.'

Although the Queen was unsparing of herself she did not believe in unnecessary heroics. She put a stop to her Lady of the Bedchamber staying on hand in London, whenever she was in waiting, whether she was wanted or not, saying it was ridiculous to be in London, waiting to be bombed, unless it was necessary. Since then the Lady of the Bedchamber has been sent for only when required.

When Buckingham Palace was damaged by bombs, and while more adequate shelters were installed, King George and Queen Elizabeth often slept at Windsor Castle, returning to the Palace during the day. A building in Fitzmaurice Place off Berkeley Square was designed as a protective shelter for the King and Queen during the war, but they never used it. When Schomberg House in the Mall was bombed, Princess Helena Victoria and Princess Marie Louise, daughters of Prince and Princess Christian, were given the use of it, and lived in a flat there for the rest of their lives.

A new pattern of life was established at Windsor. 'We now sit and eat in the Equerries' room at night,' wrote the Lady-in-Waiting, 'and the King and Queen eat in the Star Chamber next door, and they always come in for a gossip before going to bed. Lord Wigram (who was Lieutenant-Governor of Windsor Castle) has covered his tin hat with a white cover, so that all may recognise him—he is known as "Lord Equinox".'

Many evenings and nights were noisy with the crump of land mines and the bark of anti-aircraft guns. A small but strong cellar was further reinforced and divided into two. King George and Queen Elizabeth had beds in one compartment. The Princesses and 'Allah' slept in the other. The Princesses used to sleep in their shelter every night, going down carrying a little blue and a little pink case which contained their most precious possessions. These cases were the dolls' suitcases from the magnificent trousseaux of the two French dolls given to them by the people of France in 1938.

'I remember being at Windsor one Sunday,' said the Queen's sister. 'The King was away, and there was an awful air-raid over the castle. She and "Allah" took the children down to the shelter, and she made it all rather a picnic instead of alarming.'

The Queen had no use for panic. Once during the war at Windsor Castle when the air-raid warning had sounded and there was a lot of gun-fire very close at hand, the King and Queen were making their way to the air-raid shelter. A Warden, alarmed perhaps by the quantity of anti-aircraft fire, tried to hurry the Queen—he was given a withering look and she continued on her way at a more leisurely pace!

When the King and Queen were at Buckingham Palace a downstairs room was used as a dining room: King George and Queen Elizabeth served themselves whenever they had no guests. When an occasional dinner party was held, usually for about twelve persons, the only ladies present were usually the Queen and her Lady-in-Waiting, and the short meal was served by elderly pages wearing blue battledress.

Relaxations were few. The Queen liked, when she found the opportunity, to go to the lunch-hour concerts in the National Gallery—where she listened to such artists as Dame Myra Hess.

In the autumn of 1944 the King and Queen, accompanied by the Princesses, went north to Balmoral. Although the invasion of France was an accomplished fact, a last-minute, desperate effort to seize the Sovereign was still possible, especially after the daring coup by which Mussolini had been rescued by paratroopers, and security arrangements could not be relaxed.

A detachment of Household Cavalry, together with the Fifth Battalion of the Manchester Regiment (T.A.) and some Scottish Home Guard were placed on duty at Balmoral, where they continued training. Tactical guards were disposed at night, while a supporting company of the Manchester Regiment occupied Abergeldie. Everything was 'Top Secret', with mail censored and 'green envelopes' issued to the troops.

The Royal family took a keen interest in the troops, who were inspected by the King and held their Church parades at Crathie Church, where the services were attended by the Royal family.

Officers dined at the Castle, dances were arranged and the Manchester Regiment's concert party was in great demand.

The Royal family was particularly intrigued by the territorials of the Manchester Regiment, with their broad Lancastrian accents, which Queen Elizabeth can imitate brilliantly. A Lancastrian expression which amused them was 'Tha' Wha', a cryptic phrase of which Colonel Wills of the Manchester Regiment wrote:

'In particular, the large Lancastrian element of the Battalion scorns to say the normal, "I beg your pardon." It even looks down on the more common "Eh?" and prefers its own inimitable "Tha' Wha." Experts inform me that this is an abbreviation of "Thou What?" and that it is used in Lancashire to express astonishment, extreme doubt or complete incredulity.'

The expression had given its name to the Regimental concert party. On October 10, 1944, the Queen and the two Princesses took part in one of its concerts and became members of the 'Tha' Wha Club'. That evening, Queen Elizabeth wore the Regimental badge of the Manchester Regiment—an ordinary brass cap badge converted into a brooch for the Queen by soldering a safety-pin on the back. I doubt if the diamond brooch of the Manchester Regiment, with which Queen Elizabeth was presented in 1947, is any dearer to her. At the end of the evening, Queen Elizabeth presented to the Manchester Regiment a silver cup inscribed 'Tha' Wha—Balmoral, 1944.'

The contact made in wartime has been maintained in peace: two years later the King appointed the Queen to be Colonel-in-Chief of the Manchester Regiment. When the Manchester Regiment and the King's Regiment (Liverpool) were amalgamated to form the King's Regiment (Manchester and Liverpool), she became Colonel-in-Chief of the combined Regiment. When she attends ceremonies at which Territorials of the Manchesters are present, she always asks to see Old Comrades who were at Balmoral.

During the last months of the war, joy at the tide of victory rolling across Europe was tempered by the reappearance of heavy bomb damage, first from the V.1s and then from the V.2s. One day in the autumn of 1944 the King and Queen watched anti-aircraft guns in operation against the V.1s and saw a V.1 which had been damaged by anti-aircraft fire finished off by a Tempest fighter.

They went up to stay at Buckingham Palace after a break at Windsor, aware that a radio beam had been laid across it from Germany, and that German air attack would be concentrating that night on that part of London. The raid took place and in it the balcony of the Palace was damaged, and a flying bomb came down at the Hyde Park Corner end of the Buckingham Palace Gardens. A picture of the King inspecting the damage in his own garden was captioned in the censored press, 'His Majesty inspecting wreckage caused by a flying bomb in the South of England.'

The Queen did not like flying bombs; like many other people she found them more disconcerting than the bombs dropped by manned aircraft.

A Lady-in-Waiting who came on duty in London at the height of the flying bomb period did not take over in person as usual, because the Queen had sent her predecessor home early in the Royal train, which was routed to pass near her home in Yorkshire, and so saved her a slower and more tiring journey. Instead, notes of instruction had been left for the relieving Lady-in-Waiting and among them was one saying, 'When the alert goes, the Queen expects you to go to the shelters.'

'So at the first alert,' recalls the Lady-in-Waiting, 'I went straight down to the shelters, not even taking a book to read. No one else came. After a bit I got tired of this and came upstairs and wandered about the ground floor, looking for someone, I met a footman, who said, "Luncheon is not until quarter past one, my lady."

'I discovered that the Queen had got used to flying bombs in a week. After that she never took shelter during the day, although she used to sleep downstairs in London, and sometimes at Windsor, in order not to be disturbed during the night if there was a raid. There is a tiny passage behind the Belgian suite in Buckingham Palace, and when a flying bomb was alerted the Queen would say, "We'll hide in there." A very large housemaid was also always sheltering there, taking up the complete width of the passage, and, I must confess, making me feel much safer.'

During the autumn of 1944 the health of the Queen's father, Lord Strathmore, began to cause anxiety, and after a short illness, he died at Glamis Castle on November 7, 1944. It was a hard blow for the Queen. Lord Strathmore was devoted to his youngest daughter, and she to him. A friend wrote in *The Times* shortly after his death, 'His manner, at once distinguished and deliberate —combined with a strikingly handsome appearance was for those who knew him well an embodiment of the noblest qualities of British aristocracy.'

Lord Strathmore was mostly interested in country things; his estates, the welfare of his family, his tenants and workers. He was a wonderful host, taking pains to ensure the well-being of his guests. He had the family ability to get on equally well with all people with whom he shared interests, which was illustrated in the cricket matches he organised (bowling himself) and the local football matches he regularly attended from Glamis, often with his head gardener, Mr. Donald McInnes.

The King and Queen went to Scotland for Lord Strathmore's funeral. Once more the sad ceremonies took place from Glamis Castle. Foresters and gamekeepers bore his coffin, covered by a Union Jack, to a farm cart drawn by two horses: pipers of The Black Watch, with which he had long been connected, played the poignant 'Flowers of the Forest' on the long walk to the family burial ground.

* * *

As the end of the war came at last into sight the King and Queen could occasionally undertake engagements not directly connected with the war. The Treasurer of the Middle Temple had approached the Queen, and she had consented to become Treasurer of the Middle Temple, an appointment without precedent. No Monarch or Consort had joined one of the Inns of Court and no woman had ever been admitted to take part in the Parliament of an Inn.

The Queen took her place as a Bencher of the Middle Temple, and dined with her fellow benchers, on December 12, 1944. She wore a full evening dress of black velvet with a square décolletée and with it the peacetime sparkle of a diamond necklace, brooch and earrings. Over this she assumed her black silk gown upon arrival.

The Middle Temple had suffered from high explosive bombs in 1939 and 1940, and from fire bombs later. The famous Temple Church was gutted, the library so badly damaged that it was classified as a total loss, and one hundred and twelve out of two hundred and eighty-five sets of chambers were completely demolished—but not a bottle was broken in the wine-cellars, just under the pavement!

The dinner was held in the New Parliament Chamber: even that room was in a bad state. The windows had been blown in and temporarily repaired. The only electric light was suspended from the middle of the ceiling by lamp flex. Half the oriel window had been destroyed. But the tables were laid in the form of an 'E' with the Middle Temple Silver, and the dinner was served in the usual form. When dinner was ended, and the candles lit, the Master Treasurer rose and welcomed, 'Our new Bencher the Queen.'

The end of the war drew near, but a further loss remained. The death, in April 1945, of President Roosevelt, who had proved himself so staunch a friend, was a sad blow to King George and Queen Elizabeth.

The King and Queen were in Norfolk when the news came of Himmler's offer to surrender to the Western Powers. Queen Elizabeth had arranged to fly to London on the following day, for the wedding of her niece Rosemary Bowes-Lyon to Edward Joicey-Cecil, but instead the King and Queen returned at once to London by train. On Sunday, May 6, they were at Windsor when the message came that unconditional surrender was expected immediately. They at once drove to London, but at 6 p.m. it was decided to postpone announcement of the surrender until May 8 to suit the Americans and Russians.

On the night before V.E. day a deep family anxiety was happily relieved when Lord Lascelles (now the Earl of Harewood) returned to England from imprisonment by the Germans; and dined with the King and Queen at Buckingham Palace. Outside the Palace the crowds gathered, and on V.E. day they reached enormous numbers. They called continually for the King and Queen. Repeatedly—eight times in all—alone or with Winston Churchill between them, the King and Queen went onto the bomb-damaged balcony which had been draped with tasselled and fringed silk hangings, although board had replaced the broken glass in the window behind them.

Only at 9 p.m. did the cheering pause, while the crowds listened attentively to the broadcast message the King had recorded earlier in the day:

> 'The Queen and I know the ordeals which you have endured . . . and we are proud to have shared some of these ordeals.
> '. . . We shall have failed and the blood of our dearest will have flowed in vain if the victory which they died to win does not lead to a lasting peace, founded on justice and good-will. To that, then, let us turn our thoughts on this day of just triumph and proud sorrow.'

There was victory in Europe, but in the Far East the war dragged on. There was desperate urgency to relieve the plight of Allied prisoners-of-war in those prison camps which lay in re-captured territory, and to free those still in enemy hands.

On July 5, 1945, the British people went to the polls and when the votes of Army and Home were counted on July 25, it was found that they had rejected Churchill, the man who had led them in war. On August 6, the first atom bomb and on August 9, the second atom bomb were dropped on Japan: unconditional surrender followed only nine days after the dropping of the first bomb on Hiroshima.

On August 15, 1945, a few hours after the Japanese surrendered, King George VI and Queen Elizabeth drove to open Parliament, over wet roads lined with huge crowds, in an open landau drawn by four grey horses, a mounted escort in Service dress.

Two Speeches from the Throne had been prepared, one for use if the war continued, the other—which was happily delivered —if news of the surrender came in time.

That evening King George and Queen Elizabeth once more stood on the balcony of Buckingham Palace. Somewhere down below them, anonymously hidden in the cheering crowds, were their daughters, Princess Elizabeth, now nineteen, and Princess Margaret, who was six days short of her fifteenth birthday.

Peace had come at last.

'The war is over,' said the King in his broadcast to his people. 'You know, I think, that those four words have for the Queen and myself the same significance, simple yet immense, that they have for you. Our hearts are full to overflowing, as are your own. Yet there is not one of us who has experienced this terrible war who does not realise that we shall feel its inevitable consequence long after we have all forgotten our rejoicings of today.'

CHAPTER ELEVEN

THE FIRST HARD YEARS OF PEACE

Let us never rejoice in aught that injures others, nor accept a life of selfish ease while others work and serve. Let us who have received most be the readiest to give

A Prayer from the Service of the Order of the Thistle, quoted by Queen Elizabeth at Glenalmond School, July 20, 1947

THE war was over. The immediate rejoicing was soon succeeded by a feeling of reaction and fatigue. Everything had been poured out into the six-year war effort; now the heavy cost had to be reckoned.

The King had been under no illusion about the difficulties which the British Commonwealth would face when the urgency of war had passed. 'Make no mistake,' he had said, 'there is a very hard time waiting for us after the war. The killing will have stopped, but our troubles will be great.' Internationally, the sky was dark. The wartime alliance with Russia dissolved almost overnight. Nationally, everyone in Britain was suddenly obsessed by the petty, cumulative discomforts which had been borne with stoicism for so long, but suddenly seemed insupportable. Everyone was tired of dull, rationed food, shabby clothes and insufficient fuel.

King George and Queen Elizabeth faced a personal renunciation. Hustled in emergency onto the throne, sustained by patriotism and courage through the years of war, they had now to face the fact that the end of war did not mean for them a return to the quiet ways they loved. Gone for ever was the comparatively private life that once might have been theirs. 'It was when the war was over,' said Sir David Bowes-Lyon, 'that the King and Queen realised that they could never go back to a secluded life. They thought it over, and they faced up to their changed life. They made the best of it, and did not waste time crying over what might have been.'

The King and the Queen themselves had greatly changed. King George at the beginning of his realm had been lost without his wife's support. Now he had grown to his full stature, and Queen Elizabeth had stepped a little to one side. Although the general public did not notice it the King had become the leading partner, to whom the Queen took her problems: she leant increasingly upon his strength and steadfastness.

For the King it was still, as always, his wife who made the sun shine and the birds sing. She brought him joy, and when his temperament spilled over into irritation, she brought him calm.

Queen Elizabeth was now in her mid-forties. She had entered the war as a young married woman: she emerged after six years of constant emotional and physical strain wearied and tired. Her physical courage in the face of danger had been flawless; now another, and possibly for her more difficult kind of courage was required.

Queen Elizabeth loves beautiful things—graciousness, comfort, a pleasant way of life, not only for herself but for everyone. Now she had to face a period in which tattiness, drabness, queues, shortages, unglamorous discomforts were not merely unavoidable hardships but appeared almost as positive virtues, under the dreary title of austerity. Nationally and domestically, the Queen looked upon a threadbare house, where the damage of war and the neglect of years suddenly become apparent, as old clothes look shabby in the first strong sunlight of spring.

The monarchy had to switch from the secrecy of wartime, where most of the King and Queen's movements had been unheralded and secret, to the openly announced and crowded engagements of peacetime, when public interest would be directed not only upon the report of an event, but upon the event itself. The technique of a modern Royal visit gradually developed. It was due to the Queen's personality that it did not become too stereotyped—well organised but not rigid. Perhaps she did not observe the provisional timetable as exactly as she might, but it made the visits more human. The Queen liked it to be arranged for her to see the people who were doing things.

First came events of rejoicing and thanksgiving. Immediately after V.E. Day the King and Queen made a victory tour of South

London by car, which was at times almost swamped by huge, cheering crowds in the badly bombed boroughs of Deptford, Lewisham, Streatham and Greenwich. Victory tours followed to the different regions of the British Isles, and also visits to the Isle of Man in July; and to the Channel Islands, newly freed from German occupation.

There were so many groups of people who deserved special recognition for their work in the war that it was some considerable time before each had its special service, march-past or other form of recognition. The King and Queen endeavoured to be present as often as they could. They also gave parties at Windsor and Sandringham for the returned ex-Servicemen who worked on the Royal estates, their tenants and employees. The Victory Party, held in July 1945 in the grounds of Sandringham House, was attended by two thousand five hundred people. The Windsor Party was held indoors in November, in the State Apartments of the Castle.

Among the first to be officially entertained at Buckingham Palace were those who had worked for the National Savings movement; they were invited to an Afternoon Party in the summer of 1946. Seven thousand people were present. King George and Queen Elizabeth came out into the grounds from the Bow Room, on the centre of the garden front, as the Garden Door was still unusable on account of bomb damage. No sooner had the King and Queen appeared than there was a concentrated rush forward towards them. The King and Queen were wildly acclaimed by guests behaving with an uninhibited enthusiasm never before seen in these sedate surroundings. Gentlemen Ushers, Yeoman of the Guard, Gentlemen-at-Arms, detectives, linked arms to do their best to hold a path clear along which the King and Queen could pass; they were battered and buffeted, but they managed to hold their line. The official responsible for organising the Garden Party thought, 'I *shall* get into trouble.' But the King said afterwards, 'I have never enjoyed anything more.' He was moved by his people's enthusiasm and not in the least put out, as he would almost certainly have been before the war.

The Queen, who was their Patron, paid tribute to the Women's

Land Army, which had provided power for the farms to a degree its initiators had hardly dared to hope, at a reception in the Mansion House for seven hundred and fifty Land Girls, each of whom had served for the full six years for which the Women's Land Army had been in existence.

It was not until ten months after V.J. Day that the Victory Parade took place in London. It was the largest military parade ever held in Britain. Every Commonwealth country, and all the Allies except Russia, Poland and Yugoslavia, who declined to participate (so swiftly had wartime unity disintegrated), were represented in the twenty-one thousand troops and civilians who took part.

Before the parade, the King and Queen with Princess Elizabeth and Princess Margaret spent a long time in the encampment which had been set up in Kensington Gardens.

On the day of the Parade, June 8, 1946, the King took the salute from a dais on the Mall, with the Queen standing beside him. Seated on the dais were Queen Mary, Princess Elizabeth in her A.T.S. uniform, Princess Margaret, Crown Prince Olav of Norway, Princess Juliana and Prince Bernhard of the Netherlands, King Feisal of Iraq and Prince Felix of Luxembourg. On benches beside the dais Prime Minister Attlee sat beside ex-Prime Minister Churchill, and the Chiefs of Staff were assembled.

Over the dais fluttered, by the King's command, a small, storm-sized and slightly torn Royal Standard which had flown in the cruiser *Arethusa*, in which His Majesty crossed the Channel to visit his troops in Normandy on June 16, 1944.

*   *   *

Meanwhile, slowly and painfully, life was resuming a more normal pattern. Everything was so shabby: progress was slow because of the shortage of manpower and materials, and the urgent priority of housing the bombed-out and returning Servicemen. Even in the Palace the State Rooms were filled with shrouded furniture, the walls unpainted, the Garden Entrance unrepaired, the grounds only sketchily maintained. The decorative railings of the forecourt had been destroyed by a bomb and replaced by temporary iron fencing.

Damaged ceilings and walls at Windsor were renovated and redecorated. The steel doors which had been installed as a wartime security were removed. Chandeliers were gradually cleaned and re-hung. The King's pictures were brought out of their hiding place and were exhibited at the Royal Academy before being re-hung at Windsor and Buckingham Palaces, often in new positions chosen by the King and Queen together. (Queen Mary never failed to note and assess the slightest change.) Precious china was washed and restored to the cabinets. Curtains were cleaned and occasionally renewed. It was the work of years. Indeed the Royal Chapel, which was bombed in 1940, was only rebuilt twenty-two years later.

As peacetime life gradually revived, the Queen encouraged her daughters to share it. Princess Elizabeth, who was nineteen, and Princess Margaret, who was fifteen in V.J. month, had led quiet, restricted lives during the war, and she wanted them to have some gaiety to offset the effect of the years of tension.

Together with Queen Mary, they went to Covent Garden Opera House—which had been used as a popular dance-hall during the war—when, on February 20, 1946, it was re-opened in its proper function with the Sadler's Wells Ballet Company in *The Sleeping Beauty*.

'It was certainly a great moment at Covent Garden when the King and Queen, Queen Mary, and the Princesses entered the royal box, and the motley of people in evening dress, dinner jackets and lounge suits stood up to applaud.

'But none could say that the glamour of pre-war Covent Garden had returned. That lush atmosphere of flashing tiaras of dowagers and of champagne in the crush bar was absent. The only real touch of the old days was the great candelabrum of the crush bar. It had been given a real clean-up, and its mass of scintillating light seemed a miracle out of fairy-land.

'. . . The glamour, of course, was on the stage. None could recall such a wonderful performance of *The Sleeping Beauty*.' (*Yorkshire Post.*)

The ballet was produced by Ninette de Valois, staged by Oliver Messel, and danced by Margot Fonteyn as the Princess, Beryl

Grey as the Lilac Fairy, Moira Shearer and Robert Helpmann. It must indeed have seemed a fairyland to the real Princesses in the Royal box.

The King occasionally took his family to the theatre, generally to the lighter and gayer pieces. They went to Cochran's *Bless the Bride*; *Annie Get Your Gun*; *Fifty-Fifty* at the Strand Theatre; *Pacific 1860*, the Royal family's first post-war visit to Drury Lane; and *The Winslow Boy* by Terence Rattigan. Sometimes they sat in a box, but they preferred seats in the first row of the circle, or in the stalls.

In 1946 Ascot was revived, with lounge suits or Service uniform the dress for men, and for women day dress with hat. *The Times* wrote:

> 'Royal Ascot has been restored to the calendar of social events, but, like much else in our new peace-time, its grandeur is great diminished . . .
>
> 'The King and the royal guests drove to the course in closed cars, but tomorrow, when the Gold Cup is run for, they will again drive in open carriages drawn by Windsor greys . . .
>
> 'Neither the royal enclosure nor the paddock had any startling note of fashion to catch the eye, nor was there any procession of elegantly dressed people to the Heath, across the course, because the Heath had none of its marquees for the sumptuous luncheons and teas of bygone days.
>
> '. . . One particularly cheerless special constable, whose job was to see that people did not stand on the seats, pointed out that before the war people's manners were enough to prevent them doing so . . .
>
> '. . . The refreshment pavilion and the lesser buffets made a brave effort to look like Ascot of former days, but of course, suffered severely from the prevailing austerity. Even so, there were strawberries and ice-cream for half-a-crown and champagne for sixty shillings a bottle, while on the course a peach could be bought from a tray for five shillings.'

In 1946 the King and Queen held their first post-war Afternoon Party in the grounds of Buckingham Palace. The King wore naval uniform, the Queen was in mauve, and the Princesses wore blue. Queen Mary was present, and the Princess Royal and the Duchess of Kent—the Duke and Duchess of Gloucester were in Australia—Princess Alice, Countess of Athlone and Queen Mary's brother, the Earl of Athlone, and Lord and Lady Louis Mountbatten. From other Royal families came King George of the Hellenes with his sister Princess Catherine and kinsman Prince Philip (who was quite unnoticed by the general public); King Peter and Queen Alexandra of Yugoslavia; King Feisal of Iraq and his mother Queen Aliya. Seven thousand guests were present. Although dress restrictions were relaxed and lounge suits were permitted for the first time, about half the male guests wore morning dress. Gradually khaki, which was at first very prominent, disappeared from formal occasions.

There was discussion about the form which the presentations of débutantes should take. During the first three pre-war years of King George VI's reign Evening Courts had been held, although, because of the great number of people attending them, this had proved a great and constantly increasing expense to the King. After the war Evening Courts became economically impossible.

For the first year or so after the war, attendance at an afternoon Garden Party was considered as Presentation at Court.

Later, when the State Rooms were re-opened, the Presentation Parties were held inside Buckingham Palace. The last of these was held in 1955.

There were also special guests to entertain from time to time. At the time of the meeting in London of four Foreign Ministers— Mr. Bevin (United Kingdom), Mr. Marshall (United States), M. Bidault (France) and Mr. Molotov (U.S.S.R.), the King and Queen gave a party for them and for the members of their delegations.

Mrs. Roosevelt was a visitor to Windsor Castle. The King and Queen had hoped to welcome both President and Mrs. Roosevelt to England after the war and a warm invitation had been sent to the President shortly before his death. In *On My Own* Mrs. Roosevelt wrote of the visit:

'There was, of course, much formality, but I was impressed by the easy manner of the King, dressed during the day in tweed jacket and slacks like a country squire relaxing at the week-end, and by the skill of the Queen in keeping their family life on a warm, friendly level even in such historic settings as Windsor Castle.'

The Queen expressed her thoughts in the speeches she made during her many public duties. These were not mere formal utterances but a public declaration of her ideals and hopes.

Here are some of the Queen's comments and judgements on the post-war world:

On the sacrifices of war:

'We must oppose with all our might any attempt to belittle the sacrifices of the last war or to lament them as purposeless. Those who laid down their lives did not ask for conditions and guarantees. They offered everything and expected nothing. Have we who have survived offered too little and expected too much? We must remain in action and be worthy of the fallen.' (To the Women's Section of 'Toc H' at the Albert Hall.)

On the difficulties of post-war youth:

'The days of war had their greatness, courage and self-sacrifice, but they contained also their meannesses, their desire to attain things by ways not always above board and, worst of all, the disaster of broken homes. Those days are over but they have left their mark on many of those who grew up during the years of war. I feel that you and your fellow Members can help to eliminate those marks, and can now and in the future seek to equip the youth of the nation with the qualities of truth, honesty and justice.' (The Queen: Addressing the Annual General Meeting of the Federation of Women's Institutes, 1954.)

On maintaining proportion in modern life:

'We live today in a technical society, and the problems which it has created affect every aspect of our physical lives. I feel, however, that we must not allow ourselves to be obsessed by the purely material complexities which confront us. They affect, also, our personal and national relationships.' (The Centenary Celebrations of Queen's College, Harley Street.)

On the second-rate:

'To the rising generation I would say two things. First, in these days when freedom is greatly curtailed, and regulation is almost universal, do not lose your own individuality; it is your most precious possession; and next, never be content with what is mediocre and ugly. You may sometimes have to accept it, but never be content with it.' (Message to the young people of South Africa.)

About the power of the individual (speaking in the Albert Hall about the Rev. 'Tubby' Clayton, founder of 'Toc H'):

'In a world where the individual may sometimes seem almost to lose his individuality, submerged beneath the mass movements of which we hear so much, we may well be heartened by remembering that we stand here today because of the inspiration of one man.'

On freedom:

'Only ordered freedom is true freedom. Nothing stands out more clearly amid the discords and conflicts of our age than the danger of the misuse of language which preaches licence in the name of liberty, or uses the phrases of democracy as a cloak for the most cruel tyranny.' (On receiving the Freedom of the City of London.)

On the future:

'Our lot has been cast in an age of great uncertainty and it is of vital concern that this should not strangle creative action. It is only by acts of courage and imagination, such as the founding of this college, that we can show refusal to adopt an attitude of resignation or fear in the face of much that threatens the spiritual as well as the material circumstances in which we live. By so doing we may, more profoundly than we know, do something to dispel them.

'In the past, men and women were mainly preoccupied by the affairs of family or local life: events and ideas taking shape abroad seemed remote and impersonal. Now, the whole world is, as it were, our village. Owing to the development of communications, words spoken today far across the world are delivered, in banner headlines, for all to read tomorrow morning. Thus we find ourselves brought into great confusion and chaos. As a result, our minds are nowadays exposed to so much that is new and perplexing that they may become numbed if they are not trained to judge what is thrust before them.

'Therefore, I would like to name the qualities which I believe we need, the three Ds—the elder brothers of the three Rs—first, discernment, the ability to judge between the false and the true, the essential and the inessential; second, decision, the power to turn judgement into action; third, design, the art of giving practical form to a plan of action.' (Opening the North Staffordshire University College at Keele.)

* * *

The Queen found ways in which she could help some of the many people who turned to her with their post-war problems. Her Ladies-in-Waiting were kept busy contacting local and national authorities for advice and aid.

Financial assistance was given, both personally and through special funds which were sometimes placed at the Queen's disposal. A considerable sum of money collected for her by the people of Canada was given by Queen Elizabeth to the Soldiers', Sailors', and Airmen's Families Association (S.S.A.F.A.), 'to be devoted to the needs of the dependents of all ranks who have lost their lives in the service of their country, or of those dependents of such Service personnel whose needs are attributable to the circumstances of the war'. The Queen specially wished to be kept informed of the way the money was used, and about those who benefited.

In 1955 she gave a further large sum to S.S.A.F.A. which 'had been placed in her hands by a number of Belgian people who had enjoyed the hospitality of this country', and this was used in a similar way. Again, in 1955, an American citizen, Mr. Daniel Greene Cary, offered to Her Majesty a gift of money to be devoted to the assistance of war victims in the United Kingdom.

The generous offer was accepted and a part of this money was allocated to S.S.A.F.A.

By 1959 the Queen's Canadian Fund was almost exhausted, and when Queen Elizabeth realised this the following letter from her Comptroller was received by the chairman of S.S.A.F.A.:

8 October, 1959.

'. . . Her Majesty notes that at the end of July you had in hand a sum of £1,300, which is less than has been your normal expenditure over some years past.

'It is Queen Elizabeth's desire now to supplement this sum by an annual donation of [and a very considerable sum was named] as it is her hope and expectation that she will be able, from a special fund which is at her disposal, to repeat this payment for the next five years.

'It might perhaps appropriately be put on record that Queen Elizabeth has been influenced in this policy by the admirable administration for which S.S.A.F.A. has been responsible over the last decade, and in the confidence that she could not more appropriately give effect to her own inclinations.'

*   *   *

The Queen's life was filling with the problems, perplexities and joys of the mother of a grown-up family. During the Royal family's annual holiday at Balmoral in the late summer of 1946 there was some speculation as to the identity of a tall, fair young man who accompanied the Royal family to Crathie Church on several consecutive Sundays. He was authoritatively and variously identified by know-all bystanders as Lord Carnegie, Lord Ogilvy, Lord Dalkeith and a variety of foreign princes, but few recognised Prince Philip of Greece and Denmark. His name was soon to be linked with that of Princess Elizabeth: it was not, however, until the following summer that the King gave his consent to the engagement.

In October 1946 the Queen, with Princess Elizabeth and Princess Margaret, went from Balmoral to the Clyde to attend the speed trials of the Cunard liner *Queen Elizabeth*. The liner the Queen had launched in the black days of Munich had done sterling service throughout the war as a troop carrier, and was being converted to her planned function of luxury passenger liner. The Queen was shown a length of teak rail scarred with initials carved by some of the wartime troops the liner had carried, which was preserved as an historic souvenir. The King was to have visited the ship, but once again he was unable to come, not this time on account of a national crisis, but because he was laid up with a cold.

It was a blustery, squally day, with the clouds racing over the purple-shadowed peaks of Arran. While the ship was completing a run over the Sannox measured mile the Queen was asked if she would care to take the wheel, and she agreed. She was first placed at the auxiliary wheel, while the quartermaster continued unobtrusively to control the ship, but the Queen was having none of that. 'What is he doing here?' she asked the Master. The quartermaster then left the wheel, and Queen Elizabeth herself turned the great ship round for another run across the mile.

Meanwhile, plans were being made for the forthcoming visit to South Africa, which would be the first—and it would prove the last—by the Sovereign to this Dominion. For the first time the whole Royal family—the King, the Queen, Princess Elizabeth and Princess Margaret—were going together on a Commonwealth tour.

H.M.S. *Vanguard*, the latest (and the last) Royal Naval battleship was chosen to carry the Royal family. The Admiral's accommodation was specially adapted for their living quarters, and extra furniture was provided from the Royal yacht *Victoria and Albert* which was lying in Portsmouth awaiting breaking-up. One of the ship's boats, a forty-five-foot diesel-driven picket boat, was converted for use as a Royal Barge.

The Royal Household chosen for the tour included three Ladies-in-Waiting, Lady Harlech and Lady Delia Peel, in attendance on the Queen, and Lady Margaret Egerton as Lady-in-Waiting to Princess Elizabeth. Major Thomas Harvey, who had recently been appointed private secretary to the Queen, was making his first Royal tour; Sir Alan Lascelles, private secretary to the King, and Major Michael Adeane, assistant private secretary to the King, both with previous experience from the

Canadian tour. Queen Elizabeth's detective, Inspector A. E. Perkins, her two dressers and her hairdresser were also among the party of twenty-nine.

The Queen's and Princesses' clothes for the tour had to be chosen with particular care. The effect of such a tour upon the clothing trade is considerable, and millinery colours that season included 'springbok', 'pale mealies', 'Rhodesian gold', 'African dawn', 'Limpopo' and 'Cape Mist'.

H.M.S. *Vanguard* sailed from Portsmouth on February 1, 1947, seven years and nine months after King George and Queen Elizabeth had sailed for Canada.

It had been hoped that the voyage would be a real rest for the Royal family, but on the very day on which *Vanguard* sailed from Portsmouth Britain was gripped by a cold spell of great intensity, which penetrated the daily life of the British people as weather had not affected them for hundreds of years.

'The King worried frightfully. He thought he ought to be at home, sharing the rigours with his people, and the newspaper reports, which were relayed on board by radio, did nothing to reassure him,' said one of the party. There was a Press agitation for his return. At that time, the people of Britain were still apt to regard the Sovereign as virtually their exclusive possession, and did not understand the equal rights of the people of the other Commonwealth countries. It would of course have been unthinkable for the King to abandon the tour, with its complex plans which involved so many thousands of his subjects, literally in midstream.

Nor could the early stages of the voyage be described as a pleasure-cruise. Britain did not have an exclusive share of the bad weather. Heavy water broke continually over the battleship. Gratings were smashed, staff cabins flooded, and the furniture, including the piano, thoughtfully installed, broke adrift. Boat-drill was cancelled. Two successive Royal Standards were whipped to tatters at the masthead, and a solitary remaining strip was kept by the King as a souvenir.

The Royal party were up and about, if some of them, like others on board, were not enjoying themselves. They spent most of the days in the sun lounge, watching the wild seas breaking over the escorting vessels; but they all struggled up to the saluting platform when the French battleship *Richelieu* passed, drenched sailors standing at attention; and later, in even worse weather, when the Portuguese sloop *Bartolomeo Dias* swept by to give the salute.

The seas were like mountains and the deck of the accompanying aircraft-carrier could be seen disappearing below the seas. One of the Household opened a door to the deck and the sea came right in over him. The furniture rolled about, sometimes with someone in it. 'The Queen hardly seemed to notice; I remember she played Chinese Checkers, though she had to hold onto the board all the time,' said one of her Ladies.

As the skies cleared off the Canary Islands spirits on board the battleship were stimulated by new surroundings and new scenes and rose accordingly. Queen Elizabeth had not left Britain for nearly eight years. The Princesses had never been overseas before. All sorts of deck games were played and there were concerts and singsongs at which the Princesses, with their gay singing of part songs, delighted their audiences.

It was at this time that observant Members of His Majesty's Household first noticed that King George's health was beginning to bother him. He had never been a robust man but he had seldom been ill, and had hardly suffered even from a cold during the war. At this time his leg was beginning to give trouble with cramp, although he did not say much about it. He had lost a lot of weight, and he had a cough which was never very bad, but which never seemed to clear up. During the world tour in 1927, the Duke of York had energetically played deck games, and the Duchess had played little. Now it was the King who rested, and the Queen who played games, especially deck tennis, at which she was quite good.

The King and Queen were eagerly looking forward to their tour: they had shared a great love for Africa ever since their first safari to East Africa in 1924–25, a time to which they always looked back with pleasure.

On February 17 the whole Royal family were up early, scanning the coastline of South Africa through glasses as *Vanguard* steamed towards Table Mountain. At 6.30 a.m. they were met by three frigates of the South Africa Navy; while Venturas of the South African Air Force droned overhead. Then *Vanguard* entered the narrow 'hole in the wall', passing from the tumbled waters of the Agulhas current into the smooth waters of Cape Town harbour. Those on board could see the vast crowds gathered on Signal Hill, on whose lower slopes school-children dressed in white formed with their still bodies the word '*Welcome*'. As the ship was edged alongside in Duncan Dock by four tugs a great cheer went up from the huge crowds.

After a few days in Cape Town, the Royal party set off on a tour of ten thousand miles through South Africa. They travelled up-country in their special White Train, through the sheep country of the North-East Cape and the grasslands of the Orange Free State, on a tour which took them to Basutoland; to Durban; as far north as the Kruger National Park in the Transvaal; to South Africa's other capital of Pretoria; and to Johannesburg and the Rand.

The long White Train and its pilot press and baggage train wound like two caterpillars along the tracks. The trains were heavy, and had to stop every two hours for water. At each stopping place, however small, there were crowds waiting, and the King and Queen, even if they were in the middle of dinner, invariably went out onto the platform.

'I remember standing in the corridor watching the Queen, in a beautiful crinoline dress, sidling along the narrow corridor, and then how superbly she stepped down onto the platform and out among the waiting people,' said a Lady-in-Waiting. 'The Queen once remarked to me, "You must *never* look at your feet, my mother always taught me that."'

The Queen had an amazing way of picking out people to talk to, and in getting them to say something interesting in the few seconds she had to speak to them. She talked to hundreds of people in this way.

The Royal party lived on board the train for much of the time. Outside by day it was extremely hot, but inside the train the temperature was controlled by air-conditioning. This was, of course, a great benefit, but even the best mechanical cooling is not without its disadvantages. No window could be opened, it was not entirely silent, and the humidity made it difficult to dry anything completely.

At night the train was stopped in a siding, which had often been specially prepared. One morning before dawn the Royal party was awakened early by singing: it was a chorus of Africans singing unaccompanied and with great beauty Handel's 'Hallelujah' chorus: Queen Elizabeth was delighted.

During the long train trips through Africa there were times when the King seemed very tired, and the Queen was seen to save him in every way she could. She was always close by him, introducing subjects of conversation in which he was interested and smoothing his path in little ways, but she never voiced her anxiety to the Household.

In Basutoland there was a display of fireworks which were let off distinctly close to the guests of honour, some of whom were obviously a little nervous (Princess Elizabeth had a small hole burnt in her dress). The Queen, looking very splendid in a blue satin dress with a tiara sparkling in her hair, sat motionless on a little wooden chair, smiling as if she were enjoying every moment of it.

At the time of the King and Queen's visit to South Africa in 1947 the party in power was led by Field Marshal Smuts, a man already well known and much liked by the King and Queen, and who had been their guest at Windsor during the war. There was genuine affection as well as respect between the Sovereign and his South African Prime Minister.

Field Marshal Smuts was said by his opponents to be 'a man who had to run the show himself', but during the South African tour he brought many different Ministers to be in attendance upon the King. They stayed in a coach attached to the Royal train, and Smuts saw to it that each had a real opportunity to get to know the King and Queen.

The Queen had a great personal success with everyone, including the formidable South African Dutch. The Nationalists would have liked to boycott the tour entirely, but did not do so, partly out of respect for Field Marshal Smuts, and the Queen charmed smiles onto many stern faces which had initially looked more than a little dour.

Once or twice the Royal family travelled by air, as on the one-day trip to Peitersburg in the Northern Transvaal, during which the King flew with Princess Margaret (their aircraft was dented in collision with a vulture) and the Queen with Princess Elizabeth, so that Sovereign and Heiress Presumptive did not fly together.

The Royal family also flew to Southern Rhodesia at the outset of their eight-day visit, which was the first of many made by Queen Elizabeth to Central Africa. They arrived in Salisbury on April 7, and afterwards visited Livingstone, the most northerly point of their tour, and saw the Victoria Falls. Their journey north had taken fifty days; when they left Bulawayo they took only four days by the direct train route to return to Cape Town.

It was in Cape Town on the following day, April 21, that Princess Elizabeth celebrated her twenty-first birthday; her parents listened to her moving broadcast and the declaration of faith in which she dedicated herself to the service of her future peoples. They must have felt great pride and a sense of fulfilment when they heard their young daughter declare the purpose of her life. Yet they must also have felt a certain sadness that her life should be filled with such great responsibilities. Mercifully they did not know that less than five years of her father's life stood between Princess Elizabeth and the fulfilment of her vow.

On April 24, 1947, the Royal family re-embarked at Cape Town in H.M.S. *Vanguard*.

'. . . It was among smiling faces that the Royal family said their last farewells to the eminent South Africans assembled on the platform and the King reviewed his South African guard of honour for the last time. The Governor-General and the Prime Minister, who had been the first to greet the King, and Queen and Princesses on their arrival were also the last to say goodbye. "God Save the King" and "Die Stam" were played, and the Royal family passed up the gangway into the ship. A few minutes later they appeared on the high platform above the forward gun turret, from which their distant figures had first become visible to South Africans . . .

'Soon the tugs had swung the *Vanguard* round, and she was

heading for the harbour mouth and the open sea beyond Table Bay. But before the change of direction carried out of sight the figures still waving from above the guns the crowds hitherto seated in the stands broke away in one great cheering multitude and came running down to the waterside to shout and cheer in their last farewell. So it was a sea of faces and a forest of hands, reaching out as if to make a last contact over the water, that made up the last sight that the King and Queen of South Africa would have of their southern people.' (*The Royal Family in Africa:* Dermot Morrah.)

It may seem that the great success of the South African tour was meaningless, because of the repudiation of the Sovereign by South Africa which took place a short time later. This would be only partly true. Such a tour reinforced the unifying features between the two countries. Afterwards, even when things go wrong politically as they did here, the personal feelings of good-will and affection engendered by such a tour help to lessen the personal bitterness and animosity which would otherwise prevail. Without the South African tour, troubles between our countries might well have begun sooner and reached greater violence.

On May 12 the Royal family returned to Britain, and were immediately busy with preparations for the announcement of the engagement of Princess Elizabeth to Prince Philip of Greece and Denmark. He had renounced his titles the previous December and become simple Lieutenant Philip Mountbatten, R.N., following his application for British nationality (to which he was entitled after serving in the Navy during the war). The young people had wished to marry for some time. An 'arranged', love-less marriage was abhorrent to the King and Queen, but they wanted their daughter to be quite certain of her choice, which would be even more vital for her than for other women, as when she became Queen her only really intimate confidant and com-panion would be her husband. King George thought it wisest for them to prove their love by time and a degree of separation.

The engagement was not announced until nearly two months after the Royal family had returned from South Africa. On May 26, a fortnight after their return, Queen Mary was entertained at a family luncheon party in honour of her eightieth birthday in Buckingham Palace, and Lieutenant Philip Mountbatten was among the guests. Yet although he had been a member of the Royal Ascot house-party at Windsor Castle in the previous year, he was not among the house guests in 1947. He was present, however, at the dance for about a hundred young people which was held in the Red Drawing Room on the last evening of the house-party, at which he danced almost every dance with Princess Elizabeth.

The persistent rumours of an engagement which were circulating at last had confirmation when a special sheet, attached to the Court Circular of Wednesday, July 9, 1947, announced:

'It is with the great pleasure that the King and Queen announce the betrothal of their dearly beloved daughter, the Princess Elizabeth, to Lieutenant Philip Mountbatten, R.N., son of the late Prince Andrew, to which union the King has gladly given his consent.'

Princess Elizabeth was twenty-one, her fiancé twenty-six. When the King finally gave his consent to the marriage, he gave it generously and willingly, while the Queen, with characteristic warmth, welcomed her future son-in-law into the close-knit family. They were thankful that their daughter's choice had fallen upon such a man. The moving letter which King George wrote to Princess Elizabeth at the time of her wedding has often been quoted:

'Our family, us four, the Royal family, must remain together, with additions of course at suitable moments!!

'I have watched you grow up all these years with pride under the skilful direction of Mummy who, as you know, is the most marvellous person in the world in my eyes, and I can, I know, always count on you, and now Philip, to help us in our work.'

Although Lieutenant Mountbatten did not accompany the Royal family to the International Horse Show on the eve of his engagement, from the time of the announcement he was immediately included in the Royal family's public activities. On the day that the public learnt of the engagement he appeared in the Royal party at the first Buckingham Palace Garden Party of the season. On July 15, he went north with them to Holyroodhouse.

The newly engaged young people received a tremendous welcome from the public of Edinburgh. King George said that he and the Queen were specially touched during the visit by the friendliness of the citizens and were 'delighted to observe the spontaneous affection towards Princess Elizabeth in connection with her betrothal'.

The Royal family went on to the west of Scotland. At the Crookston old people's home outside Glasgow Lieutenant Mountbatten, unperturbed by his first public duties, made what was soon to be recognised as a characteristic quip when he said to a girl reporter who had stationed herself among some of the patients in a ward, 'Aren't you a little young to be in here?' In this imaginatively planned home, many of the old people were accommodated in independent cottages.

'The King and Queen went separately into two of the homes, and when they met coming out the King, who liked the homes very much, jokingly said to the Queen: "I have put our names down for one of these".' (*Yorkshire Post.*)

Preparations for Princess Elizabeth's wedding increasingly dominated the time and thoughts not only of the Royal family, but of the whole country. The wedding broke into that rather dreary time like a bright day in winter. At last there was something pleasant to think and talk about.

The King decided, in line with Government policy, that there should be no lavish display in connection with the wedding. He also decided that he would pay from the Privy Purse all the wedding expenses with the exception of street decorations in Whitehall and the Mall, and that he would undertake the expenses of the married establishment of Princess Elizabeth for two years after the wedding.

It was rumoured that the wedding would be held in private in St. George's Chapel, Windsor, and there was general pleasure when it was announced that the wedding would be celebrated in

Westminster Abbey, like that of the bride's parents. A popular newspaper put a 'referendum' to its readers: 'Should the Princess's wedding day be selected as the first post-war occasion to restore to Britain the traditional gaiety of a gala public event?' Over eighty-six per cent of the readers replied, 'Yes.'

The wedding was planned to resemble as closely as possible that of the bride's parents, twenty-four years before, although regulations for dress were relaxed for the guests, and full dress was not to be worn. The usual State Dinner on the eve of the wedding was replaced by a buffet supper.

When King George was told the widespread wish of ordinary people to be allowed to share in the Princess's wedding, he decided to relax the usual rule that presents could be accepted only from those personally known to the Royal family. Wedding presents poured in. Princess Elizabeth's Grenadier Guards—she was immensely proud to be their Colonel—were kept busy unpacking wedding presents in St. James's Palace. These were of every imaginable kind: jewellery—King George and Queen Elizabeth gave their daughter a ruby and diamond necklace and two pearl necklaces; the King also gave her a personal present of French-cut diamond chandelier earrings—a home-made plastic brooch from a thirteen-year-old schoolgirl; a thoroughbred filly from the Aga Khan and a Siamese kitten from a district nurse; kettle-holders knitted by old-age pensioners; valuable furniture; silver and china; and a bed of rhododendrons, to be chosen and planted at a later date. The wedding presents were catalogued, and the catalogue printed. As it had to end somewhere and presents kept arriving, the number of presents listed was the same as the telephone number of the Lord Chamberlain's office at St. James's Palace—3,007. The presents were shown to the public, who queued in their thousands to see them in St. James's Palace.

On August 15, King George gave Sunninghill Park near Windsor Great Park as a grace and favour house to Princess Elizabeth, but only a fortnight later it was destroyed by fire. Clarence House, which had not been used as a private residence since the death of the Duke of Connaught in 1942, was to be their home, but it had been damaged by bomb blasts and required much renovating. Princess Elizabeth would therefore bring her husband to share her parents' home, like many other newly married people of the time.

A few days before the wedding the King invested Princess Elizabeth as a Lady of the Garter, as he wished her to have precedence in the Order over her future husband, who was himself invested as a Knight Commander of the Most Noble Order of the Garter on the eve of his wedding, and created Duke of Edinburgh, Earl of Merioneth and Baron Greenwich of Greenwich in the County of London.

Thursday, November 20, 1947, the day of the wedding, was grey and reasonably mild. The Mall was lined with thirty-two tall poles, hung with yellow and white banners bearing 'E' in gold and red medallions.

> 'The crowd was enormous, nothing like it had been seen in London since the Coronation ten years ago. And it was a happy, good-tempered crowd obviously determined to enjoy its brief escape from what we have come to call austerity. Flags and streamers flowered from every other hand, and countless periscopes—most of them little mirrors fixed on pieces of stick—danced like crystallised sunshine above the tightly packed heads.' (*Country Life.*)

The first members of the Royal family to leave Buckingham Palace for Westminster Abbey were the Queen and Princess Margaret, who was principal bridesmaid. Queen Elizabeth wore a long dress of apricot and gold lamé, falling in cape folds at the back to a short train. Her hat was of gold lamé veiled in apricot tulle, with ostrich feathers shading from apricot to amber falling over one shoulder. She wore the riband of the Garter, and the Garter itself round her left arm, and also the Imperial Order of the Crown of India and the Family Orders of King George V and King George VI. Queen Mary, magnificent in aquamarine blue chenille velvet woven with gold, with a swathed blue toque with a blue ostrich plume, who had driven from Marlborough House, was joined at the west door of Westminster Abbey by Queen Elizabeth and they made their way in procession to their places in the sanctuary. The foreign guests included Princess Andrew of Greece, the bridegroom's mother; King Haakon VII of Norway; King Frederik IX and the Queen of Denmark; the Queen of the Hellenes and King Michael of Rumania. The Duchess of Gloucester wore delphinium blue; the Duchess of Kent, pink and silver brocade.

The bride drove to Westminster Abbey with her father in the Irish State Coach, drawn by two grey horses and escorted by a Sovereign's escort of the Royal Household Troops in full dress, their polished cuirasses flashing for the first time since 1939. The Guard of Honour at the west door of the Abbey was formed from the Royal Navy, the bridegroom's service, and from the three Regiments with which the bride was connected—the Grenadier Guards, of which she was Colonel; the 16th/5th Lancers, and the Argyll and Sutherland Highlanders, of which she was Colonel-in-Chief.

It was the first celebration in English history of the marriage of an Heiress Presumptive who was later to become Queen.

Queen Elizabeth, her husband's empty chair beside her, saw the bride's procession approach, led by the choir boys of the Chapel Royal in scarlet and gold; the Lay Vicars in scarlet and white; the Canons and Minor Canons in green and gold; the Dean of Westminster in cloth of gold.

Princess Elizabeth wore a wedding dress of ivory satin, woven in Scotland, with fitted bodice, long, tight sleeves, and a full skirt. The dress was richly embroidered with pearls in a design of roses, stars and ears of wheat; the gossamer fifteen-foot-long train was appliqué-ed with the same design in white satin. Princess Elizabeth carried a bouquet of white orchids, which had caused a last-minute flurry when it had been temporarily mislaid. On her head was her mother's sunray diamond tiara, and, as a Royal bride, her veil was flung back. She looked young, radiant and sure.

The two trainbearers, wearing the kilt in Royal Stuart tartan, were Prince William of Gloucester and Prince Michael of Kent.

Eight bridesmaids followed, wearing pearl-coloured tulle dresses, lightly appliquéd with satin stars, over pearl-coloured under-dresses of stiff satin. Behind them came Princess Elizabeth's Household, her Ladies-in-Waiting in draped dresses of cyclamen and sea-green crêpe.

At the steps of the sanctuary waited the bridegroom, in naval Service dress, with his best man and cousin the Marquess of Milford Haven.

The wedding service, conducted by the Archbishop of Canterbury and the Archbishop of York, who preached the sermon, was the normal marriage service of the Church of England: the bride promised to obey her husband.

After the ceremony the bride and groom drove in the Glass Coach, with a Captain's escort, back to the Palace, followed by King George and Queen Elizabeth in the Irish State Coach, with a Sovereign's escort. The bridesmaids and the other guests went by car straight to the Palace, where a simple reception was held, very different from that held by King George V and Queen Mary for the Duke and Duchess of York.

Although it was a chilly November afternoon the bride and bridegroom drove to the station in an open landau (four hot water bottles were hidden under the rugs) with *Crackers*, Princess Elizabeth's corgi, an unexpected third. As the carriage moved off, the King and Queen and the wedding guests pelted them with rose petals, following them through the archway to the forecourt. There the thousands of spectators saw the King and Queen stand looking out along the Mall after their daughter, until Queen Elizabeth put her hand on her husband's arm and they went back into the Palace together.

That evening the Palace was floodlit, and the excited crowds, reluctant to go home, milled round the Palace, calling repeatedly for the King and Queen to appear on the balcony, as they did several times. Only when the lights were turned off at 11 o'clock did the crowds disperse, after a day of pageantry and peaceful rejoicing, which the country had not seen since before the war.

CHAPTER TWELVE

THE LAST YEARS OF KING GEORGE VI

It has been an unforgettable experience to realise how many thousands of people there are in this world who wish to join in the thankfulness we feel for the twenty-five years of supremely happy married life which has been granted to us

King George VI, broadcasting on his Silver Wedding Day,
April 26, 1948

KING GEORGE VI and Queen Elizabeth celebrated their Silver Wedding on April 26, 1948. In the morning, they drove in bright sunshine in an open landau, with Princess Margaret seated opposite them, through streets lined with troops and cheering crowds to St. Paul's Cathedral. There a special Service of Thanksgiving was held; in the afternoon the King and Queen toured in an open car through twenty-two miles of London streets, acclaimed wherever they went.

Messages of goodwill were received from all over the world, and the King and Queen received gifts from many public bodies. The Cabinet presented two Georgian sauce-boats, and the City of London a silver épergne and a pair of Battersea enamel candlesticks. The Mother's Union gave the Queen a seventeenth-century silver bell, and a clock which told the hour, day, months, seasons and leap year. The London Gardens Society sent a miniature alpine garden; the Dean and Chapter of St. Paul's presented a casket made from an oak cut at Welbeck in the seventeenth century, when the timber was presented to Sir Christopher Wren for the roofing of his new Cathedral.

A cake was baked, a gift of the National Association of Master Bakers, Confectioners and Caterers. It was three-tiered, coloured red, white and blue and weighed two hundred and forty pounds. The bottom tier was decorated with pictures of Sandringham, Balmoral, Windsor and Glamis. The middle tier depicted the King's hobbies of shooting, stalking, camping and flying, while the small top tier was surmounted with crowns topped by silver rings on which two doves were resting.

For the King and Queen this day of thanksgiving began with the private celebration of Holy Communion; its heart and meaning was, as Queen Elizabeth phrased it in her broadcast that evening, thanksgiving for 'our twenty-five years of happiness'.

She went on to speak revealingly of her philosophy of life:

'The world of our day is longing to find the secret of community, and all married lives are, in a sense, communities in miniature. There must be many who feel as we do that the sanctities of married life are in some ways the highest form of human fellowship, affording a rock-like foundation on which all the best in the life of the nations is built.

'Looking back over the last twenty-five years and to my own happy childhood, I realise more and more the wonderful sense of security and happiness that comes from a loved home. Therefore at this time my heart goes out to all those who are living in uncongenial surroundings and who are longing for the time when they will have a home of their own . . .'

In July 1948, the King and Queen entertained at Buckingham Palace the three hundred Archbishops and Bishops attending the Lambeth Conference. Their Majesties stayed in London into August to go to the Olympic Games, and on Queen Elizabeth's forty-eighth birthday, at Wembley Stadium, the assembled crowd of eighty thousand spectators sang 'Happy Birthday to You'.

Back in London after their autumn holiday at Balmoral the King and Queen, together with the Princess Royal and Princess Alice of Athlone, attended the first Thanksgiving Harvest Festival held in Westminster Abbey in living memory. Land-workers who had received the Royal Agricultural Society's medal for more than forty years' service were present, and young farmers carried baskets of corn, roots, seeds, vegetables, fruit and flowers to the altar. A young West Sussex farmer led the congregation in thanksgiving:

'For the blessing of seed and soil . . . for the mist of autumn mornings and the keen freshness of an English day, with the

smell of frost in the air and bonfires burning in the woods . . .
for the hum of the thresher . . . for the splendour of the harvest
moon, and the calm of the harvested field.'

*   *   *

Different memories were stirred at Westminster when the King
and Queen attended the re-opening of the eighteenth-century
Westminster College dormitory, which had been burnt out after
bombing. Scholars of Westminster School conducted the re-
opening entirely in Latin, and the King replied, 'I thank you,
gentlemen, for the scholarly, and, as far as I can understand it,
very friendly welcome which the King's Scholars have given to
the Queen and myself.'

Outwardly it was a normal, busy, politically worrying and
domestically happy time, although joys and anxieties were
sharpened for the two families living under one roof at Buckingham Palace, because Princess Elizabeth was shortly expecting her
first child.

During the last days of waiting for the birth of her grandchild,
the Queen faced a new anxiety: her husband's health.

Although the King seemed to have recovered from the fatigue
which had oppressed him towards the end of the South African
tour, and was looking fit and vigorous, he had for some time
been suffering from cramp in his feet.

King George consulted his doctor about the pain on October
20. Then the King and Queen of Denmark came to stay. Afterwards, on October 20, specialists were called in. Far from dis-
pelling anxiety, the specialists took much more serious a view of
the King's illness than had been anticipated. King George was
adamant that the bad news should be kept from Princess Elizabeth
until after her child was born.

Two weeks later, on November 14 when Prince Charles was
born, his grandfather lay ill in the same house. Queen Elizabeth
disseminated cheerful serenity to the patients at a time of continually growing anxiety.

A further complication was the extremely important tour, the
first by the Sovereign, of Australia and New Zealand, which was
to take place early in 1949, and which had been announced as long

ago as March 1948. The King was still determined to go, if only for a shortened and lightened tour, but the doctors said it was impossible. At last he gave way, and the Prime Ministers of the United Kingdom, Australia and New Zealand were at once informed.

The announcement to the public was made on November 23:

'As a result of advice based on a very thorough examination which has been tendered to the King by his medical advisers, and which has been endorsed by his Prime Ministers in the United Kingdom, Australia and New Zealand, His Majesty has agreed to cancel all his public engagements over a period of some months.

'This decision involves the indefinite postponement of the visit to Australia and New Zealand which the King and Queen had undertaken to pay, with Princess Margaret, during the first half of next year.

'Their Majesties wish to express to the people of Australia and New Zealand their profound regret and bitter disappointment which they themselves feel at the abandonment of their tour, and which they know will be shared by all those who were preparing to welcome them.'

There was danger of gangrene in the King's right leg, and the doctors feared amputation. The news came as a bombshell to the King, the Queen and the public alike. There was a sense of shock that a comparatively young man—King George was not quite fifty-three years old—should be faced with so serious an illness.

The Queen was thrown into a fever of anxiety, but she held herself in iron control. 'One must have no self-pity,' she said to one of her sisters at this anxious time. To her husband and her daughters, to her Household and friends and to the public the Queen presented a serene and untroubled countenance.

The Queen was of great help to the surgeons: they found their duties lightened by her calmness.

She continued to undertake her public duties. 'It was in character that she should carry on,' said one of her Household. 'She would never consider a personal anxiety, however acute, a reason for not undertaking any duty.'

Even on the day on which the state of the King's health was made public he had been due to pay a private visit to the Royal Naval College at Greenwich, to see a collection of portraits of war leaders: although it could reasonably have been cancelled as it was not an official occasion, Queen Elizabeth took his place.

When the King had reluctantly accepted the fact of his illness, he became a very good patient. The King had to rest. He found to begin with that he was so tired that he was content to rest, and he could and did continue his constitutional paper-work in bed. But all his outdoor activities were suddenly cut off, and his future became uncertain. As an additional discomfort, his room had to be kept at a level temperature—not at all to the liking of a man who loved fresh air. Keeping him pleasantly and restfully occupied took much of Queen Elizabeth's time and ingenuity, aided by her daughters.

Fortunately the King's initial response to treatment was good, almost unexpectedly good to his doctors. He was able to go to Sandringham for Christmas, and to make his broadcast at Christmas.

'The past year has been a memorable one for me. In the course of it, I have had three vivid personal experiences . . . In April I celebrated my Silver Wedding, then in November I welcomed my first grandchild; and finally I have been obliged to submit to a spell of temporary inactivity . . . The first two . . . are things that should bring happiness into any man's life, as I know they have into mine.'

At Sandringham House he was able to go outside for a minute or two to thank the carol singers and later in the month he was even able, from a sitting position, to do some shooting. When King George and Queen Elizabeth returned to London in February, the King managed to carry out an investiture. He walked slowly into the Ballroom of Buckingham Palace, and remained seated during the one-and-a-half-hour ceremony.

The Queen continued with her round of duties, and the public was beginning to breathe more easily when a disquieting bulletin was issued as a result of consultation between the King's doctors on March 3, 1949:

'While the King's general health continues to be excellent,

'In the left leg the flow of blood has been restored to the main arteries to a satisfactory degree.

'In the right leg the main artery is still obstructed, and the circulation is being carried on, less efficiently than in the left leg, through a collateral circulation.

'With a view to improving the blood supply to the right foot, and to safeguard this for the future, we have advised His Majesty that the operation of lumbar sympathectomy should be performed on his right side.

'The King has accepted this advice and the operation will be performed at an early date.'

It was signed by six doctors.

Again Queen Elizabeth allayed public anxiety by a public appearance. Just before the issue of the bulletin she had visited the Marylebone Housing Association flats in Cochrane Street, St. John's Wood, where she had tea with Mrs. Margaret Denton, wife of the caretaker.

The operation was planned to take place in Buckingham Palace on Saturday, March 12. Early that morning the Queen, with her daughters, took Holy Communion in the Chapel Royal, St. James's Palace. All went well, and the results of the operation fulfilled the hopes of the doctors.

But a prolonged period of convalescence was considered necessary, and it was now clear that the King would have permanently to modify his life and work. There would be fewer and less strenuous visits at home and abroad; more work would have to fall on other members of the Royal family.

One of the worst blows to the King and Queen was that Princess Elizabeth could not be shielded, even during the early years of her married life, from heavy responsibilities. It must also eventually make it impossible for her husband to continue in his cherished naval career.

Queen Elizabeth had now to leave her husband to carry out many public duties on her own, more than she had ever done before. However, what must be, must be. 'The Royal family got on with it,' tersely commented one of the King's Household.

Queen Elizabeth's own character flashed out when she spoke during this time 'of the person who once prayed to be granted not a lighter load, but a stronger back.'

As soon as it was at all possible the King took up a modified round of public duties. He took the salute at his Birthday Parade, which, for the first time since 1939, was a full-dress occasion for all ranks taking part. The Colour of the First Battalion, Welsh Guards, was trooped. The King, in uniform, drove in an open carriage; Princess Elizabeth, Colonel of the Grenadier Guards, rode sidesaddle behind the landau.

From this time forward King George's health was always in doubt, though he planned and carried out a number of public engagements, and he fulfilled his desk-work. Some of the engagements made in hope had to be postponed, and reposponed, and finally abandoned because of his precarious health.

The Queen was fifty years old on August 4, 1950 and spent her birthday in London: *The Times* in a leader commented:

'. . . It would be impossible to over-estimate the reinforcement that the King has derived from the serene and steady support of the Queen. She has sustained him in sickness and in health, at all times taking her full share in the burdens of royal service and in the time of great anxiety that befell her during the King's grave illness, piling new duties upon her already overcrowded programme in order that no good cause that had been promised the encouragements of royal patronage might be avoidably disappointed.

'She speaks to all men and women on the level of common experience . . . She is never afraid to challenge the over-sophisticated of the age in which she lives; she ignores the cynics and the pessimists and holds up for admiration the things that are lovely and of good report.

'She would commend to all what she told the University of Cape Town were the four cardinal virtues of academic life: honesty, courage, justice and resolve, the whole sustained upon the simplicities and the profundities of faith.'

Princess Anne was born at Clarence House on August 15, 1950. King George had gone north a few days earlier, but Queen Elizabeth remained in London to be near her daughter. Before the notice of the birth had been posted outside Clarence House Queen Elizabeth drove in at the gate and her smiling face told the news to the waiting crowds. 'A lovely baby,' she said of her grand-daughter.

After his rest on Deeside, the King was well enough to act as host during the State Visit of Queen Juliana and Prince Bernhard of the Netherlands, which took place in November 1950.

In April 1951, King George was happily able to make quite an extensive tour of those estates of the Duchy of Lancaster which lay in Lancashire. The Duchy of Lancaster was united with the Crown in 1399, when the King of England and the Duke of Lancaster were combined in the person of Henry IV, son of John of Gaunt. From that time onward the lands of the Duchy of Lancaster have been inherited by each King or Sovereign Queen, and he or she has enjoyed the incomes from that estate.

The Royal Standard was broken over the Norman keep of Lancaster Castle for the first time for a century, when its three historic keys were handed up to the King by the Constable of the Castle, Lord Sefton. The oldest and largest key, which is ten inches long, was presented to John of Gaunt, son-in-law of the first Duke of Lancaster, in the fourteenth century; the second to Queen Elizabeth I in 1588, and the most modern to Queen Victoria in 1851, on the five hundredth anniversary of the Dukedom.

*   *   *

The Festival of Britain was planned to take place in the centenary year of the famous Exhibition of 1851, to be a visible sign of British recovery from war. The King, both as Head of State and as the great-grandson of the man who had been responsible for the Great Exhibition, should obviously take as prominent a part as health would permit. Standing on the steps of St. Paul's Cathedral, he declared the Festival of Britain open on May 3, 1951.

Later the Royal family toured the exhibition on the South Bank, under the shadow of the old Shot Tower. It was a wet day in what proved to be a wet summer. The rain that had already fallen flooded the cables for the television cameras, so that only one camera would work. The homing pigeons released to mark the opening refused to fly. Nevertheless the Royal family, although Queen Mary had eventually to take to a wheelchair, indefatigably toured the Dome of Discovery and the other exhibition buildings.

In the following week the King and Queen received King Frederik and Queen Ingrid of Denmark on a friendly and successful State Visit. A visit for the North of Ireland was planned for June, and departure on the already-postponed tour of Australia and New Zealand was replanned for December.

On May 24, the King installed the Duke of Gloucester as Great Master of the Order of the Bath, and in the afternoon went on to the Imperial Institute. But he was not feeling well, and he went to bed that evening with a temperature. The doctors found that the King was suffering from catarrhal inflammation of the lung, and he was ordered a complete rest for four weeks. In the event, the King undertook no public engagements from May 24 until July 7.

On June 6, 1951, King Haakon VII of Norway was due to arrive in London on an Official Visit. An Official Visit, less formal than a State Visit, had been preferred, both because King Haakon was within two months of his eightieth birthday, and because of King George's poor health. King Haakon's visit was not put off, but his entertainment was carried through by the other members of the Royal family. Queen Elizabeth met King Haakon at Westminster pier, drove with him to Buckingham Palace, and sat at his side at the State Banquet. Princess Elizabeth read her father's speech. Queen Elizabeth went with King Haakon to the Royal Tournament, at which the massed bands played 'Here's a Health unto his Majesty', a wish which was not, alas, fulfilled.

Eventually, on the eve of the King and Queen's departure for Northern Ireland, it had to be announced that the King was not well enough to go.

The Queen, accompanied by Princess Margaret, carried on without him.

The engagement in Northern Ireland would have been a particularly happy one for the King and Queen, not only because they enjoyed the uninhibited welcome they always received from their Ulster subjects, but because the Governor's wife, Lady Granville, was Queen Elizabeth's much-loved sister Rose. Queen Elizabeth went through the four-day tour with great *éclat*, and her off-duty moments became a happy family party with her sister and brother-in-law, yet her anxiety for the King was never far from the surface. She was in constant communication with the Palace on the telephone, and took some of the good Ulster food back to the King, to tempt his appetite.

The King was still not fit when he went north to Balmoral on August 9. The Royal family could not disguise from themselves that he was much more easily tired than he had been. The threat of his arterial disease was always present. Rumours about the King's health were also circulating in public, although one newspaper leader pooh-poohed them:

> 'Now and then in some quarters we read disturbing comments on the King's health. They hint mysteriously that if (come a little closer) the writer told all he knew (make sure the door is shut) there would be a strong case for pressing His Majesty to cut down his duties and go more carefully. It is even being said that some people are saying that he would be wise to cancel his visit to Australia and New Zealand. What nonsense!'

Alas, for once rumour was right. At the beginning of September two specialists flew from London to see the King.

During the following week the King travelled by overnight train to London, where he was X-rayed. The King returned to Balmoral by air on the following day; that Sunday he and Queen Elizabeth went to Crathie Church, smiling and waving to the crowd of about two thousand. Yet once more Queen Elizabeth was plunged into acute and rising distress about the health of the King—an anxiety his subjects were soon to share, when the newspapers reported that:

> 'On the advice of his doctors the King is to return to London at the end of the week to undergo further treatment for his lung condition.'

Public anxiety was somewhat allayed when Queen Elizabeth was persuaded to remain in the north. King George travelled to London on the night of September 14–15: he was never to return to Scotland.

The bulletin which created real alarm was issued from Buckingham Palace on the evening of Tuesday, September 18:

'During the King's recent illness a series of examinations have been carried out, including radiology and bronchoscopy. These investigations now show structural changes to have developed in the lung. His Majesty has been advised to stay in London for further treatment.'

It was signed by nine doctors.

As soon as she had received the doctors' report, Queen Elizabeth, accompanied by Princess Elizabeth and the Duke of Edinburgh, immediately flew to London. Princess Margaret and the Royal grandchildren remained at Balmoral. The Queen, Princess Elizabeth and the Duke of Edinburgh entered Buckingham Palace at 9.45 p.m., by the gate off Constitution Hill, in order to avoid the crowd of several hundred people who were waiting in silence in front of the Palace. The Queen felt she could not face even the most sympathetic scrutiny: it is one of the very rare occasions on which she has ever evaded the public.

There was great sympathy for both the King and the Queen. People became suddenly aware of how fond they were of this quiet man, and how they had come to rely upon his steadfastness and courage.

On Friday evening of that week, September 21, a sober bulletin was issued from Buckingham Palace.

'The condition of the King's lung gives cause for concern. In view of the structural changes referred to in the last bulletin, we have advised His Majesty to undergo an operation in the near future. This advice the King has accepted.'

Preparations for an immediate operation in Buckingham Palace were pressed forward. Medical equipment and oxygen cylinders arrived at the Palace. Princess Margaret flew south. Queen Mary and other members of the Royal family visited the

Palace. A stream of callers crossed the forecourt to show their sympathy by signing the Visitors' Book. From all over the world came telegrams and letters. Doctors came and went, and nurses were in attendance. A large and silent crowd massed outside the gates.

During that week Queen Elizabeth left the Palace only once. King George's operation took place on Sunday, September 23: early that morning the Queen, with her daughters and the Duke of Edinburgh, drove to the chapel of Lambeth Palace, where they prayed for the King's recovery in a special service held by the Archbishop of Canterbury, Dr. Fisher. All over the world, in churches and places of worship of many denominations and religions, special prayers were said for the King.

Those close to Queen Elizabeth—even her own family—were never allowed to know whether she understood the full implications of the doctors' reports upon the King's health. Although unbearably anxious, she devoted herself to keeping up the spirits of her husband and family. She saw to it that everything was done for the comfort of the nurses who were looking after the King. She spoke always with optimism. The operation must—was going to be successful: she summoned every ounce of courage to make it so.

The operation began at 10 a.m., and occupied most of the morning. It was performed in a room on the first floor of the north wing of Buckingham Palace, which had been stripped and equipped as an operating theatre. Not far away the Queen waited, with Princess Elizabeth and the Duke of Edinburgh, through the interminable hours until at last the surgeons came to tell her that the operation was over.

Immediately Queen Mary, who was waiting at Marlborough House with the Duke of Gloucester and the Princess Royal, was told by telephone, and a telegram was sent to the Duke of Windsor.

At 4.30 that afternoon the crowd surged forward to read a hand-written bulletin, signed by eight doctors, which was attached to the railings at Buckingham Palace:

'The King underwent an operation for lung resection this

morning. Whilst anxiety must remain for some days, His Majesty's post-operative condition is satisfactory.'

A second bulletin at 9.15 p.m. read:

'The King's condition continues to be as satisfactory as can be expected.'

Five doctors remained in the Palace overnight: a continuous, silent file of people passed by the bulletin boards.

Reading and answering the messages of sympathy which poured in to the Queen helped to fill the hours when she could not be with her husband. From the leaders of all parties in the House of Commons came the following message:

'Madam, at this time of anxiety we wish with our humble duty to assure your Majesty that our thoughts are with you and the Princesses. It is our earnest prayer that His Majesty the King may soon be fully restored to health.

'Your Majesty's humble, obedient servants—C. R. ATTLEE, WINSTON CHURCHILL, CLEMENT DAVIES.'

The Queen replied:

'My daughter and I are so grateful to you, to Mr. Churchill and to Mr. Davies for the kind message that you have sent us and for your prayers for the King's restoration to health.

'We are deeply touched by your thought of us at this moment of anxiety.

ELIZABETH R.'

As the King battled his way slowly back to life, Queen Elizabeth's confidence and optimism were renewed. Although the bulletins never gave a prognosis of complete cure, the King was winning his first battle. There was, however, a slight setback in the night of September 25, and the bulletin the following morning read:

'The King has had a less restful night, but his Majesty's general condition this morning is good and progress is maintained.'

Soon afterwards, it was announced from Clarence House that Princess Elizabeth and the Duke of Edinburgh had gratefully accepted the suggestion of the Canadian Government that the beginning of their Canadian visit should be postponed, so that they would not need to leave London until late on October 7 and start their tour in Quebec on October 9, twelve days later than originally planned.

By September 27, although only Queen Elizabeth and his family had been able to see him, the King was able to sign the warrant authorising the appointment, under Letters Patent, of Counsellors of State. The Counsellors appointed were the Queen, Princess Elizabeth, Princess Margaret, the Duke of Gloucester and the Princess Royal. The King also signed, with a remarkably firm hand, the Proclamation proroguing Parliament, one of the few powers which could not be delegated to the Counsellors of State.

Gradually the King grew stronger. At the end of September, Princess Margaret rejoined her nephew and niece at Balmoral. On October 7, without further postponement, Princess Elizabeth and the Duke of Edinburgh were able to leave for Canada, although the Heiress Presumptive had to take with her all the preparations for Accession to the Throne including a draft Accession Speech, in case her father's illness suddenly took a fatal turn.

During the King's illness, the Queen worked untiringly to do everything she could to lighten her husband's work load, while the King's Private Secretary attended to the public side of his work and kept the flow of official documents moving, through the services of the Counsellors of State. While the King was alive, the Queen's conception of her duty was to support the King. She took the minutest interest in running her house and in keeping things smooth for him, never so much as when he was so very ill.

Just a month after the King's operation, the Queen took up her engagements again. Constitutionally, there is much which a Queen Consort cannot do, nor did she attempt to undertake the King's public duties, but she resumed as much as possible of her own busy pattern of public engagements.

'One would wish [said one sympathetic newspaper leader] to express the hope that after her anxious vigil, Her Majesty will not herself undertake too numerous a list of engagements.'

The Queen's first engagement was, appropriately enough, to open an extension of the Royal Free Hospital School of Medicine of the University of London. Before a medical audience who included Sir Daniel Davies, one of the King's doctors, she said, 'I am happy that my first engagement since the King's illness should be at an institution closely connected with the relief of suffering, for it seems a suitable place to pay tribute to the skill, devotion and patience of doctors, surgeons and nurses. Words cannot describe our gratitude for the loving care with which the King has been surrounded. I am glad to be able to tell you that he continues to make steady progress.'

Some years later, at Queen Mary's Nurses' Home, she said to nursing staff of the Westminster Hospital and Westminster Children's Hospital, 'I shall never forget the gentleness, the skill and the devotion with which nurses from Westminster cared for the King in his illness.' Her initials, as well as those of King George, are incorporated in the brooches which the King gave to each of the nurses who looked after him, asking that they might be allowed to wear them when in uniform.

Queen Elizabeth asked Sister Doreen Pearce and Sister Ruth Beswetherwick, who were off duty, to come as guests in her party when she went to the Royal Variety performance at the Victoria Palace. 'I was there,' commented a senior Member of the King's Household, 'and I shall never forget the thunder of applause from the audience when those two nurses in uniform entered the box. The audience at a performance of that sort is pretty sophisticated, and their spontaneous welcome to the two nurses was most moving. One felt that everyone was trying to convey their respect, gratitude and admiration. I am sure there were lumps in many people's throats at the ovation: I know there was one in mine.'

On Sunday, December 9, prayers of Thanksgiving for the recovery of the King were given in the services of all Christian Churches throughout the Commonwealth. December 11 was the fifteenth anniversary of his accession, December 14 was his fifty-sixth birthday. The King chose that day to knight his surgeon, Mr. C. Price Thomas, and his doctor, Dr. Geoffrey Marshall, and he enjoyed a family luncheon party at which guests included Queen Mary, the Duke of Gloucester and the Princess Royal.

He had so far recovered that plans for the future could be made once more, and it was arranged that the King and Queen would leave Portsmouth on March 10, 1952, and sail in H.M.S. *Vanguard* for Cape Town, where they would stay at Botha House, in Umdoni Park on the south coast of the Union, which had been generously put at the King's disposal by Dr. Malan, the Prime Minister of South Africa.

Although his lung resection had left him with problems 10 breath control, and he could talk only in brief phrases, King George with characteristic courage decided to give his usual Christmas broadcast, but to pre-record it at Buckingham Palace. He was able to go to Sandringham for Christmas, and there, free from the tension inseparable from his broadcast, to enjoy Christmas Day with his family, attending morning service and taking Holy Communion in Sandringham Church, and afterwards walking back across the park. In the afternoon he sat with his family to listen to his own words:

'I myself have every cause for deep thankfulness, for not only—by the grace of God and through the faithful skill of my doctors, surgeons and nurses—have I come through my illness, but I have learned once again that it is in bad times that we value most highly the support and sympathy of our friends . . . You are most of you now sitting at home among your families, listening to me as I speak from mine. At Christmas we feel that the old, simple things matter most. They do not change, however much the world outside may seem to do so.'

That January the King seemed specially to be enjoying the company of his family and of a few close friends at Sandringham. He delighted in the countryside; he was even able to go shooting again with a special light gun. He felt much better. He said to one of the Household: 'This just shows that an operation is not an illness—I am now all right.' The Queen had always been buoyed by an inward belief that things might not be as bad as they seemed; it looked as if the King's courage and the doctors' skill had thrust death from his doorstep for a few more years. At last the Queen felt she could relax her vigilance and begin once more to enjoy the happy tenor of their days together.

Princess Elizabeth and the Duke of Edinburgh were to undertake, in the King and Queen's place, the postponed Australian tour. The King and Queen returned to London to see them leave by air for Kenya, on the first leg of their journey. The King stood bareheaded in the keen wind, watching his daughter's aircraft disappear in the distance. Those who saw him for the first time for some months noted, with dismay, his worn and much-aged appearance, but those who had been with him constantly during the recent months of pain saw rather his greater vigour and marvelled that he could be there.

On February 5, King George enjoyed the kind of open-air day he liked best in his Norfolk home. It was a frosty, still and sunny February day. He was out shooting hares with friends and farmers, and was pleased to be using a slightly heavier charge in his new light gun, which he felt would lessen the chance of not killing cleanly. The Queen and Princess Margaret drove to Ludham to see the home and paintings of Edward Seago, the artist. At dinner that night the King was in particularly good form, joking and laughing about incidents of the day.

The King retired to bed in the ground-floor room which he had used since his illness to spare him the effort of climbing the stairs. In his sleep that night King George VI died without suffering. The fates had given him their final boon—a happy last day of life, surrounded by those he loved, and a peaceful death.

But it was an appalling shock for those dearest to him—for his younger daughter; for his elder daughter and heir, thousands of miles away in Africa; and more—most of all—for his wife, who had been close to him in work and leisure, in hope and danger through twenty-eight years.

Queen Elizabeth met the blow with utmost courage. 'I never knew a woman could be so brave,' the Member of the Household who had to break the news of the King's death to her wrote to his wife that night. Queen Elizabeth considered and remembered everyone who had been close to King George VI and who was also suffering from his loss. She told them that she and they must feel gratitude for what had been, rather than distress for what had been lost. She wrote to many of them during the sleepless hours of her first grief.

The mourning of Royalty is not like the mourning of other people. It has to be endured in a blaze of publicity and in the public view.

Queen Elizabeth's family, including her elder daughter, who had so suddenly become Sovereign Queen, drew from her courage and strength to go through their ordeal. 'If only Queen Elizabeth could break down,' said one of the Royal doctors. 'This incredible self-control will take its toll.'

* * *

The widowed Queen's inevitable reaction was, as he foretold, the more severe as a result of her initial iron control. Queen Elizabeth, now the Queen Mother, was plunged into a desolation of loneliness. Her life had been shared so fully and completely by her husband that there was no part of it, no place, no plan, no thought, which did not give her pain because he was no longer there to share it.

From the first, however, Queen Elizabeth resolved to continue along the road she must now travel alone. The work which had been interrupted by her husband's death must go forward. Her service must now be given to her Sovereign and daughter.

One of Queen Elizabeth's first actions after her husband's death was to write the following words: 'I want to send this message of thanks to a multitude of people, to you whom from all parts of the world have given me sympathy and affection throughout these dark days. I want you to know how your concern for me has upheld me in my sorrow, and how proud you have made me by your wonderful tributes to my dear husband, a great and noble King. No man had a deeper sense than he of duty and of service, and no man was more full of compassion for his fellow-men. He loved you all, every one of you, most truly. That, you know, was what he always tried to tell you in his yearly message at Christmas; that was the pledge he took at the sacred moment of his Coronation fifteen years ago. Now I am left alone, to do what I can to honour that pledge without him.

'Throughout our married life we have tried, the King and I, to fulfil with all our hearts and all our strength the great task of service that was laid upon us. My only wish now is that I may be allowed to continue the work that we sought to do together.

'I commend to you our dear daughter: give her your loyalty and devotion: in the great and lonely station to which she has been called she will need your protection and your love.

'God Bless you all: and may He in His wisdom guide us safely to our true destiny of peace and goodwill.

ELIZABETH R.'

CHAPTER THIRTEEN

REBUILDING A LIFE

My only wish now is that I may be allowed to continue the work
that we sought to do together

*Queen Elizabeth the Queen Mother in her message to the people
after the death of King George VI on February 6, 1952*

WITH the death of her beloved husband, Queen Elizabeth's world
crashed. The closeness and happiness of the married life of King
George VI and his wife were apparent to all who knew them—yet
even those in close contact with them had not realised how
deeply Queen Elizabeth relied upon her husband, whom all the
world knew depended so greatly upon her.

The shock of the King's sudden death at the early age of fifty-
six was all the greater because marriage lasting into the serene
years of old age was the natural pattern of Queen Elizabeth's
family. She had rejoiced with her parents when they celebrated
their Golden Wedding at Glamis in 1931; and had been at least a
nominal subscriber to the clock that still ticks away in their great
dining room at Glamis, the gift to her grandparents from their
children and grandchildren to commemorate their Golden
Wedding in 1903.

When King George VI died Queen Elizabeth's devastation was
as great as that which had overcome Queen Victoria on the death
of the Prince Consort. But Queen Elizabeth held to a very different idea of her duties and future—one initially more difficult, but
ultimately greatly rewarding.

*Labour well the Minute Particulars, attend to the Little Ones,
And those who are in misery cannot remain so, long.*

These lines of William Blake were of particular significance to
Queen Elizabeth at this time: she came upon them in the annual
report of the North Islington Infant Welfare Centre, of which she
is Patron, and commended them to others.

Even on the day after the death of her husband Queen Elizabeth came down to play with her grandchildren as usual, saying to one of the King's Household, who thought it would be too much for her, 'I have got to start sometime, and it is better now than later.' The late Princess Marie Louise once spoke to her of her marvellous composure. 'Not when I am alone,' said Queen Elizabeth sadly.

During the long months following the death of the King, Queen Elizabeth had to fight the reaction from years of wartime and post-war strain; from the tension of the King's illnesses; and from the shock of his sudden death as well as his ever-present loss. King George VI was a person whose influence grew upon you. All who knew him, all who served him, grew to admire and love him. They found that they felt his loss more deeply and more lastingly than even they would have anticipated. 'I am shaken to find how much I miss the King still,' said one of his Household, ten years after his death. 'I have a persistent feeling that I am going to see him, especially at Sandringham, walking with those long strides of his, or using his beautiful hands so deftly and skilfully.'

Queen Elizabeth fought against her dreadful sense of loss. Attending to the 'Minute Particulars', she strove to maintain a normal life, taking interest in the things around her—the weather, the countryside, the dogs, and above all her grandchildren. 'Her daughters were wonderful with Queen Elizabeth during that dreadful time,' said one who knows her very well, 'but her guiding beacon in her loneliness has been what her husband would have wished her to do. Throughout her terrible sorrow and sadness, Queen Elizabeth has made a great effort to remake her life. Everything she has done as a widow is because she knows the King would like her to do it.'

The challenge came early when, in May 1952, the First Battalion of The Black Watch was ordered to Korea. Whenever possible, she had always wished her Regiments God-speed before they went on overseas service. Although it was only three months after the death of her husband and she was far from well, Queen Elizabeth flew from Windsor Castle to Fife, to inspect the First Battalion of The Black Watch at Crail. If she had dreaded that

315

first duty, and had feared for her composure, there was no outward sign of it that day.

Five hundred men paraded. Each officer wore a dark mourning armband. Queen Elizabeth was in black; she wore in her lapel, as always when she visited the Regiment, the diamond Black Watch Badge presented to her in 1937 by General Sir Archibald Cameron, when she became the Regiment's Colonel-in-Chief.

She undertook to speak to the troops and spoke without hesitation, although she did not trust herself to make any reference to the late King. 'The Black Watch,' she said, 'so dear to my heart and to many of my family who have served with the Regiment, has for more than two hundred years played a distinguished part in the battles of our country. I am proud to think that the traditions which have made you great are cherished and upheld today, and I know well that whatever may face you, you will win new honour for The Black Watch and for Scotland.'

Queen Elizabeth shirked no part of the programme, speaking to relatives and Old Comrades, visiting the Sergeants' Mess and being photographed with the officers. A soldier in 'B' company spoke for everyone on parade when he wrote, 'Her Majesty Queen Elizabeth's visit was a great success and we appreciated it more than words can say.'

Her visit impressed a wider public than those present. Resolved though she was to continue the work she and her husband had started together, Queen Elizabeth did not and could not foresee the great and important rôle she would undertake in the future. There have been many Dowager Queens in our history, but they have never before taken such a prominent part in public events—although of course most were considerably older when they were widowed.

Queen Elizabeth's status as Queen Consort was clearly defined in the Constitution (unlike that of the male consort of a Sovereign Queen), but when she became Queen Dowager many of her special prerogatives ceased. No longer was she protected under the law of treason. She ceased to be eligible to serve as a Counsellor of State, until under Queen Elizabeth II's Regency Act of 1953 she was again made eligible and has often fulfilled this duty while the Queen has been overseas.

Queen Elizabeth's financial position was, however, secured

under the Civil List of King George VI and of Queen Elizabeth II, by which she received an annual income of £70,000, subject to tax.

As Queen Dowager, she maintains her own Household, and was the only Member of the Royal Family, other than the Sovereign, to have a Lord Chamberlain. Although Queen Elizabeth has gradually allowed the number of her Ladies-in-Waiting to decrease as the older members among them have retired, in fact work has increased for her Household since she became Queen Mother.

Never before, in this country, has there been a Queen Dowager whose daughter is Queen Regnant, nor a mother and daughter who have both been crowned.

Queen Elizabeth chose to be known as 'Queen Elizabeth the Queen Mother' on the death of King George VI, just as the widow of King George V had chosen to be known as 'Queen Mary the Queen Mother'. But, because her daughter is named after her, she is generally known to the public as the 'Queen Mother', although those who are closer to her always call her 'Queen Elizabeth', and her daughter 'The Queen'.

In the early days of Queen Elizabeth's widowhood she went to the very north coast of the mainland of Scotland to spend a holiday with her girlhood friend Lady Doris Vyner (sister of the Duke of Richmond) and her husband at their isolated home, the House of the Northern Gate on the coast of Caithness.

One afternoon Queen Elizabeth and her hosts made a visit to the old Barrogill Castle, which had recently been put up for sale, but without attracting a purchaser. It was feared, Queen Elizabeth was told, that the Castle would soon be demolished. 'Pull it down? Never!' exclaimed Queen Elizabeth. 'I'll buy it!' And buy it she did, restoring it to its ancient name of the Castle of Mey.

In Queen Elizabeth's own words, when she later received the Freedom of Wick: 'I found the Castle of Mey, with its long history, its serene beauty and its proud setting, faced with the prospect of having no one able to occupy it. I felt a great wish to preserve, if I could, this ancient dwelling. It is too common an experience to find that once a house becomes deserted its decay begins and it is a happiness to me to feel that I have been able to save from such a fate part of Scotland's heritage.

'It is a delight to me now that I have a home in Caithness, a country of such great beauty, combining as it does the peace and tranquillity of an open and uncrowded countryside with the rugged glory of a magnificent coastline—the remote detachment of country villages with the busy and independent life of your market towns.'

Her spontaneous gesture was the first spark of returning interest in life. The Castle of Mey was something to think about and plan for which was not part of the lost life which it was now so painful to remember. It was also an isolated and lonely retreat where Queen Elizabeth could live withdrawn from the world, if there should prove to be no place for her in public life. For Queen Elizabeth, like every woman surviving a happy marriage, felt sometimes insecure and apprehensive after the withdrawal of the devoted protection of a husband.

Castle of Mey lies just north of John o' Groats; it was built in the sixteenth century by the fourth Earl of Caithness, a small, turreted castle a field's span from the sea, with a fine walled garden famed through the centuries for flowers and fruit, which can flourish so far north only because of the warm Gulf Stream flowing past it.

Queen Elizabeth loves Caithness, an austere county which has often been dismissed as black and monotonous, but which has a beauty of its own in the sweep of the land and the gold of the bog grasses, and especially in the magnificent colours of the Pentland Firth, with its two tumbling whirlpools, the 'Men o' Mey' and 'The Well of Swona', which Queen Elizabeth likes to call by their local names of 'The Swirlies' and 'The Twirlies'. She likes walking in the invigorating winds which almost always sweep the land. One cold day she stood for a long time on the cliff-top, watching a little coaster hardly able to make headway as she battled to breast the tide-race through the Firth. Queen Elizabeth is an expert at finding the tiny coral-pink cowrie shells known as 'groatie buckies' in the sand of the lonely shore. She never tires of watching the seals, and was enchanted when by singing Scottish ballads to them she brought them closer and closer inshore to listen. She likes fishing for salmon on the Thurso River or the Forse River. She is proud of the croft she has bought beside Mey, on which she keeps a few sheep. On Sundays she worships in the little whitewashed parish church of Canisbay, sitting in the pew of the Earls of Caithness, for so long the owners of Mey, or going occasionally to Dunnet Church, one of the few pre-Reformation churches in Caithness.

Queen Elizabeth appreciates the way in which the people of Caithness have made her welcome without encroaching on her pirvacy, and she has responded to their quiet gestures of friendship and loyalty in a way which has endeared her to them. It was as 'a neighbour' that she thanked the postman for his gift of some white heather he had found on the moors.

Her contacts with the local people have been marked by the spontaneous friendliness so characteristic of her. One day she was motoring along the main road which runs a couple of miles north of the isolated town of Halkirk, and the local schoolchildren had been taken by their teacher to see Queen Elizabeth pass. They were still quite some distance from the road when the Royal car came in sight, but Queen Elizabeth had seen them, and had the car stopped to wait for them.

It was some time after buying the Castle of Mey before Queen Elizabeth could live there, as repairs and decoration were required, but in the meantime she stayed several times with the Vyners at the House of the Northern Gate. It was not until October 1955 that Queen Elizabeth moved into the Castle of Mey, when her first guests were fittingly Commander and Lady Doris Vyner.

The Castle of Mey is of modest size. 'It has no back door, and you never know what you won't see out of the window,' said a guest. 'It is an enchanting house.' It is also a house of dignity and character, built in the great days. 'They were wearing velvet and drinking claret in Caithness before they did so in the south,' remarked the late Sir Arthur Penn.

Queen Elizabeth repaired and refurnished the Castle of Mey with loving care. First of all it was made secure against the gales, and given new electric wiring and central heating. Because there would be much passing from outside to indoors the hall and staircase has been left bare to the Caithness flags or covered with coconut matting. The bedrooms are close-carpeted. They have magnificent views.

Some of her own furniture could be used, but the small rooms demanded furniture to scale; Queen Elizabeth always receives the catalogue from Christie's and Sotheby's and marks items which interest her, which are then viewed for her by one of her Household. She bought some furniture for Mey through the London salerooms, and also visited antique shops in Caithness.

Castle Mey has many turrets, with winding staircases and small rooms. Queen Elizabeth's sitting room is in one of these towers, a room reminiscent of the older part of Glamis: the ceiling is barrel-vaulted, the windows are deep in embrasures. Queen Elizabeth has rush matting covering the entire floor, with a Stuart tartan fireside rug, chintz-covered easy chairs, and a cheerful colour combination of red curtains and white walls.

Queen Elizabeth finds she has less time to spend in Mey than she originally planned, although she comes here two or three times a year. 'Mey is tiny and enchanting, with a wonderful atmosphere of peace,' said a relative who has stayed there with her. 'It remains for Queen Elizabeth a haven from the world.'

*   *   *

In London, Queen Elizabeth had to make a less welcome change, because she had grown accustomed to and even fond of Buckingham Palace, into which she had moved so reluctantly in 1937. In effect, if not in size, Buckingham Palace is a 'tied cottage', and for reasons of convenience, security and administration, it must be occupied by the Sovereign. Marlborough House was occupied by Queen Mary, widow of King George V. Clarence House, where Princess Elizabeth had lived until her Accession, became therefore Queen Elizabeth's future home.

When Queen Mary died Clarence House had already been altered for Queen Elizabeth although she had not yet occupied it, and it was not wished to incur extra expense by making alterations to Marlborough House. Now Marlborough House has been given by the Queen as the meeting place of the Commonwealth Prime Ministers in London and is unlikely ever to be used again as a Royal residence.

Clarence House has drawbacks: it is really three houses, the front house standing back to back with two smaller houses in Ambassador's Court, and abuts onto St. James's Palace, with which it has a connecting door. Inevitably this makes it a house with awkwardly-sited doors connecting its two halves, and many passages, difficult to work and to live in.

The Queen and the Duke of Edinburgh and their children moved back into Buckingham Palace almost immediately after the King's death, but before Queen Elizabeth could move out some changes had to be made at Clarence House to make it suitable for her and Princess Margaret. Meanwhile Queen Elizabeth continued to occupy her own apartments in Buckingham Palace, while the Queen and the Duke of Edinburgh lived in the Belgian suite on the ground floor, which had been designed for King George IV, and is now used by visiting Heads of State. The three Households disposed themselves as best they might in the Palace office accommodation, which had been ample for the lesser exigencies of the Victorian Empire, but which was barely adequate to contain just the Staff of the Head of a Commonwealth, whose duties were of a quantity and range which would have astounded the Victorians.

It was not until May 18, 1953, that the Standard of Queen Elizabeth the Queen Mother flew for the first time over Clarence House.

On Deeside Queen Elizabeth made a happy exchange when she moved out of Balmoral Castle back to Birkhall, the much smaller country house built in 1718, and owned for many years by the Gordons of Abergeldie, from whom it was bought by Queen Victoria for her eldest son. Queen Elizabeth and her husband always loved Birkhall, which lies on the River Muick about eight miles from Balmoral Castle. Birkhall is lower and quite noticeably warmer than Balmoral, and has a delightful, irregular garden, much of it on a steep slope, which was largely planned by the late King and Queen Elizabeth when they lived there as Duke and Duchess of York.

The tall, plain white house is not over-large. At first, Queen Elizabeth hit upon the ingenious plan of using a luxurious caravan, which had been Lord Mountbatten's in wartime, for her guests.

In 1958, however, she built a new wing containing six bedrooms.

The Royal Lodge in Windsor Great Park continues to be Queen Elizabeth's country house near London, and only there does she continue her life in the setting which she and her husband made together: for that reason it is particularly dear to her.

* * *

The Coronation of Queen Elizabeth II took place on June 2, 1953. Queen Elizabeth the Queen Mother was present, following the precedent set by Queen Mary. In place of her embroidered Coronation robe Queen Elizabeth wore a Royal Princess's robe of purple velvet. Her dress, which was made by Norman Hartnell, was of stiff white satin with a very full skirt. It was embroidered with a delicate design of trailing ostrich feathers, their stems glittering with diamanté, each frond embroidered in gold, silver and crystal. Her jewels included a triple diamond necklace and big drop-diamond earrings, and a diamond waterfall stomacher. She wore the Riband of the Garter and the Family Orders of her husband and her daughter.

Sitting in the centre of the front row of the Royal gallery, she was only the second person in British history (Queen Mary was the first) to watch her child take part in the long Coronation ceremony, a ceremony in which she had herself been crowned.

Shortly before the act of crowning there was a little stir, and Prince Charles, who was four and a half years old, took his place in the Royal gallery between his grandmother and Princess Margaret. He pointed at the splendid scene and asked about the great gold dish on the altar. Queen Elizabeth bent down to him, smiling, as she explained.

Very shortly after the Coronation, Queen Elizabeth made her first overseas journey since the King's death.

Air transport now makes visits to the Commonwealth possible on a scale never known before. The Queen's programme would astound King George V, let alone Queen Victoria. Yet the Queen cannot make more than widely-spaced visits to the Commonwealth countries and to the Colonies. The Duke of Edinburgh complements and supplements the Queen's visits, as well as accompanying her on all her tours, but much remains to be undertaken by other members of the Royal family. Queen Elizabeth is in great demand to go to all parts of the Commonwealth, and she has travelled far more widely in the decade of her widowhood than in the twenty-eight and a half years of her married life. Her journeys as Queen Mother make an impressive list:

1953   Southern Rhodesia
1954   The United States and Canada
1956   France
1957   The Federation of Rhodesia and Nyasaland
1958   Canada, Honolulu, Fiji, New Zealand, Australia, Mauritius, Uganda, Malta
1959   Kenya and Uganda; Italy and France
1960   The Federation of Rhodesia and Nyasaland
1961   Tunisia
1962   Canada
1963   France
1964   The Caribbean
1965   Jamaica, France, Canada and Germany
1966   Canada, Honolulu, Fiji, Australia and New Zealand
1967   Canada

Later Journeys

June 1974   CANADA for the presentation of new Colours to the Toronto Scottish Regiment in Toronto and a visit to The Black Watch (Royal Highland Regiment) of Canada in Montreal.

April 1975   IRAN, including visits to Tehran, Shiraz, Persepolis and Isfahan. One-day visit to CYPRUS on the way home.

October 1976   PARIS to open the British Cultural Centre.

November 1978   2-day visit to her Regiments in Germany.

June 1979   CANADA, visits to Halifax, Nova Scotia and Toronto, Ontario.

July 1981   CANADA, to Toronto and Niagara-on-the-Lake, Ontario.

May 1982	PARIS to open the new Wing of the Hertford British Hospital.
July 1982	2-day visit to her Regiments in Germany.
March 1983	GERMANY for the presentation of Shamrock to the Irish Guards on St. Patrick's Day.
July 1983	NORWAY for the celebrations to mark the 80th birthday of the King of Norway.
March 1984	GERMANY for the presentation of Shamrock to the Irish Guards on St. Patrick's Day.
October 1984	ITALY to see the work of the Venice in Peril Fund in Venice.

On this first journey, together with Princess Margaret, she flew in a Comet to Salisbury, Southern Rhodesia. 'The airport was not even officially opened,' said one of the organisers of the tour. 'Hers was the first jet aircraft to land at Salisbury.'

The main object of her visit to Southern Rhodesia was to open the Rhodes centenary exhibition at Bulawayo. It was unseasonably cold that year, and at the opening the biting wind whistled across the dais. The men, though wearing morning coats, felt distinctly chilly. Queen Elizabeth was wearing a thin silk dress, but when asked afterwards 'Were you not absolutely frozen, Ma'am?' she replied, 'Oh no, I was perfectly all right.'

It was another breezy day when Queen Elizabeth and Princess Margaret attended a centenary service for Cecil Rhodes at his grave in the majestic Matopa Hills, and there Princess Margaret caught a severe chill which laid her up so that she had to break off the tour and return to Salisbury to rest for a few days. Queen Elizabeth fulfilled the whole programme with verve and success, returning with Princess Margaret to London on July 17.

Queen Elizabeth's next overseas journey was alone, and it was perhaps a turning point of her life. In November 1952 a fund to commemorate King George VI had been launched in the United States by Lewis Douglas, the former American Ambassador in London, and had been warmly supported by President Eisenhower. A very comfortable sum had been collected which would be spent in the technical training in the United States of young people from the Commonwealth.

It was naturally wished that Queen Elizabeth herself should come to the States to receive the Fund, but it is perhaps not too much to say that she dreaded this visit, especially as no other Member of the Royal family could go with her. Queen Elizabeth felt, however, that it was due to her husband's memory that she should go, and she sailed for New York on October 21, 1954, in the liner *Queen Elizabeth*, which she had launched in 1936.

The visit was not an easy one to arrange. When Queen Elizabeth had been in New York before, it was as Queen Consort accompanying the King upon a State Visit. Now her status was less clearly defined. There were those in official positions in the United States who said bluntly, 'No American is going to be very interested in the middle-aged widow of a King.'

Queen Elizabeth was particularly nervous of the well-known American ordeal of the Press Conference, and of the enterprising methods of the American Press photographers. However the Press Conference went off well, and afterwards the New York reporters and photographers were all on her side.

When Queen Elizabeth went to Washington she had to cope with a fresh set of Pressmen and Presswomen. There was a Press Reception, which was a little stiff to begin with, so Queen Elizabeth moved down among the company, and was absolutely hemmed in: her suite could not get near her. Afterwards her Household were relieved to discover that she had enjoyed it.

In New York her success was astonishing. Each day more and more of the public crowded to see her. Cab-drivers and truck-drivers stopped and waved and called, 'That's ma Queen!' The officials were astounded. 'The attitude towards our country is changing and warming day by day,' reported one Britisher.

The cheque for the King George VI Fund was presented to Queen Elizabeth at a banquet in the Waldorf-Astoria Hotel, said to be the world's tallest, largest and most expensive hotel, and so often used for important functions that it is called New York's unofficial Palace. Queen Elizabeth, wearing full evening dress with the most wonderful jewels, found herself at dinner on a raised dais under brilliant lighting, and being televised throughout to a wide network of American viewers. Her Lady-in-Waiting, sitting more comfortably out of camera range, observed, as she ate her excellent dinner, that the Queen Mother was only toying with her meal. Afterwards, Queen Elizabeth returned to the home of Sir Pierson and Lady Dixon where she was staying, and her hostess asked her if should would care for some refreshment. Queen Elizabeth hesitated, and then asked if it would be possible to have something like scrambled eggs, 'but only if it would be no trouble'. 'I am afraid the cook was probably woken up,' said one of Queen Elizabeth's Household. 'And as the dining room was set for breakfast, the supper was served on trays in the drawing room: Queen Elizabeth, in tremendous form, took off her tiara and laying it on the sofa beside her ate supper from a tray in a lively picnic atmosphere.'

Queen Elizabeth was eager to see the famous New York shops, but her tremendous popularity with the crowds made it an unexpectedly difficult project. She wanted to go to Sak's department store, to look at the exciting costume jewellery displayed on the ground floor and which she had heard about from her Lady-in-Waiting. But word had leaked out, and when Queen Elizabeth arrived the whole place was packed and the display cases were hidden behind crowds of people.

The Royal party battled through to the lifts, and, as one member of the party described it, 'We shot up and down in the lift, just like a Marx Brothers film, trying to find a floor where there was not a crowd waiting. Eventually we managed to get out at some improbable floor, but after a little while we were traced again.' Then the distracted Manager arranged that Queen Elizabeth should go into a little boutique off the main hall, where things were brought to her. There she made her selection, but the main object of seeing a New York store was never really achieved.

After her United States visit Queen Elizabeth spent a few days in Canada before returning to New York to sail home on board the *Queen Mary*.

The effect of the visit to the United States and Canada upon Queen Elizabeth was deep and lasting. Her personal success had stimulated her, and she could no longer deny to herself her continuing importance to the work of the Royal family and the prestige of the Commonwealth.

Queen Elizabeth made her first visit to Rhodesia since it had become part of the Federation of Rhodesia and Nyasaland in July 1957. In Salisbury she was installed as President of the University College of Rhodesia and Nyasaland and in Bulawayo she opened the King George VI Memorial Centre for Physically Handicapped Children. She also visited Nyasaland for the first time, and went north to Northern Rhodesia into the Copper Belt, where she went below ground in the Roan Antelope mine, 'but was more interested in the people than in the machinery', observed one of her entourage. She enjoyed watching a mine-training school for Africans, where the men are taught by chanting the names of the tools and their uses. She spent a happy and amusing hour listening to the chanting of the auctioneer at the Rhodesia tobacco auction, and asked if it were possible to have a recording of his call. Again, she asked for a recording of some strange wooden instruments, akin to drum and xylophone, which accompanied the dancing by the Africans from Mozambique, which she had enjoyed.

During one crowded day, involving many changes between car and aircraft, it was discovered, when the Royal party was airborne, that the dread of an Equerry's life had occurred—that the brief-case containing Queen Elizabeth's next speech had been left behind. Carried in a car boot, it had been overlooked when the luggage was transferred. There was nothing for it but to construct a substitute speech, which was hurriedly copied out on a portable typewriter on very flimsy paper. Royal speeches are always typed on heavy paper, which is easy to control. At the next stop, in spite of the thin paper whipping in the high wind, Queen Elizabeth spoke with unflurried grace. As she handed her speech back to her Equerry she said with a twinkle, 'I think we did that rather nicely, didn't we?' There were no recriminations.

One evening Queen Elizabeth, wearing one of her beautiful crinoline evening dresses, was at a dinner party given by her host, Sir Robert Tredgold, the Acting Governor-General, at Government House, Salisbury. The Tredgolds had a vast dog, *Timmy*, a cross between a great dane and an airedale 'which looked as if a lion had come round the corner', and with which she had become great friends. At the end of dinner, when the ladies were withdrawing, there was an unexpected pause. Then Queen Elizabeth said, 'I'm terribly sorry, but I can't leave the table, because *Timmy Tredgold* is sitting on my dress.'

Queen Elizabeth's most extensive tour was to New Zealand and Australia in 1958. This was the first time a Member of the Royal family had flown round the world, and it was extremely strenuous. A long air journey most wonderfully compresses distances, but however smooth and helpful the organisation—and both B.O.A.C. and Qantas took great trouble and were most thoughtful—some strain upon the traveller must remain. For Royalty there is no let-up period after landing, instead they are plunged at once into an official welcome, introductions to large numbers of new people and the impact of great crowds. The pace of modern living puts enormous strain upon all public persons, statesmen no less than Royalty.

Queen Elizabeth (who incidentally had just recovered from influenza) flew almost without a pause from London to Auckland, a distance of twelve thousand seven hundred miles. Because she was flying with the sun in a fast aircraft, each day was stretched by several hours, so that a schedule which appears exacting enough in terms of 'local time' was in effect even more tiring. The fatigue suffered by all members of her party remains a vivid memory.

The aircraft landed in a snowstorm at Montreal, where snowploughs had been working all day to keep the airfield open. Queen Elizabeth, wearing a fur-coat, was met by a snow-covered official party, led by the Lieutenant-Governor of Quebec and Mrs. Gaspard Fâteux.

'The newsreel film of the occasion shows an aeroplane taxiing to a halt in a Canadian airport. A blizzard is blowing, and the notabilities on parade to welcome the plane stand upright with difficulty.

'The plane's principal passenger emerges despite the snow, her coat is thrown back on her shoulders in the familiar way.

'Despite the wind, not a hair, not a smile is out of place.

'And for a second, the very elements, which have almost

overwhelmed lesser mortals, seem so disconcerted that they, too, hold their breath.

'This more successful Canute is the lady known to millions, with the irreverence which is the British tribute to character, as the Queen Mum.' (*This Great Lady:* article by Laurence Thompson.)

The aircraft took off from Montreal to fly across the Prairies and the Rockies, a journey which took a week in the 1939 tour of Canada. They landed at Vancouver in pouring rain. Queen Elizabeth came down the aircraft steps carrying an open umbrella and exclaiming 'What rain!' The Lieutenant-Governor of British Columbia and Mrs. Frank Ross, and the Mayor of Vancouver and Mrs. Frederick Hume, were waiting to greet her. Most unusually Queen Elizabeth confessed, 'I am very tired,' but added, 'but so glad to be here.'

Because of the storm official greetings were cut short, but there remained a drive of thirty-five minutes and twelve miles from the airport to the home of the Lieutenant-Governor, the Hon. Frank Ross and Mrs. Ross, as Government House in Victoria had been destroyed by fire in the previous year. There her hosts had prepared a welcoming supper party. Queen Elizabeth retired to bed after a day in which the journey alone lasted twenty-two hours and twenty-five minutes.

After a short stop at Honolulu to refuel, the Royal party arrived at Nandi Airport, near Lautoka in Fiji, on a grey but warm tropical day.

By this time everyone was almost punch-drunk with fatigue. At a small dinner party one Lady-in-Waiting addressed the other and got no reply: she was sound asleep.

There was a delightful display of Fijian native dancers, which the entourage watched in a kind of trance, from which they emerged from time to time to hear Queen Elizabeth saying all the proper things.

The 'trouper' qualities of Queen Elizabeth are underlined by the following account from *The Times*:

'Her Majesty showed great interest in the ceremonies and often asked the Governor, Sir Ronald Garvey, or Ratu Sir Lala

Sakuna, the Speaker of the Legislative Council, to explain the symbolism. She won the hearts of the Fijians by her ready smile and flashes of humour. Being presented with a bowl of kava, the slightly bitter traditional drink, she partially drained her cup and then turned to Sir Ronald Garvey with a triumphant smile. He, however, indicated that this was not enough, whereupon she drained it completely to enthusiastic applause.'

Queen Elizabeth spent the night in the thatched Fijian-style country cottage or *bure* of the Governor. There was only room for one Lady-in-Waiting to accompany her. When Queen Elizabeth went to the bathroom her Lady-in-Waiting heard a gasp, and hurried to see what was amiss—she found Queen Elizabeth staring at a doorstop in the shape of a gigantic frog. Then it winked: it was a living frog!

Next day was roastingly hot, a brilliantly sunny tropical day. Queen Elizabeth, wearing a white nylon dress and blue hat, made a short tour of Lautoka township, and accepted a bouquet from the daughter of Mr. Choy Copal, the first Indian Mayor of Lautoka. Afterwards she was seen off by a large crowd, singing the beautiful Fijian song of farewell, 'Isa Lei'. The party left Lautoka Airport for New Zealand in a Britannia 102.

That afternoon the plane landed at Auckland Airport in the North Island of New Zealand to be greeted by vast, cheering crowds in holiday clothes, by the Governor-General Lord Cobham and Lady Cobham, and by the Prime Minister of New Zealand and Mrs. Nash.

After ninety-one hours, split into four days and only three nights (although owing to crossing the date line, five calendar dates were involved) and forty-five hours, fifty minutes in the air, London was half a world away. The legs and feet of many of the party were very swollen, and fingernails had become brittle, while the change of climate—though it was certainly most welcome to exchange a London winter for a New Zealand summer—was too sudden for comfort.

Yet this journey was only a prelude to the work of the tour, into which Queen Elizabeth at once entered with great energy and enthusiasm.

New Zealanders know how to make their visitors feel truly welcome. Mr. Holland, former Prime Minister of New Zealand, had spoken for the Dominion as a whole when he said before Queen Elizabeth's visit 'a most loyal, most warm—indeed a royal welcome will be accorded her during her stay with us'.

Queen Elizabeth, dressed in palest blue and carrying a parasol against the sun, drove the fifteen miles from Whenuapai Airfield to Auckland, and the enthusiasm of the large crowds so slowed the car that thirty-five minutes were added to the time estimated for the journey: the tour was off to a flying start.

Queen Elizabeth had only one nagging worry. Ill-health had interrupted her tour of the South Island of New Zealand thirty years before; would history repeat itself? That was why, when affected by the heat in the crowded, kauri-wood Cathedral Church of St. Paul in Wellington (although she managed to continue through the service) she took greater precautions than she might otherwise have done, abandoning a picnic planned for the afternoon and resting on the advice of her doctors. This apprehension disappeared when she passed the point of the tour at which she had become ill in 1927, and thereafter she went from strength to strength.

Public enthusiasm exceeded all expectations. At Invercargill, towards the close of the tour, Mr. Keith Holyoake, former Prime Minister, said, 'It's tremendous! She's terrific! There are no adjectives left to do justice to this tour. It is simply amazing to think what she has achieved in two weeks, not only in spreading happiness wherever she goes, but in strengthening—as she has said herself—the bonds that tie us to the Mother country. Look at all these people,' he said with a sweep of the arm which included a great happy crowd, 'she has done something wonderful for them.'

Queen Elizabeth's Household observed how deeply touched she was by her welcome in New Zealand, and she said in her farewell broadcast: 'The heartfelt affection with which you have surrounded me throughout this tour has been quite overwhelming. I can never hope to tell you how deeply I have been moved by your welcome.'

At Christchurch goodbyes were said to the New Zealanders,

and the Australians took over. Queen Elizabeth flew the Tasman Sea in a Qantas Super Constellation which had been adapted to take her bulky wardrobe trunks, and was beautifully decorated with Australian orchids. The flight to Canberra took five hours, forty-five minutes.

Queen Elizabeth was able, by landing directly at the Federal capital, for the first time to by-pass the headache of previous Royal tours to Australia, that of passing through State territory before arriving in Federal territory.

It was a day of memories for her—the sixth anniversary of the death of her husband, with whom she had visited Canberra May 1927, when it had been only the shell of the future capital, a town of mere seven thousand people. Now she visited an ample, well-built capital city with a population of nearly forty thousand.

The tour had been arranged so that Queen Elizabeth could open the fourteenth Conference of the British Empire Service League in Canberra on February 17. This League, founded at a meeting convened by Lord Haig in Cape Town in 1921, is a Commonwealth bond between the ex-Servicemen's organisations of all the Commonwealth countries and had then twenty-four member nations.

This tour, like so many before and since, 'just growed'. At first it had been intended that Queen Elizabeth should visit only the eastern States of Australia, but she agreed to an Australian invitation to lengthen the tour and take in all the States. It was not possible to find time for her to visit the Northern Territory, although she did meet many people from there, and a group of children were brought specially to meet her from the outback and from Australia's outlying territories, Papua, New Guinea, Norfolk Island and Nauru.

'It was Queen Elizabeth's wish to meet the *people* of the country, and because we were able to say it was her wish, we were enabled to do a lot more to make it a fact,' said one of the organisers, 'to cut down the people formally presented and make it a rule that everyone would be presented *once* only, if as a Cabinet Minister, then not again with the Members of Parliament and so forth, which halved the number of formal presentations and greatly increased the time available for meeting fresh people.'

In Australia, Queen Elizabeth's success was at least the equal of the warmth she had aroused in New Zealand. An official closely concerned with her tour said afterwards, 'The Australian tour was most carefully planned, and of course bad planning could have ruined it. But it was her own personality that made it—briefly, she aroused devotion—devotion to those who served her and those who saw her. This was particularly noticeable with the Press. It is said that the Australian Press is pretty frank, but I don't think there was ever an unkind word or phrase addressed in her direction, and that was emphatically not just because she was a member of the Royal family. People felt she was interested in *them* and in their friends. She seemed to regard even the most crashing bore as a challenge with whom she must and did get on. She kept her own counsel about what she liked best, she is far too intelligent ever to compare one State with another. But we did feel she was enjoying it.'

As always with Queen Elizabeth's tours there were many spontaneous incidents. During her last, fantastic day in Sydney when one hundred and twenty-five thousand children assembled to cheer her (and what a din they made!) she also unveiled a plaque in an unfinished building devoted to Mother and Infant Welfare in the grounds of Sydney University. She walked over the rough concrete floor to speak to the building foreman, who was wearing working clothes with open-neck shirt, and commented that he was much more suitably clad for Sydney's hot weather than the professors and official guests in their morning suits.

There was a wildly successful Government House Garden Party in Sydney, with some unorthodox behaviour on the part of the guests, who short-cut across the flower beds in order to see her—some distinguished Australians suddenly discovered they could climb trees almost as well as in their childhood days.

At Brisbane almost an inch of tropical rain fell in two hours, but ten thousand people packed themselves loyally into the Brisbane Exhibition Grounds for the evening's entertainment arranged for Queen Elizabeth, which included wood-chopping and rough-riding. She arrived to a delirious welcome, and the crowd roared approval when they heard over the loudspeakers that she had requested the cancellation of any item which might endanger those taking part. In spite of this, there was an accident when a wood-chopper, working fifteen feet from the ground slipped and fell heavily, his axe flying to the ground. Queen Elizabeth was much disturbed, and had enquiries made at once, and again the following day. Happily, he was not as much hurt as he might have been.

The tropical downpour continued for some days. Queensland was badly flooded: to the north of the State the floods were extremely serious. As Queen Elizabeth drove through the heavy rain along the wet bush roads, hundreds of people, huddled under umbrellas and canvas covers, waited to cheer her. Queen Elizabeth responded warmly, with a smile and wave to each and every group. The procession of cars was stopped again and again to accept unofficial bouquets.

On her return journey there were still crowds—at Ipswich for example, thousands of inhabitants turned out in the rain to cheer her on her second visit through the town.

Even with all Queen Elizabeth's care she missed one group on her outward journey, when, at a migrant camp at Rocklea, the children had assembled in their various national costumes, but had not been seen in time for the cars to stop. Queen Elizabeth asked her Equerry to telephone to the camp, to say how disappointed she had been to miss them, and that she would stop there on her return journey. Then five little girls from five countries presented her with bouquets and baskets of flowers, and the National Anthem was sung in sixteen languages. Indeed, the welcome along the roads disorganised the timetable considerably.

The programme was very heavy. In Adelaide, Queen Elizabeth had fifteen separate engagements in one sixteen-hour day. Yet in Melbourne, when she had a free Sunday, after attending church (as she does invariably wherever she is) she drove to Ballarat to see the town's famous flowers, and asked that a dinner party be arranged for her that evening especially to meet the 'young marrieds', a group with whom she found she did not come in as close contact as she would like.

One of the most beautiful of all the ceremonies was in Adelaide, where Queen Elizabeth sailed in a barge along the River Torrens between lines of decorated and illuminated small craft. She was seated in a chair in the stern of the vessel. Suddenly the lights below the canopy were switched on and the crowds saw Queen Elizabeth in a sparkling evening dress of white silk organdie, wearing diamonds and ruby tiara, earrings and necklace. Thousands of voices took up a single shout of 'God Bless Her Majesty'.

Queen Elizabeth flew with Qantas across the desert from Adelaide to Perth. When she landed en route at the twin gold towns of Kalgoorlie and Boulder there was immense excitement, all work stopped and almost the total population was at the airport. One hundred thousand people lined the nine-mile route from Perth Airport to Government House. The Governor-General, Sir William Slim, and the Prime Minister, Mr. Menzies, flew in to Perth to say goodbye to Queen Elizabeth, as did the Opposition Leader, Mr. Evatt, while the whole country joined in their farewells. Australians remarked that inter-State jealousies and disputes were swept aside in all-Australian pride and Commonwealth loyalty.

'In the three weeks I have been in Australia,' said Queen Elizabeth, 'I have found around me a spirit of courage, confidence and enterprise which I feel promises well for the future of this great country. United in devotion to the Throne and in loyalty to the British Commonwealth, I pray that Australia may ever find peace and prosperity in the years to come.'

Queen Elizabeth took off from Perth Airfield at 5.45 p.m. local time, on the evening of Friday, March 7, in the Qantas airliner the *Southern Sea*. Routed by way of the Cocos Islands, Mauritius, Nairobi (where she had public engagements and a night would be spent) and Malta (another night stop) her aircraft was expected to land at London Airport at 3 p.m. on Monday, March 10, after a flight of three days, five hours, fifteen minutes.

This was a proud day for Qantas Airways; they had planned and prepared for this honour for many months, and everything had been checked and rechecked.

But it is not only for mice and men that plans go wrong. When *Southern Sea* was two hundred miles from Port Louis, Mauritius, a brand-new cylinder seized in a newly-overhauled engine, and several cowling pieces were broken open. This failure had occurred on only five previous occasions in twenty-five million miles of engine operations; Qantas had only *one* previous failure of this nature. Captain Uren asked Group Captain Mitchell of the Queen's Flight to inform Her Majesty of the mishap, and he returned to assure Captain Uren that Queen Elizabeth was calm and unconcerned. The aircraft flew without difficulty on three engines to Mauritius, where a spare engine was available.

But, as bad luck would have it, there was no spare engine cowling. A new cowling was immediately put on board an aircraft at Australia, but the aircraft carrying the spare part had to turn back from the path of a cyclone, and so was grounded in the Cocos Islands. A delay of hours became a matter of days, during which Queen Elizabeth stayed at Le Reduit, the home of the Governor of Mauritius and Lady Scott. Although she could not now arrive at Nairobi in time to fulfil her engagement to open the new airport there, she did not allow her disappointment to appear. Queen Elizabeth sent a message to the Governor of Kenya, saying that she was greatly distressed not to open the airport but that 'on another voyage, which I hope will not be too far in the future, my aircraft will land at your new airport'. Queen Elizabeth fulfilled her promise in the following year.

Alternative means of transport were now offered to Queen Elizabeth to take her back to London, but she firmly stood by the Australian crew of the Qantas airliner, who had been so very proud to carry her and were so bitterly disappointed by the delay.

When the relief plane arrived, the engineers of the aircraft and the staff at Mauritius worked in the torrential rain from the tail end of the cyclone throughout the night to install the new engine. Queen Elizabeth took off just after 5 p.m. on Tuesday, March 11. Her route home was shortened by omitting the call to Nairobi. The red and silver Super-Constellation was seen approaching Entebbe Airport just before 1 a.m. on Wednesday, March 12, local time, for what was scheduled to be a very short stay.

Queen Elizabeth was met by the Governor of Uganda, Sir Frederick Crawford, and driven to Government House. About 2.15 a.m. she returned to the aircraft, which was expected to take off immediately. But a slight fault had developed in the ignition of the replacement engine, probably due to the appalling cyclone

weather in which it was fitted, and at 2.45 a.m. the aircraft was
still motionless.

"When the aircraft struck trouble on the ground at
Entebbe," wrote captain A. J. R. Duffield, "its engineers,
sweating in the heat of the equatorial night and working
on the engines with the usual flow of language, were startled
when they realised that Her Majesty had left the aircraft and
was standing beside them. But she was not fazed in slightest,
and the engineers reported that her sympathy for them and
her remarkable technical knowledge of what they were
trying to do, gave them an immense lift."

'For three-quarters of an hour she walked about the runway,
peering into tool boxes, inspecting a distributor, and talking to
officials and engineers standing in the luminous glare of arc-
light. She appeared completely unruffled by the now protracted ordeal.

'It was known all along that a Britannia aircraft was standing
by at Nairobi, but it appeared to be everyone's wish and not
least Her Majesty's own, that the Australian aircraft should see
her safely home to London.' (*The Times.*)

At 3 a.m. Queen Elizabeth returned to the aircraft. At 4 a.m.
the engines were started up, but Group Captain Mitchell and
Captain Duffield were still not satisfied. Shortly after 5 a.m.
Queen Elizabeth left the aircraft and drove to Government House,
where she spent the day quietly. It was not until 6.30 local time
that evening that the fault had been put right and the aircraft took
off for Malta, but at Malta a further delay of twelve hours was
forecast due to hydraulic trouble, and Queen Elizabeth agreed
reluctantly to transfer to a Britannia aircraft of B.O.A.C.,
inviting Sir Robert Laycock, Governor of Malta, who had
remained in Malta to greet her but was due to go to London for
Governmental talks, to accompany her.

Queen Elizabeth landed at London Airport at 11.11 a.m.
G.M.T. on March 13, 1958, sixty-eight hours behind schedule.
To the disappointed Qantas Airlines manager in London, who
apologised to her, she said, 'It could have happened to anyone. I
feel very sorry for the crew; they all worked so hard.'

To the Governor-General of Australia, Sir William Slim, she sent a message which read:

'Deeply regret that owing to a most unusual series of misfortunes it was not proved possible for me to complete my homeward journey in a Qantas aircraft. The crew had been wonderful and I send my warmest thanks to all those who have worked so hard on my behalf during the flight.

ELIZABETH R.'

* * *

Queen Elizabeth had flown 25,800 miles in her journey round the world. No Queen—or King—before her had ever flown round the world.

From her first flight, when as Duchess of York she flew with her husband to visit the International Exhibition at Brussels in 1935, Queen Elizabeth has always taken air travel in her stride, indeed 'she gets on with airmen like a house on fire' in the words of a pilot of 600 (City of London) Squadron of the Royal Auxiliary Air Force, of which she was the enthusiastic Air Commodore.

Early in Queen Elizabeth's widowhood she enjoyed a flight in a de Havilland Comet I jet airliner, which she made only a fortnight after Prince Philip had made the first ever Royal flight in a jet aircraft. Princess Margaret and the Marquess and Marchioness of Salisbury, with whom she was staying at Hatfield, went with her. They lunched as they crossed France, saw Mont Blanc and the Jungfrau, turned west along the south coast of France and then along the north Pyrenees to Bordeaux, crossed the Channel over Brighton, and so back to Hatfield after a flight of four hours.

Immediately Queen Elizabeth returned to Hatfield she sent a telegram to her 600 (City of London) Squadron which read:

'I am delighted to tell you that today I took over as first pilot of a Comet aircraft. We exceeded a reading of 0·8 mach at 40,000 feet. Thoughts turned to 600 Squadron. What the passengers thought I really would not like to say.

ELIZABETH R.
Hon. Commodore 600 Squadron.'

On the ground Queen Elizabeth has been shown how to handle the controls of the giant Brabazon II, when she visited the Bristol Aeroplane Company's works at Filton, and in the air she also handled the controls of a Viking of the Queen's Flight. She had her first helicopter flight in April 1956, from Windsor to Biggin Hill, and since then has often used helicopters for awkward cross-country journeys.

When she kept her promise to revisit Nairobi in 1959, she also visited Narok, Mombasa and the White Highlands of Kenya during her twelve-day stay. It had been a terribly dry season, and rain so often accompanied or closely followed her tour that she was called 'The Rainmaker', a title considerably more popular in Africa than it would be in Britain. At the Western Kenya cattle show at Eldoret it was raining heavily, but as an ox-wagon of the type used by the early Afrikaner settlers passed before the Royal box Queen Elizabeth signalled it to stop, and went out, shielded from the heavy rain only by a parasol, to inspect wagon and oxen at length.

Much of the travelling about Kenya and Uganda was by train, and everywhere Queen Elizabeth received a tremendous welcome.

'As the Royal Train carrying Queen Elizabeth the Queen Mother covered the 70 miles between Nakuru and Eldoret on Thursday afternoon and evening, the Royal lady, sitting for nearly seven hours on the observation platform, witnessed an incredible series of demonstrations of loyalty and affection.

'At Maji Mazuri and Equator stations, both of which were reached in daylight, crowds were expected, but few can have anticipated that at every road crossing, at every halt, at the water stop at Timbora, at dozens of other places along the route, little clusters of people of all races would have waited patiently in the deep blackness of a Kenya night to cheer the long white Royal train.

'Those in the train could barely discern the faces of the people beside the track and as the train approached those patient Kenyans may, perhaps, have been justified in feeling that they were merely cheering the train, but when the Royal Lady in light blue, sitting on the illuminated observation platform, came into sight the redoubled cheers indicated that they felt the long wait had been justified.

'And the Queen Mother appears quite tireless . . .' (*Sunday Post* of Kenya.)

Queen Elizabeth found a tremendous change in the country since her first visit to Kenya and Uganda thirty-four years before, and she was surprised at the size of the harbour of Kilindini near Mombasa, and the tremendous new buildings in Nairobi. Her mind must often have dwelt upon the happy weeks of safari with her husband; indeed, she described her tour as 'nostalgic'.

On this tour, too, she saw many wild animals, now far rarer than during her earlier tour of Kenya. She stayed one night in Treetops Hotel, not in the little house in the branches of a giant figtree in which her daughter had kept vigil on the night on which King George VI had died: the tree and hut had been burnt down in the Mau-Mau revolt, and only the charred stump remained, but in a substitute house in the trees. She did not see any elephants, but she did see rhino, buffalo, bushbuck, waterbuck, giant forest hogs and dozens of baboons, and on her way back the next day she saw young zebra, wildebeest, Thomson's gazelles and impala. Even on the way to the airport she saw a family of giraffes near the road.

In 1960 Queen Elizabeth paid her second visit to the Federation of Rhodesia and Nyasaland, and her fourth to the territory of Southern Rhodesia, when she flew out for a nineteen-day visit. An official who has been responsible for organising the tours remarked, 'It is getting quite hard to show Queen Elizabeth anything new in the Federation. She has been to so many places never before visited by a member of the Royal family. She is always eager to see everything. You don't need to be shy with her, just say straight out what you would like her to do.'

The main object of this 1960 was to open the Kariba Dam, which provides hydro-electric power for the Copper Belt, and which—despite disastrous floods in 1957 and 1958—was constructed in only four and a half years. The day of the ceremony presented a difficult problem in transport, as about one thousand people had to be flown in and out of the limited airstrip at Kariba on that one day. Queen Elizabeth was greatly impressed by the immensity of the Kariba Dam project, and by the power-house a large as a cathedral carved under the grey granite mountain. It was difficult to make the ceremony appropriately impressive for the crowds outside, as water would not be dramatically released but instead would be fed quietly into the giant turbines. So it was arranged that after Queen Elizabeth had spoken and had pressed the switch to start the generator, a recording would be broadcast of the water rushing through the turbines. Then, so that everyone could see her, Queen Elizabeth walked out along the road on the top of the dam which, narrow though it appears from the air, is wide enough for four streams of traffic.

Although there was political unrest at the time, Queen Elizabeth carried out her projected tour of the Copper Belt.

In April 1961 Queen Elizabeth sailed in *Britannia* from Portsmouth for her first visit to North-West Africa, where she spent two days as the guest of President Bourguiba of Tunisia.

* * *

In June 1962 Queen Elizabeth visited Canada for the third time when she flew to Montreal for an eight-day visit in a Trans-Canada Air Lines jet aircraft, in order to present new colours to all three battalions of The Black Watch (Royal Highland Regiment) of Canada at an impressive parade in the Percival Molson Stadium at McGill University. Unusually for a Royal stay, it took place just before the Canadian General Elections, but the date had long been fixed by the centenary celebrations of The Black Watch of Canada.

Queen Elizabeth left London Airport on June 7, aboard a Trans-Canada Air Lines D.C.8 jet aircraft. This was her first trip in a regular commercial airliner, although the forward section had been re-fitted and reserved for her and some of her party. During the seven-and-a-half-hour flight Queen Elizabeth went through to the other sections, to talk to some of the airline's regular passengers.

The largest Officers' Mess dinner ever held by the Regiment

took place in the Grand Salon of the Queen Elizabeth Hotel in Montreal, when over three hundred past and present officers of the Regiment were present, many of whom had come from very distant parts. They included veterans of the Boer War, both World Wars and Korea. About one-third were in the scarlet mess jackets of The Black Watch, the remainder were in evening dress with miniature decorations, and there were present forty-five Regimental holders of the D.S.O. or M.C., as well as Lieutenant Dinesen, V.C., from Denmark, who had served in the ranks of the Forty-Second Royal Highland Regiment of Canada. Regimental tradition was observed, the haggis was piped in, to be cut with a dirk, and the snuff was passed.

* * *

Side by side with Queen Elizabeth's overseas tours have gone a great number of public engagements in Britain, far too many even to list. To each, she brings freshness and a feeling of warm interest. Her programme is varied—attending an agricultural meeting, and dining at the Middle Temple, opening a new home for Distressed Gentlewomen and speaking at the centenary of a boys' school. 'She is always at great pains to say to boys nothing long, but something they can carry away in their minds, although it is legitimate to say the same truths to recurring generations. Perhaps it is impossible to say anything immensely original, but the same truth shines through her words to them. Her simplicity is essential to herself and it is astonishing the effect she has. She has an extraordinary gift with people,' said a member of the Household.

Her Patronages encompass a wide range of interests, big and small. The Aberdeen Angus Cattle Society and the Aged Christian Friends; the Bar Musical Society and Birkhall Women's Institute; the Gardens Society and the Georgian Group; she is a Friend of Manchester, Norwich and St. Paul's Cathedrals and of many churches. Societies of which she is Patron figure largely in her engagement book.

Queen Elizabeth is particularly good with children, speaking them with that unaffected sincerity which they so readily distinguish from pomposity. Something of the magic is caught in the essays of war orphans who were at the seventieth birthday party of the Soldiers', Sailors', and Airmen's Families Association held in St. James's Palace on April 14, 1955, from which this account has been jig-sawed:

Robert Burns, Kirkconnel, Dumfriesshire

'The highlight of our two days' visit was, as you may suppose, the tea party with Her Majesty Queen Elizabeth the Queen Mother.'

Mavis Screen, West Bromwich

'At the party there was the giant cake with seventy candles, the spring flowers on each table, the thick red carpet, the beautiful paintings in their gilt frames, in the background beautiful music that was just loud enough to make this like a scene out of a fairy story.

'Then suddenly the fairy story came to life . . .'

Frances Elaine Richards

'I loved her. She spoke to me and shook hands with me because I had been chosen to present a bouquet to her. The Queen gave me a lovely smile and asked me what I was called . . .'

Robert Burns

'Her Majesty was charming and when she spoke to me, said that she knew Kirkconnel very well. I was thrilled to know that Her Majesty knew of this small village which is my home.'

Helen McKnight, Glasgow

'She asked me if I enjoyed myself. We had sausage rolls, buttered buns, sandwiches and assorted iced cakes and ice creams.'

Peter Corbeth, who won a rabbit in a race

'I could barely stand the excitement of it all and every now and then had to pinch myself to make sure that I had not dreamt it all. When I think of it now it gives me a wonderful feeling.'

Queen Elizabeth's mail is continually increasing. When she was Duchess of York she was only just beginning to be known to the public, and she received comparatively few letters. When she became Queen Consort she received many more, and her mail increased enormously after her husband's death, especially from those who were bereaved or in need. People feel that she understands family problems. Some letters are from people who appeal to almost everyone for help, others from those who have never turned to anyone before. 'She is good and practical at thinking out how those in trouble or need can best be helped. She knows when to give, and when to withhold. She looks individually at each *case*—which is a word she does not much like—and suggests the organisation most likely to help. She grew up watching her mother, who was the daughter of a clergyman and a very practising Christian, caring for people, visiting them in their homes and caring for them on a small, personal scale,' said one who is associated with her charities.

Queen Elizabeth helps many of those who even today 'fall between two stools'. She recognises that help, if it is effective, must be sufficient completely to cover the gap—partial help is of very little service. Yet she knows also when it is strengthening to remove help which, if continued permanently, would result in a state of perpetual dependence.

Very few, even of those close to her, are aware of the range of Queen Elizabeth's private charities—only she herself knows their full extent. One worker from a charitable organisation in which Queen Elizabeth takes a real interest wrote to me: 'I think the outstanding point is Her Majesty's interest in everyone who appeals to her—those whose claim and life are unspectacular in every way—those who might seem dull and uninteresting with comparatively small anxieties, but affecting an individual: an elderly couple in their last years, a widow, the spinster who has worked all her life and prided herself on independence. But perhaps most of all Her Majesty's deep concern is for a family, and if at all possible, in its restoration to a happy family life.

'Her generosity is obvious but her generosity of heart cannot be known except by those who experience her concern for all sorts and conditions of people.'

It is when personal and family dilemmas fall outside the scope of the organised sources of help that Queen Elizabeth herself, time and time again, has come anonymously to the rescue. Most of the people whom she helps in this way have no idea that it is Queen Elizabeth who has helped them. A report of the progress of all those whom she helps goes to Queen Elizabeth regularly. Once it arrived on the morning of her birthday. 'Although Queen Elizabeth was very busy with her birthday happiness,' Sir Arthur Penn told me, 'she at once read it.'

An individual, even a Queen, does not have a bottomless purse; Queen Elizabeth cannot possibly take the burdens of every individual upon her back, but by piloting some who are overwhelmed and bewildered into the right channels, by personal giving wherever she can, and above all by *caring*, she has shown the truth of her own belief in the power of one man or one woman to do real good.

In widowhood Queen Elizabeth's life still burgeoned with new interests.

She became Chancellor of the University of London in November 1955, in succession to the Earl of Athlone.

Dame Helen Gwynne-Vaughan was one of the first who interested Her Majesty in the University of London:

'My first contact with Her Majesty was in, I think, 1935. The Girl Guides Association was having a big function at which the Duchess of York took the salute. At that time I was chairman of the Guide executive, it was my duty to attend the Duchess and we had some time to wait together before the marching Guides appeared. In reply, no doubt, to an enquiry, I told her I was a professor in the University of London and seized the opportunity to speak of Birkbeck College where I held my chair and of our students who were earning by day and gave their evenings to study and research. I asked her to persuade the Duke of York to accept our Presidency. She was interested and in fact everything was in train when the Duke succeeded to the throne and the plan collapsed. It must have been one of her first contacts with the University of London of which Her Majesty is now Chancellor.

345

'I remember so well the beauty of her turn out and wide hat with trailing pale blue ostrich feathers in delightful contrast to the rather sombre Guide kit (she said she had outgrown hers). To the children she was sheer fairy-tale.

'My next contact with Her Majesty was in the summer of 1939. I had been appointed Director A.T.S. at the War Office. The Queen had sent for me and told me she intended to appoint one of her three sisters-in-law to each of the three Services. Ours was the Princess Royal who was already a "County Commandant" in the A.T.S.

'In 1955, I had the pleasure of being one of Her Majesty's nominators for the office of Chancellor of the University of London.'

Queen Elizabeth quickly showed that hers was to be no token contact with London University. She has regularly attended all sorts of university occasions, and she has taken every opportunity to meet the students. She has hammered home, whenever she could, her belief that more than book-learning is needed to make a fully developed and complete person.

To the Second Presentation of Graduates in May 1959, she said, 'But I hope that, while the University will take its full share in training the increasing numbers of scientists and technologists which our country so urgently needs, it will not become too preoccupied with scientific and technological matters.

'As civilisation advances, it becomes progressively more complicated and more intricate to manage. We now stand in greater need than ever before of men and women with wide intellectual interests and broad human sympathies to fill the many responsible posts on which our society depends for its smooth and successful functioning.'

Queen Elizabeth was the first Chancellor to confer University of London degrees in Africa. In the open air, in very different surroundings from the Albert Hall, presentation of degrees was made to thirty-six students of Makerere College in Uganda in 1959. The Chancellor wore the prescribed black damask robe with gold trimmings. The robe made for her predecessor, the Earl of Athlone, had weighed between nine and ten pounds, but a considerably lighter version had been made for Queen Elizabeth. However, she afterwards remarked, 'I felt that I was breaking new ground at any rate in our respect, for I was assured that the Chancellor's robes had never been to Africa before. However that may be, I can certainly vouch from personal experience that they were not designed to be worn with comfort on the Equator.'

Another of Queen Elizabeth's special interests stemmed from a letter published in *Country Life* just after the war, an appeal for those with country houses to give plants to the bombed, so that they could re-start their gardens. It was written by Sir Wyndham Deeds on behalf of the London Gardens Society, and the Society was electrified to receive a letter saying that the Queen had read this with great interest, and would they like a collection of plants from Sandringham or a donation, as Her Majesty would like to be associated with this helpful and healing work.

The London Gardens Society was formed in 1934 by the late Lord Noel Buxton who conceived the idea of linking together the many gardening guilds in and around London. The Society's main aim is to encourage people to beautify London by the growing of flowers everywhere, and particularly by the use of window-boxes and hanging plants where proper gardens are not possible. It was re-formed in 1946, with Queen Mary, who was also keenly and personally interested, as Patron. On her death she was succeeded by Queen Elizabeth.

Nothing deters Queen Elizabeth from keeping her appointment with the Society. One year she arrived in very bad weather, and got out of the car to a roll of thunder, at which she laughed and held out her foot showing that she was wearing transparent waterproof bootees over her shoes; when the rain came she carried on in a raincoat. She happened to drop her handkerchief in a puddle, from which it was retrieved wringing wet by the owner of the garden, and returned to her. Queen Elizabeth looked at it doubtfully and said, 'Perhaps you would like to keep it as a souvenir?' The monogrammed and crowned handkerchief, ironed and framed, now hangs in a Stepney sitting room.

She always has tea alone with one family. One year the organisers wanted her to see an extra garden, and she was approached to ask if she would forgo her tea. Back came the answer that 'Her Majesty loved her tea, and that she would see the extra garden "as well" but not "instead".'

Another time the wife of a retired Merchant Navy man said over tea, 'Ma'am, I hope you have a happy time on August 4.' 'How kind—but why do you mention it?' 'It is my birthday too.' Nothing more was said, but on August 4 a telegram of birthday good wishes arrived for the lady from Queen Elizabeth.

In one house there was a punchball and Queen Elizabeth asked the teenage boy what he did besides boxing. 'I sometimes write poetry.' 'I should love to see one of your poems.' A search ensued, without success, for a poem. 'Never mind—send it to me at Clarence House', and when this was done the poem was later returned to him with an appreciative comment.

Always interested in how people live, when she was taken to see the outside of a mews flat in Paddington which was not to be visited because of a difficult outside stair, she insisted on going up to see the flat as well. Indeed there have been many occasions when the timing of the whole tour has been endangered by Queen Elizabeth's interest in house as well as garden.

Through years of public duties she has retained her freshness and sense of enjoyment, because, although *things* are often the same—the ribbon to cut, the stone to lay, the key to turn, the speech to make—*people* are always different, and people are her abiding interest.

CHAPTER FOURTEEN

INDIAN SUMMER

PLEASURES A myriad to rehearse! . . .
The likely horse . . . The lucky 'hand' . . .
The leaping trout . . . The living verse . . .
The favourite waltz . . . The floodlit dome . . .
The crowds, the lights, the welcome . . .
—and (sweet as them all) the going home!

DUTIES!—The emblazoned document . . .
The microphone, while nations listen . . .
The moments when the ranks present . . .
This tape to cut . . . That stone to lay . . .
Another Veuve Cliquot to christen
The great bows that slide away! . . .

*From an engraved crystal engagement holder designed by Laurence
Whistler, given to Queen Elizabeth by her Private Secretary,
Major T. D. Harvey, C.V.O., upon leaving the Royal House-
hold.*

How our attitude to growing old has changed—is changing! It
is most vividly illustrated in comparing Queen Elizabeth the
Queen Mother—lively, involved, attractively dressed in delicate colours, and at ease with any generation—with the forbid-
ding and gloomy image of the elderly Queen Victoria. Yet
Queen Victoria was the younger woman.

Queen Mary, widow of King George V, remains at present
the longest living of any British Queen, a distinction that
Queen Elizabeth will not attain until May 1986. Queen Mary
was 85 years and ten months old at the time of her death on
March 24, 1953.

The span of life has considerably increased in this century,
and there is a royal sidelight to illustrate this. As is well known,
the Queen sends a message of congratulation to those who
have become centenarians—the highlight of that rare cele-

bration. When the Queen first sent such telegrams in 1952 they numbered 200 a year. In 1982 no fewer than 1,750 centenarians received their message of congratulation. No doubt part of the increase is due to more applications being made, but it does show that attaining even 100 years is not so rare as it once was.

Of far greater importance than the length of a life is its quality. We are just coming to terms with the whole altered lifespan which increased longevity is giving us, and which requires a reappraisal, a replanning of life itself. The three long-living Queens—Victoria, Mary, Elizabeth—were each doughty ladies, retaining personality and individuality, but the kind of activity and involvement enjoyed in later life has changed dramatically.

A quarter century after the official age of retirement for women Queen Elizabeth retains her zest for life, her appetite for hard work, and—in full—her charisma. Consistently she retains her contacts with, her interests in her previous pursuits. She sees no reason to give something up if she is still wanted and needed, still interested and involved, just because of a date in the reference books. She thinks young, therefore she is young.

The rewards of her long, outgoing life are being reaped. In her mid-eighties she is still in demand, still unable to accept more than a fraction of the invitations and requests for her patronage, her presence. Thus she has been spared the worst affliction of the elderly—that of not being wanted.

Yet life has not muffled its blows. Queen Elizabeth has suffered her fair share and more of sadness and sorrows. She was only 51 when she lost her cherished husband. She has survived all her six brothers and three sisters, of a particularly close-knit family. She has even outlived some cherished younger members; and especially the gaps left by a brother and sister, nephew and niece, Lord Elphinstone and Miss Elizabeth Elphinstone, remain sadly unfilled. The close friends among her contemporaries are, to a large measure, no more. Those few who do remain are frail, and often live at a distance.

Sudden tragedy has hit hard, especially the murder of Earl Mountbatten, who was her senior by only six weeks, and with whom she shared many memories.

Queen Elizabeth had confronted the dark side of life early on, when she met in her home turned hospital young men whose health, hopes and future had been shattered by war wounds and shellshock. During the Second World War she supported her husband in his time of stress, and silently sustained her own burden of anxiety for the safety of her children. Queen Elizabeth has her own way of dealing with these terrors. She faces them with a characteristic lift of the head and with unswerving fortitude. She ignores them—not for her the unburdening of her troubles in how-dreadful, what's-to-be done chatter. In the Scottish phrase 'she hauds her wheesht'.

The general pattern of her year has altered little. Around the time of her birthday, August 4th, Queen Elizabeth goes north, first to Castle of Mey and then to Birkhall for the longed-for and longest break of the year, spending many hours each day out of doors ridding herself of exhaust fumes, and breathing the sparkling Highland air.

In the autumn her public engagements draw her south, spending the weeks at Clarence House and the weekends at Royal Lodge. In London the round of public duties and the preparation for these duties is enlivened by visits to National Hunt meetings. The year ends and begins at Sandringham, a family festive season with an ever-increasing influx of young children and many dogs. The midwinter break lasts almost through January, with brisk walks in the crisp frost or splashing through rain and mud. This is very much a family time.

Back in London for a further round of public engagements, the coming spring brings new growth to look for and enjoy during the weekends at Royal Lodge (which was formerly referred to as The Royal Lodge). Queen Elizabeth and other members of her family gathered at Windsor meet at the morning service in the little church in Windsor Great Park, close to the gates to Royal Lodge. It has become the custom for the Queen and the rest of her family to come back to Royal Lodge for a pre-lunch sherry and a chat. Queen Elizabeth likes to do a certain amount of personal entertaining at Royal Lodge, and always has a large party for owners, trainers and riders connected with the Grand Military meeting, held at Sandown Park in March.

Once upon a time the year was planned round Queen Elizabeth's overseas trips, much enjoyed but exhausting both in preparation and execution. The invitations still come: Canada, which she has visited so often over the years, is particularly pressing with suggestions.

Visits to Europe are another matter. Queen Elizabeth is in the habit of visiting France privately for a few days each year, staying in a château, with expeditions to places of interest in the neighbourhood. She visits Germany, especially in connection with visits to the Irish Guards, whom she annually presents with their ritual shamrock on St. Patrick's Day.

In the spring, on a date dictated by the spate (if public engagements permit), she goes north to Deeside for a few days of salmon fishing. And she still dons waders and goes into the water. Her delight in walking for long distances, in any kind of weather, continues unabated and she can and does still exhaust her Household.

Although many of her public engagements take place at longer intervals, there are certain annual events she never misses, if she can help it—the Annual Remembrance Service in November, Trooping the Colour to celebrate the Queen's official Birthday, Services of the Order of the Garter, Royal Ascot, Badminton Horse Trials, the Cheltenham National Hunt Meeting . . .

Recurrent engagements often involve the Regiments of which she is proud to be Colonel-in-Chief, in each of which she takes a fierce personal interest, as senior War Office pundits will confirm, if the future or wellbeing of one of Queen Elizabeth's Regiments is threatened. This year, when the 300th anniversary of so many British Regiments is celebrated, involves special Regimental occasions. Several Regiments with which the Queen Mother is officially connected will celebrate their Tercentenaries in 1985. Plans under way had not been made public at the date of going to Press. The Regiments involved are the Queen's Dragoon Guards, the Queen's Own Hussars, the Royal Anglian Regiment and the Light Infantry.

The full list of regiments, squadrons and corps with which Queen Elizabeth is presently connected is as follows:-

Colonel-in-Chief
   The Black Watch (Royal Highland Regiment)
   The Black Watch (Royal Highland Regiment) of Canada
   Canadian Forces Medical Services
   The King's Regiment
   The Light Infantry
   1st The Queen's Dragoon Guards
   The Queen's Own Hussars
   The Royal Anglian Regiment
   Royal Army Medical Corps
   Royal Australian Army Medical Corps
   9th/12th Royal Lancers (Prince of Wales')
   Royal New Zealand Army Medical Corps
   Toronto Scottish Regiment

Honorary Colonel
   Inns of Court and City Yeomanry
   The London Scottish
   The Royal Yeomanry
   University of London Officers' Training Corps

Honorary Air Commodore
   University of London Air Squadron

Commandant-in-Chief
   Royal Air Force Central Flying School
   Women's Royal Air Force

Women's Royal Army Corps
Women's Royal Naval Service

'When I copy Queen Elizabeth's diary of public engagements,' one of the clerical staff at Clarence House remarked to me, 'I just can't imagine how she fits it all in.'

The most important—indeed virtually the only—public appointment which Queen Elizabeth has given up is the Chancellorship of London University, which is now held by her granddaughter Princess Anne. A rare new commitment is in becoming President of the Victoria Cross and George Cross Association in the summer of 1984, an appointment which she celebrated, in typical style, with a party for the Committee held at Clarence House.

Continuity and loyalty mean a great deal to Queen Elizabeth. Her mainspring is her family and must always be the heart of her life. She is at the apex of a family of two daughters, four grandsons and two granddaughters, three great-grandsons and one great-granddaughter. She does not expect—or want—everyone to be alike but she knows the strength and joy that comes from the interdependence of a family.

Her Household, the people around her whom she sees most frequently, and on whom she relies for loyalty and support, has remained virtually unchanged throughout the years except where death has intervened. Her private secretary remains Sir Martin Gilliat. Captain Alastair Aird, her Comptroller in place of the late Lord Adam Gordon, was formerly her Equerry. Her Press Secretary continues to be Major A. J. S. Griffin.

Clarence House is of necessity her base for most of the year, although it is not her favourite home. But it would be impossible for her to carry out her round of engagements from distant Castle of Mey, Birkhall on Deeside, or even Royal Lodge. (She may recall those fogbound, eerie journeys lost in the spaces of Richmond Park in the very early years of her married life, when, as Duchess of York, she lived at The White Lodge.)

When Queen Elizabeth returns to Clarence House her car turns off the Mall, enters Stable Yard Road and turns sharp right between the solid, black-painted wooden gates that protect the limited privacy of Clarence House's modest garden, up the few yards of gravelled drive, to draw up under the pillared, cream-painted portico. Then her Royal Standard, lengthened by the punning Arms of Bowes-Lyon, is hoisted onto the bare flagpole.

One step of white marble leads up into the small hall. Here stands the musical clock, surmounted by the Scottish lion on a crown, made by 'John Smith of Pittenweem, North Britain' which was the wedding present of the citizens of Glasgow to the Duke and Duchess of York in 1923.

Three further steps lead into the broad inner hall or lower corridor. This is lit by two fine Regency chandeliers, with ormolu centres which look like garden fountains, over which the crystal drops fall like water. A jardinière filled with flowering plants—Queen Elizabeth loves massed flowers—stands before an early seventeenth century tapestry from Italy. Halfway down the hall stand two tall Nubian figures, originally used as torchères, made from Italian walnut early in the eighteenth century. A fine ormolu clock, decorated with a Chinese man holding an umbrella hung with bells, stands on a table—as usual Queen Elizabeth's sense of fun has directed her choice.

In a large display cabinet is set out a splendid service of Worcester china, originally presented by George IV to the King of Hanover. King George IV himself selected the scenes painted on the porcelain—mostly of classical subjects, they include a surprising number of death-beds. They are painted with great skill by Humphrey Chamberlain, inside a gold-sprigged, dark-blue surround. The finest plate is judged to be that showing three children, painted after Sir Joshua Reynolds.

Clarence House is by no means large, and was in fact designed to be smaller still, consisting as it does of three small houses back-to-back and arbitrarily connected. It is very different in scale from Buckingham Palace or Windsor Castle. The portraits in the hall were designed for larger rooms, but they look well here in close-up. A Lely portrait in an oval frame is of James, Duke of York, afterwards King James II, wearing the robes of the Order of the Garter. Two portraits by Allan Ramsay are of George III, also in Garter robes, and of Augusta, wife of Frederick, Prince of Wales, who is wearing a pink dress under a black lace cloak, in a garden setting. These two portraits came from Marlborough House. A portrait of Queen Charlotte, wife of George III, also shows her in a pink dress, over which she wears a blue cape trimmed with ermine. A contrast in styles and eras—but still with the Order of the Garter theme—is Simon Elwes' painting of King George VI investing Princess Elizabeth, the present Queen, with the insignia of the Garter.

The first door on the left of the inner hall opens into the morning-room, a pleasant place. Special cabinets have been built on either side of the chimneypiece to accommodate part of Queen Elizabeth's magnificent collection of Red Anchor Chelsea. The cabinets reach to ceiling height and break up the design of the Nash plasterwork, so that the ceiling is asymmetric. In this room Queen Elizabeth is surrounded by some of her favourite pictures, including an Augustus John study of the head of George Bernard Shaw. (These have already been described in Chapter One.)

Opening off the morning-room is a small, square room, which is now the library. The walls are lined with Queen Elizabeth's books, many of them uniformly bound in deep-blue leather. There is a fine rosewood table, set round with Chippendale chairs. Queen Elizabeth often lunches here when she is alone, or with members of her Household, or when she has only one or two guests. This was the original entrance-hall of Clarence House, then entered from Stable Yard and not, as now, from the garden front.

The dining-room proper can be entered from the library or from the hall. It is a long room, with a delicately moulded Nash ceiling. Pleasant Edwardian wall panels are set with portraits which have looked down on the diners for many,

many years. There are ten Kit-cat portraits of the Duke of
Clarence (later King William IV) from whom the house takes
its name, and of his parents, brothers and sisters. These
pictures have been displayed here since the Duke of Clarence
himself dined in this room. His father George III and his
mother Queen Charlotte are painted in their Coronation robes
by Sir William Beechey, who also painted two of the portraits
of his brothers, and two of his sisters. Hoppner however
painted the portraits of the Duke of Kent, father of Queen
Victoria, and of the Duke of Clarence himself. The splendid
1770 chimneypiece of white and grey marble was installed
during the occupancy of Queen Elizabeth.

Queen Elizabeth's dinner parties are usually for twelve
people, seated round the long table of Spanish walnut. Dinner
is timed for 9 pm, but it is not unusual for it to be a little
delayed. At luncheon or dinner parties the dining- and side-
tables display some of Queen Elizabeth's fine collection of
plate. This is normally kept in tall, green-baize-lined cabinets
in an underground silver vault, where it is cared for—mostly
with elbow grease—by the Yeoman of the Gold and Silver.

One very old and rare casket made of mother-of-pearl and
silver-gilt was made in Targau in Saxony in 1570. Standing on
four fluted crystal-ball feet and still lined with the original
tapestry, each of the mother-of-pearl scales which adorn the
outside is held by a gilded belt, with pierced and chased
silver-gilt mount. This was the present of John Brown's
shipyard after Queen Elizabeth had launched the liner bearing
her name in 1938. Many of Queen Elizabeth's treasures are
linked with great public occasions. Others are family gifts,
lovingly chosen to mark birthdays and Christmases.

Queen Elizabeth also used to buy items which particularly
appealed to her from the famous London salerooms. Her
Comptroller for so long, Lord Adam Gordon, an expert and
connoisseur, used to visit Christie's or Sotheby's to inspect
objects which Queen Elizabeth thought might interest her, and
to advise her. Since his death, although the catalogues are still
sent to her, she has become less active in her purchases. She has

however, always liked to buy pictures or pieces of silver which had at some time belonged to her family, and which have come onto the market. She has acquired, for instance, a very fine ewer and dish hallmarked 1718 made by David Willaume, one of the earliest of the Huguenot silversmiths to come to this country after the revocation of the Edict of Nantes in 1685. These bear the arms of George Bowes of Streatlam Castle, whose heiress daughter married the ninth Earl of Strathmore in 1767 and brought Bowes to Lyon.

Queen Elizabeth has been a collector of Regency wine-coasters, which she finds hard to resist. Among the Royal silver are some fine pieces which she has inherited from Queen Mary's collection. It is a curious development, however, that the famed collections of Queen Mary, consisting often of exquisitely wrought and elaborate items in the continental style, are not so much to the modern taste as Queen Elizabeth's personal collections of silver, portraits and porcelain.

A favourite possession, often displayed, which was chosen for and not by Queen Elizabeth, is the set of four attractive silver-gilt conch shells, with dolphins playing around them, designed by Leslie Durbin, of which she is very fond. They were presented to her by the Federal Power Board of Rhodesia and Nyasaland when she opened the Kariba Dam.

Like the Queen, Queen Elizabeth is always quick to incorporate among the possessions on display anything which forms a particular link between her guests and herself. When she entertains her friends from the world of horse-racing she often has racing cups on the table, perhaps the Tote Investors Cup won in 1957 by *Double Star* or the cup won by *Manicou* at Kempton Park in 1950. Her greatest racing triumph was the Whitbread Gold Cup, won by a short head by *Special Cargo* in 1984. This original and historic cup has been generously presented to Queen Elizabeth to keep, and future winners will be rewarded with the tenure of a replica cup.

She possesses a replica of the Lanark Silver Bell, won by King George VI's horse *Kingstone* in 1946. The Lanark Silver Bell was the prize for one of the oldest—sometimes claimed to be *the* oldest-British horse race. According to legend it was founded by King William, the Lion of Scotland, who reigned from 1165 to 1214. Early history is somewhat misty, but at least the name of the winner is known as far back as 1661, and the present Bell probably dates from 1718. Lanark racecourse is now closed and the race was not transferred to another course but is at present suspended. The King was not present to see his horse win, and the Cup was borne south by his racing manager Captain Charles Moore. At the end of the year, when it had to be returned to Lanark, a replica was made to be given to the King, and it is this replica which is in Queen Elizabeth's possession.

The first floor of Clarence House is reached by a staircase (at the back of the hall), and turning right. The walls of the upper corridor are crowded with pictures of personal choice and family interest, with diverse themes and styles. Perhaps this part of the house mirrors more clearly than any other the pressures of space experienced when moving from very large palaces to a more modestly proportioned house.

We see a serene Duchess of York, painted by S. Sorine in 1923, the year of her wedding, in which she is wearing an ivory-coloured dress and a large matching hat with an emerald green ribbon. Opposite hangs a portrait of Princess Elizabeth, also by Sorine, and painted in the year of her marriage. Close by is the full-length portrait of King George VI in the uniform of the Eleventh Hussars, presented in his memory to Queen Elizabeth by the Officers of the Regiment.

Other pictures from Queen Elizabeth's notable collection of the works of modern artists hang in the upper corridor. These include an Augustus John, an Ethel Walker depicting the sea on an October morning, an unusual Lowry of a Fylde farm, and a splendid Sisley of the Seine near St. Cloud on a misty morning. The two still-life pictures are an unusually bright Matthew Smith of jugs and apples, and a bottle, basket and marrow by the Scottish artist Peploe.

Both her family and her personal interest in the thorough-bred horse are naturally well represented. Queen Elizabeth's family were distinguished both as breeders and owners of racehorses. Is it any wonder then that she and her elder daughter and only granddaughter should have such a great interest in horses?

Most successful of all was her kinsman, John Bowes of Streatlam Castle in County Durham, who was born in 1811 and died in 1885, the son of the Earl and Countess of Strathmore. His father, a noted man across country after hounds had won the 1803 St. Leger with *Remembrancer*. Young John Bowes was left a number of mares by his father, including *Emma* the dam of *Myndig* and *Cotherstone*, winners of the Epsom Derby in 1835 and 1843 and grandam of *West Australian*, who won the Derby in 1853. John Bowes also won the Derby with *Damiel O'Rourke* in 1852, and in all won eight English classic races, a remarkable record. It is said that John Bowes, a shrewd man even in his youth, discovered that *Myndig* (whose name means Coming of Age) was being heavily backed to win the Derby by his guardians. Bowes confronted them with proof of their bets, and stated that he would withdraw the horse unless the bets were transferred to him. This was done, the horse ran and won—by only a head—and young John Bowes cleared about £20,000, which was then a considerable fortune. *West Australian* was the first horse ever to win the Triple Crown, that is to say the three of the five English classic races open to three-year-old colts and fillies (the other two being confined to fillies)—the Two Thousand Guineas run at Newmarket, the Derby run at Epsom and the oldest of them all, the St. Leger at Doncaster, run over gradually extending distances, between May and September.

Queen Elizabeth bought and has hung in the upper corridor at Clarence House a delightful and very personal souvenir of this kinsman's successes. It is an ornate gold frame specially made to contain the portrait of *Cotherstone*, surrounded by the individual portraits of six of his ancestors, by Herring, all painted on the same canvas. Queen Elizabeth loaned the unique picture to the Antique Dealers Fair in Grosvenor House in 1962. She also has a portrait of *West Australian* by Harry Hall.

Throughout Clarence House one is continually reminded that this is the home of a person with strong family ties and affections allied to a love of beauty—and with a sense of humour which shows itself in many characterful and comical ornaments. It is also the home of someone who has moved from a larger into a smaller house, where treasures are now shuffled into a place beside neighbours of another age or style, where each and every piece is retained because it is too well loved to discard.

The west side of the first floor of Clarence House is taken up by a double drawing-room, with Queen Elizabeth's private sitting-room on the corner overlooking the garden. The double drawing-room was originally designed as two rooms by Nash. The division of the rooms is marked by a pillar on each side. The splendid moulded plaster ceilings remain, and are picked out in gold. The walls are pale cream. The rooms are lit by two magnificent Waterford crystal chandeliers. On the floor are two rich Aubusson carpets, and the furniture is eighteenth-century French gilt-wood.

Above the chimney-piece on the north side of the room hangs an Augustus John of Queen Elizabeth wearing a silver and rose evening dress. This painting was begun in peacetime, but because of the war sittings were moved from Buckingham Palace to Windsor Castle and became unduly protracted. A member of Queen Elizabeth's Household told me drily that he suspected the artist found residence at Windsor congenial and so was in no great haste. Eventually the project was suspended and the artist took the unfinished portrait away with him to the country for safety. It was discovered twenty years later with many other John pictures in the cellar of his house, and was first seen, among *Pictures not previously exhibited by Augustus John* at Tooth's Gallery in Bruton Street in 1961. The portrait was presented to Her Majesty, to her great delight, by Viscount Knollys, the chairman of Vickers-Armstrong, after she had launched the Shaw Savill liner *Northern Star* at the

361

Vickers shipyard at Walker-on-Tyne in June 1951. This is the third Augustus John painting on the walls of Clarence House.

Another personal picture on the walls of the double drawing-room is a delightful portrait of three Victorian school-age children, each with long chestnut hair and delicate colouring, wearing russet-coloured dresses. The girls, who are very alike, are the three beautiful Misses Cavendish-Bentinck, Queen Elizabeth's mother and her two aunts.

The Royal connection is indicated in two portraits of Queen Victoria: an unfinished sketch for an equestrian portrait is by Sir Edwin Landseer. A Wilkie of *Queen Victoria's First Communion* shows her with her Mother, the Duchess of Kent, who also lived at one time at Clarence House—and includes, somewhat surprisingly, Queen Victoria's fox terrier.

Other favourite modern artists of Queen Elizabeth's, although their paintings are not always on the walls of Clarence House, are Edward Seago, John Piper and Claude Muncaster. King George and Queen Elizabeth commissioned Edward Seago to paint their favourite views round Sandringham. Similarly John Piper, who painted the picture of the Church of Santa Maria della Salute in Venice, which does hang on the walls of the double drawing-room, was commissioned to do two series of striking and dramatic pictures of and around Windsor Castle. Claude Muncaster has recorded the Deeside scenery round Balmoral, and also scenes in Windsor Home Park.

There is a grand piano in the drawing-room upon which stands a stitched and framed sampler, with an animal for each Commonwealth country, and a verse which begins:-

In stitching we here record
The crowning of Our Sovereign Lord.

When Queen Elizabeth is alone, she very often sits on a sofa at the south end of the drawing-room, in front of the red lacquer silver cabinet which used to be in her sitting-room at 145 Piccadilly. Sometimes when she is alone she will dine here.

Her own television—there are others used by Household and staff in other parts of Clarence House—stands in front of the sofa, and she is known to watch quite a number of programmes, and to display knowledge of them when she meets the appropriate actors or producers.

The south west corner of the first floor of Clarence House contains Queen Elizabeth's private sitting-room. A piece of furniture familiar and all too necessary in all palaces and great houses is the draught screen: here a black lacquer screen protects the door leading from the corridor. Again the ceiling is by Nash. The walls are hung with the same blue silk decorated with vertical swags of flowers that Queen Elizabeth had chosen for her private sitting-room at Buckingham Palace. The fine grey and white marble chimney-piece dates from the reign of George II. The dark-blue Persian carpet on which roam tigers, deer and other animals, was in the morning-room of 145 Piccadilly, and afterwards on the floor of Queen Elizabeth's sitting-room at Buckingham Palace. The easy chairs are covered in blue silk.

On the walls are some small pictures particularly dear to her, including the study of her husband made by Simon Elwes for his large picture of *The Investiture of Princess Elizabeth with the Order of the Garter by King George VI*, which hangs in the lower corridor. Queen Elizabeth likes the spontaniety and vigour so often caught in an artist's sketch for a great painting, and here she has hung a similar study by Terence Cuneo of her daughter the Queen, in her Coronation robes. There is also a painting by E. Moynihan of Princess Elizabeth in blue. The *Madonna and Child Enthroned* by Fra Angelico is one of the early Italian masterpieces collected by Albert, the Prince Consort.

Here also are some of the objects which Queen Elizabeth has enjoyed collecting over the years, some miniature furniture—more often samples of the furniture-maker's skill than furnishings made for luxurious dolls' houses—and some fine Battersea enamel, including the two tea caddies given to Queen Elizabeth when she received the Freedom of the City of London by the Lord Mayor and Aldermen. The cases contain several of the peapods and small vegetables in Red Anchor Chelsea which were presents aptly chosen for her by Princess Elizabeth and Princess Margaret when they were young girls.

Queen Elizabeth reads a great deal, and there are always books lying about, which will include illustrated art books about architecture, pictures, furniture, china and other achievements of man-made beauty, while others record the countryside, gardens and flowers.

Invariably, in any room of any house occupied by Queen Elizabeth there are flowers—not one or two blooms but massed flowers, filling the air with their scent. In spring there are great bowls of daffodils, and often tubs containing flowering shrubs. The bouquets which Queen Elizabeth has recently received are undone and rearranged in vases or bowls. Both King George VI and Queen Elizabeth disliked wired flowers, and made haste to release the blooms from their bondage.

But in the private sitting-room the eye is drawn inexorably to the large mahogany desk placed with its back to the west window, which is lit, with brusque efficiency, by a modern anglepoise lamp. On it are all the tools required for desk work—paper-opener, a basket filled with pens (including a gold quill pen which is never used), and a pile of wicker-work baskets labelled *Private Secretary* and *Lady in Waiting*.

Paperwork is not Queen Elizabeth's favourite way of spending her time, and she sweetens the pill by surrounding her desk with reminders of those she loves. She has always had photographs on her desk, but in recent years these have greatly increased in number. There are many of the King, notably an amateur photograph taken in profile during the South African tour, others of her daughters, grandchildren and great-grandchildren at various ages, and some of her own family, including her beloved brother Sir David Bowes-Lyon.

Facing her in the centre of the desk is an object both beautiful and practical. It is the gilt and crystal screen shaped liked a triptych and designed by Laurence Whistler. It was the inspired gift of her former Private Secretary, Major Harvey, upon leaving her service. The centre panel is of the exact size to hold the sheet of Royal letter paper on which her day's engagements are typed out. Each side has a trophy, a verse and, at the foot, a little engraved scene. One side commemorates *Pleasures*, the other *Duties*. The apt verses are quoted at the beginning of this chapter. In the trophy for *Pleasures* are a landing-net, a pair of raceglasses, musical instruments and the mask of Terpsichore, the muse of dance. Below is depicted the drive in an open landau drawn by postilions on mounted greys up the course at Royal Ascot. The *Duties* cleverly and decoratively incorporate microphone, drums, trowel, mortar-board, scissors and key. The scene below depicts the Royal car driving out of the gates of Buckingham Palace.

Perhaps there are fewer recent additions to the treasures in Queen Elizabeth's room and her house, but she delights in the associations of the possessions by which she is surrounded. She still gets the catalogues of the great salerooms, but since the death of Lord Adam Gordon, for so long her Comptroller, who was her adviser on the antiques which he loved and knew so well, she has bought little. It is interesting to observe that the possessions which Queen Elizabeth acquired often before they had taken the experts' fancy have increased fantastically in value, probably more than the more formal collections of Queen Mary who was, in her lifetime, generally thought to be the greater expert.

If something in a catalogue interested Queen Elizabeth she was in the habit of asking Lord Adam to take a look at it and give her his opinion. If his verdict attracted her she would ask to have the item sent to her for her inspection at Clarence House. For example she liked the description of some Japanese porcelain cats, and, when she saw them, found them charming. 'Then there was the challenge of assessing a bid, the excitement of the day of the auction, and the pleasure when the attractive cats were knocked down to her representative,' commented Lord Adam. When she is overseas she often asks to have the work of local artists sent to her, and selects from their work pictures which she likes, and which remind her of places visited. Sometimes, of course, she is presented with such mementoes. For instance, after she had visited the colony of wild albatrosses on Otago Head in the South Island of New Zealand, she was amused by a cartoon which appeared in a local paper, showing an exceedingly proud albatross sitting on her nest, while fellow albatrosses jealously discussed her. '. . . And so when it's hatched, she's going to call it Elizabeth!', read the caption. She was delighted to accept the original drawing, when it was offered to her by Sir Leonard Wright, the Mayor of Dunedin.

But perhaps the interest which is liveliest in her mid-eighties is in racing. Every day, every race-card, every result is new, and endlessly exciting, as well as reviving memories of friends and horses of yesteryear. Queen Elizabeth has six to ten horses in the care of Mr. Fulke Walwyn at Lambourn, all jumpers. This is fewer than she had in training even ten years ago, but because of the ever-increasing cost of keeping horses in training, does not represent any great saving. At a peak Queen Elizabeth had sixteen jumpers in training, spread amongst several trainers. Peter Cazalet's death was a great blow to Queen Elizabeth because he was not only her trainer but also a personal friend, and she had always enjoyed her visits to Fairlawne in Kent to see her horses in training. Now that they are with Fulke Walwyn she spends more time at Lambourn in Berkshire. Jack O'Donoghue at Reigate has long been one of Queen Elizabeth's trainers, specialising in 'the awkward squad', but as Sir Martin Gilliat, Queen Elizabeth's Private Secretary, who shares her knowledge of and interest in the sport, remarked, 'we have no problem children just now.'

Queen Elizabeth is a considerable expert on conformation, action and form in a racehorse. She loves a good race. It is said by those who should know that the Queen will go anywhere to see a stud, and the Queen Mother anywhere to see a good race, especially over jumps. She remains today as enthusiastic as ever, and her fondness for National Hunt racing is undiminished. Queen Elizabeth reads *The Sporting Life* regularly, and when she was in Venice in 1984 special arrangements were made so that she could obtain her daily *Life*. She consults *The*

Racing Calendar, studies the form book and reads articles and books about racing. The novels of Dick Francis are among her favourites.

Together with her daughter she is a Patron of the Jockey Club (which only recently opened its doors to women members). For a long time the Queen and Queen Elizabeth were the only women included. An event which gave Queen Elizabeth particular pleasure was the private luncheon party at the Savoy which the Stewards of the Jockey Club held to mark her twenty five years as an owner, and to which the Queen came as a guest.

Queen Elizabeth had been named Patron of the National Hunt Committee in 1954 and when that Committee, which was responsible for the conduct of jumping, was amalgamated with the Jockey Club under the newly-created Turf Board in 1965, she became joint Patron.

She is also Patron of the Injured Jockeys Fund, originally founded to help those injured in jump-racing but now extended to all those injured in racing. For their part the National Hunt jockeys, not a sycophantic company, have demonstrated the high regard in which they hold her by requesting—and being granted—permission to adopt her racing colours for their National Hunt Jockeys Cricket Club. Queen Elizabeth hears how her team is faring through reports from their captain, ex-jockey and trainer David Nicholson, and delights, whenever possible, in coming to watch their 'needle' match against Ascot in May each year. Queen Elizabeth's presents to those who work for her in racing are personally and aptly chosen. It is rare for her to arrange to be photographed, but this is what she did before Terry Biddlecombe rode for her for the last time before his retirement from the saddle. She then signed and presented to him the colour photograph which showed her with Fulke Walwyn and Terry in the paddock at Cheltenham.

The continuing story of Queen Elizabeth's involvement in horseracing as an owner began in the season of 1949/50. The Queen, as she was then, was fired with an interest in racing through Lord Mildmay, a celebrated amateur rider who had on two occasions narrowly, and unluckily, failed to win the Grand National. Peter Cazalet, who trained Lord Mildmay's horses, found *Monaveen*, a promising Irish half-bred, which was owned jointly by the Queen and Princess Elizabeth, and ran in Princess Elizabeth's name and colours.

Monaveen won his first race for the new Royal partnership on 10 October 1949, the three-and-a-quarter mile Chichester chase at Fontwell, ridden by Tony Grantham. The race, incidentally, was worth a mere £204 to the winner—a similar race is worth ten times as much today. *Monaveen* went on to win them three further races, and finished fifth of the seven finishers in *Freebooter*'s Grand National, after leading to the 14th fence, when a bad blunder put him out of it. The luck was too good to last. In the following season *Monaveen* was knocked into when jumping the water at Hurst Park, fell, broke a leg and had to be destroyed. He is buried on the racecourse. Princess Elizabeth, who was living in Malta where her husband was stationed, was heartbroken; she has never again owned a jumper, concentrating her involvement in horseracing on the Flat.

However Queen Elizabeth, although saddened by the loss of *Monaveen*, persevered in her ownership of National Hunt horses, even though a greater blow still had followed with the death by drowning of lord Mildmay. She decided to perpetuate his interests, and bought his best horse *Manicou* which continued to be trained by Peter Cazalet. She raced *Manicou* in her own name, and in her family colours of blue, buff stripes, blue sleeves, and black cap with a gold tassel. (The colours had been made up to match those shown in an old racing print. They proved disappointingly drab, until the picture was cleaned, and the original, much brighter, colours were revealed and reproduced in a new set of colours).

When *Manicou* won the Wimbledon Steeplechase at Kempton Park on 24 November 1950 it was the first occasion that a horse owned by a Queen and running in her colours had won in Britain since a horse called *Star* owned by Queen Anne had won at York in 1714. It was also the first time ever that a horse owned by a Queen had won under National Hunt rules. *Manicou* went on to win the prestigious King George VI chase at Kempton Park on Boxing Day 1950 before breaking down and being retired to stud, where he became a successful sire of jumping horses.

Queen Elizabeth's next really successful horse was *Devon Loch* a very useful chaser who won six races, but will always be associated with his extraordinary defeat in the Grand National of 1956. *Devon Loch* led over the last jump. On the long run in, he was well in the lead from the tiring *E.S.B.* when, only thirty yards from the post, he suddenly faltered and sprawled to the ground. The huge crowd, who had been lustily cheering him home, was instantly silenced. When *Devon Loch* struggled to his feet he seemed unharmed, and no-one has really explained what happened. Queen Elizabeth's joy was dashed into bitter disappointment but she was the first to recover her serenity. She swiftly sent messages of comfort to her disconsolate jockey Dick Francis and her dispirited trainer Peter Cazalet. Nor did she omit warmly to congratulate the lucky owners of *E.S.B.* As it happened Mr. Malenkov and Mr. Gromyko, and other visiting Russian dignitaries, were present at Aintree. As Graham Stanford wrote in *The News of the World*, 'It was probably the most typical British occasion Mr. Malenkov has yet seen. And—above all else—he saw for himself the intense personal disappointment of the huge crowd in a Royal defeat when victory seemed certain.'

There was a happier by-product of this strange incident. When Queen Elizabeth's jockey Dick Francis was injured shortly afterwards and had to retire from the saddle, he was asked to write his autobiography—largely because of the public interest generated by *Devon Loch*'s collapse. This became *The Sport of Queens* and was followed by international success with his detective novels.

Incidentally *Devon Loch* continued perfectly fit, and was for some years lent as a hack to trainer Noel Murless at Newmarket.

One of Queen Elizabeth's most successful horses was *The*

Rip, which she bought on her own judgement, although he had a slightly twisted foot which might have discouraged other experts. He was by her own horse *Manicou* out of *Easy Virtue* and was bred by J. A. Irwin of the Red Cat Hotel, North Wootton near Sandringham, where Queen Elizabeth went to see him. After buying him, she kept him at Sandringham until he was sent to Peter Cazalet to be trained. In all *The Rip* won thirteen races for her. *Double Star*, an early favourite, won seventeen races, as did *Chaou II*, a French-bred horse, which caused chaos at Clarence House when he got loose when brought to Clarence House for Queen Elizabeth's inspection while she was convalescing after an operation. *Game Spirit* was another prolific winner.

The last winner trained by Peter Cazalet for Queen Elizabeth was *Inch Arran*, winner of the Topham Trophy and first winner at Liverpool in 1973. Unfortunately the trainer, who died in May of that year, was not well enough to attend the race.

Fulke Walwyn, who took over as Queen Elizabeth's principal trainer, is distinguished both as a rider, amateur and professional, winner of the Grand National on *Reynoldstown*, and as a top trainer of National Hunt horses who has trained such great horses as *Mandarin*, *Mill House*, *Team Spirit*, *The Dikler* and recently *Diamond Edge*, while the great races he has won would fill a whole page.

The first two big races Fulke Walwyn won for Queen Elizabeth were particularly aptly named—the Fairlawne Chase, named after Peter Cazalet's stables, with *Game Spirit* at Windsor, and the Reynoldstown Pattern Hurdle at Wolverhampton with *Sunyboy*—*Reynoldstown* had been ridden by Fulke Walwyn to win the Grand National in 1936. This was followed in February 1975 by the Schweppes Hurdle at Newbury, always hotly contested, which was won by *Tammuz*, trained by Fulke Walwyn and ridden by Bill Smith. Queen Elizabeth was present and received a tumultuous welcome and three cheers from the delighted race crowd. The race was worth £9,727 to the winning owner.

This remained Queen Elizabeth's most valuable win until April 1984, when *Special Cargo*, an eleven-year-old bay gelding by *Dairialatan* out of *Little Tot*, won the Whitbread Gold Cup, value £25,472 to the winning owner, in a dramatic race. The Whitbread Gold Cup, the first sponsored race of modern times, is run over three miles and five furlongs at Sandown Park as the last big race of the jumping season. It is a race which has produced some magnificent finishes up the Sandown hill, none more so than in 1984. Let Brough Scott tell the story in a brilliant piece which originally appeared in the *Sunday Times*.

'*HER MAJESTY'S PLEASURE*—*a Whitbread special . . . the race of a lifetime*.

It was as near as we'll get to the ultimate horse race. Three-and-a-half miles travelled, twenty-four fences crossed, four brave horses straining up the Sandown hill for a double photo-finish, with victory finally going to jump racing's best-loved colours, the blue and buff silks of Queen Elizabeth the Queen Mother.

The Whitbread Gold Cup was the royal lady's biggest success as an owner, and some repayment for her many years devotion to the jumping game. But it was much more than that. It was final proof that within the confines of a horse race you can sometimes experience enough twist on the emotions to make any script-writer blush.

Each of the first four home deserved a chapter to himself. The winner, *Special Cargo*, came from an impossible position two fences out, and from two years' lameness before that. The second *Lettoch*, came from being almost knocked over after half-a-mile. The third, *Diamond Edge*, came within two short heads of a record third Whitbread, and, in fourth place, *Plundering* came within two lengths of finally laying the hoodoo that has haunted Fred Winter as jockey and trainer in this race.

The stories go on. *Special Cargo* was an unprecedented seventh Whitbread win for 73-year-old Fulke Walwyn, who also saddled the 13-year-old *Diamond Edge* on whom *Special*

Cargo's regular jockey Bill Smith was making a magnificent, if heartbreaking, final appearance. *Lettoch* trainer, Michael Dickinson, is also quitting National Hunt after the most meteoric career in the game, and if *Plundering* had collected, Winter would have won the season's long duel with Dickinson for the trainer's title.

On the second circuit, where the fences come close together, *Diamond Edge* was in the lead but frequently challenged.

Seven times the young challengers pushed up to match strides with the old champion. Seven times *Diamond Edge* saw them off, only to give way like some ageing stag, as *Plundering* and *Ashley House* pressed on towards the Pond fence three from the finish. At this stage *Lettoch* was the clear danger to the leading pair, and only their loyalist supporters could have really fancied either *Diamond Edge* to throw off the years or, further back, for his stable companion *Special Cargo* to put spring into his battered old legs, as Kevin Mooney urged him forward.

Crossing the second last, *Lettoch* had taken over, and as *Plundering* raced with him, the stage seemed set for the expected Dickinson—Winter trainers' duel. One fence to go, and it was desperate stuff.

Plundering was the first to crack, rolling away to *Lettoch*'s left and leaving a gap through which Bill Smith drove *Diamond Edge* with the knowledge that this was the absolute final throw for horse and rider. A hundred yards to go and *Diamond Edge* was only a neck down and gaining. But now another twist, *Special Cargo* was within two lengths and Mooney had him flying.

All three were together as the post flashed by. First thoughts were that none could be a loser. A few minutes later, when *Special Cargo*'s name had been called and his owner stood in the victory circle, her pale blue coat matching Mooney's silks, you had to think that perhaps we had the right result.'

The Sunday Times, 29 April 1984

This splendid win secured for Queen Elizabeth the Lanson Award as Racing Lady of the Month. *Special Cargo* already stood high in his owner's affections, after his win in the Horse and Hound Grand Military Gold Cup, at Sandown Park a month earlier in which he was ridden by Gerald Oxley. This was the young officer's second ride and first win under Rules. He is the son of John Oxley who formerly trained in Newmarket and was serving in Germany with the 13th/18th Royal Hussars. *Special Cargo* won this race for the second time, March 9th, 1985.

Although Queen Elizabeth's racing interests are firmly centred upon National Hunt racing she also enjoys the Flat, and has had several Flat racing horses. Outstanding was *Bali Ha'i III*, who was presented to her in New Zealand and won her several good Flat races, notably the Queen Alexandra Stakes at Royal Ascot which, at two miles and six furlongs, is the longest Flat race in the British calendar, and is always associated with the great *Brown Jack*.

Up to the end of 1984 Queen Elizabeth had won no fewer than 351 jumping and three Flat races.

*   *   *

Queen Elizabeth has fished for most of her life. But it is only comparatively recently that she became a really keen salmon fisher. She still fishes for salmon, and she still, in her mid-eighties, dons waders and wades out to reach into the best waters. She likes to go up to Birkhall for a week or ten days of fishing every spring—the Dee is at its best in spring—but because of her many engagements the date has to be fixed some months in advance, so there can be no guarantee of perfect conditions.

Encouraged by the gillies, who are enthusiasts as well as experts, Queen Elizabeth is out on the river all day, sometimes changing beats, and sometimes, after coming back to Birkhall for tea, going out again later on. Occasionally she goes out after tea without even a gillie to accompany her.

Once, when the river had been very low and Queen Elizabeth had been waiting all day for water, the gillies reported improving conditions around six o'clock. Queen Elizabeth changed and went out at once. It grew dark, dinner time came and went. Still there was no sign of Queen Elizabeth. A search party was hurriedly organised and, equipped with hurricane lamps, was about to set out when Queen Elizabeth arrived, hauling along—she would not let the gillie handle it—a great twenty pound salmon.

'This is what kept me late,' she exclaimed in triumph.

Once—to her pride—she was featured in *The News of the World*—as landing the biggest salmon of the week.

Queen Elizabeth is probably happiest at Royal Lodge or at Sandringham, or in Scotland at Birkhall or the Castle of Mey. There she can wear old clothes and spend hours in the open air, whatever the weather. 'Sometimes,' said a woman relative, 'you think it's too frightful, we shan't go out today. But Queen Elizabeth always does. "The dogs are looking for their walk," she says, and out she goes.'

'They're tough,' said an ex-member of the Household, 'tough as can be. There is nothing shilly-shallying or weak about them, and in this the present Queen greatly resembles her Mother.'

Only recently, when revising this account for the new edition, a long-standing member of the Household, asked if Queen Elizabeth walked as far and as long as ever, said somewhat ruefully, 'She can still walk the legs off all of us.' She does find standing more tiring than she did, and at receptions or ceremonies her Household will endeavour to find chairs, so that she may sit and chat with people of interest. She goes to fewer of the routine receptions interminably given by the Heads of foreign missions to celebrate National and Independence days.

But if there is a special or personal reason for attending any ceremony or function, going to any meeting or marking any anniversary, she will be there, indefatigable, always interested, lending her own special sparkle to what could be a dreary routine function. Other women of her age began drawing their pensions a quarter of a century ago. She carries out a programme which many a woman half her age would find demanding. She remains fresh, interested and cheerful after *sixty-two* years of laying foundation-stones and inspecting hospital wards. Impossible to calculate how many hands she has shaken, how often she has turned aside for an extra word, how many factory floors she has visited, how often she has paused or retraced her steps to allow a harassed photographer to get his picture.

Of course her programme is ridiculously overloaded for a woman of her age, in a way that quite alarms those who love and serve her. She really does far too much, partly because of the continually increasing number of duties pressed upon the Queen and all other members of the Royal Family today; partly because it is in Queen Elizabeth's nature to say 'yes' more often than is strictly necessary, rather than cause disappointment; above all because she so dislikes severing the link of long-lasting association and friendship.

Queen Elizabeth is always reluctant to give anything up. Her Ladies-in-Waiting and others around her often urge her, as best they can, to cut down her engagements and suggest dropping this or that. Each member of the well-meaning Household will put forward a different organisation or event for the axe. The answer is invariable: 'But you have selected the *one* thing that I really *enjoy* doing!' exclaims Queen Elizabeth.

Queen Elizabeth's visit to Venice in October 1984 may serve to illustrate both her appetite for all that is new and stimulating, together with her unfailing execution of her public duties, whether or not of major importance.

Queen Elizabeth had last been in Italy as long ago as 1959, when she had unveiled a statue to Lord Byron in the Pincio Gardens in Rome, but she had long wished to revisit Italy, and especially to see for herself some of the work carried out by the organisation *Venice in Peril*, which is endeavouring to repair the ravages of the 1966 floods, and of time itself.

She travelled by air to Ancona, and then on to Venice in the royal yacht *Britannia*, which was at that time in the Mediter-

ranean. *Britannia* berthed—in dense fog—at the Riva dei Mar-
tiri on 25 October 1984. The anticipated view was, of course,
obliterated. The visit was expected to coincide with exceptionally high water, but in the event there was not too much,
but too little, water.

Lady Clarke, wife of Sir Ashley Clarke the former British
Ambassador to Rome, who as joint vice-chairman of the
Venice in Peril Fund was closely concerned with every aspect of
the visit, wrote '. . . atmospheric pressure induced quite the
opposite conditions to what had been forecast and frantic
signals from the Naval Attaché hurried the party in the flotilla
of motorboats at top speed along the Giudecca canal to reach
S. Nicolo dei Mendicoli, a church surrounded by notoriously
shallow canals, before the tide ebbed too far.

'Only by lightening the royal motorboat of all passengers
save Her Majesty could it be brought alongside steps where she
could be handed ashore into the Campo surging with euphoric
parishioners . . .'

Although the visit was official, both the Italian and the
English Press—but not the citizens of Venice—initially
announced that it was private. Indeed *Corriere Della Sera*
headed its first report 'La Sovrana visiterá la cittá della Laguna
in forma strettamente privata' ('Strictly private visit to the City
of the Lagoon by the Queen Mother'). Considerable crowds
had, however, gathered to greet her and from the beginning
the people responded to her, and to her characteristic acknowledgement of the people collected both to port and starboard.
'Those who met her found her "delicious", in other words
friendly, lively and with a natural pleasure for conversation.'

The long-laid plans for the day of her arrival, 25 October
1984, had to be hurriedly changed because of the fog. In the
event the day included listening to a long address of welcome
in Italian in a packed church under the heat of television lights;
receiving with apparent delight a newly-washed and dripping
bunch of grapes from a stallholder; touring the Doge's
Palace—remarking in admiration of the many sculptured lions
that she too 'was a Lyon'. She visited the basilica of SS

Giovanni e Paolo, where she especially admired the restoration of the great stained-glass window, undertaken by *Venice in Peril*. In St Mark's Lady Clarke observed 'the glowing mosaics, the newly-restored bronzes of the Capella Zen, the precious enamels of the Pala d'Oro, and the Nicopeia Madonna, all received her unhurried attention.'

By the next day—26 October 1984, the main day of her short visit—all confusion over whether this visit was private had been dropped. *Il Gazzettino di Venezio* simply referred to it as 'Elizabeth Day'. The Queen Mother's programme was packed with commitments. There was the reopening of the Oratorio dei Crociferi, which featured an ecumenical service, held for reasons of space in the Church of the Gesuiti. She met with the widows from the hospice of the Oratorio dei Crociferi, from whom she received handmade gifts. This was followed by a large Governmental luncheon at the Locanda Cipriani in Torcello, presided over by Minister Visentini. There followed a brief visit to the Cathedral of Sta. Maria Assunta, where Queen Elizabeth was greatly impressed by the wonderful mosaics, before hurrying back to *Britannia* to change, and receive individually 200 guests at a reception on board.

Everywhere Queen Elizabeth was accompanied by hordes of press photographers, bent on recording the tumultuous reception she was now receiving from the citizens of Venice. As so often with Queen Elizabeth, the day included little incidents which delight a photographer's heart—such as the single rose with which she had been presented, and was carrying. But what would underline definitively to the public at home that this was a Venetian visit? Why of course, a picture of Queen Elizabeth seated in a gondola! The security men were none to happy; they refused, argued, protested.

The *Corriere Della Sera* (to whom this is a decidedly hackneyed setting) recounted: 'British press and television won! Despite some long and strenuous resistance the staff who protected the Queen Mother during her visit to Venice finally gave in. Smiling, the Queen agreed, though for less than five minutes and for a distance of less than one hundred metres, to board a gondola, escorted by *Britannia*'s Admiral.' (Rear Admiral Paul Greening, Flag Officer Royal Yachts, will, incidentally, take up his appointment as Master of the Queen's Household in April 1986.) The *Corriere Della Sera* concluded '. . . she waved happily in this most classic Venetian scene.'

The following morning Queen Elizabeth made the rounds of *Britannia*, visiting all departments, and including the traditional stirring—with an oar—of the monster Christmas pudding. One final and agreeable duty: Queen Elizabeth, on behalf of the Queen, invested Lady Clarke with the O.B.E. which had been awarded to her in the Honours List for her work for *Venice in Peril*. Queen Elizabeth then returned by air to London.

Such is the spirit and the endurance of Queen Elizabeth the Queen Mother, aged eighty-five years old.

Queen Elizabeth represents the warm and vital mother-figure, the ideal grandmother and great-grandmother to the many thousands who have met her and who cherish their special memories, and to millions who have seen her only in the newspapers or 'on the box'. She shows us that duty is absolute, but that it need never be dull, and that it is always rewarding to meet all manner of men and women. Born in the last year of Queen Victoria's reign, a child in the time of Edward VII, married to a son of George V, the sister-in-law of Edward VIII, wife of George VI and mother of Queen Elizabeth II, Queen Elizabeth has lived through the best part of a century of change. Always she has served her sovereign and her country.

'Bring out the warmth that shines through her,' said a senior member of Queen Elizabeth's Household. 'It has not only been a privilege to serve her, but such fun to be with her.'

INDEX

ELIZABETH LONGFORD

ELIZABETH R: A BIOGRAPHY

Now is the time for a major reappraisal of the Queen's life and reign by a leading biographer. Elizabeth Longford, the highly respected and superb historian, has painted a fresh, compelling portrait, blending new information with lively anecdote. Through interviews with a great many of those who have served or known her – both past and present – a picture emerges of Elizabeth II as wife, mother, queen and leader of the Commonwealth. ELIZABETH R is a brilliant and penetrating study of the development of Queen Elizabeth II's character and the evolution of her own very special style of monarchy.

POST A LITTLE HAPPINESS

Post·A·Book

A Royal Mail service in association with the Book Marketing Council & The Booksellers Association.

Post·A·Book is a Post Office trademark

CHRISTOPHER WARWICK

PRINCESS MARGARET

Written with the full co-operation of Princess Margaret, this is the first authorised biography of one of the most remarkable members of the Royal Family. Drawing on numerous conversations with her, this fascinating account gives the most authentic record yet published of the Princess's private life and public duties. Christopher Warwick dispels the media-created legends and reveals – at last – the woman glass-cased inside the Princess.

CORONET BOOKS

A. J. P. TAYLOR

A PERSONAL HISTORY

After writing twenty seven books on history and biography A. J. P. Taylor now turns to his own story. Born in Birkdale, Lancashire, in 1906, he was educated at Bootham School, York, and Oriel college, Oxford. He spent two years in Vienna studying modern and international history and then became a lecturer at Manchester University for nine years. Thereafter he was a Fellow of Magdalen College, Oxford until 1976. At the same time he achieved spectacular success in broadcasting and journalism. A life long radical, once a Communist, A. J. P. Taylor is now a loyal member of the Labour Party. He has been married three times, has six children and now lives in happy retirement with his third wife in Kentish Town, London.

CORONET BOOKS

ALSO AVAILABLE FROM CORONET